FINANCIAL STABILIZATION IN MEIJI JAPAN

**A volume in the series
Cornell Studies in Money**

Edited by Eric Helleiner and Jonathan Kirshner
A list of titles in this series is available at cornellpress.cornell.edu.

FINANCIAL STABILIZATION IN MEIJI JAPAN

The Impact of the Matsukata Reform

Steven J. Ericson

CORNELL UNIVERSITY PRESS   ITHACA AND LONDON

First published 2019 by Cornell University Press

Library of Congress Cataloging-in-Publication Data

Names: Ericson, Steven J., 1953– author.
Title: Financial stabilization in Meiji Japan : the impact of
    the Matsukata reform / Steven J. Ericson.
Description: Ithaca : Cornell University Press, 2019. | Series: Cornell studies
    in money | Includes bibliographical references and index.
Identifiers: LCCN 2019015731 (print) | LCCN 2019018064 (ebook) |
    ISBN 9781501746925 (pdf) | ISBN 9781501746932 (epub/mobi) |
    ISBN 9781501746918 | ISBN 9781501746918 (cloth)
Subjects: LCSH: Finance, Public—Japan—History—19th century. |
    Economic stabilization—Japan—History—19th century. | Japan—
    Economic conditions—1868–1918. | Matsukata, Masayoshi, 1835–1924.
Classification: LCC HJ1393 (ebook) | LCC HJ1393 .E75 2019 (print) |
    DDC 339.50952/09034—dc23
LC record available at https://lccn.loc.gov/2019015731

To Solveig

Contents

Acknowledgments

My interest in this topic began when I wrote a paper on the Matsukata financial reform for a modern Japanese history course taught by the late William Wray during my first year as a graduate student at Harvard University. Several years later, at the urging of Teruko Craig, with whom I was editing history articles for the *Kodansha Encyclopedia of Japan* (1983), I turned that essay into the encyclopedia's entry on the "Matsukata Fiscal Policy"; I added some lines about continuities between the financial programs of Ōkuma Shigenobu and Matsukata Masayoshi but otherwise presented what was then the common understanding of the Matsukata reform in the English-language literature. In the meantime, other than revisiting that early graduate school paper for the encyclopedia, I had shelved "Matsukata finance" and begun working on Meiji railroads for my doctoral dissertation, which became my first book, *The Sound of the Whistle: Railroads and the State in Meiji Japan* (1996).

Like Charlie of "The MTA Song," who rides "forever 'neath the streets of Boston," I seemed to be stuck on the railroad, writing articles on Meiji railway history for journals and edited volumes well into the new century. I owe a huge debt of gratitude to Mark Metzler for getting me "off the train" when he invited me to present a paper on the Matsukata deflation in a panel he was organizing on nineteenth-century financial crises for the 2012 World Economic History Congress. Drafting that paper helped rekindle my interest in the Matsukata reform and gain fresh perspectives on it.

Brill Academic Publishers, the *Journal of Japanese Studies*, *Monumenta Nipponica*, and *Japan Forum* kindly gave me permission to incorporate material from articles of mine that they had published: "'Poor Peasant, Poor Country!' The Matsukata Deflation and Rural Distress in Mid-Meiji Japan," in *New Directions in the Study of Meiji Japan*, ed. Helen Hardacre, 387–96 (Leiden: E. J. Brill, 1997); "The 'Matsukata Deflation' Reconsidered: Financial Stabilization and Japanese Exports in a Global Depression, 1881–85," *Journal of Japanese Studies* 40, no. 1 (2014): 1–28; "Orthodox Finance and 'The Dictates of Practical Expediency': Influences on Matsukata Masayoshi and the Financial Reform of 1881–1885," *Monumenta Nipponica* 71, no. 1 (2016): 83–117; and "Smithian Rhetoric, Listian Practice: The Matsukata 'Retrenchment' and Industrial Policy, 1881–1885," *Japan Forum* 30, no. 4 (2018): 498–520. I am grateful for financial support from Dartmouth College, the Japan Foundation, the Japan Program of the

Social Science Research Council, the Northeast Asia Council of the Association for Asian Studies, the Japan-United States Friendship Commission, and the Marion and Jasper Whiting Foundation. I also wish to thank the library staffs at the University of Tokyo Faculty of Economics and at Senshū and Hitotsubashi Universities as well as Mr. Suzuki Yasuhiro of Senshū University's Historical Documents Section (Daigaku Shi Shiryō-ka) and Professor Hyōdō Tōru of Daitō Bunka University's Research Institute for Oriental Studies (Tōyō Kenkyūjo). I am indebted to a number of Dartmouth undergraduate students who have provided invaluable research assistance over the years, including Mutian Liu '11, Juan Carlos Freile '12, Bonnie MacFarlane '13, and Ezra Toback '14. For generous advice and encouragement, in addition to Mark Metzler, I want to thank Steven Bryan, Simon Bytheway, Janet Hunter, Dick Smethurst, and my colleagues in the Department of History at Dartmouth. I am also grateful to the two anonymous reviewers for extremely helpful recommendations on reframing the manuscript. Roger Haydon and his colleagues at Cornell University Press, Michelle Witkowski and Robert Griffin of Westchester Publishing Services, and Rachel Lyon, who created the index, worked with exemplary professionalism and dispatch. Solveig Grønning Ericson deserves special thanks for her unflagging patience and support. All errors and omissions are my responsibility.

FINANCIAL STABILIZATION IN MEIJI JAPAN

Introduction

DEPARTURES FROM ORTHODOXY

In 1880–1881 the Japanese government embarked on a pivotal program of financial stabilization and reform that came to bear the name of Matsukata Masayoshi (1835–1924; fig. 0.1), who brought the program to fruition after he became minister of finance in October 1881. The main objective was to deal with the severe inflation and paper currency depreciation that had begun in 1878–1879—exacerbating ongoing foreign trade deficits and specie outflows—when the government and U.S.-style "national banks" had thrown huge new issues of inconvertible (fiat) paper notes into circulation.[1] Because of the fixed land tax, still overwhelmingly the main source of state revenue, the inflation brought financial crisis to the Meiji regime,[2] jeopardizing the government's nation-building efforts. Under Matsukata, the Ministry of Finance helped end the crisis by accelerating the retirement of unbacked notes and the accumulation of specie reserves. It did so mainly by floating domestic bonds, selling rice overseas, and underwriting private exports of raw silk, tea, and other primary products at a time of sluggish imports between 1881 and 1885. By January 1886, the regime had succeeded in establishing a sound, silver-backed currency system centered on the Bank of Japan, which Matsukata had founded in 1882.[3]

The program of financial reform that Matsukata carried out has figured prominently in narratives of modern Japanese history as a transformative event in the country's modern economic development. The English-language literature, in particular, has portrayed the reform as an example of a highly successful "orthodox" program of financial stabilization. This view owes much to Cold War–era modernization-school studies, such as an oft-cited 1966 article by Henry Rosovsky,[4]

FIGURE 0.1   Matsukata Masayoshi (1835–1924). *Photo from* https://commons
.wikimedia.org/wiki/file:MatsukataMasayoshi.jpg.

which continue to influence textbook coverage of the Matsukata reform.[5] Rosovsky,
for instance, while proclaiming that, as finance minister, Matsukata "cleared the
decks, and made it possible for modern economic growth to begin," asserts that
he had developed "a strong belief in financial orthodoxy" and applied ideas of
conservative finance such as austerity and budget balancing "when his hour came."[6]

The "orthodoxy" to which Rosovsky refers was a mid-nineteenth-century version of British economic liberalism, the principles of which Matsukata purportedly learned through a French filter while leading the Japanese delegation to the
1878 Exposition Universelle in Paris. In Britain at the time, financial and economic
orthodoxy called for policies of debt reduction through spending cuts and tax
hikes, currency convertibility with paper money backed by specie and with an
independent central bank to manage the currency, and both free enterprise and

free trade with minimal state involvement in the economy.[7] British classical economists beginning with Adam Smith (1723–1790) and his cohort had largely developed the underpinnings of such policies, elaborating the concept of laissez-faire that French physiocrats had introduced earlier and, most important for financial policy, emphasizing the need for hard money, with paper currency redeemable in gold or silver. As J. Taylor Vurpillat has noted, after 1850 British supremacy in global trade and investment "conferred enormous prestige upon Britain's liberal economic doctrines," and advocacy of the gold standard "held particular sway . . . among statesmen in emerging nation-states with ambitions to follow the British model toward power and prosperity."[8]

Some scholars have also regarded the Matsukata financial reform as a self-imposed, nineteenth-century antecedent of the kinds of "neoliberal" reforms pressed on former Soviet bloc countries and other transitioning or developing nations in the late twentieth century as a condition for loans under the so-called Washington Consensus. Promoted by institutions based in Washington, D.C.—the International Monetary Fund (IMF), the World Bank, and the U.S. Treasury Department—these reforms ranged from programs of fiscal austerity and increased taxation to privatization of state-owned enterprises, currency stabilization, and the creation of a central bank.[9] Most English-language accounts present the Matsukata reform as having contained all of these measures, whose introduction, as Rosovsky has argued, not only ended the multiple crises of rampant inflation, a sharply depreciating currency, and chronic trade deficits but also established a foundation for Japan's successful economic growth. Mark Metzler has in fact suggested that the Matsukata financial reform may have been the world's first comprehensive, IMF-style structural adjustment program.[10]

Following this kind of interpretation, policy-oriented faculty at Harvard University showed great interest in the Matsukata reform in the 1980s and 1990s. Harvard Business School invoked the reform as a prominent case in its MBA course "Business, Government, and the International Economy," doing so at least until the bursting of the late 1980s bubble sent Japan into a prolonged economic slump after 1990.[11] The supplements students received in that course drew considerably on Rosovsky's 1966 article. Even Jeffrey Sachs, while preparing to advise postcommunist states on their efforts to reduce debt, control inflation, and transition to market-based economies after 1989, reportedly considered the Matsukata reform as a possible model.[12]

This book challenges the view that the Matsukata financial reform unfolded along the lines of mid-nineteenth-century British-style orthodoxy or the late-twentieth-century IMF version. Building on Japanese scholarship of recent decades,[13] it presents a view of the Matsukata reform that diverges from that of older Japanese- and English-language literature, which has continued to shape understandings of the reform outside of Japan. The evidence shows that, in practice, most of the measures Matsukata took after 1881 differed from both classical liberal and neoliberal programs in ways that actually resembled "heterodox" approaches to development.[14] Like contemporaries in many other countries, Matsukata combined financial stabilization with economic nationalism in adapting liberal orthodoxy to changing conditions. While influenced by British economic liberalism in French translation, his reform paralleled the programs of contemporary statesmen elsewhere who tailored or eschewed classical liberal doctrines to meet nationalist and developmentalist goals.[15]

Matsukata was never a full advocate of British-style liberal orthodoxy. True, the one aspect of orthodox finance on which he did follow through was establishing a convertible currency, achieved in 1886—although at that time on a de facto silver standard, which Matsukata regarded as merely a detour on the road from the legal bimetallic system that had been in effect since 1878 to an official gold standard, finally adopted in 1897.[16] In devising his monetary reform, however, he drew not only on British-style economic liberalism but also on Japan's own experience with currency stabilization, especially in the early eighteenth century. In addition, upon becoming finance minister, Matsukata intended to carry on the program of fiscal retrenchment that his predecessors had initiated, ordering government ministries to freeze their budgets for three years, but once in office he demonstrated flexibility in response to circumstances, belying his reputation as an unyielding adherent of financial orthodoxy. Rather than reducing government spending, he in fact increased it and moved relatively quickly from conservative to positive policies such as export promotion and public bond issuance, even attempting to sell bonds overseas, despite having vigorously opposed foreign borrowing only a few years earlier in the lead-up to his appointment as finance minister. Furthermore, Matsukata canceled the plan adopted under his predecessor Sano Tsunetami (1822–1902) to set up a central bank patterned after the independent Bank of England that would rely on British capital and management and instead based the Bank of Japan on the statist models of Belgium and Germany; in the early 1880s he also called for a parastatal industrial bank, and eventually the government would found both hypothec and industrial banks under close state supervision around the turn of the century. In this regard, as in his advocacy of tariff protection in the 1870s and his support after 1881 of continued government intervention in the economy, albeit of an increasingly indirect nature, Matsukata revealed that he had come under the influence not just of British liberal economic doctrines but of nationalist and statist traditions both at home and from abroad. From this perspective, even at the start of his tenure as finance minister, he committed to austerity to some extent for unorthodox, nationalist reasons. His departure from fiscal retrenchment beginning in 1883 reflected not so much a shift in worldview away from orthodoxy as it did a pre-existing, somewhat unorthodox mindset shaped by his study of ancient Chinese Legalism and his exposure to pre-Meiji mercantilism in his home domain of Satsuma as well as to the ideas of Western economic nationalists in the 1870s.

The concept of economic nationalism has undergone serious scholarly study only since the late 1990s, paralleling growing critiques of Washington Consensus policies, especially in the wake of the Asian financial crisis of 1997. Politically the concept has become inescapably prominent today, as the 2008 crash and its aftermath, with echoes of the period between the world wars, have set the stage for the rise of Brexit and Trumpism and intensified pressures on free-market globalization stemming from a contagion of debt crises as well as China's pursuit of a nationalist development strategy not unlike what industrializing countries in the West and elsewhere followed in the nineteenth century.[17]

During that century, the person most responsible for developing the notion of economic nationalism was the German economist and later American immigrant Friedrich List (1789–1846; fig. 0.2). As Eric Helleiner and others have shown, the core of List's ideas centered not on his advocacy of nonliberal policies such as infant industry tariff protection, for which he is most famous, but on his valorization of the nation and nationalism.[18] This focus contrasted with the universalizing cosmopolitanism of mid-nineteenth-century economic liberals such as Richard Cobden (1804–1865) who maintained that the largely unfettered actions of individuals would lead to global unity and prosperity. According to List, a less industrialized nation must organize its economy to serve nationalist goals and pursue a developmental strategy befitting its particular stage of development; only at some later stage could a follower nation become "an industrial society ready for free trade."[19] For Meiji leaders, List's larger emphasis on the crucial role of state activism in a nation's transition to industrial maturity held greater relevance than his call for infant industry protection. After all, raising tariffs was not an option for the Japanese government until 1911 when it finally regained tariff autonomy from the Western powers that had imposed unequal commercial treaties on Japan in 1858, although in the 1870s Matsukata would repeatedly call on the government to press for treaty revision so that it could engage in tariff protection.

Another insight derived from this more recent attention to the nationalist content of nineteenth-century economic nationalism, as opposed to its nonliberal policy prescriptions, is that the concept encompassed a variety of approaches to strengthening the nation, ranging from autarchic to liberal economic nationalism.[20] In this typology, Matsukata would seem to fall in the strand of what Helleiner has labeled the "'the liberal nationalist' position."[21] Though Matsukata's commitment to reform drew on classical British economic liberalism, it also stemmed heavily from nationalist concerns. These concerns emerged partly from

FIGURE 0.2   Friedrich List (1789–1846). *Photo from AF archive/Alamy stock photo.*

his study of Asian statist and mercantilist traditions and partly from his early experience in the Meiji government and his exposure to Listian thought in the 1870s. Matsukata appears to have been a liberal nationalist particularly in his monetary policy. Like statesmen in many other less economically developed countries in the late nineteenth century, he pursued the "orthodox" policy of establishing a convertible currency, ultimately on the gold standard, not for liberal reasons but for nationalist ones. Rather than the liberal economic goal of minimizing state involvement in monetary matters through the automatic adjustment mechanisms of the gold standard, the nationalist aim was the exact opposite: to bolster the state's control over the monetary system and its ability to further the economic development and unity of the nation.[22]

Many have likened Matsukata to an earlier economic nationalist, the first U.S. secretary of the treasury, Alexander Hamilton (ca. 1755–1804), whose ideas and policies influenced List. The Hamilton reference began as early as 1885 when the

American minister to Japan, John Bingham, sent a letter to Matsukata, congratulating him on the virtual completion of his currency reform, in which Bingham explicitly compared Matsukata to Hamilton.[23] Similarly, a eulogy published in a U.S. magazine following Matsukata's death in 1924 was unabashedly titled "The Alexander Hamilton of Japan."[24] During his tenure as treasury secretary from 1789 to 1795, determined to establish a fiscally robust federal government, Hamilton issued public bonds to pay off national debt and founded a government-supervised central bank with the goal of setting up a sound, specie-backed paper currency, much as Matsukata would do nearly a century later. In addition, Hamilton championed higher tariffs to protect fledgling industries and further U.S. economic independence from Britain, an approach Matsukata would also advocate for Japan.[25]

Like Hamilton, Matsukata was dealing with the challenge, shared by many of his contemporaries, of establishing a modern financial system in a developing state emerging from warfare and aiming to industrialize. Steven Bryan points to a number of statesmen in late-comer nations who pursued "Listian developmentalism," particularly in the late nineteenth century. The examples he cites include the Russian minister Sergei Witte (1849–1915) and the Argentinian president Carlos Pelligrini (1846–1906), both economic nationalists who put their countries on the gold standard. Witte was a devotee of List's ideas on state-directed industrialization and protective tariffs, even publishing a book that introduced List's work to Russian readers in 1889.[26] Meanwhile, Pelligrini advocated programs of "infant-industry protection, export promotion, and industrial developmentalism" that reflected the ideas of Hamilton and List, among other exponents of economic nationalism.[27]

Matsukata fell squarely in the Hamilton-List lineage; if not for the treaty powers' enforcement of a low fixed tariff, he would have practiced tariff protection as well. At least on monetary policy, his economic nationalism was of the liberal nationalist variety like that of state leaders in other late industrializers who were transitioning from silver, bimetallic, or paper currencies to the gold standard in the latter part of the nineteenth century.[28] In the late 1870s and early 1880s, Matsukata's predecessors as finance minister, Ōkuma Shigenobu (1838–1922) and Sano, had actually proposed or introduced almost all of the "orthodox" measures for whose origination Matsukata has usually received credit: note redemption and specie accumulation, fiscal retrenchment, and support for free enterprise (through privatization). Those measures were all on the books or in progress by early 1881.[29] Yet at the height of the Matsukata reform, central government expenditures rose, taxes stagnated, and hardly any state enterprises passed into private hands; at the same time, financial policy moved unmistakably in an economic nationalist direction, as state-led export promotion and domestic borrowing—rather than austerity and taxation—largely enabled the Ministry of Finance under Matsu-kata to retire fiat notes and to create a unified, convertible currency under the new central bank.[30]

In the end, Matsukata emerged as a practitioner primarily of *unorthodox* policies from the standpoint of both nineteenth- and late-twentieth-century versions of financial and economic orthodoxy. He differed from those orthodoxies in his policies, as he boosted government spending, established a state-controlled central bank, promoted exports, issued public bonds, implemented economic reforms in which privatization played a minimal role, and followed an incremental rather than a shock-therapy approach to financial stabilization. He also departed from orthodox mindsets in his pursuit of statist and nationalist priorities, his commitment to made-in-Japan solutions, his reliance on local intellectual tradition, and his willingness to be flexible in response to "the dictates of practical expediency,"[31] as he would proclaim in 1886.

In the chapters that follow I elaborate on these departures from orthodoxy. Chapter 1 examines the transition from the expansionary policies of Ōkuma to the contractionary ones of Sano as background to the Matsukata reform, which in large measure ended up combining his predecessors' approaches. Chapter 2 looks at the experiences and ideas that influenced Matsukata both in his commitment to aspects of mid-nineteenth-century British economic orthodoxy and in his predilection for unorthodox policies on certain issues. Chapters 3, 4, and 5 address the financial and economic programs that made up the Matsukata reform, highlighting the ways in which Matsukata diverged from contemporary British-style economic liberalism in his fiscal, industrial, and banking policies. Chapter 6 discusses the Matsukata deflation and its impact on domestic agriculture and industry and on foreign trade, suggesting that Matsukata's deviations from orthodoxy helped to ameliorate and shorten the deflation-induced depression. The conclusion returns to the notion that Matsukata merged the positive and negative policies of his predecessors along liberal nationalist lines, pursuing a kind of "expansionary austerity" during the Matsukata deflation.

FROM "ŌKUMA FINANCE" TO "MATSUKATA FINANCE," 1873–1881

Beginning in 1878, Japan suffered mounting inflation and currency depreciation triggered by the huge issue of additional inconvertible notes to pay for suppression of the Satsuma Rebellion of 1877, the last and greatest samurai uprising following the Meiji Restoration.[1] In response, the Meiji regime took tentative steps toward a program of retrenchment in 1879, Ōkuma Shigenobu's last full year as finance minister. During that year, total government notes in circulation, which had continually increased since the start of the Meiji period, began a steady decline until their complete replacement by central bank notes two decades later.[2] It was under Ōkuma's successor as finance minister, Sano Tsunetami, however, that the government embarked on austerity in earnest. In late 1880 and early 1881 the Council of State adopted practically all the components of both classical economic liberalism and what in the late twentieth century would become IMF-style neoliberal orthodoxy: fiscal retrenchment, increased taxation, privatization, and currency stabilization. Later in 1881 the government, despite having rejected a proposal made by Ōkuma a year earlier that it raise a large foreign loan to redeem its fiat notes, would approve a new plan he submitted with Itō Hirobumi (1841–1909) to sell domestic bonds abroad and establish a central bank on the British model.

That 1881 plan embodied the critical difference between the Ōkuma and Matsukata approaches to financial policy. Ōkuma sought to engineer a rapid currency reform using the proceeds from overseas bond issuance while applying the savings from austerity to continue the expansionary economic policies he had pursued as finance minister. The adoption of his new foreign-borrowing scheme in the summer of 1881 signaled a softening of official commitment to fiscal retrenchment. Matsukata intended to continue the Sano initiatives with the exception of borrowing abroad and founding a British-style central bank. Yet in practice he would diverge from much of the Sano austerity program in ways that differed from both classical and neoliberal orthodoxy.

Financial Policy in the Early Meiji Period

In the first two decades after the Restoration, Japan experienced a financial roller coaster. The country lurched from a precocious but unsustainable gold standard, which the regime adopted in 1871, to a legal bimetallic monetary system in 1878—but, in practice, no metal standard, as government notes became inconvertible in 1872, as did U.S.-style national bank notes in 1876. Starting in the fall of 1881, Matsukata would put Japan on track toward a functioning, de facto silver standard (even as the country remained officially bimetallic) and ultimately a return to gold convertibility in 1897. Meanwhile, the economy moved from mild deflation in the middle of the 1870s to sharp inflation in the years 1878–1881, followed by an equally intense deflation during the Matsukata reform. Foreign trade also swung from persistent deficits through 1881 to surpluses, with a surge in exports, especially of raw silk, and a decline in imports during the Matsukata deflation. Then came a decade of inflation, as the global price of silver continued to fall, boosting Japanese trade with Western gold-bloc nations and largely insulating silver-standard Japan from the long-term deflationary trend among those nations.

In 1871, a decade before the Matsukata reform, the Meiji government began working to establish a gold-backed monetary system on the recommendation of Vice-Minister of Finance Itō Hirobumi, who was then studying financial systems in the United States. Itō presciently observed in a letter to his colleagues in Tokyo that the "trend of opinion in Western lands" was in favor of the gold standard.[3] He thus predicted that countries in the West with silver or bimetallic standards would follow Britain's lead and go for gold, as in fact many did after Germany officially adopted that standard in 1873. Also, in 1871 the Meiji state established the yen as the official monetary unit and began the process of replacing more than sixteen hundred varieties of pre-1868 domain notes (*hansatsu*) with its own yen notes.[4] Furthermore, in 1872 the government accepted Itō's proposal to organize a decentralized U.S.-style system of "national banks" chartered by the state to issue notes exchangeable for gold from the banks' reserves. The banks would deliver 60 percent of their capital stock in the form of government notes to the Ministry of Finance and could issue up to that amount in their own notes but had to keep the remaining 40 percent of their capital as a reserve in gold coins, resulting in an "extraordinarily high" ratio of specie reserve compared to the experience of most Western banks.[5]

The government itself minted not only gold coins but also silver ones for foreign-trade purposes because the Western powers insisted on the use of silver—East Asia's de facto trade standard—in the treaty ports. Consequently, despite being legally on gold for most of the 1870s, Japan in practice had a bimetallic currency system—silver for international transactions and gold for internal ones—until the government made the bimetallic system official in 1878 when it decreed silver coins to be legal tender domestically as well.

In 1886, after the Matsukata deflation, Japan would go on a de facto silver standard with both government notes and newly issued Bank of Japan notes fully convertible to silver. In 1897 the country would return to gold after the government had successfully negotiated a phased revision of the unequal treaties and secured an enormous indemnity in specie from China following Japan's victory in the Sino-Japanese War of 1894–1895. Japan would thus follow the precedent Germany had set after the Franco-Prussian War a generation earlier of using war reparations to leverage its adoption of the gold standard.[6]

In the 1870s, however, the Meiji government was unable to maintain the gold side of its de facto and, from 1878, legal bimetallic currency system. With the price of silver entering a long-term decline, as other countries followed Germany in going on the gold standard, foreign merchants in the treaty ports began exchanging silver for gold coins, which the exchange rate the regime established in 1871 undervalued. Thus, as Mark Metzler notes, "Japan, like other bimetallic countries, experienced an outflow of gold and was pushed onto a de facto silver standard"[7] (though the nation would not have an operational silver standard until 1886, by which time Matsukata had sufficiently contracted the bloated money supply and built up the Treasury's specie reserve). In the early to middle 1870s, the gold flight compounded the country's lack of specie needed to back the official, pre-1878 gold standard. From 1872 to 1877 Japan hemorrhaged on average over ¥5 million in gold coins a year. The gold outflow persisted in the first three years under the legal bimetallic system at an average annual rate of nearly ¥5 million (see table 1.1).

Shortage of specie, together with the onerous reserve requirement, also impeded the founding of national banks, only four of which had opened for business by 1876. In the first week of August of that year, the government announced both a revision of the national bank regulations and the compulsory commutation of samurai stipends into interest-bearing public bonds. Under the banking revision, the regime dropped the convertibility requirement for national banks, allowing them to issues notes for up to 80 percent of their capital in the form of public bonds deposited at the Treasury and to hold the rest of their capital as a reserve in unbacked government notes. The government hoped these changes

TABLE 1.1 Japanese foreign trade, 1872–1881 (yen)

DATE	EXPORTS	IMPORTS	BALANCE OF TRADE	NET SILVER EXPORTS*	NET GOLD EXPORTS
1872	17,026,647	26,174,815	−9,148,168	−1,895,401	789,385
1873	21,635,441	28,107,390	−6,471,949	1,442,237	600,148
1874	19,317,306	23,461,814	−4,144,508	4,799,881	8,123,590
1875	18,611,111	29,975,628	−11,364,517	3,788,819	10,629,860
1876	27,711,528	23,964,679	3,746,849	−2,742,431	5,150,891
1877	23,348,522	27,420,903	−4,072,381	1,208,276	6,059,496
1878	25,988,140	32,874,834	−6,886,694	1,538,712	4,600,840
1879	28,175,770	32,953,002	−4,777,232	5,626,091	4,017,969
1880	28,395,387	36,626,601	−8,231,214	3,717,207	5,867,556
1881	31,058,888	31,191,246	−132,358	3,387,661	2,246,739

Source: Matsukata, *Report on the Adoption of the Gold Standard*, 37–38.
*The net inflow of silver specie in 1872 resulted from the 1871 sale of bonds in London for state railway construction in the amount of ¥4.88 million (£1 million). The figure for 1876 reflects a doubling of raw silk exports in response to the collapse of sericulture in France and Italy and a jump in silk export prices.

would not only invigorate the national banking system but also provide a safe investment for members of the former ruling class, who would receive a staggering ¥174 million in commutation bonds.[8] The remedy had the desired effect: 21 new national banks opened in 1877. But the government's decision the next year to make the bonds transferable opened the floodgates: as a Western observer declared in 1882, national banks "have sprung up like mushrooms" until their number had reached 153 by 1880, at which point the Ministry of Finance stopped issuing new licenses.[9]

The national banks have generally received a bad reputation as a failed experiment in decentralized banking, for they ended up exacerbating inflation by issuing inconvertible notes worth more than ¥32 million after 1876. For example, according to Fujimura Tōru, the doyen among postwar Matsukata experts, with the abandonment of convertibility, the national banks "lost the proper function of banks and became troublesome (*yakkaina*) entities"; they "looked good but in fact had become usurious entities unable to make any contribution to the expansion of production."[10]

Ishii Kanji, however, presents a contrary view. He points out that the banks' newly issued notes "circulated smoothly" at first, supplying the funding needs of "various developing industries"; in his view, "the history of the national banks should not be treated as an unnecessary mistake."[11] To redeem unbacked government notes, the regime had to improve public finances by slashing its enormous outlay on ex-samurai stipends. The 1876 revision of the national bank regulations proved "indispensable" to the accomplishment of that task. Paying those stipends had accounted for as much as a third of government expenditures until 1876; the commutation, however, reduced the cost of supporting the former samurai by half. Adopting the national banking system may have been a detour on the road to establishing a central bank, which even Itō Hirobumi, the champion of that decentralized system, admitted in the early 1870s might be the eventual outcome, but, as Ishii suggests, changing the system to permit the use of commutation bonds as the basis for note issuance was "an effective strategy" for government leaders "to take feudal privileges away from their colleagues as peacefully as possible." (Granted, that strategy failed to avert the most serious samurai rebellion from breaking out in 1877!) Ishii cogently concludes that creating a standard, centralized currency system was "not only an economic issue but a highly political one."[12]

The issuance of unbacked national bank notes certainly helped stoke the fires of inflation, but the government compounded the problem by printing fiat paper on an even greater scale to help pay for its extensive nation-building efforts, ranging from the creation of a Western-style military to the initiation of modern industries. Meanwhile, chronic trade deficits caused silver to flow out of the country as well, so that even nominally specie-backed paper money became inconvertible in practice. From 1873 to 1880, Japan imported more than it exported in every year but one—the deflationary year of 1876—averaging an annual trade deficit of ¥5.3 million, while silver specie likewise drained out of the country every year during that period, again save for 1876, at the average annual rate of ¥2.4 million (see table 1.1).

The issuance of both government and national bank notes leaped in 1878, when the regime settled expenses from its quelling of the 1877 Satsuma Rebellion (see table 1.2). Putting down that rebellion cost the government nearly ¥42 million.[13] This amount was four times the government's aggregate expenditures to quash all other uprisings—peasant and samurai—from the Restoration to mid-1876 and almost equivalent to the regime's total ordinary spending for fiscal 1877. The government met the cost of suppressing the rebellion by borrowing ¥15 million in newly issued notes from the Fifteenth National Bank and printing ¥27 million in government notes. The Fifteenth National Bank, also known as the Peers Bank (based on the investment of commutation bonds by former daimyo and samurai), accounted for fully half of the notes issued by all 153 national banks. It opened in the midst of the rebellion after concluding a contract to lend the Ministry of Finance ¥15 million for building railways and redeeming bonds the government had floated abroad in 1871 and 1873. The Finance Ministry, however, ended up diverting the loan to help pay for subduing the 1877 uprising instead.[14]

The government could have covered the cost of putting down the rebellion without issuing ¥27 million in additional fiat notes. Instead, the Finance Ministry

TABLE 1.2   Notes in circulation, 1871–1886 (yen)

DATE (END OF MONTH)	GOVERNMENT NOTES	SUPPLEMENTAL NOTES	NATIONAL BANK NOTES	BANK OF JAPAN NOTES	TOTAL NOTES IN CIRCULATION
Dec. 1871	60,272,000	0	0	0	60,272,000
Nov. 1872	64,800,000	3,600,000	0	0	68,400,000
Dec. 1873	77,281,014	1,100,000	1,362,210	0	79,743,224
Dec. 1874	90,802,304	1,100,000	1,995,000	0	93,897,304
Dec. 1875	91,283,869	7,788,000	1,420,000	0	100,491,869
Dec. 1876	93,323,156	11,824,426	1,744,000	0	106,891,582
Dec. 1877	93,835,764	11,961,327	13,352,751	0	119,149,843
Dec. 1878	119,800,475	19,618,116	26,279,006	0	165,697,598
Dec. 1879	114,190,804	16,118,116	34,046,014	0	164,354,935
Dec. 1880	108,412,369	16,528,116	34,426,351	0	159,366,836
Dec. 1881	105,905,194	13,000,000	34,396,818	0	153,302,012
Dec. 1882	105,369,014	4,000,000	34,385,349	0	143,754,363
Dec. 1883	97,999,277	0	34,275,735	0	132,275,012
Dec. 1884	93,380,233	0	31,015,942	0	124,396,175
Dec. 1885	88,345,096	0	30,155,389	3,653,272	122,153,757
Dec. 1886	67,800,846	0	29,501,484	39,025,779	136,328,109

Source: Fujimura, *Meiji zaisei kakuritsu katei no kenkyū*, 440.

could have applied budget surpluses totaling ¥23 million that it had deposited in its reserve fund in fiscal 1876 and 1877 and, for the rest of the military expenditures, have drawn on the ¥28 million the fund held at the start of fiscal 1876 as well as borrowed from the national banks. The budget surplus had resulted partly from a drop in military outlays in fiscal 1875 following the suppression of a major samurai uprising in Saga in 1874 and the conclusion of the Taiwan Expedition that year.[15] In addition, the switch in payment of samurai stipends from rice to money in 1875—in advance of the stipends' compulsory commutation to public bonds—produced a dramatic fall of ¥9 million in that expenditure, as the average price of rice declined from ¥7 per *koku* (about 330 pounds) in 1874–1875 to ¥5 in 1876–1877 (see fig. 1.1). The slump in the rice price, in turn, stemmed in large part from the flooding of the rice market with the monetization of both samurai pensions and the land tax, which the government also changed from a payment in kind to a payment in cash under the land tax reform of 1873. Then, beginning in 1877, servicing the commutation bonds would yield a further reduction of several million yen in annual disbursements to members of the former ruling class. In the event, government expenditures plunged from ¥69 million in fiscal 1875 to ¥59 million in 1876 and then to ¥48 million in 1877.[16]

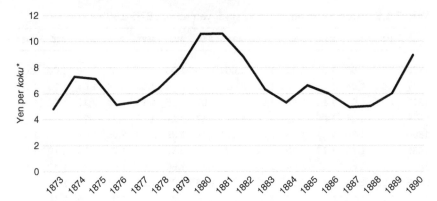

FIGURE 1.1   Average annual wholesale price of medium-grade rice in Tokyo, 1873–1890 (yen per *koku**). *Source:* Matsukata, *Report on the Adoption of the Gold Standard*, 36, 103.

*A koku of rice weighs about 330 pounds, considered in premodern times the amount of rice sufficient to feed one male samurai for a year.

Finance Minister Ōkuma Shigenobu, however, wanted to use the reserve fund for industrial promotion and therefore turned to expanded note issuance to meet the rebellion-related expenses. Yet, because the economy was in a deflationary mode before and during the Satsuma uprising, the jump in military outlays connected to the rebellion did not immediately trigger inflation. Farm household consumption, the biggest component of total demand, fell with the drop in the rice price, canceling the inflationary effect of increased military expenditures and acting as "a powerful deflator of the national economy as a whole."[17] At the same time, the slump in the price of rice heightened the burden of the fixed land tax on rural communities, prompting a spike in riots against the land tax reform; in response, the regime decided in January 1877 to lower the tax rate from 3 percent of the assessed value of land to 2.5 percent, a decrease that factored into the retrenchment in government spending. Furthermore, a majority of the ¥42 million in paper money issued in 1877–1878 went into the reserve fund or the ordinary budget and thus stayed within the Treasury for a time. Consequently, Japan experienced a considerable time lag between the end of the Satsuma Rebellion and the start of severe inflation in 1879. Ōkuma continued his expansionary financial policy against the backdrop of this lag, which became a major factor in his dogged pursuit of that policy.[18]

In any event, the sudden increase in unbacked notes in 1878 set Japan on the path to mounting inflation and currency depreciation. Total paper money in circulation leaped from ¥106 million in January 1877, when the Satsuma uprising

TABLE 1.3 Average monthly paper/silver yen ratio, 1876–1885

	JAN.	FEB.	MAR.	APRIL	MAY	JUNE	JULY	AUG.	SEPT.	OCT.	NOV.	DEC.	AVE.
1876	1.02	1.02	1.00	1.01	1.00	1.00	1.00	1.00	1.00	1.00	1.00	1.00	1.00
1877	**1.01**	1.04	1.03	1.03	1.02	1.02	1.03	1.05	1.05	1.04	1.04	1.03	1.03
1878	1.05	1.08	1.11	1.08	1.07	1.07	1.07	1.08	1.11	**1.15**	1.13	1.22	1.10
1879	1.22	1.25	1.26	1.25	1.16	1.10	1.12	1.17	1.16	1.23	1.29	1.34	1.21
1880	1.37	1.39	1.44	1.55	1.37	1.37	1.38	1.39	1.49	1.65	1.69	1.66	1.48
1881	1.73	1.75	1.77	**1.80**	1.62	1.63	1.63	1.63	1.69	1.73	1.69	1.70	1.70
1882	1.70	1.65	1.55	1.54	1.55	1.57	1.57	1.66	1.61	1.59	1.48	1.40	1.57
1883	1.33	1.40	1.41	1.36	1.33	1.33	1.26	1.21	1.19	1.15	1.10	1.11	1.26
1884	1.11	1.16	1.13	1.09	1.09	1.07	1.05	1.05	1.05	1.06	1.06	1.15	1.09
1885	1.17	1.20	1.19	1.07	1.02	1.00	1.00	1.00	1.01	1.01	1.00	1.00	1.06

Source: Matsukata, "Shihei seiri shimatsu," 120.

started, to ¥163 million in October 1878, when the government completed settlement of rebellion-related expenses.[19] From January 1877 to October 1878, paper money depreciated only moderately in terms of silver, falling by 14 percent; by the time it hit bottom in April 1881, however, it had depreciated a further 57 percent (see table 1.3). Similarly, the average monthly price of rice, the key indicator of inflation, would not peak until December 1880, by which time it had risen to ¥12.5 per koku, but the rice price had already climbed from ¥5.6 at the start of 1878 to ¥7.4 by the end of that year (see table 1.4). The rise in the price of rice was naturally a boon to farmers, but the inflationary movement presented a growing crisis to the government as the proceeds from its principal funding source, the fixed land tax, paid almost entirely in paper money, dropped in value.

Ōkuma responded to the crisis by retiring a portion of the government's fiat notes. By early 1880, however, he had made only a small dent in the total supply of paper money in circulation, having permitted the issuance of additional national bank notes.[20] At the same time, he severely reduced the Treasury's reserve fund, whose main purpose was to support the paper currency. In 1872 Vice-Minister of Finance Inoue Kaoru (1836–1915) had established that fund to redeem Treasury notes, to acquire gold and silver to back paper in circulation, and to "invest . . . in some useful industry, so that the Fund may be augmented."[21] As finance minister, Ōkuma emphasized the reserve fund's investment function, committing a large part of the fund to industrial lending, and in fact depleted much of the remaining specie reserve by selling off silver currency beginning in April 1879. He did so in the mistaken belief that the appreciation of silver was the cause of inflation, failing to recognize that in fact the rise in both silver and commodity prices had resulted largely from the overissue of inconvertible paper

TABLE 1.4 Average monthly wholesale price of medium-grade rice in Tokyo, 1878–1883 (yen per *koku*)

	JAN.	FEB.	MAR.	APRIL	MAY	JUNE	JULY	AUG.	SEPT.	OCT.	NOV.	DEC.	AVE.
1878	5.60	6.00	6.30	6.30	6.60	6.50	6.40	6.40	6.20	6.70	7.30	7.40	6.48
1879	7.40	7.15	7.20	7.35	7.40	7.60	8.20	8.80	9.00	9.00	8.50	8.50	8.01
1880	8.40	9.10	9.50	10.20	10.60	10.90	11.50	12.20	11.50	11.50	12.20	12.50	10.84
1881	12.10	12.00	11.90	11.40	11.00	11.25	11.20	10.70	10.20	10.30	10.90	11.50	11.20
1882	10.50	10.40	9.80	9.05	8.30	8.20	8.20	8.70	9.10	9.25	8.60	7.10	8.93
1883	6.25	6.60	6.50	6.35	6.70	6.80	6.70	7.25	6.60	5.80	4.90	4.65	6.26

Source: Nōrin Shō, *Beikoku tōkei nenpyō*, cited in Muroyama, *Matsukata zaisei kenkyū*, 123.

TABLE 1.5   Government reserve fund, 1876–1885 (yen)

DATE (END OF JUNE)	SPECIE IN THE RESERVE FUND	NOTES AND BONDS IN THE RESERVE FUND	TOTAL	GOVT. NOTES IN CIRCULATION (A)	RESERVE SPECIE AS % OF (A)
1876	19,025,550	9,315,866	28,341,416	105,147,583	18.09
1877	15,332,266	23,699,271	39,031,538	105,797,092	14.49
1878	14,965,891	36,301,089	51,266,981	139,418,592	10.73
1879	13,988,333	38,298,982	52,287,316	130,308,921	10.73
1880	9,071,627	42,253,888	51,325,515	124,940,486	7.26
1881	8,691,914	47,101,584	55,793,498	118,905,195	7.31
1882	14,514,151	40,772,704	55,286,855	109,369,014	13.27
1883	18,405,528	35,006,482	53,412,011	97,999,277	18.78
1884	28,494,024	18,492,168	46,986,192	93,380,234	30.51
1885	38,325,178	8,250,118	46,585,297	88,345,096	43.38

Sources: Takahashi, *Meiji zaisei shi kenkyū*, 87; Matsukata, *Report on the Adoption of the Gold Standard*, 29, 96.

money.[22] Ōkuma may have acted on the advice of Fukuzawa Yukichi (1835–1901), the founder of the future Keiō University and the leading popularizer of Western knowledge in the Meiji period, who in March 1878 urged the finance minister to "put one million worth of Mexican [silver] dollars on the market to stabilize it."[23] But the silver that the Ministry of Finance placed on the market, far from checking the metal's appreciation and bringing hoarded silver into circulation, flowed out of Japan on account of continuing foreign trade deficits, causing a further rise in the silver price. By 1880 the ratio of specie in the reserve fund to government notes in circulation had dropped from 14.5 percent in 1877 to a precarious 7.3 percent (see table 1.5), while the value of paper money had fallen to the point where a one-yen paper note fetched only two-thirds of a yen in silver for the year as a whole.[24]

Dealing with the Financial Crisis, 1880–1881

In 1880–1881, the Meiji leaders grappled with proposals for financial stabilization that ranged from foreign borrowing to retrenchment. Ōkuma, wishing to avoid deflation and to continue the expansionary industrial policy he had pushed as finance minister, proposed in May 1880 that the government redeem inconvertible paper money and restore the value of the yen in one stroke by floating a ¥50 million loan in London. While most of the other leaders also wanted to avoid deflation, they deadlocked over Ōkuma's plan, whereupon they turned to the emperor; like many of the state councilors, the Meiji emperor viewed foreign borrowing as too risky and cast the deciding vote against the proposal. In late 1880, the government acted under Sano Tsunetami, who had succeeded Ōkuma as finance minister earlier that year, to reverse inflation and currency depreciation by hiking consumer taxes and reducing state spending. Yet the Council of State (Dajōkan) soon grew wary of full retrenchment, and in the following year, in a surprising move, it approved a recycled version of Ōkuma's plan, which he had made more palatable by labeling it a scheme for selling domestic bonds abroad rather than raising a foreign loan.

The regime was about to implement that plan, over Matsukata's vigorous objections, in November 1881, at which time Itō, who had cosponsored Ōkuma's proposal, was completing a final draft of the plan.[25] In the previous month, however, the dominant Satsuma and Chōshū leaders[26] had ousted Ōkuma from the government for what they considered his radical call for a British-style parliamentary system (Ōkuma hailed from the domain of Hizen, a junior partner in the Restoration coalition). Preoccupied with the political crisis, the leaders finally acceded to the request of Satsuma colleague Matsukata that he replace Sano as finance minister. The Council of State had slated Itō to succeed Sano but at the last moment appointed him to draft a constitution instead. Itō's fellow Chōshū colleague, Inoue Kaoru, the other principal alternative to Matsukata, accepted the position of foreign minister and focused on treaty revision negotiations. Sano, also a Hizen native and typically depicted as an Ōkuma proxy, had in fact distanced himself from his compatriot by forcefully opposing Ōkuma's first foreign loan scheme and, before supporting his recycled plan, by advocating a program of note redemption through retrenchment on a scale bigger than what even Matsukata proposed. Rather than departing with Ōkuma upon his expulsion from the government, Sano remained in the regime as vice-chair of the Genrō-in, the early Meiji body that reviewed legislation.[27] Once ensconced as finance minister with the emperor's full backing, Matsukata convinced the other leaders to drop the overseas bond-selling scheme and to achieve financial stabilization and currency convertibility by continuing the austerity measures the regime had initiated a year earlier.

A common view in the English-language literature is that, once the Meiji leaders had rejected Ōkuma's 1880 scheme for raising a foreign loan to tide over the inflationary crisis, they turned to Matsukata's program as the "only alternative."[28] Matsukata then appears as the savior of the Meiji miracle, the great architect of Japan's modern financial system, who "cleared the decks" for modern economic growth to begin.[29] Meanwhile, Ōkuma Shigenobu comes across almost as the reverse of Matsukata—a financial bungler who tried to fight fire with fire by pushing an expansionary policy at the height of a violent inflation and coming up with a wild-eyed scheme to resolve the crisis by borrowing massively from abroad. Most accounts portray the other leaders as having been aghast at the radical nature of Ōkuma's plan, some citing Minister of the Right Iwakura Tomomi (1825–1883) as wondering aloud whether Japan might have to give up Shikoku and Kyushu to the foreigners to repay the loan;[30] Iwakura and his colleagues therefore rallied to quash Ōkuma's proposal for overseas borrowing and instead adopted Matsukata's program, which combined austerity with economic nationalism. Ōkuma appears as a loner not only in his radical constitutional opinions but also in his financial policies. In this view, it was his isolation on both counts that led to his ouster from the government in 1881, paving the way for the Matsukata financial program.

Some of Matsukata's contemporaries, however, had less-than-flattering things to say about Matsukata himself, portraying him as a second-rate bureaucrat who had risen to prominence only because of his Satsuma origins and the patronage of Ōkubo Toshimichi (1830–1878), the most powerful of Meiji leaders in the mid-1870s and de facto prime minister until his assassination in May 1878. Often quoted, for example, is Ōkuma's famous putdown that, if it were not for his Satsuma pedigree, Matsukata "would at best have become a prefectural governor."[31] Matsukata in fact did begin his post-Restoration career as governor of a prefecture in Kyushu, far from the seat of power. He then joined the central government in 1870 as junior deputy minister of civil affairs, several grades below peers such as Ōkuma, who had already been serving as assistant minister of finance.[32] Mutsu Munemitsu (1844–1897), like Ōkuma a government official without Satsuma-Chōshū credentials (he was from Wakayama domain), noted unkindly that one of the most remarkable things he had ever encountered was that someone so mediocre could have risen so far.[33] Similarly, a leading member of Ōkuma's later political party, Ozaki Yukio (1858–1954), claimed that Matsukata had had the good fortune of having "all his superiors" die "one after the other" and so had gotten his turn to represent Satsuma "through no particular merit of his own."[34] Insofar as these men were referring to Matsukata the politician rather than Matsukata the financial leader, these assessments have some measure of validity. Matsukata was notably ineffective as a prime minister, in which capacity he served briefly on two occasions in the 1890s.[35] But, when it comes to Matsukata in the financial realm, these statements were clearly off the mark.

Actually, Matsukata received little in the way of favoritism from Ōkubo, who deliberately held up his fellow clansman's advancement in order to show "impartiality in personnel matters."[36] When Matsukata transferred from the Civil Affairs Ministry to the Finance Ministry in July 1871, Ōkubo demoted him from junior deputy minister to the much lower rank of assistant director of the Taxation

Bureau and later that year passed over Matsukata for the bureau's top position in favor of the more junior Mutsu. Ōkubo then tried to prevent Matsukata's promotion to vice-minister of finance in 1875, reluctantly agreeing to it only at the insistence of Councilor Kido Takayoshi (1833–1877). Furthermore, Ōkubo refused to let Matsukata burnish his résumé by going on study tours of the West until the land tax reform was well under way.[37] It was only after Ōkubo's assassination and Matsukata's return from Europe in 1878 that he finally emerged as a prominent figure in the Meiji regime. Even then he faced resistance from other members of the Satsuma clique, who were dead set against the deflationary program Matsukata was advocating. In early 1880, they made sure that he was appointed home minister rather than minister of finance. Only in October 1881, when Matsukata at last gained the Finance Ministry portfolio, did the other leaders admit him to the top decision-making group as a councilor of state (*sangi*). He thus joined the inner circle a decade after younger members of his cohort such as Ōkuma and Itō had begun holding high-level leadership positions.

In 1880, at the height of the inflationary crisis, the government faced more than just the two options of borrow from abroad or retrench. A third proposal—a reactionary one—also emerged calling for a return to collecting part of the land tax in kind rather than in money. According to advocates of this plan, particularly Iwakura, the root of the financial crisis was the skyrocketing price of rice, which had fattened the farmers and sent them on a spending spree on imported luxury goods. The idea, then, was for the government to soak up much of that rural surplus and thereby depress demand for imports in the countryside by collecting a portion of the land tax in rice. In 1877 the regime had established a voluntary program whereby it permitted farmers to pay up to half of their land tax in kind, but the new plan would have mandated that land owners meet a fourth of the tax in rice. This proposal was redolent with vestigial samurai attitudes: basically, it was a scheme to put the peasants in their proper place and secure funds to help out struggling members of the former ruling class.[38] This plan, however, met defeat at the hands of the more progressive leaders, especially Ōkuma and Itō, who were not about to turn the clock back to the feudal age.

In Ōkuma's view, the causes of the inflation and trade deficit were not soaring agricultural prices and excessive imports; rather, the rising silver price and inadequate exports were to blame. In particular, he maintained, it was the underdeveloped state of export industries that had resulted in the serious trade imbalance, leading to an outflow of specie and a jump in silver and other prices. What the government needed to do, therefore, was to continue, if not expand, the policy of industrial promotion that it had been pursuing throughout the 1870s: in other words, to pump more money into the economy, to issue more paper currency—not less—in order to foster domestic production, especially of exports. Admittedly, the retirement of government notes began under Ōkuma in 1879; however, even as Ōkuma was redeeming government paper, he was simultaneously permitting a large increase in national bank notes (see table 1.2).[39] By no means did Ōkuma abandon his expansionary, interventionist policies. True, he was eventually forced to compromise and to go along with retrenchment and currency redemption as expedients, but to the bitter end he remained wedded to his activist, industrial promotion approach.

By late 1880 government leaders with the exception of Ōkuma seemed to be in agreement, however reluctantly, that they needed to follow a conservative course of austerity and deflation. Nonetheless, as late as November 1881—a month *after* Ōkuma's ouster from the regime—the government was preparing to implement a policy of foreign borrowing that would have obviated the need for deflation. By then, Matsukata had become the only senior official who advocated a program that included austerity. Nearly all the other government leaders were in favor of an activist industrial policy aimed specifically at boosting exports.

Kuroda Kiyotaka (1840–1900) of Satsuma, the main supporter of Ōkuma's program and head of the Hokkaido Colonization Commission (the Kaitakushi), also sought to provide employment to the former samurai and thereby undercut the Popular Rights movement, which disgruntled members of the samurai class had launched in 1874. Did Matsukata, in carrying out his deflationary policy after 1881, have the same political motive, that is, to undermine the Popular Rights movement, which by that time had broadened to include farmers riding the crest of the inflationary wave after 1878? Matsukata certainly realized that his program would inflict hardship on rural communities, and it may have had the side effect of financially weakening and dividing the political opposition,[40] but such adversity was collateral damage in his eyes, determined as he was to restore the value and convertibility of paper money. Ironically, however, the more politically conservative among the backers of Ōkuma's expansionary, pump-priming policy in the 1870s did have that opposition-busting goal. Men like Kuroda and Iwakura explicitly linked industrial promotion to the quelling of political dissent; Ōkuma's program would have helped curb opposition by creating jobs for the former samurai who were struggling to survive on fixed incomes.[41] The problem was that those two goals—promoting industry through an inflationary policy of unbacked note issue and offering relief to the former samurai—ultimately conflicted; as much as Ōkuma's investments created jobs, inflation hurt the samurai.

To Ōkuma's credit, he was the first among the proponents of expansionary finance to recognize that, with inflation getting out of hand, it had become impossible to pursue his industrial promotion policy through an aggressive program of note issuance. He had come to this conclusion by 1880. In February of that year, the other leaders, blaming Ōkuma for the financial problems besetting Japan, forced him to resign as finance minister. Under an administrative overhaul that remained in effect until October 1881, they also suspended the concurrent holding of positions as senior councilor (*sangi*) and head of a ministry. Ōkuma would continue as a councilor but would have to share financial decision-making with fellow councilors Itō and Inoue while his nominee, Hizen compatriot Sano Tsunetami, would serve as finance minister. At this point, Ōkuma decided that the only way to continue with an activist industrial policy was to borrow from abroad. Accordingly, in May 1880 he presented his proposal for raising a huge foreign loan in London in the amount of ¥50 million to carry out the immediate recovery of all inconvertible paper money so as not to jeopardize his cherished industrial policy.[42]

Though several government leaders regarded this proposal as a radical plan and called for rejecting it as too risky, a majority of the senior councilors actually supported it, with almost all the Satsuma men approving Ōkuma's proposal and the Chōshū men generally opposing it. Home Minister Matsukata, though not a councilor, broke ranks with his Satsuma colleagues and voiced strong opposition. To Ōkuma's surprise, his handpicked successor as finance minister, fellow clansman Sano, also objected to the plan.[43] But most of the Chōshū councilors were not opposed to Ōkuma's interventionist industrial policy; far from it, they were very much in favor of the active promotion of manufacturing and exports and had almost the same understanding—or misunderstanding—of the financial crisis as Ōkuma, one of them even recommending that the Finance Ministry just continue with the bankrupt policy of expanded note issue.[44] These men were simply against large-scale foreign borrowing as entailing too many risks. Itō and Inoue were in fact willing to compromise, stating that, if it was absolutely necessary and was prudently arranged, they might agree to borrowing from abroad perhaps a fifth of what Ōkuma had proposed.[45] Even Sano, who advocated a drastic reduction of paper money in circulation through a multiyear program of retrenchment and bond issuance, recommended taking a foreign loan of ¥15 million, using it, however, not to redeem fiat notes but to address the trade deficit by underwriting exports.[46]

Matsukata was the only government leader to present a coherent argument against the plan for a foreign loan. In a memorandum he submitted to the Council of State in June 1880 at the request of Chancellor Sanjō Sanetomi (1837–1891), Matsukata called for creating a sound, convertible currency not through what he asserted would be an "extremely difficult and dangerous" program of foreign borrowing but rather through the gradual redemption of inconvertible paper and steady accumulation of specie in the reserve fund. In doing so, Matsukata outlined the basic contours of the economic and financial policies that he would attempt to carry out after 1881, although many of the specific measures he rec-ommended in this document, such as having the government undertake the export of rice to acquire specie and establishing a "specie bank" that would lend paper money to export merchants and collect repayment in silver and gold coins, actu-ally built on ideas that Ōkuma and Sano had already implemented or proposed.[47]

Virtually none of the other leaders shared Matsukata's views on currency reform, but they were split over Ōkuma's foreign loan proposal. If the govern-ment had followed protocol and left the decision to the senior councilors, they would likely have approved the Ōkuma plan. But Sanjō decided to solicit the opinions of ministry heads, including Matsukata and Sano.[48] As Sano was the minister in charge of finances, his views carried considerable weight; Iwakura, for instance, remarked that, "although we received various opinions, Sanjō said that he favored Sano's position." The final tally, however, was eight for Ōkuma's scheme and eight against it; essentially the emperor broke the tie, stating in a June 1880 rescript that the plan would be "most improper at the present."[49]

Following the defeat of Ōkuma's proposal, as much as government leaders wanted to avoid retrenchment, that course seemed increasingly to be the one they would have to take. The army and particularly the Satsuma faction resisted; after all, the national budget had already shrunk in real terms owing to inflation, so where could they make additional cuts? The only option, it seemed, was to in-crease taxes. At this point, Iwakura put forward the reactionary plan to collect a quarter of the land tax in kind; backing him were all of the Satsuma leaders, save Matsukata. For Ōkuma, this plan would have meant abandoning his expansion-ary program, which tended to favor farmers—the originators of the major ex-port items of silk, tea, and rice—and giving priority to assisting former samurai at the farmers' expense; that is, to reverse the flow of income, directing it away from farmers to the state and by extension to the former samurai. In this case, Ōkuma broke with his erstwhile Satsuma allies and voted with the Chōshū lead-ers against the land tax proposal.[50]

With his foreign loan plan shot down, Ōkuma realized he had no choice but to seek funds for industrial promotion through a hike in taxes and a curtailment of government expenses, but he was determined to prevent those measures from being linked to note redemption. In September 1880 the Council of State formally approved a new proposal submitted by Ōkuma, in cooperation with Itō and Inoue, that the government secure needed funding through tax increases and spending cuts.[51] The leaders also adopted plans to sell off state enterprises and to streamline the administration of economic affairs by establishing a new Ministry of Agriculture and Commerce. These steps seemed to mark a dramatic shift away from the previous expansionary course. Yet Ōkuma made sure that the regime postponed a decision on how it would use the resulting surplus, giving him time to come up with a separate plan for currency reform, one that would enable the government to avoid deflation and maintain an activist industrial policy.

These changes in policy appear to have laid the rails on which Japan would move full speed into the Matsukata financial reform. Yet, in early 1881 Ōkuma set out to roll back those rails by putting forward a new loan proposal to finance note redemption and specie acquisition in one stroke so the government could invest the funds resulting from the retrenchment program in new industrial projects. This time Ōkuma was careful not to label it a proposal for a foreign loan; rather, he presented it as a plan to float public bonds that would be open to subscription by foreigners and never once used the term "foreign loan." The government was to apply the proceeds from this bond issue to setting up "a great bank" managed by a hired British expert that would acquire specie from abroad and carry out the immediate conversion of paper currency.[52] Despite its appearances, this initiative was nothing but a recycled version of Ōkuma's earlier foreign loan scheme, for he explicitly prioritized overseas sales as a way "to make gold and silver flow in from abroad."[53] Nevertheless, by April 1881 Ōkuma had secured the consent of Finance Minister Sano as well as Itō and, with Itō's cosponsorship, proceeded to submit the bond proposal to the Council of State in July. At the end of that month the government formally approved the proposal with hardly any debate, immediately began to work out the details of the plan, and, as noted, by November, *after* Ōkuma's ouster from the regime in the Political Crisis of 1881, had reached the stage just prior to implementation.[54]

How does one explain this apparent 180-degree turn in state financial policy? For one, the fact that Ōkuma did not present his scheme as a foreign loan proposal made it more palatable to government leaders. Moreover, several who had voted against Ōkuma's first proposal were not opposed to foreign borrowing in principle, while no one was against floating public bonds. Second, Ōkuma had no problem with the Satsuma and military leaders, who were delighted with the revival of his loan proposal. Its near-unanimous acceptance was simply another indication of the extent to which state leaders were in favor of a more activist industrial policy and wanted to avoid retrenchment and deflation if at all possible.

Unsurprisingly, the one leader who was not pleased with this turn of events was Matsukata. After Sano agreed to back Ōkuma's new plan, Matsukata became the only government leader to oppose foreign borrowing and to advocate financial reform through Japan's own efforts. In October he came out with his famous "Proposal on Finance" (Zaisei gi), typically described as a formal statement of his reform program. More than a prospectus, this document represented Matsukata's counterattack against the sudden change in financial policy. In it, he offered a consistent, systematic argument in favor of gradual currency reform without recourse to foreign capital and expressed his surprise and anger over the reversal of the previous year's decision against foreign borrowing.[55] If Japan, legally and commercially handicapped by the unequal treaties, were to borrow from the Western powers, it risked "falling into a pitiful state like Turkey, Egypt, and India." Instead, what the country urgently needed, Matsukata declared, was to "establish a center [that is, a central bank] for currency operations, build up the fund for redeeming paper money by accumulating specie, and restrain imports by encouraging production."[56]

Fortunately for Matsukata, the Sat-Chō leaders joined together to expel Ōkuma from the regime shortly after Matsukata submitted his Proposal on Finance, but even Ōkuma's ouster did not mean the immediate adoption of the Matsukata plan for financial reform. Itō, who in November would complete a concrete plan for implementing the bond flotation program, intended to become finance minister himself and recommended that Matsukata continue as home minister.[57] With the new priority on constitution-making, however, Itō ended up heading that effort instead, and so the Finance Ministry portfolio finally came around to Matsukata.[58] He immediately pressed the Council of State to approve his financial reform measures and, as a guarantee against deviation from his program, obtained the emperor's endorsement as well.[59] The Meiji government thus dropped the plan for bond issues; and, with Matsukata in control of state finance, it embarked on a full-scale program of note redemption and specie acquisition.

The Sat-Chō leaders drove Ōkuma out not so much because of his financial views or his defeat in the *financial* debate; rather, it was mainly what they perceived to be his unduly progressive ideas on constitution-making that led to his ouster. In addition, his criticism of Kuroda's proposed fire sale of government properties in Hokkaido at the time made him a darling of the Popular Rights movement, raising suspicions of collusion with the political opposition and sealing his fate. Shortly after the government appointed Matsukata finance minister, the situation changed dramatically in his favor, the upshot being abandonment of Ōkuma-style positive finance. Further paving the way for Matsukata was that, in addition to expelling Ōkuma, the Council of State forced Kuroda, the leader of the Satsuma faction, to resign over the Hokkaido scandal. Thus, the two principal advocates of financial and economic activism had left the scene, creating a political environment conducive to the execution of a deflationary program. Moreover, it was a case not so much of Matsukata's having won the day with a persuasive counterattack as of the other government leaders' being so preoccupied with the political crisis that they essentially left it to Matsukata to deal with problems of finance.[60] At the same time, the Sat-Chō leaders may well have felt indebted to Matsukata for contributing to Ōkuma's ouster by directly attacking his financial policies, something Itō, for instance, could not have done, for, although he was Ōkuma's rival in the political arena, Itō had cooperated with him on financial matters.[61] Hence, for all the insight and sophistication of Matsukata's arguments—and unquestionably they far surpassed the level of debate at the time on note redemption—it was almost a case of "Matsukata finance" by default; or, as Muroyama Yoshimasa puts it, "Matsukata ended up assuming the position of finance minister-cum-*sangi* by a process of elimination."[62]

On the much-debated question of continuities and breaks in financial policy between Ōkuma and Matsukata,[63] one can view the proposal that Ōkuma submitted with Itō's support in July 1881 as representing a significant shift in his policy approach and a "bridge" to the Matsukata financial reform.[64] Both the Ōkuma-Itō proposal and Matsukata's 1881 proposal called for promoting exports and accumulating specie, for retiring fiat notes, and for establishing a convertible currency managed by a central bank. Accordingly, one could claim that by the summer of 1881 Ōkuma, working with colleagues, had set the basic course for the reforms Matsukata would execute. Their programs would then appear to differ mainly in tempo—go-fast versus go-slow.

Nonetheless, a fundamental divergence characterized their approaches. Ōkuma, like statesmen in other developing countries at the time, called for dependence on foreign capital and even foreign management; the Council of State in fact approved a recommendation by British minister to Japan Sir Harry Parkes that it hire a British banker to run Ōkuma's proposed central bank.[65] Matsukata countered with a plan that, in its nationalist emphasis, was unorthodox for its time, for he rejected foreign involvement, insisting on a more gradual program of financial reform through reliance on Japan's own efforts.

ORTHODOX FINANCE AND "THE DICTATES OF PRACTICAL EXPEDIENCY"

Influences on Matsukata

Matsukata was the only Meiji leader who in the late 1870s and early 1880s consistently advocated monetary and fiscal policies that mirrored mid-nineteenth-century British orthodoxy, but his policies also had roots in illiberal traditions of East Asia. In Matsukata's thinking, the practice of "financial orthodoxy" meant, above all, the pursuit of policies (1) to restrain spending by the central government and generate adequate revenue for it, thereby enabling it to balance the national budget or, better yet, create a budget surplus and (2) to establish and maintain a stable, national currency backed by specie—a hard currency with paper money convertible into silver or gold coins. Matsukata clearly followed through on the second point, and his pronouncements in favor of austerity and laissez-faire economic policy suggest, at least at a rhetorical level, a more general commitment to classical financial and economic liberalism. By the time he succeeded Sano Tsunetami and sought to implement such policies, most of which his predecessors had introduced, Matsukata had come to embrace aspects of financial orthodoxy based on multiple influences: his pre-Restoration study of ancient Chinese and early modern Japanese financial reforms, his experience as an official in the new Meiji government, and his exposure to Western ideas and precedents in the 1870s.[1]

Yet once he became finance minister, Matsukata would display a flexibility in financial management, adjusting to "the dictates of practical expediency," as he would declare in 1886. In showing such adaptability, he would depart significantly from classical liberal approaches to fiscal and industrial policy as well as differ from neoliberal projects of the late twentieth century. The program Matsukata ended up carrying out would feature practices that were *heterodox* from a liberal or neoliberal perspective such as a larger state role in the economy, incrementalism in building upon reforms that were already under way, and reliance in part on non-Western intellectual traditions.

Still, a widely held view is that, as finance czar, Matsukata rigidly applied the theories of orthodox finance he had learned from French economists during the nine-month trip he took to Europe in 1878.[2] Some historians likewise claim that French scholarship and example provided the overall pattern for the Matsukata reforms of the 1880s.[3] For the most part, however, French tutelage simply reinforced ideas that Matsukata had been developing since the Restoration, drawing on both Sino-Japanese and Western sources, ideas that he would go on to implement pragmatically after 1881. Granted, he and his subordinates in the Ministry of Finance did rely heavily on the French recycling of classical British liberal economics. Yet what they found attractive about this French rendering was not its free trade or laissez-faire prescriptions but its down-to-earth, policy-oriented views on monetary and fiscal matters. Matsukata and his brain trust had no single model for financial reform; rather, they participated in a global circulation of ideas and practices regarding public finance, including currents not only of Franco-British liberalism but also of German and U.S. economic nationalism.

Sino-Japanese Sources of the Matsukata Reform

Most accounts of the ideas and practices that informed the Matsukata financial reform emphasize the European influences the future finance minister absorbed during his overseas sojourn in 1878. Yet—as only a few historians have detailed, but as one might expect of someone who had received a traditional samurai education as a youth—Matsukata also drew on indigenous and Chinese sources for his views on public finance. John Sagers and others have pointed out that Matsukata and his contemporaries in the Meiji regime emerged from a homegrown mercantilist tradition whereby the Tokugawa shogunate and domain governments had sought to amass specie by promoting import substitution and the production of export goods; indeed, Katalin Ferber suggests that the written work and advice of the Western experts Matsukata encountered in 1878 largely confirmed ideas that the Meiji oligarchs had already formed in pre-Meiji times.[4] More specifically, during his formative years in his home domain of Satsuma, Matsukata had studied the Confucian classics and works on Japanese and Chinese history. Muroyama Yoshimasa writes that, although Matsukata "was not particularly fond of reading," his favorite books included the ancient Chinese compilation *Guanzi* and the writings of the Tokugawa-period shogunal adviser Arai Hakuseki (1657–1725).[5]

The encyclopedic *Guanzi*, named after the philosopher and politician Guan Zhong (ca. 720–645 BC) and probably written in the mid-third century BC, is regarded as a precursor of Legalism for its practical prescriptions on political economy.[6] From this work Matsukata would have learned that Guan Zhong, as prime minister of the state of Qi from 685 BC, introduced a number of economic reforms, including a uniform tax code and state monopolies on salt and iron. He may also have been struck by *Guanzi*'s emphasis on investigating the past to understand the present, a dictum that Matsukata had clearly taken to heart by the time he entered the Ministry of Finance in 1871 as assistant head of the Taxation Bureau.

According to Muroyama, the most decisive Asian influence on Matsukata's financial thinking was the Confucian scholar-official Arai Hakuseki, who became the leading shogunal adviser in the 1710s. Muroyama cites the journalist Tokutomi Iichirō as observing in a eulogy for Matsukata that "in financial matters he adored Arai Hakuseki."[7] Muroyama claims, moreover, that the financial and currency reform the shogunate carried out with Hakuseki's input was "the model for the Matsukata reform."[8]

The parallels between the Hakuseki and Matsukata reforms as well as the crises that preceded them are indeed striking. Beginning in 1695, the Tokugawa shogunate, which initially had minted gold coins (*koban*) of high quality, sought to cover burgeoning government expenses by repeatedly reducing the precious metal content of its currency. In a scenario similar to what Japan would face in the late 1870s, successive reminting set off rampant inflation, causing speculation to soar, imports to rise, and specie to flow out of the country. As a member of the shogun's advisory group from 1693, Hakuseki remonstrated against debasement, charging that it had, among other deleterious effects, led to the hoarding of pre-1695 coins and violent fluctuation in the gold-silver exchange rate, much to the disruption of private commercial transactions. Inflation, he pointed out, had erupted because the shogunate had not only depreciated the currency but also increased the amount in circulation. Hakuseki then helped bring about a dramatic, albeit short-lived, reversal of policy in 1713, when the shogunate embarked on a program of retrenchment and deflation aimed at restoring the value of the currency by reminting coins to their original standard of purity and reducing the amount of money in circulation.[9]

In public addresses as minister of finance, Matsukata clearly showed the influence of his study of Hakuseki and of public finance in pre-1868 Japan. In discussing the history of Japanese currency and monetary standards, he would typically begin with the minting of hard money at the start of the Tokugawa period before moving on to the economic disruptions at the turn of the seventeenth century and again at the end of the shogunate.[10] This narrative strengthened his conviction that establishing a solid, specie-backed currency system was absolutely essential for the government to achieve economic and financial stability.[11] To say that the Hakuseki-inspired reform was the "model" for his financial program may be an exaggeration, but precedents from premodern Japanese financial history certainly weighed heavily in Matsukata's thinking.

Another parallel between the monetary reforms associated with Hakuseki and with Matsukata has to do with their practical approach. Kate W. Nakai states that the shogunate's post-1713 reform "was as much a pragmatic response to the socioeconomic problems of the day as an outgrowth of intellectual theory," specifically of Hakuseki's bullionism.[12] Despite his adherence to bullionist theory, Hakuseki himself, according to Tessa Morris-Suzuki, was "a man with a strongly practical and empirical turn of mind," whose method of dealing with a social or economic issue was "not so much to refer to the writings of the Confucian sages" as "to collect detailed information on its causes and implications."[13]

Nakai's description of shogunal monetary policy as embodying a "flexible pragmatism in trying to deal with ongoing problems"[14] would apply perfectly to Matsukata's mode of operation as well. Muroyama asserts that, as assistant head and then chief of the Taxation Bureau in the early to middle 1870s, Matsukata sought to design and implement a land tax reform suited to the actual conditions of Japan, drawing not so much on economic theories imported from the West as on his study of Japan's premodern tax systems and the current state of Japanese agriculture.[15] As Muroyama puts it, a "homegrown policy gene" animated Matsukata's reform ideas, and even after his tutelage in Europe in 1878 he found Western theories useful only insofar as they fit the realities of the Japanese economy.[16]

A similarly pragmatic attitude informed Matsukata's position on currency standards. In his view, that Japan would ultimately adopt a gold currency system was only self-evident: Japan had privileged gold in its currency since the beginning of the Tokugawa period, and by the 1880s most advanced Western countries had gone on the gold standard. "For him, from both historical and practical perspectives, the gold standard was the indispensable factor" for creating a sound financial and economic environment.[17] Yet as of the early 1880s Matsukata also understood that Japan's shortage of gold and the continued use of silver as the currency of trade in Asia necessitated adoption of the silver standard. Thus, in a speech to the Japanese Bankers' Club in his fifth year as finance minister, he defended the government's choice of silver as the standard instead of gold—even as he conceded, as it was later reported, that the gold standard was superior "from a purely scientific point of view"—declaring that "the aim of the Administration is to adapt itself to the dictates of practical expediency, rather than to the theories of abstract science."[18] As he summed up his approach to financial policymaking shortly before he left Europe in 1878, "No matter how superior the scholarship, no matter how advanced the logic, if it does not conform to reality, then it is of no use to the state whatsoever."[19]

Early Financial Experience

Matsukata, writes Muroyama, "had no formal training in finance or economics" and "had not been involved in any specialized line of work" in those fields prior to the Meiji Restoration in 1868, when he was 33 years old.[20] Yet Muroyama's assertion that until 1868 Matsukata lived the life of a "typical samurai" with "hardly any connection to financial or economic matters" is not entirely accurate.[21] In fact, by then he had acquired a considerable amount of what we might call, in the overused parlance of academia today, "experiential learning."

Before and during the Restoration of 1868

As a teenager in the early 1850s, Matsukata served as a clerk in the domain's treasury. Then, in the waning years of the Tokugawa period, he was dispatched by the Satsuma authorities to the shogunate's naval training center in Nagasaki, where he diligently studied Western mathematics and surveying techniques as well as the operation and outfitting of warships.[22] If not for his recruitment as a prefectural governor in 1868 and civil administrator in the central government in 1870, after the Restoration he might well have become the architect of the imperial Japanese navy, largely the work of fellow Satsuma men.

Some scholars, including Takahashi Makoto and Yoshino Toshihiko, have suggested that a decade before his direct exposure to Western thought and practice Matsukata learned the principles of financial orthodoxy from a native guru, an expert in Western studies by the name of Yamamoto Kakuma (1828–1892).[23] The son of a high-ranking samurai of the Aizu domain, Yamamoto moved to Edo in 1853 to study Western military science with Sakuma Shōzan (1811–1864) and Katsu Kaishū (1823–1899), among other specialists. Back in Aizu, he taught in the domain academy and in a newly established school of "Dutch studies." In 1862 Yamamoto accompanied the daimyo of Aizu to Kyoto, where two years later he set up his own school of English and Dutch studies. At the time of the Restoration, with his domain fighting on the shogunal side, he was captured by imperial forces and held at the Satsuma mansion in Kyoto.

During his captivity, Yamamoto, who by that time had lost his eyesight, dictated a lengthy treatise summarizing his opinions on a range of policy issues for presentation to Shimazu Hisamitsu (1817–1887), father of the Satsuma daimyo. In the section titled "Kahei" (Currency), Yamamoto stressed the dangers of inconvertible notes, arguing that the government must back paper money with specie.[24] According to an early biography of Yamamoto, by the late 1870s he had come to advocate the adoption of the gold standard and the establishment of a central bank that would issue convertible paper.[25]

Although Matsukata had served as an aide to Hisamitsu and his son in the mid-1860s, he was in Kyushu during Yamamoto's house arrest and likely did not see the 1868 treatise when it was written. As finance minister, Matsukata did seek out Yamamoto's advice and later remarked to Fukai Eigo (1871–1945), who became Matsukata's private secretary in 1900, that the two teachers he admired the most were Yamamoto Kakuma and Léon Say (1826–1896), the French minister of finance who had personally tutored him during his time in Paris.[26] This pronouncement has led one historian to proclaim that "Yamamoto was the father of the Matsukata financial reform, Say the mother."[27]

That this Western studies expert had a significant formative impact on Matsukata seems doubtful, however. Yamamoto does not appear to have come to Matsukata's attention until 1882, soon after the founding of the Bank of Japan, when the prominent Kyoto businessman Hamaoka Kōtetsu (1853–1936) reportedly told Matsukata that as early as 1877 an acquaintance named Yamamoto Kakuma had already stressed the need to establish a central bank. Surprised to learn that "such a farsighted person" (*sonna senkakusha*) existed, Matsukata asked Hamaoka to arrange a meeting so that he and Yamamoto might "exchange views." When the meeting took place in Kyoto that year, Yamamoto heartily endorsed the finance minister's currency and banking reform, urging him to "resolutely carry out your intentions no matter what hardships you may face," though he also warned that in doing so Matsukata would be risking his neck. Matsukata replied that he had been prepared for the worst from the start and parted with the rather dramatic statement that "either paper money will have my head, or I will have its" (*shihei ga Masayoshi no kubi o kiru ka, kono Masayoshi ga shihei no kubi o kiru ka da*).[28] Though hardly the "father" of the Matsukata program, Yamamoto clearly made a deep impression on the finance minister, who years later recalled that "when public opinion was vociferously against me, only a few people besides this Yamamoto Kakuma told me they approved of what I was doing."[29]

Governorship of Hita

Matsukata's real on-the-job training in finance and economics began after the Restoration with his appointment as governor of Hita Prefecture, previously the largest territory in Kyushu directly controlled by the shogunate.[30] During his tenure from 1868 to 1870, he dealt with a range of fiscal, monetary, and commercial issues and twice memorialized the central government on the urgency of establishing a sound, unified currency system.

In April 1868, before Matsukata assumed office, the new Meiji regime had adopted the policy of issuing inconvertible "Council of State notes" (*dajōkan satsu*) to fund local economic development and make up budget deficits. Soon after Hita Prefecture began receiving its share of the notes in the fall of 1868, Matsukata faithfully followed the central government directive to place them in circulation at a fixed rather than market rate, but Hita merchants complained as the new paper money depreciated. To further impede matters, notes printed by neighboring domains were also flowing into Hita and falling in value, causing inflation and business stagnation. Many of Hita's villages were paying taxes in this domain paper, and the merchants who collected the tax money to use as loan capital pending delivery to the authorities accordingly petitioned the prefecture to guarantee the convertibility of the domain notes.[31]

In response to these problems, Matsukata sent two memoranda to the central government, one in November 1868 and the other in March 1869.[32] In the first, he called on the Council of State to unify the nation's currency, remarking that the job "will not be finished if currency remains unstandardized even in the remote corners of rural areas" (*kahei no gi wa hekikyō hisū made ichiyō narazu sōrō tewa aisumazu*).[33] Matsukata further recommended that the council either set a redemption deadline for all domain notes or direct localities to return the notes to the issuing domains in exchange for specie and thereafter restrict the use of such notes to their respective domains of origin. In the second, he criticized the decision the central government had made a month earlier to switch from a fixed to a market rate for *dajōkan satsu*, arguing that the change in policy risked causing prefectural residents to lose faith in the new regime.

Through his practical experience with Dajōkan and domain notes in Hita Prefecture, Matsukata thus became aware of the need both to ensure the smooth circulation of currency and to establish a sound monetary system at the level of national policy. At this early stage, his understanding of these issues was admittedly limited: in his two memoranda, he offered neither a theoretical rationale nor concrete measures for achieving a stable national currency, going no further than to emphasize the moral obligation to maintain consistency of policy based on "fidelity" (*shingi*). Yet the local experience that Matsukata gained during his brief stint as Hita governor would, to a considerable degree, help prepare him for the national financial responsibilities he would undertake after joining the newly formed Ministry of Finance in 1871.[34]

Knowledge of the West

Once he entered the central government, Matsukata began to develop more so-phisticated ideas on finance. Muroyama contends that until Matsukata went abroad in 1878 he "was ignorant of conditions in the West" and "had had no ex-posure to modern finance or economics."[35] This assertion, however, needs qual-ification. Granddaughter Haru Matsukata Reischauer claims that Matsukata had read translated works by Léon Say before he sailed to Paris and met the French finance minister.[36] Although the first book-length translation of a work associ-ated with Say—*Dictionnaire des finances* (1889–1894), which he edited—did not appear until a dozen years after Matsukata's European sojourn,[37] the in-house li-brary of the Ministry of Finance, to which Matsukata would have had access, boasted the second-largest government repository of books from Western coun-tries (the largest being that of the schools that would later merge into the prede-cessor of Tokyo Imperial University). This library held a number of translations of Western economics textbooks, in particular from Britain, the United States, and France, reflecting the ascendance of classical liberal economics in the first de-cade and a half of the Meiji period, before the turn to the German historical school of economics.

In the early 1870s the available Japanese translations, most of them in abridged form, included William Ellis's *Outlines of Social Economy* (1846), Francis Way-land's *Elements of Political Economy* (1837), and Millicent Fawcett's *Political Econ-omy for Beginners* (1870). Of these, the Ellis translation, produced by Kanda Takahira (1830–1898) in 1867 from a Dutch rendition of the original English, rep-resented the first systematic introduction to Western economics in Japanese. A scholar in the shogunate's Western Studies Institute (Bansho Shirabesho), Kanda later drew on the work's taxation section to author an 1870 proposal that influ-enced the land tax reform largely carried out under Matsukata in the mid-1870s.[38] Meanwhile, translations of chapters from Wayland's book as well as from *Cham-bers's Educational Course: Political Economy, for Use in Schools, and for Private In-struction* (1852) figured in the best-selling *Seiyō jijō* (Conditions in the West; 1867–1870) series by Fukuzawa Yukichi. Fukuzawa's former student Obata Tokujirō (1842–1905) embarked on a full translation of Wayland in 1871; begin-ning in 1872, both the Wayland primer and Arthur Latham Perry's *Elements of Political Economy* (1865) were adopted by the Department of Translation of the Ministry of Finance for use in teaching political economy and financial practice. By 1870, an abridged version of Perry's book had also become available in Japa-nese translation.[39]

For knowledge of current trends in the West, Matsukata would also have been able to turn to the Western experts—nineteen in 1872 and twenty-seven two years later—whom the Ministry of Finance kept on its payroll.[40] Illustrating his basic awareness of these trends, Matsukata noted in an 1874 memorandum that France had faced no interference from its neighbors when it increased tariffs to pay off the indemnity it had incurred after the Franco-Prussian War of 1870–1871.[41] In fact, the French government had cleared the indemnity (by the autumn of 1873) not through tariffs but through bonds issued in both domestic and international markets.[42] Protectionist sentiment was, however, clearly on the rise in postwar France, as in the early 1870s the authorities did what they could to raise import duties that were not restricted under the treaties France had concluded with leading European countries during the free trade movement before the war.[43] Matsukata's point was that Japan, then burdened by tariff restrictions imposed by the Western powers in 1858, ought to have the same right to set its own customs duties. In any event, his argument shows that he did have some knowledge, however incomplete, of recent financial developments in Europe.

The growing maturity of Matsukata's views on financial policy is evidenced by a lengthy memorandum he presented to the Council of State in September 1875. In this document he urged the government to economize on administrative expenses, to bolster the faltering gold standard by reducing the amount of paper money in circulation and augmenting the Treasury's gold reserves, and to stanch the hemorrhaging of specie from Japan by promoting both import substitution and exports.[44] In particular, how to deal with the nation's "enormous" (*kyota*) quantity of inconvertible notes, Matsukata asserted, was "the most difficult among extremely difficult tasks" (*shinanchū no saishinan*), but he warned that "each day that we neglect this [problem] inflicts another day of harm" (*ichi nichi kore o okotareba ichi nichi no hei ari*).[45] By pointing out that the excessive issue of fiat notes was the cause of paper money depreciation, Matsukata displayed a level of discernment "that had not been seen in the memorials of finance officials to that point."[46] Finance Minister Ōkuma Shigenobu would incorporate Matsukata's recommendations on note redemption and specie accumulation into a proposal he submitted to the government the following month.[47]

In his call for shrinking the supply of paper money to stabilize its value, Matsukata may well have been inspired not only by his study of public finance in early modern and contemporary Japan but also by the advice of foreign employees in the Ministry of Finance and by his reading of Western works in translation. While in Europe, he would gain further confirmation of this position from Western sources elucidating the quantity theory of money, and as minister of finance he would go on to implement a dramatic reduction of the paper money in circulation in 1882–1883.

In addition to his exposure to the principles of classical economic liberalism in the 1870s, Matsukata also showed the influence of Friedrich List's ideas during that decade. In a battery of memoranda he submitted to the government in 1874–1875, including the one in which he referred to French tariff protection, Matsukata urged the government to press for the recovery of tariff control; moreover, in a little-known aspect of his 1878 travels around Europe, he exhorted Japanese consuls to push for treaty revision so that Japan could increase customs duties to aid fledgling domestic industries and raise revenue for the Treasury.[48] According to Reischauer, Matsukata told Say that "he was a great admirer of Adam Smith's laissez-faire economics and hoped that the day would come when Japanese industry would be strong enough to make those policies feasible in his country, but protectionism was more appropriate for Japan at that time. In fact, throughout his life, Matsukata often referred to the protectionist policies of the German economist Friedrich List as more suitable then for Japan than Adam Smith's ideas."[49] A Japanese translation of List's *Das nationale System der politischen Ökonomie* (1841) did not appear until 1889, but as early as 1872 the Ministry of Finance had published a book by Wakayama Norikazu (1840–1891) that included a partial translation of *Principles of Social Science* (1858–1859), a three-volume work written by the U.S. champion of infant industry protection, Henry Carey (1793–1879).[50] In his work Carey "made liberal use" of List's *National System*.[51] Hence, from the early Meiji period, even if Japanese officials were unable to read Western-language editions of List, they had access to a recycled version of his ideas, which Japanese writings were reflecting as early as the mid-1870s.[52] And Matsukata was surely aware that the Tokugawa shogunate had clamped down on imports from the early eighteenth century, when currency crises had resulted from the outflow of specie to pay for Chinese silk and other foreign goods and from the depletion of Japan's metal mines.

True, the book translations available in Japan in the early to middle 1870s were mostly introductory, and Matsukata had to await his trip to Europe for immersion in theoretical and applied finance of a more advanced nature. Yet those circumstances hardly meant that he went abroad totally uninformed about currents in Western financial and economic thought and practice.

The French Connection

Matsukata's long-held wish to travel abroad finally came true when he was appointed head of the Japanese delegation to the 1878 Exposition Universelle in Paris. Held from May to November on a scale greater than that of any previous world's fair, the Paris Expo celebrated the recovery of France from the Franco-Prussian War; during his trip, which lasted from March to December, Matsukata took advantage of his appointment to tour much of western Europe, investigating financial, economic, and transportation systems and meeting with scholars and officials in France, Britain, Germany, Switzerland, and the Netherlands. As Henry Rosovsky notes in his influential study of early Meiji economic development, the nine-month European sojourn by the future leader of Japanese finance "had considerable intellectual consequences."[53]

Léon Say

The pivotal figure in Matsukata's overseas journey was the economist Léon Say (fig. 2.1), grandson of the Adam Smith disciple Jean-Baptiste Say (1767–1832). Like his grandfather, Léon Say was a fervent advocate of free trade who opposed

FIGURE 2.1   Léon Say (1826–1896). *Photo from Sowa Sergiuez/Alamy stock photo.*

"state interference of any kind"[54]—although he could also be flexible, as he showed in backing the Freycinet Plan, the vast program of public works centering on railroad, canal, and port construction launched by the Third Republic in 1878. Even more than Say's endorsement of public support for infrastructural and especially railway development, his consistent disapproval of state indebtedness would have resonated strongly with Matsukata, who considered indebtedness "a form of servitude" and later recalled visiting his father's grave in Satsuma after paying off the family debt in 1857 as "one of the most satisfying moments of his whole career."[55] Say, as "practically the autocratic ruler of the French finances" for much of the 1870s,[56] had displayed his financial acumen during his first term as finance minister in 1872–1873 by completing payment of the massive Franco-Prussian War indemnity of ₣5 billion (£200 million) a full year and a half ahead of schedule. When Matsukata arrived in 1878, Say, who was in his third term as finance minister, was on the verge of clearing the debt of ₣1.5 billion that the French government owed the central bank.[57]

Matsukata's time in Europe also coincided with two international meetings held in Paris on pressing financial matters. In August 1878 Say presided over an international monetary conference, one of a series of such assemblies in the latter third of the nineteenth century, which convened at the French foreign ministry to deliberate on measures proposed by the United States to reintroduce bimetallism and halt the depreciation of silver. The global silver slide that had begun in 1871 had accelerated two years later when Germany adopted the gold standard, a move that threatened to inundate neighboring countries with demonetized silver and prompted France to retaliate by limiting silver coinage.[58] The conference failed to reach agreement on a single monetary standard or a new gold-silver exchange rate, ensuring a continued drift toward gold among Western nations. Then in October, two months before Matsukata's departure from Europe, the member states of the Latin Monetary Union, which had formed under French leadership in 1865, met in Paris and resolved to completely stop the minting of silver coins. This decision gave a further push to the "limping bimetallism" that had begun with the total suspension of silver coinage by France in 1876.[59] Matsukata clearly set foot in Europe at an eventful time for French as well as international finance.

Shortly after arriving in Paris, Matsukata toured the Tobacco Monopoly Bureau, which was under the supervision of the finance ministry. Learning of Matsukata's perceptive questioning of officials at the bureau, Say invited the Japanese delegation leader to call on him. On that visit, as Matsukata later recounted, the finance minister told him, "We'll place a desk for you next to mine; bring an interpreter, and let's talk from time to time."[60] So Matsukata received his own private tutorial from the French statesman.

Rosovsky speculates that Say may well have advised his Japanese guest to seek balanced budgets and to bear in mind the important role of a sound, gold-backed currency in establishing a nation's reputation for creditworthiness.[61] As Jean Garrigues points out, "budget-balancing" was indeed "the watchword" of Say's financial administration;[62] in a speech to the Chamber of Deputies in late 1875, for instance, Say declared that "it is only on a balanced budget that one can base the credit of a country, and without credit no governing is possible."[63] But on the question of currency standards, over which advocates of gold monometallism and bimetallism were then "locked in bitter dispute worldwide,"[64] Say took a cautious, ambivalent public stance. He announced at the August monetary conference that the French attitude was one of "expectancy": his country held itself "in readiness to adopt the single gold standard or to revert to the double standard, according to circumstances."[65] At the same time, he suggested that France would restore the free minting of silver if the silver market stabilized and assured U.S. representatives that "France was sincerely bimetallic at heart."[66] In making these pronouncements, Say undoubtedly was showing consideration toward his longtime associate Alphonse de Rothschild (1827–1905) and other directors of the privately owned Bank of France, who vigorously defended bimetallism out of a desire to prevent the bank's large silver holdings from further losing value as well as to maintain the steady income private banks derived from arbitrage between the two metals. Owing to the strong opposition of the Paris financial community to gold monometallism, "the French government never renounced bimetallism in principle."[67]

Still, by 1878 France and almost every other western European country had gone on a de facto, if not official, gold standard. In his private conversations with Matsukata, Say may have advised that Japan also go for gold, although in view of his public statements he likely emphasized convertibility over any particular monetary standard. Nonetheless, Matsukata would have been struck by reports of comments from the August international monetary conference identifying gold with modern industrial nations and silver with backward, "uncivilized" countries. The Swiss representative expressed a common sentiment among gold monometallists when he declared that "silver was an inferior metal, ill adapted to the needs of higher civilization, . . . only fit as a standard for backward nations."[68] Five years later, as minister of finance, Matsukata, in a speech to Japanese bankers about his program to replace the country's inconvertible paper money with silver-backed notes, would wax poetic on his ultimate goal of moving Japan into the ranks of the "advanced" gold-bloc nations by returning it to the abortive gold standard of early Meiji: "Even though it has become a silvery world, one day we will see a spring when golden flowers bloom again" (*shirogane no yo to wa nare domo, itsuka mata koganebana saku haru o min to wa*).[69]

Whatever the French finance minister might have advised regarding currency standards, he would certainly have disapproved of the issuance of unbacked paper by Japan's government and national banks. Rosovsky concludes, "Judging by Matsukata's subsequent actions, Say must have . . . been a persuasive advocate of his own ideas."[70] Matsukata himself would write of his debt to Say in an 1883 letter upon the Meiji emperor's conferral of a decoration on the Frenchman: "In taking responsibility for the public finances of imperial Japan, I have had the opportunity to put into practice what you previously taught me . . . [and] from the beginning have followed the principle of hard currency (kōka no shugi)."[71]

Matsukata was unduly generous in his expression of gratitude, for he had been championing similar ideas from before he went to Europe. For the most part, Say merely offered empirical and theoretical support for the policies his Japanese guest had already been recommending to the Meiji leadership. Say's main original contribution was to impress on his visitor the importance of establishing a central bank, a feature that had been missing from Matsukata's proposals before 1878. In the course of their discussions, on learning of Japan's decentralized system of national banks, Say counseled that it was "inadvisable for various kinds of banks to operate separately without coordination" and that it was "definitely best to establish a central bank under the aegis of the government."[72] Say's advice seems to have had a decisive impact on Matsukata, convincing him that Japan needed to overhaul its banking system along centralized European lines to secure the convertibility of its currency and the provision of credit to private enterprise.

Matsukata proceeded to make a special point of examining the leading central banks of Europe, spending two full days visiting the National Bank of Belgium.[73] Say had recommended that institution as an appropriate model for Japan owing to the relative lateness of its founding, which, as Matsukata explained later, had enabled its creators "to consider fully the mistakes as well as the successes of older banks."[74] Matsukata ordered a subordinate, Katō Wataru (1847–1889), to remain in Brussels to study the history and organization of the Belgian national bank; Katō would return to Japan three years later to play a key role in the establishment of the Bank of Japan in 1882.[75]

Pierre Paul Leroy-Beaulieu

Matsukata's connection with Léon Say is fairly well known, but less so is his relationship with another Frenchman, a prominent economist and disciple of Say by the name of Pierre Paul Leroy-Beaulieu (1843–1916; fig. 2.2). Say introduced Matsukata to Leroy-Beaulieu and his writings, in particular Traité de la science des finances, published just the previous year.[76] Scholars sometimes argue that one of the keys to Matsukata's success and longevity as financial czar was the firm

FIGURE 2.2   Pierre Paul Leroy-Beaulieu (1843–1916). *Photo from The History Collection/Alamy stock photo.*

theoretical grasp he had of his field as one of the few Japanese in early Meiji to have mastered the science of public finance.[77] Yet one would be hard-pressed to characterize Matsukata as a genius in financial theory. His forte was decidedly in the area of practical or applied finance; hence the huge attraction of French scholarship—especially that of Leroy-Beaulieu, who was very much an authority on the practical application of orthodox financial theory.[78]

In actuality, the person most responsible for popularizing Leroy-Beaulieu's work in Japan, and specifically for making it accessible to government officials, was not Matsukata but a junior bureaucrat in the Ministry of Finance named Tajiri Inajirō (1850–1923; fig. 2.3).[79] Tajiri was the first Japanese student sent overseas to major in finance. He spent eight years in the United States during the 1870s, eventually earning a bachelor's degree from Yale College and staying on for a year of graduate study there. Under his primary mentor at Yale, the sociologist William

FIGURE 2.3   Tajiri Inajirō (1850–1923). *Images of Yale individuals, ca. 1750–2001 (inclusive). Courtesy of Manuscripts & Archives, Yale University.*

Graham Sumner (1840–1910), Tajiri learned "the latest theories on state finance, monetary policy, and currency stabilization."[80] An impassioned proponent of hard currency, Sumner frequently gave public lectures on "the evils of inconvertible paper money," including one at the invitation of the New Haven Chamber of Commerce during Tajiri's freshman year at Yale.[81] As Sumner had declared in his 1874 book *A History of American Currency*, "an irredeemable paper currency is a national calamity of the first magnitude. . . . It is like a disease in the blood, undermining the constitution and spreading decay through all the arteries of business."[82] H. A. Scott Trask writes that Sumner also believed in "the systematic study of history" as a method of understanding economic laws and, in *A History of American Currency*, maintained that the U.S. colonial experience "demonstrated

the validity of . . . the quantity theory of money."[83] As Sumner stated in the conclusion to that book, "the whole story which precedes goes to show that the value
of a paper currency depends on its *amount*."[84]

It was Sumner who recommended that Tajiri peruse Leroy-Beaulieu's 1877
Traité de la science des finances—the same book Say introduced to Matsukata on
the other side of the Atlantic, at nearly the same time—which spelled out in plain
language the importance of budget balancing and currency convertibility, among
other orthodox principles. As Tajiri noted in the preface to his first partial translation of *Traité*, published within half a year of his return to Japan in 1879, Sumner was of the opinion that "anyone who wants to understand political economy
need only read Mr. Beaulieu's financial treatise."[85] Of greater interest to Tajiri (and
Matsukata) than the Frenchman's opposition to tariffs and direct state intervention in the economy was his classic position on public finance, specifically on the
positive role that official monetary and fiscal policies could play in stabilizing
financial conditions. According to Marc Flandreau, in *Traité* Leroy-Beaulieu articulated the contemporary "consensus view" on monetary systems, emphasizing, as did Sumner, the quantity theory. "The domestic supply of banknotes determined the value of the currency," which would depreciate if banks created
paper money "out of proportion" to their reserves; the public would then lose
trust in the currency until the government turned to "the fiscal machine [i.e.,
taxation and budget control] rather than the printing press . . . to finance public
expenditure."[86]

Tajiri entered the Ministry of Finance in early 1880, soon after his return to
Japan. From then to 1884 he and his colleague Komai Shigetada (1853–1901), who
had also studied public finance in the United States, worked to translate most of
Leroy-Beaulieu's treatise. The translation they produced of the chapter on the budget, for example, presented such sound prescriptions as "annual expenditures
should not exceed revenues" (*mainen no keihi wa sono shūnyū ni chōetsu sezaru o
yōsu*).[87] The Japanese editions of Boriyū (as Tajiri and Komai chose to shorten
and transliterate Leroy-Beaulieu's tongue-twister of a surname), then, became the
financial bible for mid-Meiji bureaucrats before the rise of the German historical
school of economics in the 1890s.[88] Tajiri went on to frame many of the components of the Matsukata reform, including, for example, the special account for
military emergencies within the Treasury's reserve fund and programs for the issuance of public bonds.[89] Tajiri would eventually rise to the position of assistant
minister of finance, serving in that capacity for a total of eight and a half years
between 1892 and 1901.[90] At Yale he had become a friend of classmate and future
U.S. president William Howard Taft—they had been seated alphabetically next
to each other in the classroom. On a visit to Japan after the turn of the century,
Taft, according to the reminiscences of his wife, learned from the spouse of Field

Marshal Ōyama Iwao that Tajiri had aspired to succeed Matsukata upon the oligarch's retirement as finance minister in 1900; but, despite having functioned as de facto head of the Ministry of Finance under his mentor, he had been passed over for the position, and "the disappointment had made Tajiri very much of a recluse."[91]

Further Western Influences: The Question of Foreign Borrowing

During his 1878 visit to Europe, Matsukata also came under direct Western influence on the question of foreign indebtedness. A common view is that he was on principle staunchly opposed to borrowing from abroad, a misperception that stems from his pronouncements and actions during the 1880–1881 debates over measures to combat the runaway inflation that had plagued Japan since 1878. The course he would actually take in the mid-1880s would reflect his basic pragmatism and flexible approach to financial policy.

By comparison, the Meiji emperor was a more principled opponent of foreign borrowing. His mid-1880 rescript ruling against Ōkuma's loan proposal declared the plan "most improper at the present time" (mottomo konnichi ni fuka naru).[92] The emperor's resolve on this issue was strengthened by previous advice from a somewhat unlikely source—former U.S. president Ulysses S. Grant (1822–1885). Grant visited Japan in 1879 during a round-the-world trip and earned the gratitude of Japanese officials for his emphatic support of treaty revision as well as his earnest counsel on various pressing matters. In a two-hour audience with the emperor, the ex-president denounced overseas borrowing as the road to national ruin, citing the unhappy experiences of Egypt and the Ottoman Empire.[93] As Grant declared, "There is nothing a nation should avoid as much as owing money abroad." If possible, Japan, which had taken two small loans from Britain in the early 1870s, "ought never to borrow any more from foreign nations."[94] In Grant's view, "loans from foreign powers were always attended with danger and humiliation," and Egypt, in particular, offered a lesson of what happened to countries that incurred enormous foreign debts: indiscriminate borrowing had made that country "a dependency to her creditors." Becoming indebted to foreign powers, he concluded, would only lead Japan "into the abyss into which Egypt has fallen."[95]

Grant's admonition made a forceful impression on the emperor and his advisers. When Ōkuma's loan proposal reached the Imperial Household, the emperor's private tutor, Motoda Eifu (1818–1891), strongly objected to it, citing Grant's warning from the year before. He and Minister of the Right Iwakura Tomomi asked whether Japan, should it fail to repay the loan, would "have to yield part of its territory—say, Shikoku or Kyushu—in order to satisfy its creditors." The emperor himself likewise noted in his rescript, "Last year Grant spoke at length concerning the advantages and disadvantages of foreign loans. His words are still in my ears. . . . Now is the time for putting thrift into practice."[96] Richard Chang concludes that Grant's influence on the emperor was "permanent and substantial." While deliberating with his ministers on the draft of the Meiji constitution shortly before its promulgation in 1889, for instance, the emperor "said over and over again, 'On this question Grant said . . . On that question Grant taught me . . .'"[97] The emperor's determination to avoid foreign loans would continue to affect state financial policy as late as 1895, following the conclusion of the First Sino-Japanese War: in a letter dated April 21 of that year, Grand Chamberlain (*jijūchō*) Tokudaiji Sanetsune (1840–1919) conveyed to Matsukata the emperor's will that he should "not float foreign loans but rely on domestic bonds. Of course, some years ago General Grant gave his opinion about the evils of raising foreign loans. . . . At this time do your utmost to restrain national expenses and keep from borrowing abroad."[98]

Meanwhile Matsukata, too, played the risk-to-national-sovereignty card in speaking out against Ōkuma's loan proposal and calling for financial reform through Japan's own resources. Influencing his position on the matter was another Frenchman he had met during his time in Paris, the politician, civil engineer, and commissioner-general of the 1878 universal exposition Jean-Baptiste Krantz (1817–1899). Krantz, who had devoted his early career to railway construction, emphasized to Matsukata the adverse effects of relying on foreign capital and management in the development of railroads, citing France's own sorry experience with British financial involvement. "If Japan is to permanently maintain national independence," Krantz insisted, "this matter is of utmost importance."[99] The Frenchman's warning hit home for Matsukata, who in a series of memoranda to his superiors in 1874 had already expressed concern over Japan's vulnerability under the unequal commercial treaties;[100] what was more, Japan, like France, had borrowed from Britain to finance its initial railway lines. In addition to Krantz, Leroy-Beaulieu may also have influenced Matsukata's position at the time through his caution in *Traité* that, under "an inconvertible paper regime," currency depreciation would render a large external debt an "untimely and painful" burden for a country: "States should thus be very careful when they borrow abroad."[101]

Yet, as his future actions would indicate, Matsukata was hardly an unyielding opponent of foreign borrowing. True, he did stand virtually alone in objecting to the recycled version of Ōkuma's loan proposal that the Council of State approved in the summer of 1881. After Ōkuma's ouster and his own appointment as finance minister in October 1881, Matsukata skillfully persuaded his colleagues, with the ready endorsement of the emperor, to shelve the plan. Matsukata's opposition to the Ōkuma proposal, however, was grounded not only in the threat that dependence on foreign money would pose to national sovereignty but also in the very high interest rate that Japan would have to pay under conditions prevailing at the time. Once those conditions changed, Matsukata was more willing to turn to foreign loans, as he did in the fall of 1883 when he proposed offering public bonds abroad in order to accelerate the accumulation of specie and the retirement of inconvertible notes and move up the timetable for resuming convertibility. By that time the price of public bonds had recovered as interest rates fell because of the depression that Matsukata himself had largely brought on with his drastic currency contraction of 1882–1883; furthermore, the severity of the economic downswing appears to have prompted Matsukata to set aside any doubts he might have had about turning to overseas capital markets.[102]

Accordingly, in December 1883 the Ministry of Finance announced regulations for two sets of bonds, one for note redemption and the other for state railway building, opening both issues to foreign buyers paying in specie. In 1884–1885, Matsukata made several attempts to sell large amounts of the redemption bonds in Europe; as it turned out, negotiations to place the bonds overseas collapsed, although brisk domestic sales more than compensated for the disappointing foreign subscriptions.[103] In any case, Matsukata was far from an unequivocal opponent of foreign borrowing, and his efforts on that front in the mid-1880s prefigured the success that Japan would enjoy a decade later in selling public bonds and raising loans overseas after it defeated China and used the enormous indemnity it obtained from the Qing regime to go on the gold standard in 1897.[104]

The German Connection

Regarding Western influence on mainstream Japanese financial thinking, Japan moved in general from a liberal Anglo-American phase in the first decade of the Meiji era to a pragmatic, technically oriented French phase in the second decade followed by a conservative German phase from the late 1880s.[105] This periodization, however, somewhat oversimplifies the actual flow of Western currents into Japan. For all the seeming hegemony of French financial thought under Matsukata, notions of national economics circulating directly from Germany and by way of the United States had already made their mark in Japan by the early 1880s. In those years, both Tajiri and his colleague Komai introduced the "older" German historical school while moonlighting as instructors at the predecessors of Tokyo Imperial University and Senshū University, respectively; although they mainly discussed classical liberal economics through a contemporary French filter, their lectures also included material from the German economist Wilhelm Roscher's *Die Grundlagen der National Ökonomie*.[106] Tajiri not only exposed his students to Roscher's work but, according to Ferber, was himself "strongly influenced" by the German's views, especially his emphasis on historical method and the state's responsibility to fashion a developmental strategy befitting the nation's particular circumstances.[107]

Indeed, one historian goes so far as to say that Tajiri by no means took France, let alone Britain, as his model; rather, he looked to Germany under Bismarck as his "rich country, strong army" (*fukoku kyōhei*) ideal. On a specific matter of urgent concern to Matsukata—establishing a system of convertible currency issued by a central bank—Tajiri called for following the German example with its elastic limit method for paper note issuance, underscoring the difficulties a fixed limit had historically dealt British banks at every outbreak of financial panic.[108] Furthermore, the Bank of Japan, insofar as it engaged extensively in the discounting of bills collateralized by the shares of state-subsidized private companies, functioned in practice more like a German investment bank than like its original model, the central bank of Belgium, "the most purely commercial national bank of its time."[109]

A Japanese attraction to German financial thought and practice in the early 1880s is perhaps unsurprising, given that during this period Japanese officials began turning to Germany for models in fields ranging from law and education to social policy.[110] By that time, as Erik Grimmer-Solem notes, the appeal of classical political economy and laissez-faire liberalism "was fading rapidly in the West" no less than in Japan, while German models, especially in scholarship and teaching, were on the rise in many countries, keeping trends in the second decade of Meiji "very much in line with international currents."[111]

Conclusion:
Models for the Matsukata Reform

Several scholars argue plausibly that France provided the basic pattern for the Matsukata reform. In doing so, they point to the influence of the practical, policy-oriented rendering of British classical economics by Leroy-Beaulieu and other French experts. In addition, they often cite the affinity between the Japanese situation and France's experience of mobilizing a sound monetary and fiscal program to surmount serious economic and financial challenges after its loss to Prussia. On the reception of French scholarship in particular, Ōbuchi Toshio writes that, because France and Japan "had experiences and problems in common, it was only natural that Leroy-Beaulieu's *Traité de la science des finances*, which empha-

sized the theoretical explanation of practical issues and featured copious examples and a lucid style, should have been singled out for extensive introduction into
Japan."[112] On the issue of foreign borrowing, Matsukata's outlook was shaped not
only by the warnings of Krantz and perhaps Leroy-Beaulieu, who reinforced his
pragmatic opposition to Ōkuma's loan schemes of 1880–1881, but also by the
practicality of Say, who floated a massive international loan in 1872 to accelerate
payment of France's indemnity to Germany. This act may well have inspired Matsukata's 1884–1885 efforts to sell bonds overseas to help advance his program of
currency reform.

Yet Matsukata and his assistants fell under the influence not only of French
and U.S. versions of British liberal economics but also of nationalist economic
ideas flowing from Germany, the United States, and other later-developing Western countries, particularly in the area of trade policy, as seen in Matsukata's call
for treaty revision to enable Japan's use of tariff protection, as well as in the field
of industrial policy. To be sure, the Matsukata program, under which the Meiji
regime sold most of its mines and factories, marked a significant shift away from
direct state involvement in the economy; one scholar goes so far as to assert that,
with the enactment of the Matsukata reform, the Japanese state adopted "a more
or less orthodox version of laissez faire."[113] Matsukata himself reflected the free
enterprise ideas of his French mentors when he stated in an 1882 memorandum,
"The Government should never attempt to compete with the people in pursuing
lines of industry or commerce. . . . It is always best . . . to leave those matters to
be conducted and developed by individual efforts and enterprise."[114] This pronouncement would have made Léon Say proud; as the Frenchman summed up
his own "liberal creed," "The true economic policy must be a policy of absten-
tion more than of action."[115]

Neither Say nor Leroy-Beaulieu, however, was a die-hard laissez-faire proponent, and the same was true of Matsukata. Say, in particular, supported the am-
bitious Freycinet Plan for state development of transport infrastructure, though
he also insisted that the government set a fixed budget for each public works project and limit the total amount of debt the treasury would incur.[116] Meanwhile, as
Dan Warshaw points out, Leroy-Beaulieu moved from a "hostile conception of
the state" at the start of his career to a moderate "acceptance of state activity": in
the 1877 *Traité*, he linked "his analysis of public expenditures to practical experience rather than to abstract principle" and "widened his earlier list of legitimate
state functions."[117] Anticipating the stance that Say, his mentor, would publicly
take in 1878, Leroy-Beaulieu wrote that government investment in railroads, ca-
nals, and ports could prove "a great benefit if the public works have been judi-
ciously conceived and executed with economy."[118] Similarly, Matsukata offered
generous subsidies to private railroad companies in the 1880s, an approach that

Krantz had recommended to him. Those and other private business subventions, combined with the financing of munitions factories and railroad workshops that the Meiji government continued to operate, kept state investment in industry at a high level even as the Matsukata reform unfolded and the government privatized most of its other industrial enterprises after the early 1880s.[119]

If one is to speak of a model for the Matsukata financial program of the early to middle 1880s, one would have to say that it was neither single nor static but rather a composite informed by a fluid array of Asian and Western precedents and typifying the pragmatic, eclectic approach the Meiji leadership took to the whole project of modern nation building. Yet to claim that financial authorities in Japan followed one Western model or another, or even a group of models, overlooks the fact that most states from the late nineteenth century to the Great Depression of the 1930s pursued basically the same set of financial policies the Meiji regime implemented after 1880: hard money, fiscal expansion alternating with contraction, and—when countries like post-1871 France and, much later, Japan were free to raise tariffs—selective protectionism. For the most part, Matsukata and his subordinates adopted foreign ideas and practices piecemeal to address immediate needs. As Kaneko Masaru cogently concludes, Tajiri chose Leroy-Beaulieu's treatise not because he had come under the sway of classical British economics or of laissez-faire ideology—far from it; rather, he recognized *Traité de la science des finances* as "a *technical work that transcended nationality*" (*mukokuseki no gijutsu sho*) and abounded in examples of problems common to nations worldwide.[120]

Japan thus entered a transnational circulation of ideas on financial issues—part of a "global traffic in ideas," as Grimmer-Solem puts it.[121] In this instance, the flow was epitomized by an American's introduction of a French utilitarian recycling of British political economy to a Japanese who would become a key player in the Matsukata reform—the thought of British classical economists as adapted by Leroy-Beaulieu and then transmitted to Tajiri Inajirō by William Graham Sumner. Metzler writes that "Japanese industrial policy had deep indigenous sources and was shaped by global currents of which Japanese statesmen were acutely conscious."[122] In view of the domestic and native-inflected Chinese influences that converged with imported Western concepts in Matsukata's thinking, this statement would seem to apply equally well to financial policy in post-1880 Japan.

AUSTERITY AND EXPANSION

The Matsukata Reform, 1881–1885

After assuming the Finance Ministry portfolio, Matsukata would attempt to carry out financial stabilization based at least in part on orthodox principles. One axiom of British-style financial orthodoxy to which he would adhere was the establishment of a hard paper currency, at this stage on a de facto silver standard. For all the gradualism of his monetary reform compared to the plan proposed by Ōkuma, Matsukata would achieve currency convertibility through a kind of "shock therapy" reminiscent of late-twentieth-century structural adjustment programs, as he would redeem unbacked government notes at breakneck speed, although he was building on note retirement that had already been under way, albeit at a slower pace, since 1879. Matsukata also intended to pay for the retirement of fiat paper and the accumulation of specie through fiscal retrenchment by freezing the budgets of government ministries.

Yet the outbreak of military crises on the Korean Peninsula, the worsening of the domestic depression brought on primarily by his own currency contraction, and other exigencies prompted Matsukata instead to *increase* government spending, generating fiscal deficits that he financed not by boosting tax revenues but by promoting exports and selling public bonds. He did raise sake brewery and other consumer taxes, but he did so to fund armaments expansion, not financial reform. Far from creating budget surpluses by slashing state expenditures and hiking indirect taxes, Matsukata presided over rising government outlays, stagnating tax revenues, and chronic budget deficits at the height of his financial reform in the years 1882–1884.

In responding to these trends through a pragmatic embrace of public bond issuance and state-led export promotion, Matsukata departed significantly from classical economic liberalism. He began turning toward such positive policies as early as 1883. In that regard, the Matsukata financial reform as it unfolded combined the contractionary program of Sano with the expansionary approach of Ōkuma. This policy mix, in turn, would help shorten a sharp, deflation-induced depression that Matsukata initially expected would continue for a year or two longer.

Note Redemption and Specie Accumulation under Matsukata

Under Ōkuma and Sano but especially under Matsukata, the Meiji government set out to raise revenue for retiring inconvertible paper money and purchasing specie from abroad, or to withdraw the fiat currency and acquire silver directly, through four principal means: cutting state expenditures, raising consumer taxes, floating public bonds, and underwriting exports. Another measure the state longed to employ, hiking import tariffs, was not an option until Japan fully escaped its semicolonial status and regained customs sovereignty in 1911. Nor was it politically possible to increase the land tax, which annually averaged two-thirds of government tax income from 1881 to 1885; in fact, the government reneged on a promise it had made in 1873 to *reduce* the land tax, fixed at 2.5 percent of assessed land value since 1877, by up to 1 percent once revenue from consumer taxes exceeded ¥2 million.[1] Of the available measures, after Matsukata became finance minister, retrenchment and taxation policies contributed relatively little; rather, it was bond issuance and export promotion that largely enabled the government to redeem fiat money and accumulate specie in quantities sufficient to resume convertibility in January 1886, a year or two earlier than Matsukata had originally anticipated.

In the event, spending cuts proved difficult to accomplish, as the government faced a series of unexpected developments, including a cholera epidemic in 1882, devastating weather conditions in 1884, the growing severity of the depression in rural areas that attended the "Matsukata deflation" and the scores of peasant disturbances it provoked between 1883 and 1885,[2] and above all anti-Japanese uprisings in Korea in 1882 and 1884 that prompted the army and navy to demand expanded military budgets. Matsukata grudgingly agreed to extraordinary military expenditures and tried to secure the necessary funds by doubling the rate of the sake tax, the most important consumer tax by far,[3] in late 1882. Because of the intensifying deflation and falling demand as well as increased home brewing and tax evasion, however, total income from the sake tax and related fees actually dropped from ¥16.3 million in fiscal 1882 to ¥13.5 million in 1883 and narrowly topped ¥14 million the following year.[4] The reported total for sake production plummeted by over a third from 1881 to 1884 and in fact never returned to the five million *koku* level of 1881–1882 until after 1912.[5] Consequently, Matsukata scrambled to raise additional tax revenue during those years, hiking indirect taxes or instituting new ones on everything from tobacco, soy sauce, and confectionaries to patent medicines and rice and stock brokering (see table 3.1).[6]

The decline in demand for sake and the resulting drop in both brewery production and tax proceeds after 1882 stemmed in large part from the decrease in farm household income caused by the plunge in the price of rice from 1881 to 1884.[7] On the Tokyo wholesale market, the average rice price halved during those years, tumbling from ¥10.6 per *koku* to ¥5.3 (fig. 1.1). But just as important as the fall in income of agricultural workers, who made up 71 percent of the gainfully employed in the years 1881–1885,[8] was the jump in the sake tax, which breweries passed on to consumers, prompting a spike in licensed and illicit home brewing as well as in tax evasion and concealment by small-scale breweries, as local tax officials made clear in their reports.[9]

In September 1880, under Sano, the Ministry of Finance had obtained Council of State approval to raise the tax on ordinary sake from ¥1 to ¥2 per *koku*, setting the price for higher grades at ¥3 and ¥4. In December 1882 Matsukata secured permission to redouble the ordinary sake tax while increasing the tax on each of the higher grades by ¥2 per *koku*.[10] Revenue from the sake tax nearly doubled from 1879 to 1881, at the tail end of the inflationary period, before surging by another 49 percent in fiscal 1882 (see table 3.2). In proposing to the Council of State that his ministry raise the sake tax again to generate funds for military expansion, Matsukata pointed to this climb in revenue, noting that, despite the 1880 tax hike, sake production and sales had both increased. In fiscal 1880, he noted, the tax increase had amounted to only 4 percent of the average retail price, but since then the price had gone up by almost 20 percent. He went on to argue that, as the profits of breweries had risen over the past two years, a further hike in the sake tax would not cause a decline in production. Brewers could pay the tax out of profits; but, even if they raised prices to absorb the tax increase, demand, far from lagging, would continue to move upward "because the people enjoy a comfortable standard of living. Therefore, now is the time to resolutely carry out an increase in the tax."[11] Matsukata would seem to have been making a disingenuous argument, for he was fully aware that his deflationary policy would drive the economy into a depression, and indeed, as it turned out, under the double blow of deflation and a heightened tax burden, sake brewery output and tax revenue both nosedived from 1882 to 1883 and plateaued thereafter.

The Ministry of Finance managed to offset the decline in the sake tax slightly with the income from brewery and home brewing license fees, which together

TABLE 3.1 Selective sources of tax revenue, 1876–1886 (thousands of yen)

TAX	1876	1877	1878	1879	1880	1881	1882	1883	1884	1885	1886
Land	43,023	39,451	40,455	42,113	42,346	43,274	43,342	43,538	43,426	43,034	43,282
Sake	1,412	3,050	5,100	6,464	5,511	10,646	16,331	13,491	14,068	1,053	11,744
Tobacco	244	227	275	270	293	276	281	2,154	1,294	905	1,236
Stamp	689	810	949	1,168	1,424	1,660	1,613	2,273	2,149	1,599	—
Patent medicine	28	87	74	79	86	84	365	495	364	282	439
Soy sauce	—	—	—	—	—	—	—	—	—	640	1,188
Confectionary	—	—	—	—	—	—	—	—	—	438	545
Rice broker	—	—	—	—	—	—	—	—	—	—	181
Stock broker	—	—	—	—	—	—	—	—	—	—	88
Total revenue	51,731	47,923	51,486	55,580	55,262	61,676	67,739	67,660	67,204	52,581	64,393

Source: Fukaya, Meiji seifu zaisei kiban no kakuritsu, 178–79.

TABLE 3.2 Sake production, revenue, and licenses, 1879–1887

	COMMERCIAL OUTPUT (1,000 KOKU*)	NUMBER OF COMMERCIAL BREWERIES	BREWERY TAX (¥1,000)	BREWERY LICENSE FEE (¥1,000)	HOMEBREW LICENSE FEE (¥1,000)	TOTAL REVENUE (¥1,000)	HOMEBREW OUTPUT (1,000 KOKU)	NUMBER OF HOMEBREW LICENSES
1879	4,483	39,879	5,251	379	0	5,631	n.d.	0
1880	4,851	27,875	9,427	837	0	10,264	n.d.	0
1881	4,714	27,082	10,260	812	0	11,072	n.d.	0
1882	5,895	25,451	15,301	761	269	16,330	245	339,581
1883	3,063	21,824	12,302	651	538	13,491	496	670,361
1884	3,189	18,387	12,991	548	529	14,068	533	659,421
1885	2,623	16,320	15	485	554	1,053	n.d.	n.d.
1886	3,023	14,660	10,757	445	588	11,790	n.d.	n.d.
1887	3,869	15,471	11,976	454	680	13,110	n.d.	n.d.

Sources: Muroyama, *Matsukata zaisei kenkyū*, 254; Fukaya, *Meiji seifu zaisei kiban no kakuritsu*, 219, 225.

Note: n.d. = no data available.

*One koku as a unit of volume equals about 73.5 gallons.

averaged about ¥1 million a year from 1882 to 1885. Proceeds from the brewery license fee had more than doubled in fiscal 1880, but by 1885 revenue from that source had slid continually, as consolidation proceeded in the sake industry with the weeding out of small producers, the total number of breweries dropping from nearly forty thousand in 1879 to fewer than fifteen thousand in 1886. Nonetheless, the home brewing fee, which Matsukata had introduced in December 1882 in a vain attempt to restrain such production and protect taxpaying breweries, netted annually over half a million yen during the 1883–1885 fiscal years (he eased this sudden imposition by waiving the fee for home brewers of less than one *koku* of sake).[12] Matsukata had further tried to minimize competition for existing breweries so they could shoulder the increased tax burden by requiring that new commercial license seekers produce at least one hundred *koku* of sake a year as well as obtain permission from the local brewers' association.[13] Home brewing, however, remained the biggest headache for both the sake industry and the government, markedly shrinking the market for taxable sake. The number of licensed home brewers rocketed from about 340,000 in 1882 to some 660,000 in 1884, while their reported output leaped from around a quarter of a million *koku* to more than half a million during those years, equaling one-sixth of the amount produced by breweries in 1883 and 1884. Moonshine was particularly difficult to police, and it was not until December 1883 that the government gave tax officials the legal authority to enter and inspect private homes suspected of brewing sake without licenses or above permitted quantities. In July 1886, though too late to help breweries and augment tax income during the Matsukata financial reform, the government finally prohibited individuals from home brewing ordinary sake and restaurants from making all grades of the liquor. In the end, actual revenue from the sake tax came up short of the budgeted amounts for the years 1883–1884 by a total of nearly ¥6 million.[14]

Scholars have typically, and somewhat misleadingly, applied the term "retrenchment" to the Matsukata financial reform. In fact, to persuade the other leaders to acquiesce in his deflationary program, Matsukata switched from demanding that all ministries adhere to a policy of economizing on expenses for five years to requiring that they freeze their spending at the 1881 level for three years, after which he would approve budget increases.[15] Because currency would appreciate during his financial reform, Matsukata in effect guaranteed real budget enhancements from 1882 to 1885 and promised absolute ones thereafter. But the successive exigencies Japan confronted in the first half of the 1880s forced him to authorize actual increases in budgets from the start. Far from "retrenching" administrative spending, Matsukata would have run budget deficits if not for transfers from the reserve fund, which the finance minister intended chiefly for note redemption and specie acquisition.[16] In November 1883, for example, Matsukata reported to the Council of State that the Ministry of Finance had had to

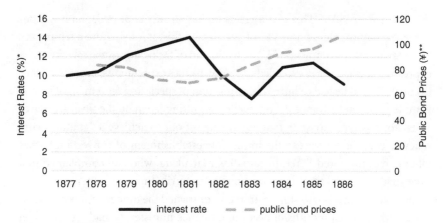

FIGURE 3.1 Interest rates and public bond prices, 1877–1886. *Sources:* Matsukata, *Report on the Adoption of the Gold Standard*, 34–35, 99–100; Matsukata, *The History of National Debts in Japan*, 58.

*Average annual rates of interest for loans of ¥1,000–¥10,000.
**Average annual prices of 7 percent commutation bonds.

appropriate ¥1.5 million from the reserve fund to cover extraordinary expenses in just the first four and a half months of that fiscal year but could face a "ruinous" deficit of ¥5.8 million at year's end, and in April 1884 he similarly noted that the ministry had already budgeted ¥1.5 million from the reserve fund to make up for a projected revenue shortfall in fiscal 1884 and expected to draw on the fund for an additional ¥0.5 million upon settlement of accounts at the end of the year.[17] In fact, the Ministry of Finance had to meet average unbudgeted outlays of almost ¥15 million a year from fiscal 1882 to 1884.[18]

Against the backdrop of flat-lining tax revenues, mounting expenditures, and worsening depression, Matsukata turned to yet another measure to advance currency reform: the issue of public bonds.[19] For all his vociferous opposition to Ōkuma Shigenobu's plans for foreign borrowing before Matsukata's own appointment as finance minister, beginning in 1884 he made several attempts to sell public bonds to foreigners in hopes of accelerating specie accumulation and note redemption. In 1881 Matsukata had opposed Ōkuma's second "foreign loan" plan, which involved offering domestic bonds to foreigners, on the grounds that, under conditions prevailing at the time, the interest rate would be too high and that dependence on foreign money would risk further loss of national sovereignty. By late 1883, however, conditions had changed dramatically. As interest rates fell owing to the depression, the price of public bonds recovered (see fig. 3.1). Furthermore, the sharpness of the economic downturn apparently caused Matsukata to overcome any misgivings he might have had about borrowing from abroad. He had reported to the emperor in 1882: "This year a recession has already appeared, and it will become even more intense next year. I anticipated this. It is by nature a temporary but unavoidable phenomenon."[20] Yet, by the end of the next year, the severity of the depression seems to have exceeded even Matsukata's expectations, prompting him to conclude that he had to hurry the acquisition of specie and retirement of inconvertible paper and advance the timetable for putting Japan on the silver standard.

Historians typically state that Matsukata set out to achieve a "gradual" currency reform, in contrast to the immediate establishment of convertibility that Ōkuma had proposed.[21] Yet, in actuality, Matsukata, who had complained in a June 1880 memorial that "the government arbitrarily turns out paper money . . . without knowing when to stop,"[22] initially contracted the money supply at a rapid pace: within fifteen months of becoming finance minister, he had redeemed all ¥14.5 million in outstanding supplemental notes, which the government had been issuing to cover temporary shortfalls in revenue since early Meiji and which Matsukata had regarded as the primary cause of the currency depreciation (see table 3.3). He secured the money to retire these notes partly by calling in loans that Ōkuma had made to industrial enterprises out of the reserve fund, a method of financing that Sano had terminated in June 1880; from October 21, 1881, the date of Matsukata's appointment as finance minister, to December 31, 1885, the reserve fund had recovered nearly ¥3 million in such loans (see table 3.4, "Loans paid back"). After relying on transfers from the reserve fund as a stopgap to make up short-term budget deficits, he obtained state approval in September 1884 to follow the Western practice of issuing Treasury bills, which the government had to redeem out of the revenue of the year of issue.[23]

Having liquidated the supplemental notes, Matsukata then started retiring regular government paper money, taking ¥7.34 million out of circulation from April to June 1883. So, in the space of just over a year and a half, he had slashed the paper currency in circulation by nearly ¥22 million, reducing the total money supply by 14 percent.[24] Needless to say, currency contraction of this magnitude and speed came as a shock to the economy, escalating a deflation that was already in progress; as the *Japan Weekly Mail* observed in early 1884, the contraction had taken place "with dangerous rapidity" and, in the eyes of some, the newspaper reported a year and a half later, "by a process so rapid as to be almost reckless."[25]

Thus, somewhat paradoxically, Matsukata wanted to speed up what was already a precipitate operation—and thereby avoid prolonging the depression that his policies had largely produced—by launching a new program of public bond issues in late 1883. This program replaced an older one that the government had begun in 1873 to recover the ¥55.5 million in convertible paper money it had issued in 1868–1870 in exchange for registered bonds bearing 6 percent interest. As the number of notes in circulation had yet to become excessive, the govern-

TABLE 3.3 Regular and supplemental government notes, November 1881–June 1883 (thousands of yen)

	NOV. 1881	DEC. 1881	JAN. 1882	FEB. 1882	MARCH 1882	APRIL 1882	MAY 1882	JUNE 1882	JULY 1882	AUG. 1882
Regular notes	105,905	105,905	105,881	105,785	105,718	105,710	105,639	105,635	105,635	105,635
Suppl. notes	14,500	13,000	9,500	7,000	7,000	4,000	4,000	7,000	7,000	7,000

	SEPT. 1882	OCT. 1882	NOV. 1882	DEC. 1882	JAN. 1883	FEB. 1883	MARCH 1883	APRIL 1883	MAY 1883	JUNE 1883
Regular notes	105,635	105,602	105,601	105,369	105,369	105,359	105,349	98,348	98,290	98,290
Suppl. notes	7,000	7,000	7,000	4,000	0	0	0	0	0	0

Source: Matsukata, "Shihei seiri shimatsu," 108–9.

TABLE 3.4 Receipts and disbursements of specie in the Reserve Fund, October 21, 1881–December 31, 1885 (yen)

RECEIPTS		DISBURSEMENTS	
Specie on hand on October 21, 1881	8,674,174	Paid in drafts	14,583,774
Foreign bills of exchange collected	18,424,395	Specie paid out in exchange	12,503,906
Drafts cashed at home	2,783,127	Bullion transferred to the Mint	19,523,849
Loans paid back	2,970,383	Bullion sold	18,304
Payments received from the sale of rice and *konbu*	1,887,437	Paid for gold and silver bullion purchased	16,737,461
Specie received by exchange	19,522,398	Miscellaneous disbursements	402,401
Balance after settlement received from the General Account	74,380		
Minted coins received	19,523,833		
Payment received for advance on drafts	8,772,782		
Gold and silver bullion bought	22,834,409		
Payment received from the sale of bullion	9,070		
Miscellaneous receipts	558,947		
Total receipts	106,035,335	Total disbursements	63,769,695
Balance	42,265,640		

Source: Matsukata, *Report on the Adoption of the Gold Standard*, 142.

ment had started that program not to contract the currency but to provide a more convenient method of paying the interest in specie that the state had promised holders of those initial notes if it had not redeemed them within five years of their issue. With government paper generally holding its value at the time, the regime had sold only ¥2.2 million in these so-called *kinsatsu* (gold note) exchange bonds by 1875. By that time, the authorities had almost completely replaced the remaining ¥53 million of initial paper with new, inconvertible government notes, which found public favor owing to their durability and resistance to counterfeiting compared to the poorly made original notes.[26] Sales of note redemption bonds resumed after October 1880 when, as part of Sano's financial reform, the government revised the program with "the express purpose of withdrawing paper money which had become depreciated owing to overissue."[27] From then until 1883, the Finance Ministry exchanged bonds totaling some ¥4.4 million for inconvertible government notes, about a fourth of that sum being redeemed after Matsukata's appointment as finance minister.[28]

In December 1883 Matsukata terminated this program and introduced a more effective one for reducing the amount of paper money and restoring its value. At that time, the Finance Ministry announced new regulations for note redemption bonds. The government planned to exchange the bonds for its fiat paper money and to redeem the bonds in silver within thirty-five years; the recovered notes were to be immediately "destroyed by fire"[29] at the Finance Ministry. At the same time, the authorities made public regulations for a second set of bonds, also redeemable in silver over a thirty-year period, to finance construction of the state's planned central trunk railway. Unlike the redemption bonds that previous finance administrations had floated, the two new ones were to be unregistered and therefore transferable, making them more attractive to subscribers, and both were to be open to foreign buyers. Not only would the bonds soak up inconvertible paper notes from domestic customers, but the redemption bonds in particular would contribute directly to specie accumulation, as foreign subscribers would purchase them with silver currency.[30]

Matsukata made several determined, though ultimately unsuccessful, attempts to sell redemption bonds abroad. In April 1884 he commissioned a British merchant residing in Yokohama, E. B. Watson, to offer £2 million sterling in such bonds to British investors at 90 percent of face value.[31] Watson began negotiations to float the bond issue in London, but he failed to reach agreement on a sterling conversion rate for the silver currency that the Japanese government would pay on interest and principal, and the negotiations collapsed. In late 1884 and early 1885 Matsukata made two more attempts to sell ¥10–20 million in redemption bonds in Europe to raise war funds during the confrontation between Japanese and Chinese troops in Korea; however, these efforts also broke down over the terms of issue.[32]

Although, to Matsukata's dismay, foreigners bought few of these Japanese government bonds, domestic sales more than made up for the disappointing foreign subscriptions. The authorities issued at home redemption bonds bearing 6 percent interest with a total face value of nearly ¥8 million—of which foreigners purchased a paltry ¥2,900[33]—and retired over ¥5 million in government paper notes between May 1884 and January 1886, in which month they stopped selling the bonds with the start of convertibility. Also, from early 1884 to mid-1885, the government successfully floated in three installments ¥20 million in 7 percent railway bonds, which Japanese buyers clearly preferred due to their slightly higher interest rate and shorter redemption period, as they oversubscribed the bonds by a large margin; in the case of the second and third issues, total subscriptions amounted to three times the sum required.[34] Like the conversion bonds, these instruments helped reduce the quantity of paper money in circulation at least in the short run, but the Treasury also appropriated some of the proceeds earmarked for future railway construction to cover temporary budget deficits, facilitating the transition from supplemental note to Treasury bill issues for making up such shortfalls.[35]

Mobilizing the Reserve Fund, Running Budget Deficits

Rather than relying mainly on the generation of budget surpluses to retire inconvertible government notes, Matsukata made heavier use of the reserve fund, based chiefly on the proceeds of bond issuance and export promotion, for that purpose.[36] Matsukata redeemed the government's supplemental notes entirely with coin from the reserve fund without touching ordinary revenue. Furthermore, he postponed until 1883 disbursement of ¥7 million that Sano had designated in the fiscal 1881 budget for recovering regular government notes, reducing the budget deficit for fiscal 1881 and obviating the need to make up the deficit by issuing supplemental notes on top of transfers from the reserve fund. By the time Matsukata had completely redeemed the supplemental notes in January 1883, the value of paper money was well on the road to recovery, with the average exchange rate of paper for silver yen that month standing at 1.33; it had been 1.73 in October 1881 (see table 1.3).[37] Only in April 1883, three months after the completion of supplemental note redemption, did the Ministry of Finance begin to retire regular government notes using the ¥7 million carried over from the 1881 budget.

Matsukata may have followed precedents set by Ōkuma in redeeming the fiat paper in circulation, but he differed markedly from Ōkuma in his use of the reserve fund. Under Ōkuma and Sano, from 1878 to 1880, the Ministry of Finance retired ¥11.2 million in regular government notes, not much less than the ¥13.6 million redeemed out of the ordinary budget under Matsukata from 1882 to 1884 (see table 3.5). As Muroyama suggests, attributing to Matsukata's initiative the ¥7 million recovered under him that the government had originally budgeted for fiscal 1881 might be questionable, as his predecessor, Sano, had put together the fiscal 1881 budget. But Sano had agreed to the plan that Ōkuma and Itō had drafted in early 1881 for note redemption through domestic and foreign borrowing. When the Council of State formally approved that plan in the summer of 1881, it effectively killed the budget line for retiring government paper. Then, once Matsukata convinced his colleagues to shelve the new loan scheme in November of that year, the council essentially resurrected the ¥7 million earmark. Matsukata, however, prioritized the retirement of supplemental notes using the reserve fund and delayed the expenditure of ¥7 million to redeem regular notes until April 1883, almost the end of the next fiscal year.[38] Accordingly, it may be appropriate to view note redemption under the fiscal 1881 budget as the starting point of Matsukata's program to retire government paper money out of ordinary revenue.[39]

Nevertheless, regarding the fiscal 1881 budget as a transitional Sano-Matsukata production and the next fiscal year as the real beginning of the Matsukata financial

TABLE 3.5 Retirement of government notes, 1878–1885 (thousands of yen)

	1878	1879	1880	1881	1882	1883	1884	1885
Ordinary budget retirements	4,310	4,857	2,000	0	7,000	3,300	3,340	0
Public bond retirements	0	0	131	3,280	0	710	948	1,573
Transferred to Reserve Fund	0	0	0	3,833	5,228	5,000	7,007	5,400

Sources: Muroyama, *Kindai Nihon keizai no keisei*, 109; Matsukata, *The History of National Debts in Japan*, 95, 101.

program makes all the more significant Matsukata's employment of the reserve fund as the pivot of his currency reform. Herein lies one of the most striking differences between the Ōkuma and Matsukata financial policies. Ōkuma employed the reserve fund to make loans to businesses and sold off a portion of its silver holdings in an abortive attempt to restrain speculation in the silver market. As a result, he nearly depleted the fund's silver reserves, which fell to less than ¥10 million, or just 6.1 percent of all notes in circulation,[40] causing a further drop in the value of paper money. By the end of his tenure as finance minister in early 1880, the fund consisted mainly of promissory notes and public bonds that were continually losing value themselves (see table 1.5). Subsequently, under Sano, the Finance Ministry terminated both lending to enterprises out of the reserve fund and unloading its silver on the market but planned to continue redeeming government paper out of ordinary revenue. By contrast, Matsukata from the start downplayed the use of budget appropriations to retire regular government notes and, to restore confidence in paper currency, emphasized instead the importance of redeeming supplemental government notes and acquiring specie through a fortified reserve fund.[41] After completely retiring the supplemental notes, Matsukata finally turned to redeeming regular government paper out of the annual budget. By this means, as noted, Matsukata ended up recovering ¥13.6 million in government notes—or just ¥6.6 million if one excludes the ¥7 million retired under Sano's budget plan for fiscal 1881—compared to the ¥14.5 million in supplemental notes he had redeemed using the reserve fund. Moreover, after disbursing the ¥3.3 million budgeted for note redemption in fiscal 1883, at the end of which the average monthly exchange rate between paper and silver yen had fallen to 1.07,[42] Matsukata broke off retiring regular government notes and moved the amounts scheduled for note redemption in the fiscal 1884 and 1885 budgets entirely to the reserve fund for acquiring specie in preparation for the resumption of currency convertibility. (The fiscal 1884 transfer actually ended up covering a

¥5 million deficit upon settlement of accounts at the end of the year in June 1885, close to the shortfall Matsukata had predicted in April 1884.[43])

Matsukata certainly did try to create budget surpluses or at least balance the government's budget. On the revenue side, two big jumps in consumer tax proceeds came in fiscal 1881 and 1882, when the total went from ¥55 million in fiscal 1880 to ¥62 million the next year and then to ¥68 million the year after, thanks to Sano's doubling of the sake tax in September 1880 and Matsukata's redoubling of the tax in December 1882. Aggregate revenue from consumer taxes, however, stagnated thereafter, as Matsukata barely made up the drop in sake tax income in fiscal 1883 and 1884 by raising other indirect taxes, especially on tobacco and postage stamps (see table 3.1). Matsukata also revised the procedure for disbursing government revenue and speeded up the delivery of the land tax to minimize temporary budget shortfalls. Previously the Ministry of Finance had handed over lump sums to the other ministries to cover their estimated expenditures at the beginning of each fiscal year before it had fully collected taxes. As a result, in the first half of fiscal 1880, for instance, the short-term deficit reached ¥22 million, an amount the Finance Ministry had to make up mainly by issuing supplemental notes. Matsukata ended this "block grant" system and mandated that from then on the Treasury make all disbursements centrally.[44] Furthermore, in November 1881, he put into effect a program that Sano had announced in February of that year to accelerate the collection of the land tax; the new system required the owners of rice fields to start paying the tax a month earlier and to complete installments two months earlier than under the previous system. Matsukata moved to hasten the delivery of tax revenue further by introducing a form of "wire transfer," ordering local tax offices to telegraph the amounts of cash payments they received for immediate recording at the Treasury.[45]

On the expenditure side of the budget, besides postponing the disbursement of the ¥7 million earmarked for note redemption in fiscal 1881, Matsukata continued the practice that Ōkuma had initiated in 1878 of shifting the burden of public works spending onto prefectural governments. Whereas Ōkuma had reduced transfers to prefectures out of the central budget, Matsukata terminated them. Consequently, prefectural budgets, which had recorded surpluses until fiscal 1881, fell into the red thereafter, as grants from the central government plunged from ¥3.6 million in 1880 to an average of ¥1.5 million from 1881 to 1884—the proceeds of public bond issues rather than central budget outlays.[46]

In nominal terms the government's year-end account was slightly in the black for each of the fiscal years 1882 and 1884, balanced for 1883, and significantly in the black for 1885.[47] The official figures, however, disguise annual expenditures that, once factored in, cause the accounts for all four years to show, in fact, substantial deficits. These additional expenditures resulted from the peculiarity of the contemporary budget system whereby the state made "annual" outlays over a period of two to three years. The reason was that the Ministry of Finance was unable to complete the collection of revenue within the July-to-June fiscal year, which the government had adopted in 1875 together with the principle that it would apply a given fiscal year's income to that year's expenditures. In particular, the deadline for payment of the final installment on the land tax, by far the government's largest source of income, was April 30, but distant localities typically delivered that payment to the Treasury after the fiscal year ended on June 30, so tax collection generally took place over two fiscal years. Similarly, installment payments for the second most important revenue source, the sake tax, the proceeds of which exceeded all other non–land tax income by a wide margin in 1882–1884, came due in April and September, again straddling two fiscal years. In addition, the government also collected taxes on goods produced in Hokkaido as well as on corporations in two installments over more than one fiscal year, while distant post offices were generally unable to forward their stamp tax revenues within a given fiscal year. Consequently, to maintain the principle of covering each year's expenditures with that year's revenue, the Ministry of Finance had to devise a multiyear accounting method whereby it collected and disbursed annual revenue over two years, and at times three years. Formally, the budget period consisted of a single year, but in practice each year's budget settlement aggregated parts of two or three years' income and outlay.[48] Muroyama has adjusted the official statistics to reflect this system and found that, far from balancing the budget or creating a surplus from 1882 to 1885, Matsukata actually engaged in "deficit financing" at the average rate of about ¥5 million a year during that time (see table 3.6). By doing so, however unintentionally, he helped alleviate, to some extent, the depression brought on by his drastic currency contraction.

Promoting Exports

The official export promotion program that Matsukata inherited from the previous finance regime also made a signal contribution to his currency reform. Under this program, the Ministry of Finance directed the Yokohama Specie Bank, which state leaders had established in February 1880, to advance paper money to merchants involved in exporting Japanese goods, primarily the leading export commodities of silk and tea, by discounting foreign bills of exchange and to receive repayment in specie that the bank's agencies collected at the export destinations.[49] Matsukata, however, made substantial changes to the initial program, which the government had based on an 1879 proposal of Maeda Masana, "the ideologue"[50] of Ōkuma Shigenobu's expansionary policies. Above all, Matsukata switched the

TABLE 3.6 Central government budget, official and adjusted, 1877–1886 (thousands of yen)

	OFFICIAL BUDGET			ACTUAL BUDGET INCOME AND OUTGO		
	Income	Expenditure	Balance	Income	Expenditure	Balance
1877	52,338	48,428	3,910	77,433	54,074	23,359
1878	62,444	60,941	1,502	64,064	64,340	−276
1879	62,151	60,318	1,834	65,583	63,053	2,530
1880	63,367	63,141	226	68,156	65,558	2,598
1881	71,490	71,460	30	70,575	64,746	5,829
1882	73,508	73,481	27	73,758	78,978	−5,220
1883	83,108	83,108	0	76,609	85,341	−8,732
1884	76,658	76,652	7	83,133	84,454	−1,321
1885	62,157	61,121	1,033	59,684	64,313	−4,629
1886	85,326	83,223	2,102	80,717	70,910	9,807

Source: Muroyama, *Matsukata zaisei kenkyū*, 282.

emphasis of the program so that, instead of acquiring foreign exchange to redeem bonds that Japan had sold abroad in the early 1870s as well as to meet overseas expenses of the government, the Ministry of Finance sought to earn specie for the reserve fund that would eventually back issues of convertible paper money.[51] He also corrected a major deficiency in the original program, directing officials to calculate each merchant's repayment amount at the exchange rate prevailing upon consignment of goods in Japan rather than upon settlement at the export destination.[52] The new method ruled out speculation over fluctuations in the value of paper money, which had previously arisen among exporters, exacerbating the ongoing inflation and depreciation of paper currency.[53] In addition, Matsukata discontinued the practice of extending a portion of the export credit directly to local producers, a practice that had conformed to Ōkuma's policy of actively promoting domestic industry.

Furthermore, in November 1882 Matsukata, building on an idea floated by his predecessor, Sano, proposed that the government itself engage more actively in the export of rice, which it had been doing since the early 1870s. His plan was to use money from the reserve fund to make annual purchases of rice for export as yet another way to accelerate the accumulation of specie. With Japan in the midst of a run of bumper crops that had begun in 1879 and would continue into 1883, the government's acquisition and export of surplus rice, Matsukata maintained in his proposal, would have the added benefit of helping "protect the income of the farmers." He followed this recommendation with another one in February 1883 calling on the government to export *konbu* (edible kelp) directly to

China.[54] Approved by the Council of State and put into effect in June 1883, Matsukata's program for official rice and *konbu* exports had by the end of 1885 netted nearly ¥2 million, which the Ministry of Finance collected in U.S. and British coins, Mexican dollars, and Chinese taels. Meanwhile, the program for discounting merchants' foreign bills of exchange brought in more than ¥18 million in specie from the date of Matsukata's appointment in October 1881 to December 31, 1885, so that together the two programs accounted for over one-fifth of the ¥97.4 million in specie deposited in the reserve fund during that time (at the start of that period, the reserve had had a paltry ¥8.7 million on hand; see table 3.4).

The merchant lending program succeeded especially after Matsukata opened it to foreigners operating in the treaty ports. The intent of both Matsukata and his predecessors had been to circumvent the Western merchant houses and promote "direct export trade" by Japanese trading companies. The regulations for discounting bills of foreign exchange that the government approved in February 1882 stipulated that every such bill "shall under all possible circumstances be discounted for a Japanese merchant," though "for reasons of necessity" the Ministry of Finance could grant "special permission" to a foreigner.[55] In 1884, after the effort to push "direct exports" yielded meager results owing to Japanese traders' lack of facilities and knowledge about foreign markets, Matsukata began turning to foreign merchants wholesale. Even at the height of the "direct export" drive, foreign trading houses had continued to handle 85–90 percent of Japan's exports. With the change in policy, foreign traders' share of the bill-discounting funds leaped from nothing in 1883 to 69 percent the next year and to more than 80 percent in 1885 and 1886. Thanks primarily to this refocusing of the program, overseas agencies of the Yokohama Specie Bank returned nearly ¥27 million in silver currency between 1883 and 1886 (the agencies had remitted only ¥4.2 million in the three previous years), and the value of specie held in the reserve fund increased by nearly 40 percent from 1883 to 1885, reaching over ¥42 million in the latter year (after deducting nearly ¥64 million in disbursements).[56]

Completing Currency Reform

Meanwhile, on the currency front, the total quantity of inconvertible government paper in circulation dropped from ¥120.4 million (including the supplemental notes) in October 1881 to ¥93.4 million in June 1884. By mid-1884, the paper-silver yen ratio was approaching parity, so at that point, as noted earlier, Matsukata stopped redeeming paper directly out of ordinary revenues and transferred all of the money budgeted for note retirement in fiscal 1884 to the reserve fund for accumulating specie. In addition, in May 1883 the Finance Ministry began steadily redeeming the inconvertible notes of the national banks, requiring them to deposit money for that purpose at the Bank of Japan, which Matsukata had established in 1882 (the new central bank also handled the public bond issues on behalf of the ministry). As a result, the amount of national bank paper in circulation fell from ¥34.3 million in May 1883 to ¥30.7 million in May 1885,[57] at which time, paper money being virtually on par with silver, the Bank of Japan made a preliminary issue of convertible government notes "as a sort of experiment, preparatory to the resumption of specie payment" in January 1886.[58]

Hence, primarily through the domestic sale of public bonds and the extension of the export promotion program to foreign merchants, Matsukata managed to shorten a process that he had expected would take until 1887.[59] He had also thought it would require a drastic contraction of the total money supply from the ¥150 million level prevailing in late 1881 to ¥100 million, the amount of money in circulation in the mid-1870s, the last time paper notes were on par with silver. In fact, however, by the time the total money supply had fallen to just over ¥120 million in mid-1885, paper had returned to parity, sparing the country a prolongation of the depression on account of currency deflation.

SPENDING IN A TIME OF "RETRENCHMENT"

Industrial Policy and the Military

The privatization of Meiji state enterprises, which most accounts portray as a key component of the Matsukata "retrenchment," did occur almost entirely during Matsukata's long tenure as finance minister, but the government adopted the program a year before he assumed that post, and almost all of the sales, including the biggest ones, took place between mid-1884 and 1896, after the deflation had largely run its course.[1] Certainly, by transferring the government's nonmilitary factories and shipyards and its mines into private hands, the Matsukata reform was instrumental in bringing about a shift in industrial policy away from direct state intervention in the economy and toward the creation of a favorable institutional setting for the growth of private enterprise. Yet, for all of Matsukata's free enterprise rhetoric—"the Government should never attempt to compete with the people in pursuing lines of industry or commerce"[2]—he deviated from classical economic liberalism by increasing industrial spending in fiscal 1881–1885 compared to the previous four years and by maintaining fairly heavy state involvement in the economy. Likewise, his industrial policy contrasts with the emphasis of neoliberal International Monetary Fund (IMF) orthodoxy on privatization insofar as the Meiji government sold off hardly any of its enterprises until late in the Matsukata financial reform, although the paucity of sales until mid-1884 was a function more of the shortage of buyers than of Matsukata's lack of commitment to supporting private initiative.

The questions this chapter addresses include the following: How did the divestiture program originate and develop, and how much did it contribute to financial reform at the height of the Matsukata "retrenchment" from late 1881 to mid-1885? Furthermore, with the decision in November 1880 to privatize most of the state enterprises and with the creation in April 1881 of the streamlined Ministry of Agriculture and Commerce, to what extent did the government actually reorient industrial policy and change its level of spending on industry, both direct and indirect, during the Matsukata financial reform?

In addition to retaining its railroads, mints, and postal and telegraph systems, the government held on to its arsenals and naval shipyards.[3] Since the early 1870s, the army had been operating a munitions factory in Tokyo on the grounds of the former residence of the Mito daimyo (the location of today's Tokyo Dome City and Koishikawa Kōrakuen Garden) and another in Osaka, which inherited equipment from the shogunate's Nagasaki Ironworks and opened on the grounds of Osaka Castle. Meanwhile, the navy was also managing two arsenals. One at Yokosuka took over the shogunate's ironworks there, and a second at Tsukiji in Tokyo obtained machinery from two shogunal shipyards.[4] Besides inheriting the Yokosuka Shipyard from the shogunate, in 1884 the navy purchased Onohama Shipyard, founded in Kobe by British merchant Edward Charles Kirby, after that works had started building the original battleship *Yamato* and Kirby had committed suicide over financial difficulties and construction delays (in 1895 the navy closed the shipyard and moved its equipment to Kure).[5]

A claim often made in earlier Japanese work on the Matsukata reform is that, in addition to stabilizing Japan's currency, Matsukata intended his financial program to create a surplus specifically to fund the government's armaments expansion efforts, including the development of these military works.[6] More recent studies have challenged the notion that military concerns drove the Matsukata reform.[7] According to these studies, although government spending on the army and navy increased substantially during the 1880s, spurred on by anti-Japanese uprisings in Korea in 1882 and 1884, the increase happened in spite of, rather than because of, Matsukata's program. A second set of questions addressed by this chapter, then, centers on the issue of how the government managed to finance a major military buildup in the midst of a so-called retrenchment and how Matsukata's currency reform succeeded despite the pressures of heightened military expenditures.

Off-Loading State Enterprises

The Meiji government operated enterprises in a range of industrial and agricultural fields mainly through the Public Works, Home, and Agriculture and Commerce Ministries and the Hokkaido Colonization Commission (Kaitakushi). The Ministry of Public Works, established in 1870, managed state-owned railways, mines, shipyards, and iron and machine works as well as glass, cement, and brick factories while the Home Ministry, founded in 1873, oversaw establishments in light industry and agriculture centering on silk-reeling factories (filatures) and textile mills, an agricultural experimental station and school, and stock farms. The Kaitakushi, which opened in 1869, administered—in addition to railroads and mines in Hokkaido—a cornucopia of works that included everything from a tannery, a sawmill, a silkworm nursery, and a horse farm to a sugar refinery, a brewery, canneries of various sorts, and cod-liver oil and miso shoyu factories.[8] After its establishment in 1881, the Ministry of Commerce and Agriculture took over the enterprises of the Home Ministry; and, with the abolition of the Kaitakushi in 1882 and the Public Works Ministry in 1885, it took charge of their industrial projects as well.[9]

The Meiji government carried out the program to sell state enterprises under Matsukata,[10] but the planning and adoption of the program took place in 1880 under the leadership of Ōkuma Shigenobu—with the cooperation of Inoue Kaoru and Itō Hirobumi—during Sano Tsunetami's tenure as finance minister.[11] During the 1870s, however, Matsukata, as an Ōkuma subordinate in the Ministry of Finance, appears to have influenced his superior's views on the matter. As early as May 1873, Matsukata, then assistant head of the Taxation Bureau, had sent Finance Minister Ōkuma an opinion paper calling for "promoting the foundation of national wealth and curtailing non-urgent expenses." In this memorandum—contradicting the image of Matsukata in the 1880s as a champion of modern industry at the expense of agriculture[12]—he had argued that "the profit arising from the fertility [of agriculture] gradually comes to be of great benefit to industry and commerce" and that "the foundation of national wealth" was "the nurturing of agriculture, which yields profit with little capital." Spending on the military was indispensable, but the government should stop "non-urgent works."[13] Whereas the early emphasis of the state enterprise program was on the development of railroads and mines and the importation of Western-style machine shops and shipyards, Matsukata was advancing a position in tune with that of his mentor, Ōkubo Toshimichi, who, as home minister in the mid-1870s, pushed for the promotion of crop and livestock farming as well as sericulture. Similarly, in 1877, when Matsukata was serving as both assistant finance minister and head of the Home Ministry's Agricultural Promotion Bureau, he submitted a memorandum to Ōkuma and Ōkubo urging that the government focus on supporting the production of raw silk, "the foundation of exports."[14] Here Matsukata was beginning to express free enterprise views, in advance of his exposure to Léon Say's laissez-faire notions in Paris in 1878.

After his return from Europe, Matsukata voiced laissez-faire views more explicitly—while pointedly urging the state to pull out of certain economic activities—in a memorandum he presented to the government in September 1879. In this document, titled "Fundamental Principles for Promoting Agriculture" (Kannō yōshi), Matsukata, using the term "agriculture" loosely to include light industry, insisted that the government should not compete with the people in economic endeavors that are "by nature" private works but should simply "assist where public knowledge is deficient." The state might have to lead the way in certain fields, but once private interests had entered such a field and achieved good results the government ought to "withdraw from that line of work and leave its advancement to the people themselves." Matsukata cited as examples the state's Tomioka filature, Sakai cotton-spinning mill, and Shimofusa sheep farm along with various agricultural experiment stations run by Tokyo Prefecture as having been "from the start temporary operations"—projects in which "the government should by no means intervene permanently."[15]

Scholars who stress discontinuity between Ōkuma's policies in the 1870s and those of Matsukata in the 1880s tend to argue that, in memoranda like "Kannō yōshi," Matsukata was criticizing his superior's activist approach, calling for a decisive change in government industrial policy away from direct involvement in the economy.[16] Ōkuma and Matsukata certainly diverged in their financial strategies for dealing with the post-1877 inflation; but, perhaps reflecting Matsukata's influence on Ōkuma, their industrial policies had a fair amount in common. In January 1875, for example, Ōkuma submitted to the Council of State a memorandum proposing measures to stabilize public finances in which he echoed the opinion paper he had received from Matsukata a year and a half earlier. One of the measures Ōkuma recommended was the sale of state enterprises. In this document, the finance minister maintained that, although the state should manage large-scale works such as shipyards and railways, to eliminate unnecessary expenditures it should gradually transfer to "proper businesses" those enterprises that ought to be in private hands.[17] This memorandum appears to mark Ōkuma as the first Meiji leader expressly to recommend the disposal of state enterprises. Nonetheless, the government divested hardly any of its industrial or agricultural ventures from 1875 to the mid-1880s—among the exceptions was the Sakai spinning mill, which the Home Ministry sold to a Satsuma entrepreneur, Hamazaki Taheiji, in 1878—and, in the memorandum, Ōkuma suggested he was counting on continued state operation of works that produced import-substituting goods.[18]

Ōkuma repeated his call for the sale of state enterprises in a memorandum he submitted to the government in May 1880, the same month in which he presented his abortive foreign loan proposal. As Matsukata did in his 1879 memorandum, Ōkuma recommended specific works for disposal, but he went beyond Matsukata's short list to propose the sale of fourteen model enterprises: all the textile mills run by the Home Ministry, factories and machine shops managed by the

Public Works Ministry, and two industrial plants operated by the Hokkaido Colonization Commission. Ōkuma estimated that the sale of the fourteen concerns he named would yield about ¥4 million, which the government would use to redeem public bonds. Whereas Matsukata in his memorandum had urged privatization from a laissez-faire perspective, Ōkuma did so with the prime objective of financial retrenchment and stabilization, but he insisted that the process not "harm or diminish government assets." Accordingly, the "Regulations for the Sale of Factories," which he attached to his memorandum, stipulated strict conditions for the proposed divestitures.[19]

In the memorandum that Matsukata issued the following month attacking Ōkuma's foreign-borrowing scheme, he at the same time reiterated support for the disposal of public enterprises. Like Ōkuma, Matsukata linked divestiture to financial reform but equally to free enterprise thinking. Under the heading "works that concern private initiative should all be turned over to private ownership," he asserted in this document: "Responding to requests from interested people, we should endeavor to hand over government enterprises that belong in the private sector."[20] Whereas in his 1879 memorandum Matsukata had limited his sale proposal to agriculture and light industry, in this document he expanded the scope of recommended disposals to state enterprises as a whole.

After the Council of State rejected Ōkuma's 1880 foreign loan proposal, he worked with Inoue Kaoru and Itō Hirobumi to come up with an alternative plan for financial stabilization. Inoue presented a memorandum in August 1880 outlining a program of retrenchment and revenue raising, adding his endorsement of the sale of state enterprises: they "should be gradually and in so far as possible sold to private buyers."[21] In September, after conferring with Itō, who recommended a fiscal program similar to that of Inoue, Ōkuma submitted a proposal, modeled after Itō's plan, for hiking excise taxes, curtailing central government expenditures, disposing of public enterprises, and streamlining the administration of the state's economic promotion activities.[22] The Council of State accepted these recommendations and began to implement them, beginning with a doubling of the sake tax in late September. Then, in early November 1880, the government issued orders for retrenchment and for the sale of state enterprises. Also that month, as part of the program to economize on administrative expenses, Ōkuma and Itō jointly proposed the founding of a "Ministry of Agriculture and Commerce" to unify and rationalize the government's economic endeavors. Basing their memorandum on Ōkuma's September proposal, they urged the government to learn from the experience of continental European countries like France and Germany where one ministry oversaw public ventures in agriculture, commerce, and industry.[23] In fact, they closely followed French precedent in drafting the rules and regulations of the proposed ministry.[24] The Council of State proceeded to establish the ministry in April 1881 with the goal of eliminating the duplication of efforts by various ministries and saving a projected ¥2 million in administrative costs. As Kobayashi Masaaki notes, the Ministry of Agriculture and Commerce "had the character of a liquidation agency entrusted with state enterprises until their sale."[25] In the long run, its establishment marked a significant change in industrial policy, as the Meiji government moved, for the most part, from a strategy of intervening directly in industry and agriculture by operating model enterprises to a strategy of developing the economy indirectly by furnishing technical assistance and subsidies to private interests. Yet, as Ishizuka Hiromichi suggests, the actions the Council of State took from November 1880 to April 1881 did not bring about an immediate change in industrial policy, other than a sharp reduction in funding transfers to local governments: until mid-1884, as the Matsukata "retrenchment" unfolded, the government sold few of its enterprises and continued to spend at a fairly high level on industrial and agricultural promotion.[26]

As Kobayashi has pointed out, the program for the disposal of government enterprises went through three phases after the Council of State announced it in November 1880.[27] Under the initial guidelines, the government intended to sell only its factories and placed emphasis on finding buyers capable not so much of managing the factories as of purchasing them at a fair price. As a result, in the early stages of the program, rather than selling off money-losing enterprises one after another at bargain-basement rates, the authorities in fact set relatively strict terms of disposal, requiring competitive bids, immediate payment for working assets, and annual installment payments for fixed assets. These requirements echoed the draft regulations Ōkuma had appended to his May 1880 memorandum. Not surprisingly, few suitable buyers appeared in the early 1880s, a situation that prompted the government in July 1884—after it had sold only two enterprises—to officially add most of its mines to the offer list and to ease the purchase requirements. This change marked the beginning of the disposal's second phase, which lasted until mid-1888. During this phase, which came *after* Matsukata had basically completed his currency deflation, the government unloaded most of the enterprises it had put up for sale. It sold the majority of these operations under long-term payment schedules at no interest and with no obligation to cover the working capital. The authorities also paid more attention to whether prospective buyers were able to stay in business, often leasing the concerns for a year or two and then completing the sales if results proved satisfactory. The third and final phase of the divestiture program began and ended with the transfer of the government's three most profitable mines, the Miike coal mine to Mitsui in August 1888 and the Sado gold mine and Ikuno silver mine to Mitsubishi in September 1896. For these mines, the government stipulated even more rigorous terms of competitive bidding and payment than in the first phase (see table 4.1).[28]

TABLE 4.1 Principal government enterprises sold from 1882 to 1896

DATE OF SALE	ENTERPRISE	CAPITAL INVESTED BY THE STATE (¥)*	ASSESSMENT OF ASSETS (¥)**	SALE PRICE (¥)
June 1882	Hiroshima Cotton Spinning	54,205	—	12,570
January 1884	Aburato Coal Mine	48,608	17,192	27,943
July 1884	Nakaosaka Iron Works	85,507	24,300	28,575
July 1884	Fukagawa Cement	} 101,559	} 67,965	61,741
July 1884	Fukagawa White Brick			12,121
August 1884	Kosaka Silver Mine	547,476	192,000	273,659
October 1884	Nashimotomura White Brick Works	—	—	101
December 1884	Innai Silver Mine	703,093	72,993	108,977
March 1885	Ani Copper Mine	1,673,211	240,772	337,766
May 1885	Shinagawa Glass	294,168	66,305	79,950
June 1885	Okuzu, Magane Gold Mine	149,546	98,902	117,142
November 1886	Aichi Cotton Spinning	58,000	—	—
December 1886	Sapporo Brewery	—	—	27,672
May 1887	Shinmachi Filature	138,984	—	141,000
June 1887	Nagasaki Shipyard	1,130,949	459,000	459,000
July 1887	Hyogo Shipyard	816,139	320,196	188,029
December 1887	Kamaishi Iron Works	2,376,625	733,122	12,600
January 1888	Mita Agricultural Machine Factory	—	—	33,795
March 1888	Banshū Vineyard	8,000	—	5,377
August 1888	Miike Coal Mine	757,060	448,549	4,590,439
November 1889	Horonai Coal Mine and Railway	2,291,500	—	352,318
March 1890	Monbetsu Sugar Refining Mill	258,492	—	994
September 1893	Tomioka Filature	310,000	—	121,460
September 1896	Sado Gold Mine	1,419,244	445,250	} 2,560,926
September 1896	Ikuno Silver Mine	1,760,866	966,752	

Source: Kobayashi, *Nihon no kōgyōka to kangyō haraisage*, 138–39.

*As of the end of 1885, except, in the cases of Hiroshima Cotton Spinning, Banshū Vineyard, Horonai Coal Mine and Railway, Monbetsu Sugar, and Tomioka Filature, investment until the sale date.

**As of the end of June 1885.

From June 1882 to June 1885, as the Matsukata deflation proceeded, the government unloaded eleven of the factories and mines earmarked for disposal, though it disposed of all but one of them in the last year and a half of that period. Against a total cumulative investment in those enterprises of ¥3.66 million, the state recouped just over ¥1 million.[29] Though that figure pales in comparison to average government revenue during that time of about ¥78 million per year,[30] the state certainly made "savings" in operating expenses and investments. Ten of the eleven divested enterprises were mines, factories, and an ironworks that had been under Public Works Ministry management.[31] When the government dissolved that ministry, finance officials calculated that most of those works had made profits over the course of their existence; they listed only the Nakaosaka mine and Shinagawa glass factory among these ten divestments as having been in the red.[32] Some of these enterprises, particularly the metal mines, contributed to the private company boom of the late 1880s, but the driving forces behind that business surge were railroads built and operated by private concerns and cotton-spinning companies that followed the model not of the government plants, which were too small to capture economies of scale, but of the larger and more efficient Osaka Spinning Company, established in 1882.[33]

Government expenditures for industrial promotion from the mid-1870s to the mid-1880s indicate the need to qualify the view that the Matsukata reform entailed a significant retrenchment in industrial spending. With the sale of the ten Public Works enterprises between January 1884 and June 1885, extraordinary spending on state enterprises did indeed plummet in fiscal 1884 (table 4.2). But such spending had been at a high level in the preceding three fiscal years, which overlapped with Matsukata's drastic contraction of the currency from December 1881 to April 1883. Owing to increased outlays for mine and railroad development, expenditures on state enterprises in those years even exceeded those made in the mid-1870s by the Public Works Ministry, especially on mines, and by the Home Ministry at the height of Ōkubo Toshimichi's campaign to promote agriculture and light industry. In fact, from fiscal 1877, in the aftermath of the Satsuma Rebellion and with mounting trade deficits and inflation, cutbacks were under way, as operating expenditures by the Home Ministry fell to about half of the average for 1875–1876—and by the Public Works Ministry to roughly a seventh—in each of the next four fiscal years, while extraordinary expenditures dropped dramatically during those years. Sustained heavy outlays by the Hokkaido Colonization Commission somewhat offset the sharp decrease in those ministries' spending, but aggregate figures for government expenditures on industrial promotion, including corporate subsidies and other indirect outlays, show that the real retrenchment took place in the years *preceding* the Matsukata financial reform: such spending totaled some ¥43 million for January 1873 to June 1877, dropped

TABLE 4.2 Central government expenditures related to enterprise promotion, 1873–1884 (thousands of yen)

		1873*	1874	1875	1876	1877	1878	1879	1880	1881	1882	1883	1884
Ordinary Expenditures of ministries	Public Works	574	282	4,777	4,343	629	598	661	565	477	468	445	502
	Home	—	—	592	1,023	393	337	387	391	—	—	—	—
	Agriculture and Commerce	—	—	—	—	—	—	—	281	1,145	1,061	911	982
	Hokkaido Colonization	761	1,035	3,972	1,904	1,496	1,719	1,912	2,184	1,358	—	—	—
	Working capital supplement	—	—	—	—	143	137	168	95	28	241	40	—
Extraordinary expenditures	State enterprises	5,997	6,400	4,111	159	800	620	1,361	1,601	6,625	7,247	6,426	1,266
	Hokkaido enterprises	227	215	298	—	—	20	26	—	—	—	—	—
	Agric. and industry loans	87	523	3,382	1,174	751	665	354	148	—	—	—	—
	Prefectural subsidies	185	109	119	—	—	—	—	—	—	—	—	—
	Corporate subsidies	—	—	1,116	—	—	—	—	—	12	86	53	133
Special Funds	Enterprise Promotion Fund	—	—	—	—	—	284	1,326	3,390	2,630	1,698	1,450	760
	Nakasendo RR bond outlays	—	—	—	—	—	—	—	—	—	—	—	299
	Industrial Promotion Funds for Samurai Relief	—	—	—	—	—	—	—	—	—	346	558	662
	Total	7,831	8,564	18,367	8,603	4,212	4,380	6,195	8,655	12,275	11,147	9,883	4,604
	4-year totals				43,365				23,442				37,909

Source: Ishizuka, *Nihon shihonshugi seiritsu shi kenkyū*, 130–31.

*The fiscal years 1873 and 1874 were calendar years. In 1875 the government changed the fiscal year to July–June; the figures for the transitional year 1875, therefore, cover the period from January 1875 to June 1876.

to ¥23 million for July 1877 to June 1881, then *climbed back* to ¥38 million for July 1881 to June 1885.[34]

Trends in Industrial Policy

Industrial spending rebounded only temporarily, however, for by the mid-1880s an unmistakable trend toward reduced and increasingly indirect state involvement in the economy had emerged. Nonetheless, Japan moved at most in a *quasi*-laissez-faire direction after the early 1880s, for the scope of government economic intervention remained substantial in subsequent years. Matsukata, for example, offered generous subsidies to private trunk-line railroads in the 1880s and especially in 1890–1891—in response to the Financial Panic of 1890—when total railway subventions peaked at over ¥1 million a year.[35] Added to this emergency increase in subsidies was the longer-term expansion of the central bank's collateral-lending program, which gave a boost to the provision of commercial bank credit to investors in railway firms and other joint-stock companies. The subvention of trunk-line railroads, the Japan Mail Steamship Company (Nippon Yūsen Kaisha or NYK), and other private businesses, combined with the financing of government munitions factories, naval yards, and railroad workshops, kept public investment in industry at a high level through the Matsukata reform and beyond. The retained government works represented an important part of the nascent modern sector of the economy. They continued long after the 1880s to be leading centers for the introduction and diffusion of advanced Western technology and management systems. They did so by furnishing both technical support and personnel to private armaments, ship, and locomotive makers, proving vital to the rise of modern engineering industries in Japan.[36]

Even for enterprises the government did sell off, disposal by no means signified the start of a hands-off policy on the part of the regime. The example of the Nagasaki Shipyard, which the government leased to the fledgling Mitsubishi combine in 1884 and sold to Mitsubishi outright three years later, illustrates continued state intervention in fields from which it purportedly "withdrew," in this case commercial shipbuilding. The success of Mitsubishi's shipbuilding venture, the basis for its subsequent diversification into a wide range of heavy industries, was partly dependent on government support. In addition to navy orders and multi-faceted technical assistance to Mitsubishi and other shipbuilders, the state provided massive subsidies to shipping companies under the Navigation Encouragement Law of 1896, indirectly subsidizing Japanese shipbuilders, particularly after an 1899 revision reduced the subvention for ships constructed overseas to half that for domestic-built ships.[37]

Furthermore, the government made a reentry of sorts into industry and business in the 1890s and 1900s. In 1896 it founded the Yawata Iron and Steel Works, Japan's first integrated steelmaker, and in the late 1890s and first half of the 1900s escalated the construction of state railways, ultimately buying out the major private railroad companies in 1906–1907. The government used nearly ¥600,000 of the indemnity it extracted from China after the 1894–1895 Sino-Japanese War to establish the Yawata works and part of the ¥3.2 million it appropriated from the reparations for transportation and communications to extend the state railway network.[38] But, as Kamiyama Tsuneo has pointed out, much of the funding for state railway building came from public bond issues. Matsukata turned aggressively to such issues as he moved from a conservative financial policy to an activist one with the virtual completion of his currency reform in fiscal 1884: from that year to 1894 the Ministry of Finance floated a total of ¥24 million in railway bonds alone.[39]

In addition, government policy under Matsukata helped make both the Imperial Household Ministry and the new European-style nobility into major sources of funding for private industry from the mid-1880s on. Under the Peers Hereditary Property Law of 1886, Matsukata and his colleagues awarded themselves and the other peers sizable grants of stock in government-subsidized companies. Also, at Matsukata's urging, the government transferred huge blocks of shares it held in banks and corporations to the Imperial Household as part of an effort to consolidate the court's financial autonomy in advance of the opening of the Diet. In 1885, the state handed over to the court ¥5 million worth of government stocks in the Bank of Japan and ¥1 million in the Yokohama Specie Bank and, in 1887, ¥2.6 million worth of NYK shares. Between 1885 and 1890 the Imperial Household acquired additional stocks in the Nippon Railway and Sapporo Sugar, among other private companies. These transfers and acquisitions served to transform that institution into basically an investment arm of the state.[40] In short, despite Matsukata's laissez-faire pronouncements, one needs to qualify the extent to which Japanese industrial policy became noninterventionist after 1881.

Matsukata did oversee a reduction in loans and subsidies to local governments, but the Council of State had already been shifting the burden of industrial and infrastructure spending onto localities since the late 1870s. In 1878, when payment for suppressing the 1877 Satsuma Rebellion came due, the government cut prefectural outlays by ¥2.5 million and eliminated public works grants to prefectures. Instead, it issued ¥12.5 million in industrial promotion bonds, but most of the proceeds, which actually amounted to ¥10 million because of a 20 percent discount on the bonds' face value, went not directly to prefectural governments but to the Home Ministry for harbor and road improvements and ex-samurai relief and to the Public Works Ministry and Kaitakushi for railroad and mine development.[41]

Under Matsukata, the central government ended transfers to prefectures out of the general budget and restricted such outlays to the special budget's industrial promotion fund drawn from the proceeds of public bond issuance. Disbursements from that fund for prefectural works nearly doubled from the post–Satsuma Rebellion retrenchment to the Matsukata deflation, going from just over half a million yen in 1877–1880 to nearly one million in 1881–1884. The recipients of these funds tended to be prefectures that produced commodities or raw materials directly tied to import substitution and exports. The change in industrial policy for localities thus involved a shift from across-the-board disbursement of central funds to targeted investment.[42]

In the first half of the 1880s the Ministry of Finance under Matsukata and the nascent Ministry of Agriculture and Commerce engaged in a heated debate and turf war over the direction of industrial policy. In the literature, Matsukata comes across as a fervent advocate of "large-scale, transplant industries and armaments expansion"[43] who in 1884–1885 eviscerated the "grass-roots, bottom-up" plan that Maeda Masana (1850–1921), a mid-level Agriculture and Commerce bureaucrat, had advanced in the first draft of his ten-year developmental proposal "Kōgyō iken" (Opinions on Promoting Industry). Maeda had carried out in-depth surveys of agriculture, industry, and commerce in all of Japan's prefectures and, based on those surveys, put forward "a detailed, staged program of institutional and financial measures" to further national economic development.[44] In his draft proposal, as Richard Smethurst notes, Maeda had given "highest priority to agriculture, sericulture, and other traditional industries, secondary importance to river transport, shipbuilding, and harbors, and lowest priority to military spending."[45] In France for most of the decade after 1869, Maeda had come under the influence of Listian ideas while studying with Eugène Tisserand (1830–1925), a French government agronomist who later became minister of agriculture and commerce. Echoing Friedrich List, Tisserand advocated the balanced development under state direction of agriculture, commerce, and industry, though, in Maeda's view, the condition of Japan's economy at the time called for preferential support of agriculture (including cottage industry), which for List "occupied a strategic position in the process of development."[46] Whether or not Maeda read the 1851 French translation of List's Das nationale System, he would, as John Sagers remarks, "have seen the implementation of Listian state activism" as championed by Tisserand.[47]

The crux of Maeda's plan was the establishment of prefectural industrial banks, or kangyō ginkō, backed eventually by a central industrial bank, that would extend loans without security for the development of traditional industries, starting with those producing the key export items of raw silk, tea, and sugar. The Ministry of Finance countered with its own proposal for an industrial bank that would lend to individuals on the collateral of real estate as well as to local governments—without security—to finance public works. The emphasis in this counterproposal was clearly on providing credit to prefectures and districts for building roads, levees, schools, and the like. Matsukata, who in 1882 had gotten the government to reject a request by the Home Ministry to reinstate Treasury grants to localities for public works, envisioned having this industrial bank instead raise funds for such works.[48]

In the end, when the official, revised version of "Kōgyō iken" came out in late 1884, it omitted any mention of an industrial bank; without a mechanism to finance the proposed program, it became a toothless, though still valuable, survey rather than an action plan. Matsukata had proposed a similar bank in both 1881 and 1882, but the government did not establish a hypothec bank until 1897, when it chartered the Nippon Kangyō Ginkō. In that year, the state also began to set up prefectural "agriculture and industry banks" (nōkō ginkō), which functioned both as agents of Nippon Kangyō Ginkō and as independent lenders. With the establishment of the Tokushima Nōkō Ginkō in 1900, all prefectures except for Hokkaido (which had its own special development bank) had such institutions. These banks offered long-term, low-interest loans mainly to farmers but also to owners of small- to medium-sized industrial enterprises, albeit with strict collateral requirements.[49]

In view of Matsukata's background in the 1870s as head of the Home Ministry bureau dedicated to the promotion of agriculture and light industry, it should come as no surprise that he by no means ignored traditional or light industries.[50] Even at the height of his deflationary policies in the early 1880s, when Matsukata was calling in the vast majority of the funds Ōkuma had lent to various enterprises and individuals out of the Treasury's reserve fund, he forgave a huge ¥300,000 loan to a direct export association of nearly seven thousand silk producers in Gunma Prefecture who were "reeling" under the impact of falling silk prices.[51] In addition, in 1883, with an eye to expanding exports of raw silk and tea, Matsukata relaxed the total ban he had initially imposed on the extension of credit by the Yokohama Specie Bank prior to the arrival of export goods overseas by permitting that bank to make advances on the security of goods before their shipment from Japan.[52] Most scholars overlook Matsukata's pragmatic response to the unexpectedly worsening depression at the time in restoring at least partially the Ōkuma-Maeda approach to promoting exports of products from the traditional sector.

Besides lending a total of ¥1.1 million to prefectures from 1881 to 1885 based on the sale of public bonds, the Ministry of Finance under Matsukata also made loans primarily for ex-samurai relief to local businesses in a variety of agricultural and light industry fields. The ministry extended almost ¥2 million in these loans between 1882 and 1885.[53] In 1884 Matsukata dispatched finance officials on an industrial inspection tour of the Kansai and Kyushu areas. At the end of that year, these officials reported on the usage of industrial promotion funds that the government had lent to local enterprises. They noted, for instance, that in Kagoshima, Kumamoto, and Saga Prefectures, which had been hotbeds of samurai discontent in the 1870s, private companies and banks or quasi-banks,[54] most of them involving former samurai, had received a total of ¥348,000 in 1884. The companies operated in fields ranging from sericulture, silk reeling, and weaving to land reclamation and livestock raising.[55] As examples of banks and quasi-banks, other sources have noted that in Kagawa Prefecture a bank founded by some seventeen hundred ex-samurai of the Takamatsu domain received an industrial promotion loan of about ¥12,000 in 1884, and a quasi-bank that engaged not only in moneylending and bill discounting but also in sugar manufacturing obtained a ¥100,000 loan that same year.[56] Under this loan program focused on samurai assistance, the authorities paid special attention to the silk industry; whereas in the 1870s the government had directed funding to advanced, machine-reeling factories, under Matsukata the bulk of support went to silkworm-raising and hand-reeling operations. Manufacturing enterprises that secured government loans—in cotton spinning, shoe manufacturing, cement production, and the like—helped lay the foundation for later development, but the majority of them, managed mostly by inexperienced former samurai, ended in failure.[57]

Financial Stabilization versus Armaments Expansion

Matsukata's effort to restrain military spending and to prevent it from interfering with his financial program in the first half of the 1880s contradicts the Marxist-influenced view of the Matsukata reform as signifying a "militarization of public finance."[58] In the "militarization" view, Matsukata retrenched on nonmilitary expenditures to generate funds for armaments expansion and military-related heavy industry. Rather, as in his staredown of the Home Ministry over its request for the revival of public works grants in 1882, Matsukata insisted that currency and budgetary reform remain inviolate even in the face of mounting demands for expanded military appropriations after an anti-Japanese uprising broke out in Seoul in July 1882 and stoked fears of armed conflict with China.

In December 1881, two months after Matsukata had taken the helm of the Ministry of Finance, the navy submitted a massive, long-term proposal for naval expansion. The proposal called for building a major new shipyard in western

Japan and for constructing, beginning in 1882, three warships per year over a period of two decades at a total cost of ¥43 million.[59] The navy's plan, however, had little chance of approval in the wake of the emperor's conferral on Matsukata of a mandate to carry out retrenchment. In his opinion paper on the fiscal 1882 budget, the recently appointed minister of finance made clear his top priority was currency reform. In this memorandum, Matsukata insisted on the cancelation of all new projects and a freeze on expenditures for three years from fiscal 1882; only after the completion of his currency reform could government ministries initiate expansion projects.[60]

The July 1882 Imo Incident, a mutiny of Korean military units that prompted the dispatch of both Chinese and Japanese forces to Korea, dramatically changed the context of financial decision making. A consensus quickly emerged among Meiji leaders about the urgency of strengthening the military to deal with external threats, specifically China, which was backing the pro-Beijing conservative faction at the Korean court. In mid-August Minister of the Right Iwakura Tomomi sent a memorandum to Council of State members urging preparations for an "inevitable" war with China.[61] Then, in September he issued an opinion paper "on expanding the navy."[62] Surprised by what he saw as the weak showing of the Japanese naval unit dispatched during the Imo mutiny, Iwakura expressed in this document alarm over Japan's national defense and called for the rapid buildup of a navy capable of confronting the Chinese threat to Japan's interests on the Korean Peninsula. Whereas previously the Meiji leaders had focused on building up the army for domestic security purposes, they now agreed that naval expansion should take center stage.

Accordingly, in mid-November 1882 the navy presented a new proposal for battleship construction, laying out an eight-year program for augmenting the fleet by forty-eight vessels, a number it considered the minimum needed to confront the Chinese navy, at a total cost of nearly ¥38 million.[63] This proposal represented Japan's first naval contingency plan for fighting a hypothetical enemy. In contrast to the navy's rejected 1881 proposal, which had centered on gradual naval expansion based on investment in domestic shipbuilding capacity, the new plan called for accelerated buildup relying primarily on imports of warships. Making this plan potentially feasible were the large trade surpluses and resulting foreign exchange acquisitions that accompanied the Matsukata deflation from 1882 on.[64]

Though Matsukata acceded to the demands for military buildup, he insisted that the government fund army and navy expansion plans out of increased consumption taxes so as not to disrupt his financial reform and that it restrict such plans within the limits of what the Ministry of Finance could raise through a hike in those taxes. In a memorandum Matsukata sent to Chief Minister Sanjō

Sanetomi on December 26, 1882, the day after the Council of State had approved the navy's plan, he declared that "there is no way we can disburse silver specie [to purchase ships] in the huge amount requested by the navy minister."[65] He estimated that additional sake and tobacco taxes would annually yield ¥7.5 million, of which the Ministry of Finance would allocate ¥3 million toward building up the navy and ¥1.5 million toward expanding the army and deposit the remainder in a new armaments fund the ministry would set up within its reserve fund. Since the disbursements would be in paper money, not in specie required for the establishment of a convertible currency, at the paper-silver conversion rate at the time, Matsukata in effect slashed the navy's request by 40 percent.[66] The army's proposed budget, which was about three-fifths the size of its navy counterpart, sustained an even bigger hit with a 47 percent cut.[67]

In a speech that he made at a meeting with prefectural governors that December explaining the need for tax increases,[68] Matsukata stated that, in view of the security challenges Japan faced, armaments expansion was necessary, but he then asked rhetorically, "Should we now turn away from the great objective of repairing public finances and focus on outlays for the navy and army?" The way to expand the military without abandoning that objective, he maintained, was to raise taxes so that the nation could "advance in parallel" financial stabilization and military expansion. He proceeded to cite the example of Italy, which he asserted had roughly the same population, geography, and "level of enlightenment" as Japan but whose people paid on average seven times the taxes that Japanese did. He concluded by exhorting the attending governors to cooperate in implementing the tax hikes, which included a doubling that month of the sake tax, by far the most important consumption tax (in fact, a redoubling of the pre–September 1880 rate).

Total revenue from the sake brewery tax, including the increase earmarked for the military, did climb substantially after the rate jump, going from ¥10.3 million in the fiscal year ending June 1882 (that is, fiscal 1881) to ¥15.3 million the next year. Income from that tax, however, fell to ¥12.3 million in fiscal 1883 before rising to ¥13 million the following year, the drop in those two years partially offset by a leap in tobacco tax returns from ¥0.28 million in fiscal 1882 to ¥2.15 million and ¥1.29 million, respectively, in fiscal 1883 and 1884. As noted in chapter 3, the decline in sake tax revenues was owing to the depression triggered by Matsukata's severe currency contraction, which led to a collapse in demand—sake production plummeted by more than a third from 1881 to 1884—and to a rise in tax evasion.[69]

Thanks to Japan's favorable trade balance during the deflation, however, specie accumulation succeeded beyond Matsukata's expectations such that from the date of his appointment as finance minister in 1881 to the end of December 1885, even after setting aside ¥42 million in silver and gold for the establishment of a convertible currency system, the Ministry of Finance was able to disburse from its reserve fund nearly ¥64 million in specie, including for the purchase of warships from abroad.[70] Consequently, consumer tax proceeds, despite their plateauing after fiscal 1882, combined with reserve fund disbursements, made it possible for military spending to surge in the first half of the 1880s. Expenditures on the army rose moderately from ¥8.25 million in fiscal 1881 to ¥10.98 million in fiscal 1884, but outlays for the navy leaped from ¥3.11 million to ¥7.51 million during those years while the armed services' share of total government spending grew from 16 to 24 percent.[71] This escalation in military and especially naval spending took place without compromising Matsukata's financial reform program.

The expanding naval budget financed a major increase in warship tonnage and naval personnel. The navy pushed to replace superannuated vessels with bigger and newer ships and by 1885 had raised warship tonnage, which had stagnated at around 28,000 in the period 1877–1882, to over 41,000. Meanwhile, the navy also augmented its manpower from about 5,500 in 1882 to 8,000 in 1885.[72] Matsukata's slashing of the naval expansion budget proposed in late 1882, however, meant that the navy would have to postpone large-scale investment in its own shipyards and limit their production to small vessels while importing Western-made battleships and cruisers.[73]

After the successful completion of his currency reform in the abbreviated fiscal year of 1885,[74] Matsukata eliminated the military reserve fund in March 1886 and moved to raise funds for naval expansion by issuing bonds, as he did for railroad development and government note redemption. As the interest rate on bank deposits fell, the value of public bonds steadily recovered, generally exceeding their face value in 1886. This recovery opened the way for the government to use bond flotation as a new source of funding for the navy. Accepting a proposal Matsukata submitted in May 1886, the state accordingly issued three sets of naval bonds totaling ¥17 million from 1886 to 1889.[75]

Nonetheless, Matsukata continued to place limits on naval spending in the second half of the 1880s. During the enterprise boom of those years, imports of machinery, raw cotton, and other goods rose, reducing the positive trade balance of the deflationary years. The resulting outflow of specie threatened the stability of Japan's recently established convertible currency, a problem exacerbated by naval expansion, which relied on the import of armored ships and the like. Consequently, despite the successful flotation of naval bonds, Matsukata continued to rein in naval expenditures even after completing his program of currency reform. Though the special budget for warship construction, for example, called for average outlays of ¥4.6 million per year for 1886–1889, the actual amount disbursed during that period averaged only ¥2.9 million a year.[76]

Scholars have invariably identified the Matsukata financial reform with the sale of state enterprises and the transition to an industrial policy of indirect support for private initiative. Some have also linked Matsukata's currency and budgetary reform to the financing of armaments expansion and of military-related heavy industry. From 1873 to 1880, Matsukata seems to have had considerable input into evolving plans for the transfer of public enterprises to the private sector, but the divestiture program itself was the handiwork of Ōkuma with the assistance of Itō Hirobumi and Inoue Kaoru. Ōkuma and Itō were also responsible for starting the process of streamlining the government's industrial promotion efforts with their November 1880 proposal for the establishment of the Ministry of Agriculture and Commerce. As it turned out, the government disposed of all but two of the enterprises it had put up for sale under the Ōkuma plan *after* Matsukata had largely completed his currency deflation. The sale program, therefore, contributed minimally to the Matsukata financial reform until the tail end of the reform.

The trend toward reduced state spending on economic activities was apparent by the mid-1880s, but the government actually cut such spending substantially more during the retrenchment after the Satsuma Rebellion of 1877 than it did during the Matsukata deflation after 1881. The rebound in expenditures in the early 1880s was mainly the result of increased Public Works investment in government-run mines and railroads (granted, those works were among the most profitable of state enterprises). The view that Finance Minister Matsukata moved the government toward a laissez-faire approach to the economy runs up against many of the policies he promoted: subsidizing large-scale businesses; lending to smaller, local enterprises; granting blocks of corporate stock to the Imperial Household and members of the peerage (including himself!); authorizing the Bank of Japan to back lending by commercial banks on the security of shares in major private railroads and other government-subsidized corporations; and setting up Japan's first integrated steelworks as well as stepping up the construction of state railroads in the late 1890s. Also, the image of Matsukata as a proponent of heavy industry at the expense of agriculture and traditional or light industry hardly fits the profile of a finance minister who provided assistance and relief to producers of rural-based exports and extended loans to a range of enterprises in agricultural and light industry fields.

Finally, military spending increased during the 1880s but not nearly as much as the army and navy wanted, as Matsukata was determined to prevent such spending from undercutting his financial reform. By slashing the navy's proposed budgets, he compelled that service to hold off on major expansion of its ship-yards and arsenals and to limit domestic naval construction, for the most part, to relatively small vessels such as torpedo boats. But, owing to continuous trade sur-pluses between 1882 and 1885, the Ministry of Finance was able to accumulate silver more quickly and on a larger scale than Matsukata had expected, making it possible for the navy to obtain specie to purchase larger, Western-made warships and to accelerate naval buildup at a time of intensified Sino-Japanese rivalry over Korea. By maintaining a separate armaments fund from 1882 to 1886, Matsukata basically siloed any military spending above budgeted amounts and made sure that military expansion would not interfere with the "great objective" of finan-cial stabilization.

FOUNDING A CENTRAL BANK

The Bank of Japan (BoJ), established in October 1882, was pivotal to Matsukata's effort to stabilize and modernize public finance, separating currency management from the state's fiscal machine but keeping it under tight government supervision. The bank opened for business as a rarity in the global history of central banking: a central bank with a monopoly on note issue that did not issue a single note until more than two and a half years after its founding. At that time, in May 1885, the BoJ initiated Japan's transition to a sound, convertible currency system with flexible note issue limits. The bank proved fundamental to the successful launch and maintenance of a de facto silver standard on Japan's journey to gold convertibility a dozen years later. But the creation of the BoJ also involved the conflict between Ōkuma's 1881 proposal for a central bank that, with British capital and managerial help, would have carried out a precipitate currency reform and that of Matsukata, who insisted on a by-the-bootstraps approach free of external interference.

After the shelving of the Ōkuma-Itō plan to issue public bonds and set up a central bank, Matsukata would follow the advice of French finance minister Léon Say and pattern his proposed BoJ after the National Bank of Belgium (NBB). The NBB especially appealed to Matsukata for being subject to greater government oversight than practically any other central bank in Europe. In practice, however, the BoJ departed from the Belgian model in significant ways, in particular by refraining from foreign exchange activities, which it left to the Yokohama Specie Bank, and by engaging in industrial financing in violation of its own legal statutes. Besides serving as cashier to the Treasury, the BoJ provided critical support to the government by taking over from the Ministry of Finance the work of re-deeming inconvertible government notes and accumulating specie. As Matsukata moved from a deflationary policy to an expansionary one in the latter half of the 1880s, the bank made vital contributions to this shift by purchasing bonds from the government and by advancing loans to private interests on the security of their public bonds, thereby facilitating both the sale of the bonds and the raising of private capital during the enterprise boom of the late 1880s.

Thus, like other aspects of the Matsukata financial reform that veered from classical financial orthodoxy, the BoJ turned out to be hardly orthodox in its structure or operations. Instead of choosing the Bank of England model with its high degree of independence from the government, Matsukata drew on the model of the Belgian central bank because it involved greater state control. Once established, the BoJ moved in an even more statist direction, assuming the task of financing industrial firms and adopting flexible German-style note issue under close government supervision rather than the orthodox Bank of England approach.

Pre-1882 Proposals for a Central Bank

The idea of establishing a Japanese central bank emerged within the Meiji regime several years before Matsukata came to embrace the concept. In 1872 state officials adopted the gist of the proposal for a decentralized, U.S.-style banking system that Itō Hirobumi had sent back to Tokyo while investigating monetary issues in the United States, but they did so only after heated debate. Foremost among those opposing Itō's plan was Yoshida Kiyonari (1845–1891), a junior assistant minister of finance, who called for setting up a British-style "gold bank" (*kinken ginkō*) as the sole note-issuing institution. In 1865 Yoshida's home domain of Satsuma had dispatched him, together with eighteen other samurai, to study in the United Kingdom.[1] Until 1870 he had immersed himself in the theory and practice of political economy, first at University College, London, and then—after moving to the United States in 1867—briefly at Rutgers College and subsequently at a preparatory school in Massachusetts. This experience had enabled Yoshida to observe and compare the British and U.S. banking systems and convinced him that British authorities had a firmer grasp of banking rules than did their U.S. counterparts and that having multiple note issuers would be inappropriate for Japan. He therefore urged the government to set up a bank with a monopoly on note issue modeled after the Bank of England.[2]

Yoshida was not alone in advocating the founding of a central bank. In February 1871, before the Council of State received Itō's memorial proposing establishment of "paper-money-issuing companies" (*shihei hakkō kaisha*) on the model of U.S. national banks, Vice Minister of Finance Ōkuma Shigenobu and Deputy Vice Minister Inoue Kaoru sent him a letter suggesting the idea of setting up a "Bank of Japan" centered on a wealthy merchant house such as Mitsui.[3] In September 1871, three months after Itō had returned to Japan, the Ministry of Finance proceeded to approve a petition by Mitsui to found a bank patterned after the Bank of England that would issue convertible notes backed by a gold reserve equal to 75 percent of the value of the notes, signifying acceptance of Yoshida's proposal for establishing a central "gold bank."[4]

Nonetheless, Itō persuaded his colleagues to overturn this decision. He argued that the government should help set up individual banks first and that, if necessary, it could unify the system at a later date—there was no reason for the government to create a centralized system at the outset.[5] He also made the case that the approved scheme for a British-style central bank focused almost exclusively on buttressing state finances by stabilizing the value of paper money whereas his plan also emphasized banks' "natural" function of providing funds for the promotion of private enterprise. Itō's argument carried the day, for in October 1872, in a meeting with Minister of Finance Ōkubo Toshimichi, Inoue, Yoshida, and other officials, he secured agreement on following the U.S. banking model. In his 1871 proposal, Itō had recommended that the government replace the inconvertible Council of State notes (*dajōkan satsu*) it had printed in 1868 with public bonds and use the bonds to establish banks that would issue notes, but, in a departure from U.S. practice, he had not specified a specie reserve requirement for the banks. The other leaders feared that his plan would simply result in a new inconvertible paper currency. Accordingly, they reached a compromise whereby, in line with the U.S. system, the national banks would issue notes against their holdings of public bonds but, to stabilize the value of the notes, would have to maintain a high-percentage specie reserve.[6]

A call for establishing a central bank sounded again in 1876, when the government removed the specie reserve requirement for national banks after only four banks had opened for business. This time the call came from a British employee of the Ministry of Finance, Alexander Allan Shand (1844–1930). Shand, former acting manager of the Yokohama branch of the Chartered Mercantile Bank, joined the ministry as an adviser on banking matters in 1872. In 1876 Shand opposed the issue of inconvertible notes under the revised regulations for national banks and instead recommended the founding of a central bank as the sole issuer of notes convertible into specie. In a written opinion, he cited the central banks of England, France, and Germany to argue that the global trend was toward centralization of note issuance; he also warned—presciently, as later developments would bear out—that ending the convertibility of national bank notes risked triggering inflation.[7]

Tokuno Ryōsuke (1825–1883), head of the ministry's Paper Currency Bureau (Shihei Ryō), dismissed Shand's recommendation, declaring that giving national banks based on public bonds the right to issue inconvertible notes was indispensable to the program adopted that year of commuting samurai stipends into public bonds and maintaining the value of those bonds. Thus, while making it easier to found national banks by eliminating the reserve requirement, the banking revisions also aimed at encouraging the use of commutation bonds as capital for the banks, thereby helping to secure the livelihood of ex-samurai. Tokuno went on to state that creating a central bank along the lines of the Bank of England, as Shand was advising, would require the withdrawal of the inconvertible notes in circulation and a resulting reduction in the compensation to members of the former ruling class.[8]

At the time, Tokuno also had to override support for a central bank from within his Japanese staff, particularly on the part of a junior bureaucrat, Taguchi Ukichi (1855–1905). Taguchi is best known for his career after he left government service in 1878 and rose to prominence as a classical liberal economist and founder of the influential *Tōkyō keizai zasshi* (*Tokyo Economic Journal*), modeled after the British journal the *Economist*. In 1872 the teenaged Taguchi enrolled as a student in the newly established Translation Bureau of the Ministry of Finance, completing courses in English, economics, and Western history in 1874. He then joined the Paper Currency Bureau as a translator focusing on bank-related issues. After the government revised the national bank regulations in August 1876, Taguchi published a two-part article in the *Yokohama mainichi* newspaper on September 22 and December 2 recommending the founding of a centralized "government-gold-handling bank" (*kankin toriatsukai ginkō*) that would redeem the inconvertible notes issued by the government. He suggested that the Ministry of Finance appoint the First National Bank to perform this task, transferring all its gold reserves to that bank.[9] After moving to the private sector, Taguchi would restate his argument in an article titled "Establish a Government Gold Bank" (*Kankin ginkō setsuritsu subeshi*) that he published in April 1879 in his newly launched journal, *Tōkyō keizai zasshi*. In neither article did Taguchi use the term "central bank," but the model he had in mind was clearly the Bank of England.[10]

By then, Matsukata protégé and fellow Satsuma native Katō Wataru was well into his study of the central bank of Belgium. Yet in late July 1881, before Katō returned to Japan and drew up the founding documents for the BoJ in early 1882, the Meiji government approved a proposal for a central bank submitted jointly by Ōkuma and Itō. In their proposal, part of Ōkuma's recycled plan for foreign borrowing, they called for setting up a "great specie bank" (*ichidai shōkin ginkō*) that would function like the central banks of England and France in service of the state. Capitalized at ¥15 million, the bank would retire the fiat paper in circulation by floating ¥50 million in domestic bonds, which would be open to foreign buyers, the expectation being that the bank would place most of the bonds overseas. It would also absorb the Yokohama Specie Bank and handle foreign exchange activities, accumulating specie on the basis of which it would issue convertible notes. In proposing the establishment of a central bank, Ōkuma and Itō apparently acted on the advice of British minister Sir Harry Parkes as well as Alexander Shand and another former manager of the Yokohama branch of a British bank, John Robertson. As Ishii Kanji notes, this proposal was about to be put into effect, so, if not for Ōkuma's expulsion from the government that October in the Political Crisis of 1881, "Japan might have gotten a central bank under strong British influence."[11]

The Belgian Model

Shortly after Matsukata became finance minister and secured cancelation of the Ōkuma-Itō plan "to newly float public bonds and establish a [central] bank," he appointed Katō head of the ministry's Banking Bureau and commissioned him to draft a prospectus for a BoJ patterned after the National Bank of Belgium as well as regulations and articles of incorporation for the proposed bank. Subsequently, three senior finance bureaucrats, Yoshihara Shigetoshi (1845–1887), Tomita Tetsunosuke (1835–1916), and Gō Junzō (1825–1910), provided input into Katō's drafts of those documents.[12] Yoshihara, a native of the Satsuma domain, had studied political science and law at Yale College from 1869 while Tomita, who hailed from the Sendai domain, had focused on economics at Whitney Business College in Newark, New Jersey, from 1867; on Yoshihara's untimely death, Tomita would succeed him as the second governor of the BoJ. After the Restoration, Gō had joined the Ministry of Finance under the aegis of Ōkuma and Itō along with other former shogunal retainers such as Shibusawa Eiichi and Maejima Hisoka. Under Matsukata, Gō initially headed the ministry's Public Bond Bureau; he would rise to the position of vice-minister of finance in 1886.

In March 1882 Matsukata presented the finished prospectus to the Council of State in the form of a memorandum, together with the other documents. In the memorandum, he compared the current state of banking in Japan to the decentralized domain system of the Tokugawa era: "While political feudalism with its particularism and separatism, with its several hundred semi-independent jurisdictions, has been happily overthrown, in financial matters we seem to be now living under a system of bank feudalism, with 150 [national] banks existing with-out correspondence with each other, . . . each one entirely absorbed with the questions of its own existence."[13] Ironically—and doubtless Matsukata had no in-tention of suggesting this point—an actual connection had developed between "feudalism" and the national banking system, for at the direction of Iwakura To-momi almost all of the former daimyo or local lords who had governed roughly 260 domains had deposited their commutation bonds in the Fifteenth National Bank, but many had also invested in other national banks, including ones in their former domains.[14] In any case, to overcome the parochial, occluded nature of the banking system, Matsukata went on to declare, Japan urgently needed a central bank, which "is to the financial system of a country, what the heart is to the sys-tem of blood circulation in a human body." Such banks were indispensable "to the constant flow of the currency," the reason why, according to Matsukata, "in all the countries of Europe we find that there are banks of this nature."[15] Whether modern central banks have actually functioned in this manner, pumping money in a "constant flow" through existing channels, may be questionable—Mark Met-zler, for instance, argues that banks have continually made and unmade credit money and decided for themselves where that credit would "flow"[16]—but Mat-sukata had clearly bought into a trope commonly advanced by Western banking experts.

The other councilors probably needed little convincing by Matsukata, as they had previously approved the Ōkuma-Itō plan for a central bank. But they might have required an explanation for Matsukata's choice of the National Bank of Bel-gium rather than the Bank of England or the Bank of France as the model for a Japanese central bank. In his memorandum, Matsukata stated that he had cho-sen the NBB because of "the lateness of its founding, which enabled it to con-sider fully the mistakes as well as the successes of older banks."[17] He admitted that the two "foremost" central banks were those of England and France: "In exten-siveness of influence and grandeur of organization, these two banks have no peer in the world." Yet, thanks to its late-comer advantage, "in point of the perfect-ness of organization and the well-regulated condition of business management, the National Bank of Belgium stands highest"; its regulations had won "praises from the financiers of the world." In short, for a Japanese central bank, Matsu-kata claimed, "no better pattern can be found than the National Bank of Bel-gium."[18] As if to confirm the appropriateness of his choice, two years later Serbia would also found its central bank, the "Privileged National Bank of the Kingdom of Serbia," on the model of the National Bank of Belgium, "which was, at the time, viewed as a paragon of a modern banking institution."[19]

The NBB was of recent vintage compared to the Bank of England and the Bank of France, founded in 1694 and 1800, respectively. But, when Matsukata ordered

Katō to investigate the NBB, over a quarter century had passed since its founding in 1850, and in the meantime several other central banks had appeared in Europe, including those of Russia (1860), Denmark (1872), and Germany (1875). Granted, Belgian authorities had updated the NBB's charter in 1872, but it was hardly a recently established central bank.[20]

According to Yoshino Toshihiko, the real reason Belgium's central bank appealed to Matsukata was that the Belgian government exercised tight control over the bank. The extent of state supervision over the NBB was certainly greater than in the case of either the Bank of England or the Bank of France.[21] Britain's central bank faced minimal state interference, while in France government supervision was indirect to a fault. Meanwhile, the central bank of the Austro-Hungarian Empire, founded in 1816 as the Austrian National Bank, was subject to government intervention only when auditors appointed by the state identified violations or actions contrary to the public good. In the case of the Reichsbank of Germany, where the government had greater supervisory authority than in Belgium, the Imperial Diet rather than the bureaucracy wielded that authority: it selected three of four inspectors as well as the bank's governor and directors. Compared to these cases, in the Belgian one, the executive branch of the government held far more power over the operation of the central bank, which was almost free of parliamentary control. Hence, for Matsukata, who wanted by all means to ensure strong administrative oversight and to avoid interference by a future parliament, Belgium's central bank system appeared the most suitable.[22]

The Belgian government chartered the NBB in 1850 after a series of crises in the late 1830s and 1840s had hit hard the two major existing banks, the Bank of Belgium and the Société Generale, which had tied up capital in industrial ventures.[23] To avoid exposure to such industrial financing as well as to minimize competition with those banks, the NBB's charter heavily restricted its business to discounting commercial bills, making it "the most purely commercial national bank of its time."[24] The bank took over the functions that the Bank of Belgium had previously performed as cashier for the Treasury, and it also managed the public debt. In addition, the NBB obtained a de facto monopoly on the issue of paper money.[25] In return, the government reserved for itself considerable powers of supervision over the bank.

Those powers were extensive. The 1850 law establishing the NBB authorized a government commissioner to supervise all activities of the bank and to disallow any action that he considered to be in violation of the law or the bank's articles of incorporation or in contravention of the national interest, ensuring that the NBB's governor "always fulfilled his obligations toward the Minister of Finance."[26] No other central bank in Europe was subject to such supervision. In addition, the Belgian king had the power not only to appoint the bank's governor but also to fire him or to suspend him from office unconditionally. The only other bank to fall under such authority was the National Bank of Denmark. The NBB's governor, in turn, had the unparalleled right to suspend any decision by the bank that, in his view, contradicted the law, the bank's articles of incorporation, or the national interest and to refer the matter to the government for arbitration.[27]

The regulations of the BoJ, which the Meiji regime authorized in June 1882, followed those of the NBB almost "word by word and article by article."[28] The BoJ's articles of incorporation largely drew on the Belgian example as well.[29] Like the statutes and charter of Belgium's national bank, those of the BoJ placed it squarely under the supervision of the state. In Japan as in Belgium, the monarch appointed the bank's governor, who had the authority to suspend the directors' decisions and refer them to the government. Like its Belgian counterpart, Japan's Ministry of Finance required the central bank to submit monthly reports and had the power to oversee all of the bank's operations and to disallow any action that the ministry deemed improper.[30]

The ways in which the BoJ's founding documents differed from those of the NBB tended, if anything, to strengthen state intervention in Japan's case. Whereas in Belgium the general assembly of the bank's shareholders selected the directors, in Japan the minister of finance appointed the directors from among nominees of the general assembly. In contrast to the Belgian king's appointment of the NBB's vice-governor from among the directors, the Japanese government, with the emperor's approval, appointed the BoJ's vice-governor separately from the directors. In fact, for the first vice-governor (Tomita), as for the first governor (Yoshihara), the Meiji regime appointed a high-ranking official from the Ministry of Finance, as would often be the case in subsequent years. Although, following the Belgian lead, the Japanese government established the BoJ in the form of a nominally independent, private joint-stock corporation, the state provided half of the bank's capital, while in Belgium the private sector furnished the entire capital. Furthermore, in Japan anyone seeking to become a shareholder of the central bank had to obtain the permission of the finance minister. Finally, the Japanese government had the right to amend the BoJ's charter whenever it decided circumstances necessitated such action.[31]

For all the Belgian state's supervisory powers, of which Matsukata was evidently so enamored, the NBB's regulations actually aimed at placing limits on state interference. As one scholar has written, the law that set up the bank in 1850 "also established barriers against the excesses of public authorities. These barriers . . . invest it with functions and rights that allow it to oppose excessive requirements and untimely interventions of the minister of finance."[32] By specifying the finance minister's authority over the bank, the NBB's charter sought to prevent him from interfering with actions the bank might have to take in response to changing conditions. Should the NBB deem the government's exercise of authority to be improper, it could appeal to judicial authorities.[33] Belgium's minister of finance had the right not to issue instructions to the national bank but only to veto decisions he regarded as contrary to the law, the bank's charter, or the interests of the state. By the same token, the bank's statutes placed tight restrictions on lending to the government: the NBB's holdings of public bonds could never exceed its paid-up capital. Meanwhile, the finance minister had no power to limit the amount of notes the NBB issued as long as the bank maintained a specie reserve—set through mutual agreement with the finance minister at the time of the 1872 revision of the NBB charter—equal to one-third of the notes' total value.[34] In short, Matsukata and his subordinates either missed or ignored this aspect of the Belgian law and the NBB's charter, learning from those documents not how to demarcate the authority of the government bureaucracy but rather how to entrench that authority.

The result was a significant modification of the Belgian model in the direction of even greater state control that, from the outset, made the BoJ essentially part of the government system. In contrast to the NBB, for which private shareholding, bank independence, and the profit motive were important, the BoJ operated almost as "a public sector, non-profit-maximizing institution."[35] The BoJ charter suggested that the government intended its investment of half the capital to be strictly temporary. In the prospectus Matsukata submitted in March 1882, he explained the need for the government to become a shareholder in the BoJ by citing the example of France, where the state had come to the aid of the central bank at its founding in 1800 by taking on a sixth of the bank's initial stock. He then stated that, much as Napoleon's regime had disposed of its shares in the Bank of France within a couple years, once the BoJ was on a sound footing, the Meiji government would gradually sell its holdings to the public as well. Instead, in 1885 the government transferred its BoJ shares to the assets of the Imperial Household, and no public sale took place, although half ownership by the Imperial Household may have led to an increase in the bank's emphasis on profits.[36] Even after the government gave up its shares, however, the Finance Ministry retained strict supervision over the bank. As Hugh Patrick has remarked, "the Bank of Japan was never able to play a really strong independent role perhaps because—rather than evolving—it was created, full-blown, at the instigation of the Ministry of Finance. From the beginning the Ministry of Finance dominated the BoJ in most ways."[37] Emblematic of government dominion over the BoJ was the extraordinary provision in the charter that the bank's governor and vice-governor, besides being imperial appointees, would have their "salaries and entertainment expenses . . . decided by the government" (Article 44), rendering them, for all practical purposes, representatives of the state bureaucracy.[38]

"A Central Bank That Doesn't Issue Notes"

The BoJ regulations also diverged from their Belgian counterpart in stipulating that the government, instead of authorizing the immediate issue of paper currency by the BoJ, would enact "separate regulations" at an unspecified future date when it would permit the bank to issue convertible notes (Article 14). In Yoshino's words, the BoJ thus started in the "rare form of a central bank that doesn't issue bank notes."[39] The government finally enacted Convertible Bank Note Regulations in May 1884, and a year later the BoJ issued its first notes convertible into silver. According to Yoshino, this "dual system" of establishing the functions of the bank, with the 1882 regulations stipulating functions other than note issuance, has no parallel "in the history of world central bank enactments."[40]

One explanation for this two-year delay in authorizing note issuance is a political one. One could make a plausible case that Matsukata rushed prematurely to establish a central bank in connection with the Political Crisis of 1881.[41] As noted earlier, that crisis centered on the expulsion of Ōkuma Shigenobu from the government by the Satsuma and Chōshū leaders, who had come to identify him with popular agitation against the regime owing to his advocacy of a parliamentary system that most of them considered excessively liberal as well as his public opposition to the government's scheme to sell assets in Hokkaido to private interests for a pittance. Also underlying the ouster of Ōkuma were personal resentments and grievances over the growing power of this leader from the "junior partner" domain of Hizen and over specific actions he had taken. For instance, as minister of finance, Ōkuma had put pressure on Mitsui, which had enjoyed special government privileges under the patronage of Inoue Kaoru, by introducing strict new banking regulations and by promoting the rival business interests of Mitsubishi; and, after stepping down as finance minister in early 1880, he had blocked Matsukata's appointment to that position by securing it for his Hizen compatriot Sano Tsunetami and was now criticizing Kuroda Kiyotaka for his controversial proposal practically to give away government property in Hokkaido, a proposal the Council of State approved in July 1881. Meanwhile, Mitsubishi began offering both subsidies to newspapers and payments to local assemblymen opposed to the Hokkaido sale, seeing it as a threat to the virtual monopoly it had established on the coastal shipping trade thanks largely to protective policies Ōkuma had instituted as finance minister. With Ōkuma's expulsion in October 1881, Satsuma and Chōshū officials, in Andrew Fraser's words, "combined to wage a vigorous campaign against Mitsubishi that brought it to the verge of ruin."[42]

Part of that campaign, Yagi Yoshikazu contends, involved the hurried founding of the BoJ. The bank started operations, without adequate preparations, a year after the political crisis. When its doors opened in October 1882, the bank had a skeleton staff of forty-four employees (besides eight directors and three members of the discount rate committee), thinly spread over thirteen departments.[43] Then, in May 1883 it proceeded to make an irregular, unsecured loan to a shipping company, Kyōdō Un'yu Kaisha (KUK), established in January 1883. The government provided this firm with extensive support to challenge Mitsubishi, according to a widely held view, because Mitsubishi was continuing to back Ōkuma after he joined the Popular Rights movement and began pressuring the government from the outside.[44] The KUK, a merger of three shipping companies, opened in the same building as the BoJ—ironically in the former headquarters of Kuroda's Hokkaido Colonization Commission, which the oligarchs had disbanded in 1882 after canceling the fire sale of Hokkaido assets in the face of public furor on the same day they expelled Ōkuma. In late November 1882, just over a month after the BoJ's founding and before the KUK had even opened for business, the shipping firm's promoters rather brazenly requested a large loan without collateral from the new central bank. As the BoJ had inherited the NBB's focus on commercial finance and its prohibition of industrial lending or investment, such a loan would have clearly violated both the bank's regulations and its articles of incorporation. Accordingly, when the officially established KUK repeated the request for a loan in early 1883 to purchase ships from Britain, the BoJ hesitated to grant approval and referred the matter to Matsukata in April of that year.[45] He quickly ordered the bank to extend the loan, which it finally did the next month. This unsecured loan—¥300,000—accounted for nearly half of the total outstanding fixed loans made by the BoJ's head office in the first half of 1883 and roughly equaled the average capital of national banks that year.[46] Five months later, the BoJ took the exceptional step of reducing the contracted interest rate on the loan from 8.5 to 7.5 percent, a half percentage below the lowest interest rate it offered any other client that year.[47]

Yagi thus argues that the BoJ was established hastily in direct response to the Political Crisis of 1881 and "was used by the Sat-Chō bureaucrats to satisfy personal grudges against Ōkuma and Mitsubishi."[48] Matsukata submitted the memorandum "Zaisei gi" (Proposal on Finance), his angry response to Ōkuma's 1881 proposal to sell domestic bonds overseas and to found a British-style central bank, not in September 1881, as the official biography *Kōshaku Matsukata Masayoshi den* mistakenly claims,[49] but a month later, just as the political crisis was coming to a head. In that sense, Matsukata was making a political statement in the context of behind-the-scenes plotting against Ōkuma, establishing his credentials as a financial authority by attacking Ōkuma's positions. Their proposals were in fact quite similar insofar as they both linked the creation of a convertible currency system to the founding of a central bank, but Yagi unfairly describes Matsukata's

"Zaisei gi" as a "rehash" (*nibansenji*) of the Ōkuma-Itō proposal.[50] Rather, as a precursor to Matsukata's 1882 memorandum that led to the establishment of the BoJ, "Zaisei gi" presented—in a section drafted by Katō Wataru, recently returned from Belgium—a different vision of central banking from that of Ōkuma's British-inspired one.[51] Nine months later, the BoJ regulations also seemed to show the imprint of the Political Crisis of 1881 in stipulating that the minister of finance had to approve any acquisition of shares in the BoJ, a requirement that, Yagi asserts, was aimed at preventing Mitsubishi from becoming a shareholder in the bank. Tomita Tetsunosuke, as a member of the bank's founding committee, objected to this provision, but Matsukata pushed through its inclusion in the regulations.[52]

The composition of the bank's ownership would seem to support Yagi's assertion. At its opening, the BoJ had 580 stockholders. After the Ministry of Finance, which owned half of the 50,000 shares, the biggest stockholder was Mitsui Hachiroemon with 1,000 shares, while two Mitsui executives held 515 shares combined. Yasuda Zenjirō and nine others affiliated with him possessed a total of 1,060 shares. Of seventy-six Osaka businessmen who had subscribed for more than 5,000 shares in all, the holders of 850 were affiliated with either Mitsui, Yasuda, or Sumitomo. Kawasaki associates held 955 shares, twenty-five Yokohama silk merchants and financiers, a total of 1,605 shares. Not one Mitsubishi-affiliated person was among the bank's initial stockholders.[53]

Regarding the lack of preparations at the time of the BoJ's founding, Yagi lists a number of points. For example, he echoes Yoshino's observation about the extraordinary character of a central, note-issuing bank that failed to issue notes until almost three years after its establishment. In addition, when the BoJ opened in 1882, it had no deposit-handling branch offices and only one in 1883; it was finally able to function as a central bank in 1884, when it counted ten such branches. Also, at the time of its opening, the BoJ had yet to establish procedures for depositing or withdrawing funds. As another indication of the rush to launch the bank, the remodeling of the former Kaitakushi offices that would house the BoJ fell behind schedule, a typhoon causing further delay, and did not wrap up until the end of October, while construction of the bank's vault began only in November; despite these setbacks, the bank doggedly adhered to opening its doors on October 10.[54] The authorities, however, postponed the formal opening ceremony for the Tokyo head office until April 28 of the next year, after the bank had finally completed the vault, while the opening ceremony for the Osaka branch took place two months later.[55]

In another irony, in 1885 Mitsubishi would surprisingly return to favor with the Sat-Chō leaders, especially Matsukata. In late summer of that year, after fierce competition between the KUK and Mitsubishi's shipping firm, the two enterprises agreed on a merger, creating the Japan Mail Steamship Company or NYK. The general director of Mitsubishi, Kawada Koichirō (1836–1896), played a key mediating role. After the hard-nosed founder of Mitsubishi, Iwasaki Yatarō (1835–1885), died of stomach cancer in February, the top executives of the company took a more flexible approach to resolving the costly rivalry with the KUK. Like Iwasaki, Kawada hailed from the former Tosa domain, which had been a junior partner in the Restoration coalition along with Ōkuma's home domain of Hizen and had been instrumental in bringing traditional enemies Satsuma and Chōshū together against the shogunate in 1866. William Wray writes that Kawada, a "huge man" who looked like a sumo wrestler, "appears in most historical accounts as the 'personification of feudal morality.'"[56] In early 1885 he entered into secret negotiations with Inoue Kaoru, who subsequently arranged for Kawada to meet quietly at a restaurant in Osaka with Matsukata and Itō Hirobumi in July, at which time he obtained their consent to a merger between Mitsubishi and the KUK.[57] Through his careful, behind-the-scenes negotiations, Kawada appears to have won the confidence of the oligarchs and helped initiate a close relationship between Mitsubishi and Matsukata in particular. The rapprochement affected the BoJ as well. When Tomita resigned as governor of the bank in 1889, Matsukata had Kawada appointed as Tomita's successor. In fact, for the next fourteen years, three Mitsubishi men in a row would serve as BoJ governor, as Iwasaki Yanosuke, brother of the late Yatarō, and Yamamoto Tatsuo, a Kawada protégé from NYK, followed Kawada in that position. Whereas the BoJ's regulations had contained a special provision purportedly meant to exclude Mitsubishi from its ownership, as soon as Kawada assumed the governorship, both he and Yatarō's son Iwasaki Hisaya became stockholders in the bank.[58]

Much as the BoJ had extended a loan to the KUK in direct violation of its legal regulations, in 1886 it also made a loan to the NYK, though in its case with collateral. For this collateral, the bank accepted NYK stock, contravening the statutory prohibition against its "lending on the security of bank or other corporate shares."[59] In the previous year the BoJ had begun accepting as loan collateral the shares of the Yokohama Specie Bank and two other corporations—the first private railway, the Nippon Railway Company, and the so-called Peers Bank, the Fifteenth National—both of which enjoyed generous public support. In November 1886, the NYK petitioned the central bank to add its stock to the list of collateral approved for BoJ loans. The bank's directors unanimously rejected the petition, citing the relative volatility of the stock's price and uncertainty about the company's finances, but when the NYK persisted, arguing that it was a special firm under government protection, the BoJ turned yet again to Matsukata. He instructed the bank not only to approve the petition but to lend on the security of NYK shares up to the full value of their paid-up portion instead of half the value,

as the bank proposed (stockholders in the NYK, as in most joint-stock companies, paid for their shares on an installment basis).[60]

Political motives of the kind Yagi emphasizes may well have contributed to the
hasty establishment of the BoJ. He speculates that, as part of the maneuvering
against Ōkuma in early October 1881, Matsukata promised to launch a central
bank within a year of his appointment as finance minister, though he provides
no evidence for such a promise.[61] That the Sat-Chō leaders, according to Yagi,
had secretly begun planning in 1881 to set up a shipping firm to rival Mitsubishi[62] and that the BoJ extended a large and irregular loan to the KUK not long
after the founding of both the bank and the company do suggest the oligarchs'
use of the bank for a political vendetta against Mitsubishi over its ties to Ōkuma
and opposition groups.

Yet alternate interpretations point to motives other than political intrigue. The
main reason for the BoJ's delay in issuing convertible notes was that in
March 1882—when Matsukata submitted his memorandum calling on the government to establish a central bank but to withhold "for some time" granting it
permission to issue such notes[63]—the difference in value between paper money
and specie was still large, even though the contraction of currency was under way,
with a one-yen silver coin fetching on average ¥1.55 in paper; paper currency depreciated even further in the months preceding the bank's establishment in October (see table 1.3). If the BoJ had started issuing convertible notes at that time,
recipients of the notes would very likely have immediately converted them into
specie, as had happened to national bank notes prior to 1876—hence, the exceptional case of "a central bank that doesn't issue bank notes."[64]

This observation still begs the question of why Matsukata did not wait to establish the BoJ until, as he put it in his March 1882 memorandum, "the national
coffers" had "enough specie to form the necessary reserve for issuing bank
notes."[65] The Political Crisis of 1881 may have hastened the BoJ's founding and
helped strengthen Matsukata's desire to ensure strict government oversight, but
he had been preparing to recommend the establishment of a central bank under
Belgian-style state supervision ever since Léon Say had convinced him to do so
more than three years before the 1881 upheaval. Matsukata seems to have staked
his reputation on putting in place a central bank—even if it was a work in progress—as the centerpiece of his entire financial program. Establishing such a
bank, he declared in his memorandum of March 1882, "lies at the foundation of
all other financial reforms" and represents a "fundamental policy through which
at one stroke financial soundness and health may be infused into the body poli-
tic."[66] Reducing the amount of currency in circulation was the most urgent task
at hand, but Matsukata may have felt compelled to follow through on founding
the BoJ posthaste after having pronounced it foundational to his reform.

In addition, Wray has questioned the view, repeated by Yagi, that the Sat-Chō leaders promoted the KUK out of a vengeful desire to weaken or destroy Mitsubishi. Instead, Wray emphasizes concerns about national security and international trade as more significant motivations for the oligarchs' sponsorship of the KUK. Whereas the government wanted "a strong commercial fleet capable of operating overseas" and especially one poised for requisitioning by the navy in wartime, Mitsubishi was increasingly focusing its shipping business on profitable coastal routes to the neglect of foreign lines.[67] Eager to promote overseas shipping for both military and economic reasons, therefore, the government drove the formation of a second company that would be more responsive to state policies. In particular, the government included in the directive it issued to the KUK numerous stipulations related to naval preparations and appointed naval officers as president and vice-president of the company. Wray's interpretation, in turn, puts into question whether the precipitance of the BoJ's founding and its loan to the KUK were part of a conspiracy directed against Mitsubishi, which, after all, continued to receive state subsidies after 1882, though with greater restrictions that ultimately led it to support the NYK merger and to withdraw from direct involvement in shipping.

Furthermore, industrial financing by the BoJ, though a violation of its legal statutes, was to a large extent a pragmatic response to economic exigencies in the 1880s and 1890s. In both "Zaisei gi" and his 1882 memorandum, Matsukata called for the creation not only of a central bank that would function as the pivot of Japan's banking system but also of an industrial bank and a savings bank. Under this proposed division of labor, following the Belgian example, the BoJ would focus on short-term commercial finance while the industrial bank would handle long-term funding of industrial, agricultural, and engineering projects and the savings bank would encourage "the spirit of thrift." But, as Matsukata declared in his 1882 memorandum, he would seek "some future opportunity" to draft regulations for the special banks.[68] He explained in a memorandum the following year that, with the current price of public bonds below par, it would be "impossible" for an industrial bank to issue bonds, which would be the basis for its lending; the government would have to wait until public bonds regained their face value before it could establish such a bank.[69] As it turned out, once the Diet opened in 1890, it did not pass laws to set up long-term credit banks until after the Sino-Japanese War of 1894–1895. A hypothec bank, Nippon Kangyō Ginkō, originally charged with providing loans primarily to the agricultural sector on the security of real estate, finally opened in 1897, and an industrial bank, Nippon Kōgyō Ginkō, which lent on the security of corporate shares, in 1902. As Ishii Kanji remarks, however, "industrialists could not wait for the appearance of banks specializing in long-term finance, so they turned to national and private banks to get long-term funding using real estate and securities as collateral, and the BoJ backed up such financing despite the prohibition against it in the bank's regulations."[70] Thus, the central bank continued to lend on the security of corporate shares, especially those of capital-intensive railroads, until after the turn of the century.

"Outsourcing" Foreign Exchange Activities

Besides undertaking industrial financing, the BoJ diverged from the Belgian model in yet another way by eschewing direct involvement in foreign exchange business until 1904. Just as in their 1881 proposal Ōkuma and Itō had recommended the establishment of a central bank that would absorb the Yokohama Specie Bank and handle foreign exchange activities, Matsukata also indicated in both "Zaisei gi" and his 1882 memorandum that his proposed bank, like the NBB, would engage in "discounting foreign bills of exchange."[71] Instead, however, as Michael Schiltz puts it, the BoJ ended up "outsourcing" foreign exchange to the Yokohama Specie Bank (YSB).[72] That bank opened for business in February 1880 on the same day the Council of State forced Ōkuma to resign as finance minister. Fukuzawa Yukichi, the educator and popularizer of things Western who was himself an accomplished private entrepreneur, seems to have originated the idea for the specie bank two years earlier, recommending the establishment of such an institution in letters he wrote to Ōkuma. Under Fukuzawa's "initiative and guidance," two government officials who had graduated from his academy, Keiō Gijuku, as well as business associates of Fukuzawa developed plans for the bank, which Ōkuma formally proposed to the Council of State in late 1879.[73] Raymond Goldsmith claims that the YSB "was the only important financial institution [in Japan] that did not closely follow a Western model."[74] As an expedient, the YSB initially operated under the national bank regulations, but its directive gave the finance minister much tighter control over the bank and withheld from it the national banks' right to issue notes. Also, unlike the national banks, the YSB centered its business on foreign exchange.

As the scale of the YSB's operations grew, the national bank regulations began to pose obstacles to its business activities. For example, those regulations forbade the transferring of funds to and from banks overseas, making it impossible for the YSB to enter into correspondent agreements with foreign banks. To remove such hindrances, Matsukata and YSB governor Hara Rokurō (1842–1933) decided in 1886 to establish regulations specific to that bank. Promulgated in mid-1887, the new regulations apparently did have a Western model—the charter of the Hongkong and Shanghai Banking Corporation (HSBC). Founded by a Scotsman in Hong Kong in 1865, the HSBC helped promote British trade with East Asia and held first place among foreign banks in Japan.[75] The Japanese authorities did pattern the YSB's provisions governing foreign exchange operations after those of the HSBC, but Ishii Kanji notes that the two banks differed considerably in organization and independence: for instance, only Japanese could be stockholders of the YSB, which the Tokyo government backed and supervised, whereas European, U.S., and other nationals held stock in the HSBC, which remained relatively free of regulation by the Hong Kong government.[76]

Ōkuma had intended the YSB mainly to help bring specie hoarded within Japan back into circulation and thereby raise the value of paper money, but the bank took on a very different function under his successors as finance minister, Sano and Matsukata. As the yen failed to appreciate in the months after February 1880, the government in October of that year adopted a program that an Ōkuma subordinate, Maeda Masana, had proposed in the autumn of 1879 whereby the YSB undertook foreign exchange operations centered on financing exports and acquiring specie from abroad.[77] As noted in chapter 3, the YSB borrowed paper money from the government and later from the BoJ and advanced it to merchants involved in exporting Japanese goods. It then received repayment in foreign moneys that the bank's overseas agencies collected at the export destinations and exchanged the foreign paper for specie, which it used to repay the government and the central bank. At Matsukata's request, the government in March 1882 expanded the program to cover exports not only of raw silk and tea but also of other goods such as rice and coal.[78] Through this scheme, by 1905 the YSB, together with the BoJ, had supplied some 80 percent of the financing for raw silk exports, Japan's number one foreign exchange earner.[79] By underwriting exports of raw silk and other commodities, the YSB played a crucial role in enabling the Ministry of Finance to accumulate sufficient specie for the BoJ to begin issuing convertible notes with confidence in 1885. With the enactment of revised YSB regulations in mid-1887, Matsukata fully abandoned the idea of merging the YSB and BoJ, stating at a government meeting in June 1887 that it would be preferable to maintain the specie bank as an independent institution handling foreign exchange business, though under the strict supervision of the Ministry of Finance.[80]

Establishing Silver Convertibility

On the question of which monetary standard he would have the BoJ support, Matsukata had hoped to put Japan back on the gold standard, which virtually all the advanced Western countries, including Japan's most important trading partners, had adopted by 1881. In that year Britain, France, and the United States alone took 74 percent of Japan's exports and provided 69 percent of its imports by yen value.[81] Much as gold standard advocates would emphasize in the lead-up to Japan's adoption of that monetary standard in 1897, convertibility to gold would therefore have lowered transaction costs and exchange rate volatility with the country's main trading partners as well as potential lenders. The exchange rate issue, in particular, would hit home when negotiations over the note redemption bonds that Matsukata aggressively tried to sell in Europe in 1884 and 1885 collapsed over the failure to agree on a silver-gold conversion rate.[82]

Nevertheless, as we saw in chapter 2, Matsukata took a pragmatic approach to currency standards, as he did in other areas of financial policy. For Japan in 1881 the silver standard was the logical choice for a convertible currency system. While demand for gold was rising and global gold production was stagnating, silver was relatively plentiful, as nations transitioning to gold standards sought to unload their silver reserves and new silver discoveries, particularly in North America and Australia, combined with improvements in mining technology, had led to more than a doubling of world silver output from 1860 to 1880.[83] The paltry ¥8.7 million remaining in the Meiji government's reserve fund in mid-1881 consisted almost entirely of silver, and at the end of 1885, by which time the specie and bullion held by the government and BoJ had reached some ¥42 million, gold accounted for less than ¥14 million of the total.[84] By contrast, at the end of the year in which Japan finally went on the gold standard, the central bank's reserve amounted to nearly ¥97 million in gold, including part of the ¥374 million in China war reparations deposited as pounds sterling in London. The 1897 reserve was equivalent to some 40 percent of the ¥226 million in convertible BoJ notes in circulation together with the ¥12.5 million in government and national bank notes still outstanding at the end of that year.[85]

Also impelling Japan to go for silver convertibility in the 1880s was that silver was East Asia's de facto trade standard, and the Western powers insisted on its use in the treaty ports, where foreign merchant houses handled as much as 90 percent of Japan's exports.[86] As Matsukata explained to the Council of State in October 1883 in recommending a shift from the legal bimetallic system to a de facto silver standard:

> At present the East has yet to reach a high level of civilization and has taken silver as its trade standard for hundreds of years. Although England is a rich and strong country that is on the gold standard and extends over the four seas, when its people come to the East, they conduct trade using silver currency. Ultimately, they conform to the actual state of affairs by using a silver standard rather than a gold one. That being the case, with our meager trade, we cannot possibly maintain a gold standard.

He went on to assert that, "although a country that dominates the trade of neighboring countries can maintain a currency standard of its own choosing, our country's trade has not yet attained that level; furthermore, because Asian lands are silver countries and our country's economy is not yet at a stage that would make the use of silver inconvenient, we must now establish silver as our currency standard."[87]

More positively, Matsukata and his colleagues anticipated that adopting the silver standard would give Japan a significant advantage in trade with gold standard countries, as the declining price of silver cheapened Japanese exports, especially of silk, tea, and rice, which were in high demand in advanced Western nations. By 1885 the price of one ounce of silver, which had remained stable until the early 1870s, had dropped on the London market by 25 percent, and the price would continue to fall until in 1897 it would stand at less than half the price in 1872.[88] Similarly, silver depreciated markedly relative to gold on the London market during this period, the silver-to-gold price ratio going from 15.63 in 1872 to 19.41 in 1885 and eventually to 34.34 in 1897.[89] As expected, from 1886 to 1895, Japan's exports to its top three gold standard trade partners—the United States, Britain, and France—did indeed surge, more than doubling from ¥34 million out of total exports of ¥49 million to ¥84 million out of aggregate exports of ¥136 million. Yet total Japanese exports to its three leading trade partners on the silver standard—China, Hong Kong, and Korea—tripled during those years, going from ¥10 million to ¥31 million,[90] suggesting that Japan's move "to the same monetary standard as its regional trade partners . . . reduced exchange rate volatility and lowered transaction costs."[91] The positive trade balances of 1882–1885, when exports held steady but imports dropped and stagnated owing to the deflation-induced depression, continued in every year during the following decade, save for the panic year of 1890 and the war year of 1894.[92]

With the global depreciation of silver and the rise in domestic prices following the Matsukata deflation, switching to the silver standard basically "insulated" Japan from the "gold-bloc deflation" of the late nineteenth century.[93] As Garrett Droppers, who had served as chair of political economy and finance at Tokyo Imperial University, wrote in 1898, "it is well known that prices in Europe and America have continuously fallen in the past twenty years—a process from which Japan has been entirely free." He then noted that, "with every decline in the gold price of silver Japanese industries had a new opportunity for expansion. The silver standard in Japan proved to be a most remarkable and peculiar protective measure—entirely free from the objections to a protective tariff,"[94] which the unequal treaties prevented Japan from applying anyway until the last pillar of the treaties—tariff control—toppled in 1911.

In an 1890 report on his currency reform of 1882–1885, Matsukata indicated that another reason the government went for silver was to hasten the buildup of the specie reserve and the establishment of convertibility. By taking advantage of silver depreciation to achieve those ends, the government could ease and shorten the economic downturn that Matsukata had anticipated his drastic contraction of paper currency would inflict on Japan: "Reducing the paper money supply and increasing the specie reserve would no doubt result in the restoration of the value of paper currency, the importation of specie, the attainment of trade surpluses, a decline in interest rates . . . and a rise in public bond prices."[95] As Matsukata explained in this report, after the government announced that the BoJ would issue notes convertible to silver beginning in 1885 and that government fiat notes would also be redeemable in silver beginning in 1886, the authorities were, in effect, able to raise the specie reserve ratio by exchanging gold coins and bullion in the reserve for silver, essentially devaluing the yen by setting paper at par with the cheaper silver coin. Under Japan's legal bimetallic system, the Treasury recorded a ¥1 gold coin as equal in value to a ¥1 silver coin in calculating its specie reserve holdings, despite the relative appreciation of the gold one yen, which was actually worth about ¥1.2 in silver at the gold-silver exchange rate in 1885.[96] Therefore, converting the nearly ¥14 million in gold coins and bullion in the specie reserve to silver in 1885, the government could raise the nominal specie reserve of ¥42 million to ¥45 million; the new figure raised the ratio of specie reserve to all government and national bank notes in circulation from about 35 to 38 percent.[97] The yen would continue to devalue steadily during the years Japan was on the silver standard, contributing to a rise in prices, wages, industrial output, and exports alike, particularly during the private enterprise booms of the late 1880s and 1890s.

Issuing Convertible Notes

Thanks in part to the YSB's foreign exchange program, combined with Japan's overall trade surplus during the Matsukata deflation, the amount of specie in the government's reserve fund rose significantly from less than ¥9 million on the day Matsukata became finance minister in October 1881 to nearly ¥34 million in December 1884. By the end of 1885, that figure had further climbed to ¥42 million, while the BoJ had accumulated an additional ¥3.3 million in its reserve.[98] The YSB program accounted for almost a fifth of the total increase in the government's holdings of specie from October 1881 to December 1885 (see table 3.4, "Foreign bills of exchange collected"). As a result of Matsukata's drastic contraction of the money supply and the marked growth in the specie reserve, which went from a lowly 8.3 percent of the value of all notes in circulation in December 1881 to 27 percent in December 1884, paper money appreciated dramatically, with the paper-to-silver ratio dropping from 1.73 in October 1881 to 1.09 in May 1884.[99]

In light of these positive trends, the government in May 1884 finally enacted regulations for the BoJ to issue convertible bank notes. In proposing the regulations in October 1883, Matsukata had recommended a maximum limit for note issuance of no more than three times the value of specie held by the bank, "following the example of European central banks."[100] Undoubtedly, then as before, he specifically had in mind the Belgian model. The National Bank of Belgium had precisely that proportional reserve requirement; unlike, say, the Bank of England, which under the Peel Act of 1844 had to back the money it issued almost entirely with gold, the NBB had the more flexible stipulation that its specie reserve equal at least one-third of the total value of notes in circulation.[101] The BoJ's 1884 regulations, however, stated only vaguely that the bank "shall keep a sufficient amount of silver coins as reserve fund for the conversion of notes," adding that the finance minister "shall determine the amount [of notes] to be issued."[102] In a July 1884 directive to the bank, the Ministry of Finance set an initial upper limit for BoJ notes of ¥2 million but stated that "the minister of finance may approve an increase in the issue when he deems it appropriate" and that he would "specify the ratio between the amount of notes issued and the reserve."[103] By the end of 1884, the bank had accumulated a mere ¥370,000 worth of silver coins, so in April 1885 it requested a loan of ¥2 million in silver from the Ministry of Finance to serve as the exchange reserve it would need upon issuing convertible notes.[104]

In May 1885, just three days before the BoJ issued its first notes, the government revised the directive, dropping the ¥2 million issue limit and indicating simply that, "depending on the state of financing, the minister of finance will specify" the maximum limit for note issuance.[105] In accordance with this stipulation, the BoJ secured Matsukata's approval for the bank to make gradual note issues of up to ¥5 million as well as for the government to lend it the requested ¥2 million in silver for its specie conversion reserve. The bank then proceeded to put into circulation its first batch of convertible notes on May 9; by the end of the year, when paper was virtually on par with silver, it had issued nearly ¥4 million in banknotes, about 3 percent of the total value of notes in circulation.[106]

Thereafter, in response to growing demand for convertible notes from both the private sector and the government, the BoJ continually obtained Ministry of Finance approval to raise the note issue limit—initially to ¥9 million in February 1886 and, only a month later, to ¥20 million and, by 1890, to ¥85 million. With the difference in yen value between paper money and silver coins having disappeared in January 1886, the issue of BoJ notes went smoothly, as the bank was able to exchange almost ¥29 million more of its notes for silver and government paper than it had to take back in exchange for silver over the course of that year. Of the nearly ¥29 million total for 1886, the amount of silver alone that the BoJ received in exchange for its notes exceeded the amount it paid out by more than ¥15 million. Although initially the bank deposited only silver coins into its reserve fund, it began to add gold coins in April 1886 and gold bullion in August of that year, partly in anticipation of the eventual return to the gold standard. The ratio of reserve specie to notes never fell below 55 percent during the three years after mid-1885, assuring the successful launch of the silver standard.[107]

In June 1883, the BoJ had assumed responsibility for redeeming national bank notes when the Ministry of Finance deprived the banks of their right of note issue and stipulated that they convert to ordinary commercial banks if they wished to continue in business after their charters expired twenty years from their founding.[108] Then, in 1886 the BoJ also took on the task of handling the retirement of the government's inconvertible notes. By the end of fiscal 1889 (March 1890), the bank had redeemed over ¥43 million in government paper money; as a result, by that time, government notes' share of all paper in circulation had plunged from 72 percent at the beginning of January 1886 to 28 percent. Not until the end of 1899, however, did the BoJ complete the retirement of government notes. Meanwhile, between January 1886 and March 1890, national bank notes' share of the total money supply declined much less—from 25 percent to 18 percent. But, after the last of the national bank charters expired in 1899, the Ministry of Finance declared the banks' remaining notes no longer legal tender, and the BoJ would finish their redemption in 1904.[109]

Despite Matsukata's advocacy in 1883 of a Belgian-style proportional reserve system, the relation between the BoJ's note issue and its specie reserve remained unclear until 1888. By then, Matsukata had changed his mind and, in another departure from the Belgian model, proposed instead a fiduciary elastic limit method of note issuance following the practice of Germany's central bank. Tajiri Inajirō had actually recommended the Reichsbank's elastic limit method (*seigen kusshin hō*) as early as August 1882, when he had sent Matsukata an opinion paper comparing different "methods of issuing paper currency," though Tajiri had rather conservatively suggested combining that approach with the Russian government's practice of limiting annual note issues to a proportion of tax revenue.[110] In fact, in June 1878, while still at Yale, Tajiri had written a lengthy paper titled "Opinion on Public Finance," in which he summarized the orthodox lessons he had learned from Sumner and others, such as the "evils of inconvertible notes" and the advantages of the gold standard but had also urged that, "following the example of the new German bank," Japan should adopt the elastic limit ("*erasuchikku-rimitto*") system as (and here he was sounding very much like a recent college graduate) "the most excellent method ever" (*mottomo senko no ryōhō*).[111] Tajiri sent his opinion paper to Yoshida Kiyonari, who was then minister plenipotentiary to the United States. Whether Yoshida forwarded the document to finance officials in Tokyo is unclear. He had taken up his position at the Japanese embassy in 1874 after helping negotiate the government's second foreign loan, which it planned to use for commuting samurai stipends. As a gold monometallist with four years of service in the Ministry of Finance, Yoshida was undoubtedly impressed with the knowledge that Tajiri displayed in his paper of financial theory and practice as well as of trends within Japan, despite his having been away from the homeland for over seven years, and he may well have recommended Tajiri to his former colleagues in the ministry. When Ulysses Grant visited Japan in 1879, Yoshida happened to be home on furlough and served as a guide to the ex-president; in honor of the general and his visit, Yoshida would name his son "Grant."[112]

Matsukata evidently mulled over Tajiri's elastic limit suggestion for several years before deciding to recommend it to the cabinet. The government accepted his proposal and revised the convertible bank note regulations accordingly in August 1888. Under this revision, the government authorized the BoJ, with the approval of the finance minister, to issue notes in excess of the issue limit—reset to ¥70 million at the time—upon payment of a tax. The bank could use as security for the notes it issued not only the silver and gold it held in reserve but also commercial and treasury bills, public bonds, and other "sound instruments." Of the ¥70 million limit, the bank had to earmark ¥49 million for retiring the remaining national bank and government notes, leaving only ¥21 million it could freely issue at the height of a private enterprise boom.[113] Consequently, the elastic-limit system, whereby the minister of finance could permit the BoJ to surpass the note limit or, better yet, establish a higher limit, was crucial in rendering the bank capable of responding flexibly to the financing needs of both private business and the government.

As the domestic economy recovered from the recession of the early 1880s and demand for financing mounted in the private sector, the BoJ steadily increased its issue of convertible bank notes, raising the total in circulation from just under ¥40 million in 1886 to over ¥79 million in 1889 and, beginning in 1886, reversing Matsukata's currency deflation.[114] The bank put into circulation a significant portion of its notes by accepting as collateral for discounting commercial bills the shares of private railroads, banks, and the Kanegafuchi Spinning Company, among other firms, thereby facilitating the provision of credit to leading joint-stock companies in the modern sector.[115] The central bank also accepted public bonds as loan collateral. In fact, from 1886 to 1889 the BoJ lent more than three times as much on the security of public bonds as on shares; during those years, the total of loans collateralized by public bonds equaled some 15 percent of the value of all convertible notes in circulation and over half of the total amount subscribers paid for the seven sets of bonds the BoJ issued on behalf of the government.[116] By accepting public bonds as loan collateral and purchasing large blocks of them from the government itself,[117] the bank contributed to the successful flotation of a series of public bonds to construct state railways, enhance the navy, and redeem inconvertible notes, as Matsukata moved from deflationary to expansionary policies after 1884.[118] The BoJ's lending on the collateral of securities, the most important of which were public bonds, played a key role in enabling Japan to experience simultaneously—and without recourse to foreign capital—currency reform, domestic bond issuance, and economic growth in the latter half of the 1880s.[119]

"POOR PEASANT, POOR COUNTRY"?

The Matsukata Deflation

In an 1886 treatise on farm insurance subtitled *Proposals for the Amelioration of the Condition of the Japanese Agriculturalist*, Paul Mayet (1846–1920), a German adviser to the Meiji government, placed on the title page an inscription that read "Poor peasant, poor country. Poor country, weak country!"—roughly the reverse of the Meiji regime's slogan "rich country, strong army" (*fukoku kyōhei*).[1] The "poor peasant" to whom Mayet was referring was the small landowning or tenant farmer suffering from the effects of the Matsukata financial reform, for, even as that reform helped pave the way for modern economic growth in Japan, it threw the country's agricultural sector into a depression. The price plunge and tax hike accompanying currency deflation and armaments buildup brought hardship and despair to many in the countryside; failing to meet their tax obligations, many owner farmers fell into a downward spiral of indebtedness leading to bankruptcy, dispossession, and tenancy. In the critical perspective, the Matsukata deflation played a major role in both the entrenchment of the prewar landlord system and the collapse of the Jiyūtō or Liberal Party, the rural-based wing of the Popular Rights movement.[2] In the positive interpretation, the rural crisis was an unavoidable but temporary by-product of an urgently needed reform; however hard hit the peasants may have been, they were not so desperate as to rise up in revolt.[3]

Regardless of whether scholars hold negative or positive views of the Matsukata reform, they have tended to overstate both the short- and long-term impact of the deflation-induced depression as well as the role of the reform itself in bringing about the "Matsukata deflation" in the first place. If Matsukata had strictly followed an orthodox program of financial stabilization, the depression would likely have been as severe as most accounts claim. But his deviations from orthodoxy—boosting government spending, promoting exports of commodities from the rural sector, and the like—helped to buffer the economy and abridge the downturn. In short, one needs to qualify the commonly held view that the Matsukata reform was "a devastating experience for millions of people."[4]

Causes of the Deflation

With few exceptions, English-language scholarship still maintains that the post-1881 "retrenchment" policies of Finance Minister Matsukata triggered the depression that gripped rural Japan from 1882 to 1885: it was a straightforward cause-and-effect relationship. In fact, however, the situation was much more complicated than such a reading would indicate, and since at least the 1980s non-Marxist scholars in Japan have portrayed the Matsukata reform as having basically reinforced and accelerated a deflationary trend that was already under way.[5] Some even go so far as to say that, no matter who had been in charge of financial policy after 1881, an economic recession would inevitably have occurred.[6]

Why, then, should Matsukata not get *all* the blame for bringing on one of the most severe deflations in modern Japanese history? Admittedly, historians agree that Matsukata's sharp reduction of the money supply from 1882 to 1884 was mainly responsible for the steep decline in prices and general depression of those years. From 1881 to 1884, while the amount of inconvertible paper notes shrank by 19 percent, Tokyo wholesale prices dropped by the same amount, with the price of rice, Japan's biggest commodity, falling by half on the Tokyo exchange.[7] But, at least in the Japanese literature, scholars have also pointed to other internal factors that preceded the Matsukata financial reform and helped trigger the deflation of the early 1880s. To begin with, Ōishi Kaichirō and others have noted that from mid-1879, when Ōkuma initiated the redemption of government notes, to the autumn of 1880, after the Council of State had accepted his retrenchment proposal, the Ministry of Finance under Ōkuma and Sano was already implementing most of the policies that would form the core of the so-called Matsukata retrenchment.[8] In other words, tax increases, spending cuts, and note retirements had all been acting to deflate the economy for at least a year *before* Matsukata became finance minister. The average price of rice on the Tokyo market, for instance, peaked in December 1880 and declined steadily into the early fall of 1881 (see table 1.4). Hence, the squeeze was on: the government, especially during Sano's tenure as minister of finance, was already soaking up the rural windfalls of the inflationary period from 1878 to 1880.[9]

Japanese historians have also observed that the speculative bubble in the rice market, the main contributor to the inflation of 1878–1880, had burst at the beginning of 1881. The regime had magnified this natural reaction to excessive speculation by announcing in February 1881 that it would accelerate the collection of the land tax, as described in chapter 3. During the four years prior to this announcement, the price of rice had skyrocketed some 220 percent, far outpacing the depreciation of paper currency, whose value had dropped "only" 44 percent during that time. Clearly, something more than currency depreciation was at work; above all, intense speculation was to blame for the soaring price of rice. The price continued to rise in spite of record harvests in 1879 and 1880. What farmers were doing was simply hoarding their bounty rather than selling it, anticipating a continued appreciation in rice prices. In this volatile, speculative environment, then, the government in early 1881 issued its new policy of accelerated land tax collection. The price of rice had begun to edge down in January of that year, as the market finally felt the effects of repeated good harvests, but the February decree on land taxes seems to have given a decisive push to the decline in rice prices. Basically, the announcement threw farmers into a panic, and, as the price of rice began to fall, they rushed to sell large amounts of hoarded rice, anxious to meet the stricter requirements for land tax payment. In short, these developments sent the rice price on a downward slide well before Matsukata launched his program of currency contraction.[10]

Besides these prior domestic causes, since the early 1980s, a number of Japanese scholars have also suggested that an external factor, the contemporaneous global depression, intensified the Matsukata deflation. They point out that in the early 1880s the global economy experienced a slowdown, one of a series of depressions in the latter third of the nineteenth century, as trade and prices fell worldwide. By that time, they maintain, Japan's exports of silk, tea, and other primary commodities had tied its economy to international market trends to such an extent that the global slump had to affect Japan.[11] This exogenous factor, however, remains understudied and largely absent from the Western-language literature.

To the extent that the Matsukata deflation and the lead-up to it constituted in large part a cyclical reaction to a speculative mania, from a macroeconomic standpoint Matsukata would appear to have pursued exactly the opposite policy he should have. One can easily make this claim with hindsight, but, when faced with an unfolding economic downturn, a government would normally avoid retrenchment and deflation, further constricting an already deflating economy; to the contrary, one would expect a government to adopt stimulus measures to bring about economic recovery. The parallels with 1930 and the disastrous deflationary policy of Inoue Junnosuke are suggestive: after his appointment in late 1881,

Matsukata sought to freeze state spending and contract the money supply as Japan was heading into an acute economic slump. Historians usually refer to the period 1878–1880 as a time of financial and economic "crisis." It was certainly a crisis for the Meiji government, and Matsukata and his subordinates, in justifying and extolling his policies, defined it as such: his program saved the Meiji miracle from a life-threatening emergency. One could just as easily turn the argument on its head, however, and call the period of the Matsukata deflation "the crisis," much as we label the panic and recession that followed the speculative boom of the late 1880s "the financial crisis of 1890."[12] One wonders whether Matsukata learned from his earlier mistakes, for he would pursue very different policies during the Panic of 1890, pumping money into the economy through the BoJ and taking other steps to alleviate that crisis.[13]

All of this speculation is somewhat moot, since Matsukata had other overriding objectives in mind. These objectives were not the political ones that scholars have often attributed to him, namely, that he set out to undercut the Popular Rights movement or to create a budget surplus for armaments expansion. Rather, Matsukata was determined above all to establish a sound convertible currency and a centralized banking system using Japan's own resources; to accomplish those goals, he had to push through a drastic program of currency deflation, come what may.

Some have argued that Matsukata underestimated the severity of the deflation and the resulting recession. He simply failed to anticipate that his program would have such an adverse impact on the economy in the short run.[14] Matsukata's efforts to accelerate currency reform from 1883 on would seem to support that view. Granted, the price of rice had been declining for almost a year when he started putting his program into effect, while the foreign trade balance had already started to improve, thanks mainly to a significant drop in rural purchasing power. But approximately a one-year lag occurred between those trends and that of the general price level, which continued to rise throughout 1881.[15] In addition, the value of paper money, which hit bottom in April 1881 at a 1.8 paper-to-silver ratio, appreciated by about 17 percent relative to silver in the middle third of the year but then dropped again in September to a ratio of about 1.7 and remained roughly at that level the rest of the year (see table 1.3). Therefore, Matsukata might well have believed that the inflationary crisis had far from passed.

Matsukata did expect his program to cause a brief but intense recession, however. His greatest fear was that, midway through, opposition to the program would become so severe that he would have to discontinue it. Accordingly, he first made certain to extract commitments from the other leaders and the emperor not to deviate from his course. As two of Matsukata's personal advisers warned him in 1882, not only might his program be jeopardized on account of popular resistance, but his own life might be endangered as well.[16] Matsukata was not oblivious to the consequences of his policies. But, as the recession unfolded, he insisted that it was merely a transitory side effect of his life-saving medicine, bringing only temporary hardship to the nation. As he reported to the emperor in 1882, he had anticipated that a recession would emerge that year and would "become even more intense" the following year, asserting that it was "by nature a temporary but unavoidable phenomenon" and that he based this assertion "not on adherence to theory" but "on the practical experience of Western countries."[17]

Prefectural governors who had to face the consequences might have required more convincing. Matsukata felt compelled to address them at the end of 1883 to allay their concerns and secure their support of his program. In his speech to the local bureaucrats, who happened to be in Tokyo for a national meeting, Matsukata repeated what he had said to the emperor the previous year and assured the officials that he had "already anticipated [the recession], which is not something to be worried about at present." Therefore, "by no means should we change the great policy of state finance."[18] Nevertheless, the steps Matsukata initiated in 1884 to hasten the completion of his "great policy" such as opening the export discount program to Western merchants and marketing public bonds both at home and abroad, suggest that he himself was taken aback by the depth and duration of the economic slump.

The Impact on Rural Communities

While the Matsukata deflation lasted, it hit rural Japan hard. For the agricultural sector, the deflation-induced depression became especially acute in 1884–1885, when a "perfect storm" of natural disasters ended the string of good harvests and a global financial panic hit Japan's main trading partners. Rice production, which had stayed at or above 30 million *koku* for five years in a row, suddenly dropped to 26 million *koku* in fiscal 1884; despite the bad harvest, the price of rice continued to fall.[19] Meanwhile, the total value of exports declined from nearly ¥38 million in 1883 to ¥33 million the following year, raw silk being the hardest hit. As frost, blight, and other natural calamities played havoc with crops, the threat of famine emerged as a widespread concern, stirring memories not so much of the fairly recent famine of 1867–1868 as of the far greater Tenpō crisis of the mid-1830s, when unusually cold weather and heavy rainfall had devastated farming communities, and tens of thousands had starved to death. In fact, national and local officials alike compared the situation in fiscal 1884 to the Tenpō famine. As the Ministry of Agriculture and Commerce warned in May 1885:

Since the opening of spring cold and heat have alternated without any order or succession, and the damage caused to crops in all districts is very great. The crop of tea has fallen five-tenths from the usual yield, and that of wheat four-tenths. A retrospect of the past shows that agricultural dearth generally occurs in this country in a cyclical period of from thirty to fifty years. This is the fiftieth year since the famine in the period of Tenpō, and the climate is so abnormal that it may well be an omen of another famine.[20]

The ministry's prescription for avoiding such a calamity consisted of the hoary bureaucratic exhortation that farmers work longer, spend less, and save more. One local headman named Ogiso Zenzaburō, who carried this message to his bailiwick in Aichi Prefecture, expressed his sense of anxiety by raising the specter not only of the Tenpō famine but also of the catastrophic North China famine of 1877–1878, in which up to thirteen million people had died. He admonished his constituents to take further precautions, lest they suffer the indignity of having to rely on foreign countries for relief aid, as the Chinese had done eight years before.[21]

As it turned out, although the Matsukata deflation brought hardship to rural areas in Japan, nothing like those earlier famines struck the country. In the bumper crop year of 1882, Matsukata had somewhat improvidently raised the government's half share of the ¥10 million in founding capital for the BoJ by disposing of central stores of famine-relief rice,[22] but the authorities had previously mandated the setting up of a local safety net. In particular, under a law enacted in 1878, localities had to establish reserves of money and grain. The twelve villages under Ogiso's supervision, for instance, had accumulated a year's supply of such reserves, which helped make their district the only one in Aichi that did not have to apply for prefectural aid in 1885. As another relief measure, in November 1883, Matsukata extended the due date for the final installment of the tax on paddy fields by a month and, in June 1885, by an additional twenty days.[23] Still, even in years of abundant harvests, conditions varied across the country: in 1883, for example, some regions had poor crops owing to "long-continued drought," and two peripheral locales, the Shima district in Mie Prefecture and Tsushima Island, "experienced actual famine."[24] Yet, according to official statistics, only 50 people died of starvation nationwide in 1884, the year of widespread crop failure, though the effects of that bad harvest intensified in the years that followed, with 212 deaths from starvation recorded in 1885 and 1,212 in 1886.[25]

Although Japan's overwhelmingly rural population may have escaped disastrous famines during the Matsukata deflation, Japanese scholars have long argued that the deflation itself had dire effects on farming communities, forcing a capitalistic "dismantling of the agricultural classes" and the consolidation of the pre–World War II landlord system.[26] Anecdotal information they often recount presents a graphic montage of peasant distress. Such information includes, for example, newspaper reports publicized by the government adviser Paul Mayet, such as stories that in one village in Yamanashi Prefecture virtually every inhabitant had been declared bankrupt for failure to pay taxes and that in Kaga Prefecture eight hundred paupers had asked the authorities to be imprisoned rather than starve to death.[27] Other sources describe grim cases in which landless peasants who defaulted on local taxes were dispossessed of everything from the traditional sliding doors of paper on wood frames (shōji) and straw floor mats (tatami) to hand mills and rice pots.[28]

The statistics scholars typically cite to support the "dismantling" argument, however, are less than persuasive. The number of land tax delinquents did increase sharply after 1881, leaping from 424 that year to almost 47,000 in 1885, though the number declined rapidly thereafter until the Panic of 1890. The total amount of delinquent land tax peaked in 1884 at ¥14,502 (see table 6.1). Furthermore, all told, between 1883 and 1887, over 300,000 people had to put up for public auction nearly forty thousand hectares of real estate to meet their land tax obligations. These figures clearly represent the growing distress of farmers caught between rising real tax rates and falling agricultural prices and income, as the overall land tax burden as a percentage of the value of rice produced in Japan shot up from under 14 percent in 1881 to 31 percent in 1884. Yet the peak annual number for delinquent taxpayers amounted to 0.9 percent of all farm households in 1885 and that for overdue land tax to 0.03 percent of the total land tax that the state collected in 1884. Meanwhile, the land forced into auction in 1883–1887 totaled 0.8 percent of all farm and residential land subject to the land tax during that period. Although thousands of farmers also lost their land for failure to repay loans—an estimated 30,000 of them going bankrupt in the peak years of 1883–1884 combined—this figure, too, represented only about 0.5 percent of all agricultural households.[29] Quantitatively, then, one can hardly say that the crushing weight of taxes and loans during the Matsukata deflation led to mass dispossession and "dissolution of the farming classes."[30]

Scholars have often used as an index of that "dissolution" the proportion of tenant-farmed land, which had increased from an estimated 30 percent of all farmland in the early 1870s to 35.9 percent by 1883 and to 39.3 percent by 1887. Thereafter the ratio continued a slow climb, topping out at 47.5 percent in 1932.[31] Although tenancy thus appears to have risen twice as fast in the first two decades after the Restoration as in the ensuing four and a half decades, this differential growth rate probably owed less to the impact of deflationary policy than to the

TABLE 6.1 Bankruptcy and tax delinquency, 1877–1890

	NUMBER OF BANKRUPTCIES	AMOUNT OF DELINQUENT LAND TAX (¥)	NUMBER OF LAND TAX DELINQUENTS	AMOUNT OF DELINQUENT SAKE TAX (¥)	NUMBER OF SAKE TAX DELINQUENTS
1877	12,599	588	280	30	5
1878	10,881	777	748	136	18
1879	9,935	3,028	194	645	31
1880	9,855	300	146	4,948	35
1881	7,789	1,097	424	33,838	104
1882	12,191	1,402	1,179	133,342	502
1883	22,492*	12,009	6,747	552,291	890
1884	27,526*	14,502	16,784	87,226	202
1885	12,483	9,687	46,692	**	**
1886	10,732	6,051	17,351	67,325	130
1887	8,756	2,656	10,005	54,226	95
1888	6,663	1,688	4,944	33,907	59
1889	5,353	1,460	4,000	73,805	106
1890	4,477	6,213	20,396	40,548	327

Source: Muroyama, Matsukata zaisei kenkyū, 248.

*Muroyama estimated that about 60 percent of bankruptcies involved farmers (p. 247)—hence, roughly 30,000 farm bankruptcies in 1883–1884 combined.

**The sake-related figures for the abbreviated, nine-month fiscal year of 1885 were combined with those for 1886.

working out of the 1873 land tax reform, which the government did not complete until the early 1880s.[32] One also finds countervailing trends: in Shiga Prefecture, for example, the sale and concentration of land had proceeded briskly during the inflationary years of the late 1870s but stagnated during the deflation when people simply lacked the money to buy land. In addition, farmers there avoided becoming tenants by engaging in various sidelines. The upshot was that tenancy actually leveled off in that prefecture during the mid-1880s.[33]

Most of the increase in tenanted land that did occur represented not the descent of independent cultivators to full-time tenant status but the conversion of owner-farmers to part-tenants after they began renting additional plots or lost a portion of their holdings to creditors. Richard Smethurst estimates that as much as half of the rise in tenancy from 1883 to 1912 resulted from the reclamation of new fields that developers leased to enterprising farmers rather than from forced sales or foreclosures.[34] For all of Japan, according to Smethurst, "pure tenants as a percentage of total farm households actually fell" between 1883 and 1887, while owner-farmers' share of the total dropped on a much larger scale during that time, so that the chief movement among categories of cultivation was from owner farming to combined owner-tenant farming, whether by choice or under duress.[35]

By far, the most serious effect of the Matsukata deflation on rural communities was widespread indebtedness. At the height of the depression in 1883–1884, farmers pawned more than 11 percent of total arable land,[36] borrowing from quasi-banks and moneylenders at rates as high as 20–30 percent a year. Paul Mayet cited debt as Japan's most pressing rural problem, asserting that, during the first half of the 1880s, peasants by the tens of thousands had been "helplessly delivered over to the blood-sucking usurer." Mayet reported a series of sensational incidents of debt-related agrarian distress, including one example from Kanagawa in which "eleven desperate farmers" had murdered a moneylender and his adopted son; deed done, the eleven had "immediately delivered themselves up to the police."[37] In one celebrated estimate, Mayet claimed that, in the three years from 1884 to 1886, "roughly one-eighth" of all Japanese farmland underwent mortgage foreclosure, though Nakamura Takafusa cautions that this figure "is a bit exaggerated because in some cases land changed hands more than once."[38] Maeda Masana, in compiling his national development plan "Kōgyō iken" for the Ministry of Agriculture and Commerce in 1884, surveyed economic conditions nationwide at the height of the deflation and discovered, for instance, that in Osaka Prefecture farmers had mortgaged half of all farmland, in Akita two-fifths, and in Toyama nearly half; for the country as a whole, Maeda estimated, 70–80 percent of farm households were in debt, and cultivators had mortgaged 30–50 percent of total arable land.[39]

In a classic example whereby a financial shock exerts longer-term effects, for many farmers, the burden of debts they had assumed during the Matsukata deflation mounted over time, so that they continued to experience distress and the threat of foreclosure for years to come, as the post-1885 rise in starvation and tenancy rates suggest. In one hamlet in Yamanashi, for instance, farmers who defaulted on loans they had taken out in 1881–1885 tended to lose their land a decade or more *after* the Matsukata deflation.[40] Hence, although the depression hardly "dissolved" the country's farming classes, it clearly had a severe impact on rural Japan.

According to one estimate, rural indebtedness in 1885, at the end of the Matsukata deflation, amounted to ¥330 million or about one fifth of total farmland value, which, one source claims, is "a quite substantial, but not disturbingly high, ratio."[41] Yet it was clearly disturbing to those carrying the debts, for—although, as Henry Rosovsky has noted, farmers may not have rioted in droves—between 1883 and 1885 scores of peasant disturbances broke out over debt-related issues; the authority on these "debt disturbances" has counted sixty-four discrete incidents, ranging from small group petitions to large-scale uprisings.[42] The participants mainly demanded reduced interest rates and deferred repayment schedules on loans, and small wonder with borrowers typically paying upward of 20 percent interest. Paul Mayet expressed amazement that one of the many so-called debtors' or paupers' parties formed during the first half of the 1880s—the one he cited had a membership of several thousand—should have been pleased to secure from a group of creditors what he considered an exorbitant rate of interest of 13 percent and a minimal deferment of three to five years.[43]

As for the connection between rural distress and the Popular Rights movement, a common argument is that the Matsukata deflation drove a wedge between the leaders and the rank and file, between landlords and tenants, and between creditors and debtors within the movement, contributing to its demise in the mid-1880s. Meanwhile, poorer peasants broke away from the movement to press economic rather than political demands through local debtors' or paupers' parties.[44] Popular rights activists were mostly members of the wealthy gōnō class and sometimes bankers or moneylenders themselves; as such, they occasionally became targets of the debtors' or paupers' parties. More often, however, they served as mediators in their capacity as trusted local leaders, along the lines of Neil Waters's "local pragmatists" in the Kawasaki region.[45] Otherwise, the debt disturbances generally had little direct connection to the Popular Rights movement; with few exceptions, the protesting debtors did not see themselves as continuing the popular political struggle by other means.

The Matsukata deflation, however, did have the effect of splitting along economic lines support for the rural-based Jiyūtō, the leading organization within the Popular Rights movement. Such division became especially pronounced among party members or backers who engaged in commercial sake brewing in the first half of the 1880s. Specifically, the interests of big brewers diverged from those of smaller producers, who suffered a bigger blow from the brewery tax hike and the shrinkage in demand for commercial sake. For Japan as a whole, sake brewers accounted for a staggering 96 percent of all delinquent taxes from 1881 to 1884. In 1884, the year in which delinquent land taxes crested at ¥14,502, overdue sake taxes exceeded ¥87,000, but, in the previous two years, the overdue sake taxes had surpassed ¥130,000 and ¥550,000, respectively (see table 6.1); the figure of more than half a million yen in 1883 equaled 4 percent of total sake tax revenue that year. Most brewery tax delinquents were small-scale producers, typically farmers making sake as a by-employment who were less able to absorb the doubling and redoubling of the sake tax in the early 1880s. As a consequence, tax defaults contributed to a huge decline in the number of breweries, which fell from just over twenty-seven thousand in 1881 to fewer than fifteen thousand in 1886, while average annual production per licensed brewery rose from 175 to 206 koku during those years.[46]

In the midst of these changes in the sake industry, the divergence of interests between big and small brewers became clear in Jiyūtō-led campaigns for tax relief, including reduction of the sake tax, in the early 1880s. In 1882 Yamagata Aritomo, soon to become home minister, proposed a national inspection program whereby the government would send envoys to localities throughout the country "to gain a broad view of political developments and to observe popular feeling"; Yamagata's goal was to use the resulting information "to suppress fractious local movements, especially the campaign for liberty and popular rights that was running at full tide" that year.[47] The inspectors he dispatched to prefectures in 1882–1883, following the government's acceptance of his proposal, reported in detail on local political activities. Their reports included considerable information on the opposition parties' agitation for tax relief, indicating in particular that the sake tax regulations Matsukata introduced in 1882, such as a minimum production requirement for new licensees, were protecting large-scale brewers while forcing many smaller producers out of business and that the regulation of home brewing was depressing the livelihood of the lower classes.[48]

The inspectors' reports on several prefectures—undoubtedly to Yamagata's satisfaction—highlighted the big brewers' undermining of the tax reduction movement. For example, in 1882, according to a report on Fukui Prefecture, sake brewers had organized under the Osaka branch of the Jiyūtō and had staged a rally demanding tax relief, but prefectural authorities had broken up the gathering. Once the government promulgated the tax increase, the participants held another rally but failed to come up with a strategy. Large brewers recognized that the tax hike would benefit them at the expense of small-scale producers and therefore broke from the movement. The author of this report emphasized that the conflict of interests between large and small brewers had ultimately led to the collapse of the antitax campaign in Fukui: "Among brewers, wealthy ones spoke publicly about the hardship imposed by the increased tax but privately tended to celebrate it."[49] Similarly, an inspector's report on Ishikawa and Toyama noted that brewers associations in those prefectures had also mounted campaigns for tax relief, but, once the 1882 increase went into effect, those campaigns failed as well. The inspector pointed out that small-scale brewers, unlike larger, full-time producers, were mostly farmers struggling to supplement declining income they derived from agricultural pursuits. While a number of small breweries had folded in those prefectures, large producers, like those in Fukui, publicly opposed the tax hike but privately welcomed the rollback of competition and "secretly agreed to prevent as much as possible" the entry of new brewers.[50] In short, the feigned support of the antitax movement by major brewers and their eventual withdrawal on account of the benefits they gained from the 1882 revision of sake tax regulations helped the Meiji government avert an escalation of the opposition parties' tax relief campaign.

While the sake tax increase, combined with the slump in demand, served to weed out small brewers, the operation of larger-scale producers actually stabilized, and both the amount of delinquent sake taxes and the number of delinquent tax-payers plummeted in fiscal 1884. As Japan's economy began to recover from the deflation that year and as the government basically collected no sake tax in the truncated 1885 fiscal year and prohibited home brewing in 1886, business conditions improved substantially for the surviving players in the sake industry.[51]

In the long run, the Matsukata reform stabilized conditions for other industries in the traditional sector as well as in the miniscule modern sector of the economy.[52] The establishment of a sound, convertible currency, with paper yen on par with silver from January 1886, and the lowering of interest rates—which in Tokyo fell on average from 14.06 percent in 1881 to 9.17 percent in 1886[53]—both contributed to setting the stage for industrial growth over the long haul.

In the short term, however, industry and commerce, like agriculture, suffered during the deflation-driven recession. Especially vulnerable were small-scale enterprises in fields ranging from silk reeling and weaving to brewing and livestock farming that had sprung up during the speculative boom of the years 1878–1880. The deflation triggered a wave of bankruptcies among such businesses. From 1882 to 1885 the total number of joint-stock companies in Japan plunged from 3,336 to 1,279.[54] In February 1883, as the currency contraction was in full swing, the *Japan Weekly Mail* ran a translation of a doleful article on trade and manufacturing that had appeared recently in the *Mainichi* newspaper: "Merchants have met with heavier losses than they had experienced for years. Owing to the poverty of the farmers, they find no demand for their goods, which are consequently piled up in their warehouses. In manufactories depression is the order of the day; the looms are idle, and the workmen unemployed. . . . [Meanwhile] sparrows are building nests in the doorways of our merchants' warehouses. . . . Most people wear a mournful aspect."[55]

Textile production trailed only sake brewing and silk reeling among Japan's most important manufacturing sectors during the Matsukata deflation. Although the production of sake fell and stagnated after 1882 and that of raw silk—most of which was still hand-reeled in farm households rather than machine-reeled in factories[56]—did the same from 1883 to 1885, the output of cotton and silk fabrics as well as woolens expanded rapidly from fiscal 1884 on, fueled by a decline in the prices of inputs. The wholesale price of cotton fiber in Tokyo, for example, dropped from ¥2.2 per *kan* in 1882 to ¥1.2 in 1884 (*kan*, a traditional measure of weight, equals about 8.3 pounds). Whereas the total value of commercially brewed sake plunged from an estimated ¥88 million in 1882 to around ¥40 million in 1883 and plateaued at that level through 1886, that of textiles shot up from ¥6 million to over ¥16 million between 1884 and 1886 and continued to soar thereafter (meanwhile, the total value of raw silk produced declined roughly from ¥23 million in 1882 to ¥16 million in 1884 and then recovered to around ¥25 million in 1886).[57]

TABLE 6.2   Major Japanese exports by value, 1880–1886 (thousands of yen)

YEAR	RAW SILK	TEA	MARINE PRODUCTS	RICE	COPPER	COAL	TOTAL EXPORTS	TOTAL IMPORTS	BALANCE OF TRADE
1880	8,607	7,498	2,392	211	461	460	28,395	36,626	−8,231
1881	10,647	7,022	2,236	262	589	395	31,059	31,191	−132
1882	16,232	7,030	1,979	1,652	827	436	37,722	29,447	8,275
1883	16,184	6,106	2,080	1,001	725	395	36,268	28,445	7,823
1884	11,007	5,820	2,557	2,170	1,387	607	33,871	29,673	4,199
1885	13,034	6,854	2,880	767	1,825	627	37,147	29,357	7,790
1886	17,321	7,723	3,110	3,301	2,149	694	48,876	32,168	16,708

Sources: Teramoto, Senzenki Nihon chagyō shi kenkyū, 22; Dai Nihon gaikoku bōeki nenpyō, 1882–1887; Matsukata, Report on the Adoption of the Gold Standard, 38, 105.

Thus, as Muroyama points out, the textile industry, which would go on to become the leading sector of economic growth in the second half of the Meiji period, had already begun to surge in the latter stages of the Matsukata reform, in advance of Japan's private enterprise boom of the late 1880s. At least for textiles, the resulting narrative differs from one that several Japanese historians have advanced, according to which the depression climaxed in 1883–1884 and continued for another year or two until the rapid expansion of exports and the outbreak of the enterprise boom in 1886–1887 brought about economic recovery.[58] Shigeto Tsuru actually observed three quarters of a century ago that, although Japan's economic output in general was "stationary" during the Matsukata deflation, "typically capitalistic enterprises" such as textiles "showed a remarkable spurt," with production in cotton-spinning firms increasing—albeit from a very low level— by 390 percent between 1880 and 1885. Tsuru cited the author of an earlier financial history of Japan as stating that this time of overall business stagnation "was nothing less than the period during which enterprises were in bud only to blossom after 1886."[59] Foreign trade would play a major role in the rise of Japanese textiles, as imports from Europe plummeted in the first half of the 1880s, but such trade would have mixed results for the agricultural sector, the source of three of Japan's top four exports during the deflation—raw silk, tea, and rice (see table 6.2).

Exports and the Global Downturn

The factors affecting the domestic depression that dealt hardship to farmers included not only the government's monetary and fiscal policies but also trends in international trade and prices. In the absence of substantial foreign loans[60] or of either inbound or outbound foreign direct investment until the turn of the century, Japan's interactions with the world economy during the Matsukata deflation centered almost exclusively on trade. Japan had run large trade deficits during the inflationary years from 1877 to 1880, as the growth of imports had outstripped that of exports. But, once the depression set in and prices dropped within Japan, imports fell while exports climbed in yen value between 1880 and 1882; and, except for a plunge in exports during the global panic of 1884, both remained roughly at their 1882 levels through the deflation, yielding a positive trade balance every year from 1882 to 1885.

With Japan's growing incorporation into the global economy through trade, the international downturn that began in 1882 naturally added to the slump already under way within the country. Yet Japan's foreign trade in 1885 accounted for only about 6 percent of its gross national product, compared to some 12 percent for the United States, 29 percent for France, and over 50 percent for Britain that year,[61] so one can exaggerate the impact of the world depression on the contemporary Japanese economy. Clearly Matsukata's drastic reduction of the money supply from 1882 to 1884 takes the overwhelming share of "blame" for the domestic depression. Still, as Mark Metzler has indicated, the global downturn of the early 1880s "was widely understood in the more industrialized countries as a crisis of overproduction and correspondingly falling prices" in international commodity markets, including those for Japan's major export items, raw silk and tea.[62] The *Japan Weekly Mail*, for instance, reported in late 1884 on "the cry of 'over-production'" in global markets: "The enterprise of commerce, we are told, has outstripped the growth of the world's wants. There is too much shipbuilding; too much mining; too much growing of tea, coffee, sugar, and wheat; too much production of raw materials and too much conversion of them into usable articles."[63] The role that trends in foreign trade, especially trends in exports, played in the Matsukata deflation, therefore, bears further examination.

In the composition of Japanese exports, raw silk and green tea dominated, but a somewhat surprising heavyweight was rice. In 1882, for example, raw silk made up 42 percent of the total yen value of exports, followed by green tea at 18 percent, but rice accounted for 4 percent of the total that year and maintained its position as Japan's fourth-biggest export item after marine products from 1882 to 1884.[64]

Export trade in fact had conflicting effects on the Japanese economy during the Matsukata deflation. On the one hand, relatively constant U.S. demand for Japanese raw silk and tea as well as European demand for Japanese rice likely served to mitigate the severity of the economic downturn in Japan, and the export-promoting policies Matsukata established between 1882 and 1884 helped lift Japan out of depression earlier than he had anticipated. On the other hand, oversupply and price competition in world commodity markets put pressure on domestic silk and tea prices, which were already in decline on account of Matsu-kata's drastic currency contraction, exacerbating the depression within Japan.

Nakamura Takafusa has shown that from the late 1870s Japanese wholesale prices, on a dollar basis, moved by and large in concert with those in major Western countries, indicating that Japan's economy had become aligned with global market fluctuations by that time, much earlier than scholars had previously imagined. As Nakamura has also pointed out, the international price of silver and the yen-dollar exchange rate, which closely followed each other throughout the Meiji period until Japan's adoption of the gold standard in 1897, both basically leveled off from 1877 through the Matsukata deflation; so Japanese exports did not receive much of a boost from a falling exchange rate during that time, in contrast to the situation after 1885, when silver depreciation resumed at a more rapid pace, becoming a major contributor to Japan's enterprise boom of the late 1880s. Therefore, Nakamura concludes, because the Matsukata deflation overlapped with a global economic downturn at a time of relative price stability for silver, "internal and external factors had a multiplying effect, giving rise to a particularly severe depression" in Japan.[65]

International prices naturally affected the domestic prices of Japanese raw silk and tea, as the country exported some 70 percent of its raw silk production and 80 percent of its tea crop in the early 1880s; but with Japan marketing overseas as much as 2 percent of the annual rice harvest at the height of the Matsukata deflation, even Japanese rice came under the influence of global price trends. As the Osaka Chamber of Commerce declared in a report in August 1885, rice had become a traded commodity whose price reflected world prices.[66]

Rice

Besides downward pressure on domestic prices, global commercial interaction also had positive effects on Japan's economy in the early 1880s. This upside was particularly true of the export-related programs that Matsukata pursued. As noted in chapter 3, in addition to promoting exports through the Yokohama Specie Bank, Matsukata expanded the government's *direct* involvement in exports, above all of rice, as yet another way to accelerate the acquisition of silver. The Meiji government itself accounted for much of the rice that Japan exported—on average one-third of the total from 1872 to 1889, the period during which the Ministry of Finance engaged in this activity. The ministry relied mainly on U.S., British, and German trading companies to handle its rice exports, Britain and Germany, in particular, being among the leading importers of Japanese rice. From 1882 to 1885, for example, nearly three-quarters of rice exports from Japan went to those two countries, although Britain reexported much of its take to the European continent, especially to Italy, Germany, and the Netherlands.[67] The Meiji government's holdings of rice resulted partly from its having permitted farmers, beginning in 1877, to pay up to half of their land tax in kind based on the average market price of rice over the previous two months. During the inflationary period, farmers had cashed in on the high price of rice, but as that price fell during the deflation—eventually by half—and farmers had to sell that much more rice to meet their tax obligations, some resorted to partial payment in kind to minimize flooding the market and further depressing the price.[68]

Silk and Tea

In European markets, Japanese rice, despite having to compete with imports from South and Southeast Asia, seems to have escaped conditions of oversupply and price competition during a good part of the Matsukata deflation. The main reason for this situation was that poor harvests in Burma led to a decline in its share of European rice imports from 85 percent of the total in 1882 to 70 percent in 1884.[69] From 1881 to 1885, the average annual price of all rice exports from Japan stayed within a range of ¥2.3–2.5 per picul, except for a drop to ¥1.9 in the global panic year of 1884.[70]

By contrast, Japan's raw silk and tea trades keenly felt the effects of international competition and overproduction throughout the first half of the 1880s. Cocoons, reeled silk, and tea leaves, however, managed to avoid the steep drop in yen price that afflicted rice domestically, thanks to fairly consistent U.S. demand through the deflationary years, although, to a much less extent, European imports of Japanese rice, especially pronounced in 1882 and 1884, may have helped to keep the home price of rice from falling even further than it did.[71] As an illustration of the difference in domestic price trends, in Tomioka, Gunma Prefecture, the average price of cocoons in 1884 had declined by only 10 percent from its peak in 1881, and that of reeled silk by 29 percent during that time, whereas the average price of rice had fallen 50 percent on the Tokyo exchange from 1881 to 1884.[72] Yet, the U.S. buffer notwithstanding, the prices and volumes of Japanese raw silk and tea exports responded sensitively to the vagaries of weather and production both at home and in the country's chief competitors in Europe and China as well as to fluctuations in Japan's major export markets.

The U.S. market played an especially important role in supporting Japan's overall export trade during the Matsukata deflation, increasing its share of that trade by value—even in the midst of the global depression—from 36 percent in 1881 to 42 percent in 1885 (see table 6.3). During that period, the United States took,

TABLE 6.3   Japanese exports by major importing countries, 1881–1886 (thousands of yen)

	TOTAL EXPORTS	GREAT BRITAIN	FRANCE	UNITED STATES	CHINA
1881	31,059	3,552	8,337	11,088 (36)*	6,303
1882	37,722	4,997	10,317	14,280 (38)	5,712
1883	36,268	4,862	9,719	13,294 (37)	5,929
1884	33,871	3,831	6,801	13,131 (39)	6,551
1885	37,147	2,453	6,740	15,639 (42)	8,242
1886	48,876	4,195	9,633	19,992 (41)	9,595

Source: Muroyama, *Matsukata zaisei kenkyū*, 276.
*Percentage of total exports in parentheses.

on average, 89 percent by tonnage of Japan's second-biggest export, green tea; and, in 1884, it passed France to become the leading customer of Japan's top export, raw silk, absorbing well over half the total by value from that year on.[73] U.S. imports of Japanese raw silk stagnated in 1883–1884 at the height of the American depression, when business activity in the United States declined by almost a fourth, but they resumed rapid growth in 1885, as the U.S. contraction ended. By contrast, imports of Japanese raw silk by France and Britain fell sharply in 1884 and recovered only slowly in subsequent years. Those two countries, together with Germany and Belgium, also "experienced severe business depressions, which began in 1882 and lasted until 1885 or 1886."[74]

In the early 1880s, Japanese raw silk faced stiff competition from the Chinese product in Japan's principal export markets in the United States and France, as did Japanese green tea in the U.S. market. Beginning in the late 1870s, an abundance of cheap Italian silk put added pressure on the values of Japanese silk exports; the price that foreign trading companies in Yokohama paid per bale of sedentary machine-reeled silk from Gunma, for example, dropped steadily from $540 to $428 in specie between 1881 and 1884. Meanwhile, during those same years, the price of Japanese tea in the U.S. market fell from $529 per ton to $368.[75]

The *Japan Weekly Mail*, a treasure trove of information that scholars have underutilized in studying Meiji foreign trade, published detailed periodic reports on domestic and international market conditions by Western silk and tea merchants operating in the treaty ports as well as articles on business trends by the paper's own editors drawing on Japanese and overseas newspapers. All through the deflationary years, the *Japan Weekly Mail* made clear that the downward trend in prices of Japanese silk and tea exports was resulting in large part from competition and oversupply. In July 1882, for instance, the paper reported that in the first half of that year Japanese silk exports had faced "keen competition" from

Italian raw silks, "which were forcing their way into consumption in Europe and America by reason of their comparative cheapness," so that Japanese silk dealers were having to dispose of stocks "at irregular but continually declining prices."[76] At the beginning of the second half of that year, observed the *Japan Weekly Mail* in February 1883, prices had continued "on a downward course": "The Italian and China crops, which at first were reported to have suffered severely from un-favourable climatic influences, had so far recovered that a fair average yield could be reckoned upon; and it was well ascertained that the supply of the raw material was fully equal to, if not in excess of, requirements."[77]

Silk overproduction, the paper suggested in subsequent years, persisted through the end of the world depression. The *Japan Weekly Mail* remarked in July 1884 that Japanese exports for the 1883–1884 season were "the largest ever known," and strong crops in China and Japan promised "an abundant supply of good and cheap raw material" for the next season. Then, in June 1885 it reported that silk prices in Europe had "fallen lower than ever before," as news arrived that "the French and Italian crops promise unusually well, while that of China is expected to be 20 percent more than in 1884. Under these circumstances, a further fall in the price of silk is generally expected."[78]

Similarly, the decline in tea prices in the U.S. market, the *New York Price Current* asserted in an article reprinted in the *Japan Weekly Mail* in February 1883, was "a question . . . of excessive competition and over-supply," which had resulted "necessarily" in "a large shrinkage in values until, with trifling exceptions, the trade has been carried on for more than a year at a steady and heavy loss." The next month the *Japan Weekly Mail* explained that Americans were annually con-suming about one and a quarter pounds of green tea per head, a rate that had held for two decades in spite of falling prices; but, in the 1881–1882 season, ship-ments of green tea from China and Japan had exceeded U.S. requirements by 10–15 million pounds. The paper concluded: "It is hardly to be doubted, then, that excessive supplies have been the chief cause of the present very low prices."[79]

Factors other than competition also affected the values and quantities of Japa-nese silk and tea exports during the first half of the 1880s. For one thing, the on-set of depression within Japan, as the *Japan Weekly Mail* reported in Febru-ary 1882, had resulted in overstocking of Japanese silk-piece goods and "great stagnation in the silk manufacturing industry of the country, which has rendered available for export large quantities of the raw material"; and a year later the paper again noted, with some hyperbole, "The Japanese themselves have taken little or no silk for home consumption so far this season, consequently the whole production of the country is available for export."[80]

At the same time, however, economic woes in the importing countries brought periodic disruptions to Japanese exports. In early 1882, for instance, the financial crisis besetting France prompted foreign merchants in Yokohama to cut back on silk purchases, though "brisk demand" from America soon revived the trade.[81] Two years later, as the U.S. downturn intensified, American demand for Japanese tea fell, further exacerbating the oversupply and price decline of the product; as the *Japan Weekly Mail* observed in March 1885, during the previous year, "the general depression in business and the consequent distress among the farmers and labourers (who are the principal consumers of Japanese Teas) had restricted consumption" in the United States.[82]

The export markets for silk and tea, products sensitive to weather conditions, responded to both actual and rumored fluctuations in the weather in Japan and abroad. In April 1882, for example, reports of frost in Italy prompted foreign exporters to make huge purchases of Japanese silk at higher prices, but by June "improved prospects for a larger yield in Italy caused buyers to hold aloof," even though prices had fallen in the meantime.[83] The disastrous weather that hit Japan in 1884 was another important, though overlooked, contributor to the drop in Japanese exports that year; even in 1885, the *Japan Weekly Mail* reported that the silk and tea crops would likely be shorter than those of the previous year, in the case of tea "owing to the damage done by late frosts."[84]

Changing government regulations and consumer tastes in the United States had equally significant, if not greater, effects on Japanese tea exports in the 1880s. In 1883 Congress passed a tea act, the first federal food law, prohibiting the importation of low-quality tea into the United States. With the enforcement of this law, imports of Japanese tea, which had deteriorated in quality "due to hasty overproduction," fell from almost 38 million pounds in 1883 to 33 million pounds in 1884.[85] Meanwhile, though the custom in many parts of the United States of drinking green tea at dinner—with milk and sugar!—continued through the early 1880s,[86] it was beginning to weaken, as U.S. consumers were increasingly turning to coffee, black tea, and cocoa; American consumption of coffee alone increased by tonnage from five times that of tea imports from Japan in 1881 to eight times in 1885. In fact, America's near-monopsony on Japanese tea exports at the start of the 1880s loosened in the latter part of that decade, when severe competition and government regulation in the U.S. market prompted Japan to shift a growing portion of its tea exports to Canada.[87]

After fiscal 1884, as the Matsukata deflation ended, Japan's economy began to rebound; industry, both traditional and modern, led the surge, but agriculture stagnated for the rest of the decade. In the industrial sector, a stable currency and low interest rates encouraged investment in enterprises centering on cotton spinning and railroad companies while the resumption of silver and exchange rate depreciation, combined with economic recovery in Japan's major Western markets, produced burgeoning export profits for traditional industries, which supplied much of the capital for domestic investment.[88] The total value of industrial production rose sharply during the latter part of the 1880s, whereas that of agricultural output slumped. The price of rice continued its downward slide of the depression years until 1888, a decline that no longer reflected currency contraction but rather a resumption of strong harvests from 1885. At the same time, however, the price of silk cocoons recovered with the expansion of raw silk exports, helping to buffer the rural economy. Tea exports also bounced back from the low point they had hit during the global panic of 1884, although the price of tea in the oversaturated U.S. market continued to fall through the remainder of the 1880s. Meanwhile, rice exports jumped dramatically at the very end of that decade, briefly surpassing those of tea, so that rice became Japan's second-biggest export in 1888–1889.[89] Despite the boost in exports from the agrarian sector, agriculture remained in the doldrums until, paradoxically, the panic year of 1890, when a bad harvest triggered a spike in grain prices, after which the total value of agricultural production rose basically in tandem with that of industry through the inflationary decade that followed.[90]

The Matsukata deflation of 1881–1885 grew intense mainly because the finance minister rapidly shrank the money supply in 1882–1883 and hiked or introduced an array of consumer taxes. Matsukata helped shorten the depression he had largely created, however, by accelerating specie accumulation through the issuance of public bonds, the promotion of exports by foreign trading companies, and the expanded sale of Japanese rice overseas, effectively restoring confidence in the yen by mid-1885. In doing so, the finance minister showed an adaptability and a responsiveness to policy misfires that are absent from most accounts of his reform. Other factors that preceded Matsukata's strict monetary and fiscal policies—the initiation of retrenchment and note redemption by his predecessors and the outbreak of panic in the rice market owing to accelerated land tax collection—also contributed to the deflation, as did roughly contemporaneous depressions in Japan's major export markets. Meanwhile, the depression in Japan hit the countryside especially hard, though scholars have generally exaggerated its impact; still, the agricultural sector continued to slump for several years beyond the start of overall economic recovery in 1885.

Although indebtedness remained a serious problem in rural areas for years after the Matsukata deflation, the average real disposable income of farmers increased markedly in the middle Meiji years, rising some 83 percent from the mid-1880s to the turn of the century.[91] Granted, this increase started from a depressed level, although Richard Smethurst suggests that the halving of the price of rice in the first half of the 1880s did not mean a 50 percent plunge in the living standard of farm households; rather, as other prices dropped, the fall in the rice price translated into about a 9 percent decrease in real income.[92] In the decades that followed, the climb in average real disposable income for agricultural workers resulted from a combination of the long-term decline in the burden of the fixed land tax and the upward trend in the price of grains, a climb that by and large continued until the severe deflations of the 1920s and early 1930s.[93]

The rise in average real income, however, masked significant differences among farmers, who ranged from full-time tenants to large landlords. Tenant-cultivated land grew from around 36 percent of all farmland in the mid-1880s to nearly 44 percent in 1903.[94] As Ronald Dore points out, pure tenant farmers got no benefit from the reduction in the tax burden, as they paid rents in kind, usually half of their rice crop, and little benefit from the increase in the price of rice, as they marketed only small amounts of their rice, especially in years of poor harvest when they were unable to capitalize on price spikes.[95] In 1891, however, such tenant farmers accounted for less than a quarter of all cultivators, whereas the largest group of agriculturalists—45 percent of the total—consisted of owner-farmers who were also part-tenants.[96] Other than full-time tenants, therefore, most farmers managed more or less to take advantage of higher prices in years of below-average yields to maintain both their own consumption of rice and their income from rice sales even if they had to reduce the amount they marketed. By the same token, in years of abundant harvests, farmers could make up for lower prices by selling more rice, cutting their personal share of the grain and yet consuming more of a bigger "pie." Nonetheless, P. K. Hall calculates that between the late 1880s and early 1900s, whereas cultivators' real earnings from the sale of rice went up in years of bountiful crops, they generally fell in bad-harvest years, despite "favourable shifts in the rural/urban terms of trade"; Hall concludes: "Thus, at the national level, . . . a good crop and an increase in sales were usually more beneficial to farmers than an enhancement of prices in poor seasons."[97] Because good harvests characterized most years from the mid-1880s through the turn of the century—rice output expanded at an average annual rate of 0.9 per cent from 1880 to 1900 and 1.7 per cent from 1900 to 1920—the farming population overall could afford to consume and market larger quantities of rice. In fact, annual per capita consumption of rice climbed inexorably in Japan: it went from less than 0.8 *koku* in the early 1880s to almost a full *koku* by the turn of the century and continued to rise thereafter, causing Japan to face persistent shortages in the domestic supply of rice and to become a chronic net importer of the grain after 1900.[98]

The Matsukata deflation commenced shortly before the global depression of the early to middle 1880s set in, with Matsukata's "retrenchment" program, like that of Minister of Finance Inoue Junnosuke a half century later,[99] coming on top of an already unfolding deflationary situation within Japan. The world depression then exacerbated the Japanese deflationary crisis. One should avoid overstating the extent of this exogenous impact, however, in view of Japan's relatively limited, albeit growing, involvement in the global economy as well as the difference in magnitude between the deflation in Japan and, for example, the contraction in the leading importer of Japanese goods at the time—one estimate places the deflation rate in Japan for the period 1881–1885 at 11–15 percent and in the United States at less than 6 percent.[100] Matsukata's policies, especially those on exports, however, pushed Japan toward greater integration with the world economy and toward heightened sensitivity to global trends, thus rendering the Matsukata deflation an important stage in Japan's transition to a more fully globalized economy.

The resumption of silver depreciation and the recovery of Western economies after 1885 basically established a pattern whereby, as Metzler notes, silver-standard Japan "was insulated from the gold-bloc deflation" thanks to "a combination of inflation internally and deflation externally."[101] Not surprisingly, in the mid-1890s export-oriented businessmen, including Shibusawa Eiichi, the "Johnny Apple-seed" of the Meiji business world, opposed Matsukata's proposal that Japan jump on the global bandwagon and switch its monetary standard from silver to gold, charging that the authorities would be foolhardy to abandon a system that was giving Japanese exports such a competitive advantage in gold standard markets.[102]

As the government stepped up plans to expand armaments, extend the railway network, and establish the country's first integrated steelworks, Matsukata was determined to go for gold so that Japan could import and borrow more easily from abroad; the failure of the attempted overseas bond issues of 1884–1885, primarily because of disagreement over the silver-to-gold exchange rate, no doubt reinforced his determination. Noneconomic concerns, however, also factored into the motivation of Matsukata and other state leaders; as an American observed in 1898, "They have their theories of the superiority of gold, of its stability, its higher intrinsic value, its expanding use in civilized countries, the demand for it as war treasure."[103] Once Japan obtained the windfall war indemnity from China, the government seized the moment and, over the objections of many businessmen, put Japan on the gold standard in 1897.

Following a series of favorable trade balances during the Matsukata deflation, Japan had continued to run surpluses during most of the subsequent years it was on the silver standard. But, with the switch to gold, the country recorded trade deficits in all but one year over the next decade[104] owing to a marked rise in imports not only of steel, machinery, and the like but also of foodstuffs and of raw cotton for the burgeoning spinning industry. Beginning with the 1890 panic, Japan substantially increased its importation of rice from Southeast Asia and Korea until by the turn of the century it had become a net importer of that commodity. Exports of raw silk and tea, however, remained largely on an upward trend through the 1890s, again thanks primarily to U.S. demand: the United States raised its share of Japanese silk exports from around 40 percent of the total at the beginning of the 1880s to nearly 60 percent by the end of the century, and, despite restrictions on tea importation, which Congress tightened in 1897, it continued to take, on average, well over 70 percent of all Japanese tea exports during the 1890s.[105] The general growth in exports of raw silk and tea notwithstanding, those two commodities accounted for a diminishing percentage of Japan's overall exports, especially as the railroad and textile industries that expanded during the enterprise booms of the late 1880s and 1890s helped make coal, cotton yarn, and silk fabrics into major export items.[106]

On the financial front, no sooner had Japan gone on the gold standard than the government, as if on cue, successfully began to sell domestic bonds overseas, and in 1899 it managed to raise a foreign loan in the amount of ¥98 million, Japan's first since the early Meiji period. But, after the move to gold, tight money triggered a panic in 1897–1898, followed by yet another financial crisis in 1900–1901. This time, in sharp contrast to its actions in the early 1880s, the Ministry of Finance pumped money into the economy through the BoJ, as it had done previously during the Panic of 1890,[107] thereby attempting to avoid a repetition of the severe depression that Japan had suffered during the Matsukata deflation.

Conclusion

THE MATSUKATA REFORM
AS "EXPANSIONARY AUSTERITY"

Matsukata Masayoshi was committed to reform and modernization of Japan's fiscal and monetary systems and to encouragement of private enterprise, but not in a categorical orthodox liberal or neoliberal sense. He certainly set out to create budget surpluses through fiscal austerity. Yet he demonstrated flexibility in response to a series of unexpected developments that compelled the Finance Ministry in fact to increase government spending. In the meantime, however, tax returns stagnated during the deflation-induced depression. Matsukata would thus have run budget deficits if not for transfers from the reserve fund derived primarily from the proceeds of export promotion and bond flotation. To a large extent, he was fortunate that, during the deflation, exports flourished and imports shrank while the price of bonds recovered, ensuring the success of both the state's direct and indirect promotion of exports and its sale of public bonds. As a result, the Finance Ministry was able to accumulate enough specie and money in the reserve fund to redeem a sizable portion of fiat notes, back the issue of convertible paper money by the Bank of Japan, and finance military expansion as well as enable the state to remain actively involved in the economy.

The package of reforms Matsukata intended to carry out bears a striking resemblance to the kinds of structural adjustment programs promoted under the Washington Consensus in the 1980s and 1990s, but the evidence presented here reveals that, in practice, the Matsukata reform differed from IMF-style neoliberal orthodoxy in a number of important ways. Indeed, the evidence even suggests that one can better view the reform as paralleling the kinds of heterodox critiques of the "neoliberal dogma" on financial and economic reform—"stabilize, liberalize, and privatize"—that have become increasingly prominent today.[1]

In policy terms, the Matsukata reform was unlike late-twentieth-century neoliberalism—let alone, mid-nineteenth-century British-style economic liberalism—in several respects. For one, government expenditures rose rather than fell during the Matsukata deflation, producing budgetary shortfalls that the Ministry of Finance met not by hiking taxes or cutting expenditures but by borrowing and boosting exports. In addition, Matsukata patterned Japan's new central bank not after the independent Bank of England but after the more state-controlled Belgian central bank. By the late 1880s the Bank of Japan had moved even further away from the orthodox British model, as it took up industrial lending and elastic German-style note issuance.

Meanwhile, privatization factored minimally in the Matsukata reform. The government unloaded hardly any of the factories and mines it had put up for sale until *after* Matsukata had essentially completed his reform, while state spending on industry had dropped to a significantly lower level during the years 1877–1881 than during the next four years on Matsukata's watch. At best, industrial policy shifted in a quasi-laissez-faire direction under Matsukata, as the government continued to pour money into railroads, military-related factories and shipyards, and eventually Japan's first integrated steelworks and as the Imperial Household and the peers served as proxy state investors in a range of private joint-stock companies.

More generally, Matsukata's approach was one of "incrementalism" rather than "shock therapy" of the kind that free market neoliberals advocated after the 1970s. In 1879–1881, under Ōkuma and Sano, the Meiji regime had planned or initiated most of the programs that Matsukata would carry through, including retiring government notes and creating a central bank, economizing on administrative expenses, raising consumer taxes, and privatizing state enterprises. Matsukata would thus build on his predecessors' reforms, although he helped shape those reforms while climbing to top decision-making positions—albeit much more slowly than many of his peers—and once he became finance minister he did more than just "continue a course that had already been established,"[2] modifying or departing from many of the programs he inherited.

"Shock therapy," however, in the sense that Jeffrey Sachs used the term, namely, ending hyperinflation in one decisive stroke through measures such as terminating the reckless printing of paper money and rapidly establishing a stable, convertible currency,[3] might apply to Matsukata's monetary reform. For all the "gradualism" of his reform compared to Ōkuma's proposal for the immediate withdrawal of government fiat notes through overseas borrowing, Matsukata in fact contracted the money supply at a frenetic pace, retiring all ¥14.5 million in outstanding supplemental notes within fifteen months of assuming the Finance Ministry portfolio and another ¥7.3 million in regular government notes over the next three months.[4] Nonetheless, note redemption had been under way for at least two years before Matsukata's appointment as finance minister, moderating the "one stroke"-like effect of his initial note retirements.

Furthermore, Matsukata's thinking was different from that of an "orthodox mindset" in several ways. He showed flexibility in changing course rather than rigidly adhering to a program of fiscal austerity. After seeing how monetary stringency had generated a severe economic downturn in 1882–1883, he stepped up programs for state-led export promotion and public bond issuance. In addition, Matsukata called for a made-in-Japan reform rather than one supported by foreign loans and foreign advisers, as Ōkuma had proposed in mid-1881 after accepting the recommendation of Britain's minister to Japan, Sir Harry Parkes, that Japan set up a "great bank" with British capital to stabilize the currency and hire a British banker to run the bank. Matsukata, by contrast, insisted on Japanese funding and management of his proposed Bank of Japan; after entering office as finance minister, armed with an imperial mandate, he pushed the Council of State not only to shelve the Ōkuma-Itō plan for floating bonds overseas and establishing a central bank but also to cancel the contract Ōkuma had negotiated with banker John Robertson to manage his planned bank.[5] Matsukata's approach in this regard was quite unorthodox, for at the time many developing countries worldwide were embracing foreign advice and assistance when hit by financial crises, and the approach also contrasted with the IMF's role in financial stabilization programs in recent decades. In addition, although Matsukata drew on the latest financial thought and practice in advanced Western countries, he also looked to the financial histories of ancient China and early modern Japan and to the statist and mercantilist traditions of his home domain.

Related to Matsukata's flexibility was the pragmatism he displayed in combining the "rules" of nineteenth-century British economic liberalism with "discretion" along economic nationalist lines. Like many state leaders in other late industrializing countries at the time, he ended up adapting or even abandoning orthodox principles in the interest of furthering national economic development and other statist and nationalist priorities. Government leaders in the 1920s, including Finance Minister Inoue Junnosuke in Japan, embraced austerity and deflation as international and moral imperatives even in the midst of recession, much as authorities would do in countries in financial crisis during the 1990s and after the 2008 financial meltdown. By contrast, their late-nineteenth-century counterparts in follower nations tended to pursue austerity ultimately for expansionary, developmentalist reasons; as Steven Bryan puts it, Matsukata followed "rules plus discretion, not rules rather than discretion."[6] The policy of "expansionary austerity," which scholars have investigated for a number of countries in recent decades, has some relevance for the Matsukata reform.[7] The policy generally involves combining domestic austerity with currency devaluation and export expansion. This oxymoronic term applies especially to when Japan went on the silver standard, effectively devaluing the yen, and silver depreciation picked up after the price of silver had by and large plateaued during the Matsukata deflation, amplifying the effects of the global depression in 1882–1885. Yet already by 1883 Matsukata had begun to move in a positive, expansionary direction by introducing programs for the Finance Ministry to export rice and edible kelp and to issue domestic bonds. Then, in 1884, he turned pragmatically toward soliciting foreign assistance to boost the ministry's accumulation of specie, opening the export-lending program to Western merchants in the treaty ports and, despite having adamantly opposed foreign borrowing in 1880–1881, attempting to sell redemption bonds overseas.

Mark Metzler has observed of Japan's financial development after 1897—using terms that Japanese scholars have also applied to the preceding Meiji years—that the government went through alternating cycles of "positive" or expansionary policies and "negative" or stabilization-oriented policies. In the period Metzler considered, it was the contradictory maintenance of empire and the gold standard, the one demanding "continued high government spending" and the other requiring "fiscal retrenchment," that drove the policy cycle.[8] In those terms, although empire and gold were still in the offing, Ōkuma pursued a "positive" policy in the 1870s and Sano generally a "negative" or contractionary policy in 1880–1881, but Matsukata in a sense combined those policies along the lines of "expansionary austerity." Matsukata had already started to adopt expansionary measures following his sharp currency contraction from 1882 to early 1883, but once interest rates had fallen, bond prices had risen, and paper money had attained parity with silver by 1885–1886, he turned decisively toward "positive" expansion, directing the Bank of Japan to increase rapidly its issuance of convertible notes and to lend actively on the security of corporate shares and especially public bonds. By accepting bonds in particular as collateral for loans, the bank facilitated the successful flotation of a series of government bond issues from 1886 to 1896, all of them at more than face value and at a favorable interest rate of 5 percent.[9]

While bringing about financial stabilization and laying the groundwork for long-term economic development primarily through the application of "unorthodox" policies, the Matsukata reform exacerbated an emerging deflation that dealt a sharp blow to the countryside, where the vast majority of the population still resided in the first half of the 1880s.[10] Matsukata's drastic currency contraction was mainly responsible for the severity of the deflation, but other internal factors preceding his reform, including the bursting of the rice market bubble and the acceleration of land tax collection, had already triggered a downward trend in the price of rice. Then the global depression that started in 1882 piled on, magnifying the domestic downturn. Agricultural households that engaged in sericulture suffered not only from the drop in grain prices but also from the volatility of cocoon and raw silk prices reflecting the ups and downs of the export trade, while those with a hand in commercial sake brewing were hard hit by increases in brewery taxes and licensing fees.[11] Farm forfeiture and tenancy, however, rose only minimally, but debt incurred during the Matsukata deflation burdened many farm families long after the mid-1880s.

Although nascent modern industries clearly benefited from Matsukata's policies, by no means did he ignore the needs of the agricultural sector. In the steps he took to relieve hard-hit rural communities, Matsukata demonstrated the flexibility that marked many of his other measures: he twice extended the deadline established under Sano for the final installment of land tax payments—in 1883 and again in 1885—and, also in 1883, lifted the ban he had imposed on the provision of credit by the Yokohama Specie Bank on the security of export goods *prior to* their shipment abroad, permitting the bank to furnish credit beforehand so as to encourage the production and delivery of raw silk and tea for export. In addition, though somewhat belatedly, in the late 1890s he would go on to establish prefectural "agriculture and industry" banks that extended low-interest loans chiefly to farmers.

In both policy and mindset, therefore, one might say that the Matsukata financial reform has been famous for the wrong reason. Many have invoked it as a successful example of "orthodox" liberal or neoliberal stabilization, but the reform, as implemented, suggests a significantly different approach. That approach is more in keeping with the ideas of contemporary heterodox critics of IMF-style orthodoxy who underscore the need for flexibility, a larger state role in adjustment, incrementalism, rejection of external interference, and reliance on local intellectual tradition.

Some writers have compared the Matsukata financial reform to a later and externally imposed reform—the Dodge Line of 1949–1950—as an equally momentous stabilization program that set the stage for sustained economic growth in Japan after World War II.[12] One study from 1992 in fact held up the Dodge Line as a "beacon for Eastern Europe and the Soviet Union half a century ahead."[13] In 1949 Detroit banker Joseph Dodge (1890–1964), who had co-designed a successful currency reform in occupied Germany the year before, arrived in U.S.-occupied Japan and enforced a drastic, "one-stroke" stabilization plan to control postwar hyperinflation. The plan required the Japanese government to balance the budget by tightening tax collection and cutting expenditures, to restrict credit, and to set a fixed exchange rate for the yen. The authors of the 1992 study maintain that, although this "cold-turkey policy" triggered a severe "but most fortunately short" recession, its timing could not have been better: a year or two earlier and it might have pushed the Japanese economy to "the brink of total collapse," whereas one or two years later it would not have been able to restrain further inflation during the procurement boom that began in 1950 with the outbreak of the Korean War. They conclude that the Dodge Line presents a model for placing a country on a "stable growth path," although their data indicate that both wholesale and consumer price inflation actually peaked in 1946 and declined steadily through 1950.[14]

On the last point, Mark Metzler has similarly noted that inflation had begun to lessen a year *before* Dodge announced his plan. He has also pointed out that Japanese authorities preserved their "fundamental monetary independence even under military occupation": after Dodge ordered abolition of the government's Reconstruction Finance Bank, which had been pumping capital into prioritized industries, Japanese authorities managed to circumvent the Dodge plan by "privatizing" the money supply process through the Bank of Japan's practice of "overloaning" to commercial banks—a supposedly stopgap measure that became a fixture of Japan's high-growth years.[15] One could well make the case that credit creation by banks and the Korean War boom "saved" the Dodge Line and set the pattern for Japan's postwar economic miracle while also acknowledging that Dodge's enforcement of a fixed dollar exchange rate at a devalued rate for the yen performed a vital role in providing Japan with an effective export subsidy until the Nixon "shocks" ended the Bretton Woods system in 1971. To some extent, one could say much the same about the Matsukata financial program: while Matsukata similarly embraced "expansionary austerity" in devaluing the yen upon Japan's adoption of both the de facto silver standard in 1886 and the gold standard in 1897,[16] inflation had already started to subside before he embarked on his stabilization policies; then, from 1882, the real net increase in government spending owing to appreciation of the yen relative to silver, the flat-lining of tax revenue, and emergency additions to ministerial budgets as well as the turn to expansionary policies in the mid-1880s served to ameliorate and shorten the deflationary downturn in macroeconomic terms (dispossessed or seriously indebted farmers certainly held a very different view!).

In financial matters, Japan in the 1880s presents striking parallels to the country in recent decades: bursting of bubbles, domestic deflation and global deflationary pressures, rising consumer taxes, and heightened government borrowing, with public bond issues under Matsukata and deficit spending under Japanese administrations since the 1970s. The differences are equally significant. Contemporary Japan, faced with a mounting demographic crisis, lacks the potential for industrial and productivity growth to deal with debt that Meiji Japan possessed with its expanding population and economy; and Japanese leaders today have no option such as their mid-Meiji counterparts had of going on a silver standard and becoming largely insulated from global deflation while enjoying trade advantages with gold-standard economies.

In both of twentieth-century Japan's major downturns following booms, in the 1920s and 1990s, the nation missed having a Matsukata, fully backed by a sovereign emperor, who could push through a painful but relatively quick financial stabilization, clearing the way for economic recovery, rather than allowing deflation to persist through indecisiveness of policy. Granted, Matsukata was fortunate to avoid challenges on the order of the Great Kanto Earthquake of 1923, the Financial Panic of 1927, or the Asian financial crisis of 1997 that served to undercut efforts to stabilize and stimulate the Japanese economy. The Korean disturbances of 1882 and 1884 did provoke a national security crisis, but the continuing trade surplus enabled Matsukata to acquire more than sufficient specie to accomplish both currency reform and armaments buildup.

The flexibility and pragmatism Matsukata exhibited along "liberal nationalist" lines at the height of the deflation reveal that he was hardly a relentless pursuer of "orthodox finance." The "cold turkey" Dodge Line resembles the Matsukata reform in its deflationary impact and stabilizing success, but Dodge may well have produced something like a "lost decade" if not for the Bank of Japan's "overloaning" and the Korean War boom. By contrast, as early as 1883, in the midst of his reform, Matsukata was already transitioning from a contractionary approach to an expansionary one.

Thereafter, Japan alternated between periods of expansion and fiscal retrenchment. The cyclical narrative of expansion, crisis, and austerity, however, is far from just a recurring Japanese story. For nations worldwide, overspending or overborrowing has repeatedly led to financial crises followed by deflation and retrenchment. The cascade of such events in the last few decades alone have included the Latin American debt crises and the U.S. savings and loan crisis in the 1980s, the Tequila and Asian financial crises in the 1990s, the dot-com bust and subprime collapse in the 2000s, and the EU debt crashes in the 2010s, along with their respective prologues and aftermaths. Japan in the Matsukata reform era differs in context from these examples at least as much as it does from Japan itself since the 1980s. Yet, recognizing Matsukata's departures from contemporary British, rules-based orthodoxy and his blending of deflationary and expansionary measures that resemble approaches suggested by critics of late-twentieth-century IMF-style orthodoxy, one might well see the Matsukata financial reform as a model of sorts after all for countries dealing with fiscal and monetary crises today. Following the "rules plus discretion"-based austerity that set the stage for Japan's adoption of a de facto silver standard in 1886, Matsukata himself would preside over the Ministry of Finance through most of the ensuing decade of inflation and economic growth, with a hiccup at the time of the global panic of 1890, as well as during the first few years of "expansionary austerity" after Japan's entry into the league of gold-standard nations.

Notes

INTRODUCTION

1. In the United States, national banks were private institutions chartered by the federal government under the National Bank Act of 1863 to issue paper currency backed by federal bonds. On the Japanese national banking system and its U.S. model, see Shigeki Miyajima and Warren E. Weber, "A Comparison of National Banks in Japan and the United States between 1872 and 1885," *Monetary and Economic Studies* 19, no. 1 (February 2001): 31–48.

2. The regime established by the elites who overthrew the Tokugawa shogunate in 1868. "Meiji" or "Enlightened Rule" was the imperial era name that officials chose that year for the reign of Emperor Mutsuhito and that continued until his death in 1912.

3. Steven J. Ericson, "The 'Matsukata Deflation' Reconsidered: Financial Stabilization and Japanese Exports in a Global Depression, 1881–85," *Journal of Japanese Studies* 40, no. 1 (2014): 1–28.

4. Henry Rosovsky, "Japan's Transition to Modern Economic Growth, 1868–1885," in *Industrialization in Two Systems*, ed. Henry Rosovsky, 91–139 (New York: John Wiley & Sons, 1966).

5. Examples of such textbook treatment include Peter Duus, *Modern Japan*, 2nd ed. (Boston: Houghton Mifflin, 1998), 119; James L. McClain, *A Modern History of Japan* (New York: W. W. Norton, 2002), 216–17; and Andrew Gordon, *A History of Modern Japan: From Tokugawa Times to the Present*, 3rd ed. (Oxford: Oxford University Press, 2013), 95.

Scholarly publication on the Matsukata reform outside of Japan remains limited. Among the few existing studies, besides Henry Rosovsky's article, Nobutaka Ike includes a chapter on the Matsukata deflation in *The Beginnings of Political Democracy in Japan* (Baltimore: Johns Hopkins University Press, 1950), 138–47, emphasizing the severity of the resulting agricultural depression and its role in undermining the rural-based wing of the Freedom and People's Rights movement; Norio Tamaki discusses the Ōkuma-Matsukata transition and the policies of Matsukata, "the wizard of Japanese banking," in *Japanese Banking: A History, 1859–1959* (Cambridge: Cambridge University Press, 1995), 49–81; and Wenkai He provides an excellent analysis of the "political economy of the Matsukata deflation" and the emergence of modern public finance under Matsukata and his predecessors in a work that stands out for reflecting recent Japanese scholarship, *Paths toward the Modern Fiscal State: England, Japan, and China* (Cambridge, MA: Harvard University Press, 2013), 78–130.

6. Rosovsky, "Japan's Transition," 132, 134.

7. On British financial orthodoxy in the nineteenth century, see, for instance, David Laidler, "British Monetary Orthodoxy in the 1870s," *Oxford Economic Papers* (n.s.) 40, no. 1 (March 1988): 74–109 (p. 106: "In the 1870s, specie convertibility was regarded as a *sine qua non* of sound monetary management.").

8. J. Taylor Vurpillat, "Empire, Industry, and Globalization: Rethinking the Emergence of the Gold Standard in the 19th-century World," *History Compass* 12, no. 6 (2014): 531.

9. On the Washington Consensus and IMF orthodoxy, see, for example, John Williamson, "The Washington Consensus as Policy Prescription for Development" (lecture delivered at the World Bank, New York, January 13, 2004), accessed August 19, 2018, https://

piie.com/publications/papers/williamson0204.pdf, and Michael Mussa and Miguel Savastano, "The IMF Approach to Economic Stabilization," *NBER Macroeconomics Annual* 14 (1990): 79–122.

10. Mark Metzler, "Japan's Matsukata Deflation in Transnational and Cross-Temporal Perspective" (paper presented at the annual conference of the Association for Asian Studies, Chicago, IL, March 27, 2009), 6.

11. Audrey T. Sproat, "Japan (A) Supplement I" and "Japan (A) Supplement II" (Cambridge, MA: President and Fellows of Harvard College, 1975); James E. Austin, "Teaching Note: Japan (A) Supplements I & II" ("Business, Government and the International Economy" course, Harvard Business School, Boston, 1987–1990).

12. Susan Pharr, personal communication, April 29, 2014, and Andrew Gordon, email message to author, March 10, 2016. Pharr recalls having received inquiries from Sachs for information on the Matsukata financial reform.

13. The most important works informing current Japanese views of the Matsukata reform are the seminal collected volume *Matsukata zaisei to shokusan kōgyō seisaku*, ed. Umemura Mataji and Nakamura Takafusa (Kokusai Rengō Daigaku, 1983); Kamiyama Tsuneo, *Meiji keizai seisaku shi no kenkyū* (Hanawa Shobō, 1995); and four books by Muroyama Yoshimasa: *Kindai Nihon no gunji to zaisei: gunji kakuchō o meguru seisaku keisei katei* (Tōkyō Daigaku Shuppankai, 1984), *Matsukata zaisei kenkyū: futaiten no seisaku kōdō to keizai kiki kokufuku no jissō* (Kyoto: Minerva Shobō, 2004), *Matsukata Masayoshi: ware ni kisaku aru ni arazu, tada shōjiki aru nomi* (Kyoto: Minerva Shobō, 2005), and *Kindai Nihon keizai no keisei: Matsukata zaisei to Meiji no kokka kōsō* (Chikura Shobō, 2014).

14. On critiques of liberal and neoliberal orthodoxies, see, for example, Harold James, *The End of Globalization: Lessons from the Great Depression* (Cambridge, MA: Harvard University Press, 2001); Ha-Joon Chang, *Kicking Away the Ladder: Development Strategy in Historical Perspective* (London: Anthem Press, 2002); Joseph Stiglitz, *Globalization and Its Discontents* (New York: W. W. Norton, 2003); and Dani Rodrik, *The Globalization Paradox: Democracy and the Future of the World Economy* (New York: W. W. Norton, 2011).

15. Works addressing nineteenth-century economic nationalism include Eric Helleiner, "Economic Nationalism as a Challenge to Economic Liberalism? Lessons from the 19th Century," *International Studies Quarterly* 46, no. 3 (September 2002): 307–29; Helleiner, *The Making of National Money: Territorial Currencies in Historical Perspective* (Ithaca, NY: Cornell University Press, 2003); and Steven Bryan, *The Gold Standard at the Turn of the Twentieth Century: Rising Powers, Global Money, and the Age of Empire* (New York: Columbia University Press, 2010).

16. On Japan's move to gold monometallism, see Nakamura Takafusa, *Meiji Taishō ki no keizai* (Tōkyō Daigaku Shuppankai, 1985), 62–77; Bryan, *The Gold Standard at the Turn of the Twentieth Century*; Michael Schiltz, "Money on the Road to Empire: Japan's Adoption of Gold Monometallism, 1873–97," *Economic History Review* 65, no. 3 (2012): 1147–68; and Simon James Bytheway, *Investing Japan: Foreign Capital, Monetary Standards, and Economic Development, 1859–2011* (Cambridge, MA: Harvard University Asia Center, 2014), 28–46.

17. On the avalanche of crises since 2008, see Adam Tooze, *Crashed: How a Decade of Financial Crises Changed the World* (New York: Viking, 2018).

18. Helleiner, "Economic Nationalism," 307–14. See also George T. Crane, "Economic Nationalism: Bringing the Nation Back In," *Millennium: Journal of International Studies* 27, no. 1 (March 1998): 55–75, and Christine Margerum Harlen, "A Reappraisal of Classical Economic Nationalism and Economic Liberalism," *International Studies Quarterly* 43, no. 4 (December 1999): 733–44. On List and Japan, see Mark Metzler, "The Cosmopolitanism of National Economics: Friedrich List in a Japanese Mirror," in *Global History:*

Interactions between the Universal and the Local, ed. Anthony G. Hopkins, 98–130 (Basingstoke, UK: Palgrave Macmillan, 2006).

19. Dieter Senghaas, "Friedrich List and the Basic Problems of Modern Development," *Review* (Fernand Braudel Center) 14, no. 3 (1991): 459.

20. See Helleiner, "Economic Nationalism," 314–22.

21. Helleiner, *The Making of National Money*, 84.

22. Helleiner, *The Making of National Money*, 84–87; Helleiner, "Economic Nationalism," 321–22.

23. Haru Matsukata Reischauer, *Samurai and Silk: A Japanese and American Heritage* (Cambridge, MA: Harvard University Press, 1986), 96. For a recent comparison of Hamilton and Matsukata, see Richard Sylla, "Financial Systems and Economic Modernization," *Journal of Economic History* 62 (June 2002): 277–92.

24. George Marvin, "The Alexander Hamilton of Japan: Prince Masayoshi Matsukata, the Valedictorian of the Elder Statesmen," *Asia* 25 (January 1925): 54–57, 81–83.

25. On Hamilton's policies, see, for instance, Robert E. Wright, *Hamilton Unbound: Finance and the Creation of the American Republic* (Westport, CT: Greenwood Press, 2002).

26. Bryan, *The Gold Standard at the Turn of the Twentieth Century*, 48.

27. Bryan, *The Gold Standard at the Turn of the Twentieth Century*, 63.

28. In lists of the monetary standards of thirty-nine countries that Barry Eichengreen and Marc Flandreau compiled, only seven states had currencies convertible to gold in 1868, whereas twenty-four had such currencies in 1908. Barry Eichengreen and Marc Flandreau, "The Geography of the Gold Standard," in *Currency Convertibility: The Gold Standard and Beyond*, ed. Jorge Braga de Macedo, Barry Eichengreen, and Jaime Reis (London: Routledge, 1996), 115, 120.

29. The common tendency to view Matsukata as the sole architect of the policies he carried out (or intended to carry out) stems in large part from reliance on the official financial history of the Meiji period, compiled after Matsukata resigned as finance minister for the last time in 1900: *Meiji zaisei shi: Matsukata Haku zaisei jireki*, ed. Meiji Zaisei Shi Hensankai, 15 vols. (Maruzen, 1904–1905). Tellingly, the compilers subtitled the work *A Record of Public Finance under Count Matsukata*, as if the first thirteen years of finance under Matsukata's predecessors had never existed. Historians have also drawn heavily on a collection of Matsukata's memorials, opinion papers, and speeches from 1868 to 1892 compiled in 1893 by his admiring protégé and future finance minister Sakatani Yoshirō (1863–1941): "Matsukata Haku zaisei ronsakushū," orig. pub. in *Meiji zenki zaisei keizai shiryō shūsei*, ed. Ōkura Shō, vol. 1 (Kaizōsha, 1931), repr. in *Matsukata Masayoshi kankei monjo*, ed. Ōkubo Tatsumasa, suppl. vol. (Daitō Bunka Daigaku Tōyō Kenkyūjo, 2001).

In addition, scholars have made considerable use of the hagiographic, official biography edited by the journalist, historian, and progressive-turned-conservative supporter of the oligarchs Tokutomi Iichirō (pen name Sohō; 1863–1957): *Kōshaku Matsukata Masayoshi den*, 2 vols. (Kōshaku Matsukata Masayoshi Denki Hakkōjo, 1935). (On Tokutomi, see John D. Pierson, *Tokutomi Sohō, 1863–1957: A Journalist for Modern Japan* [Princeton, NJ: Princeton University Press, 1980].)

Some historians have looked as well at the unpublished papers of Matsukata, particularly the huge collection of financial policy-related documents that the family deposited at the Ministry of Finance and has been available on microfilm from Yumani Shobō since 1987: Matsukata ke monjo, 67 vols., Ministry of Finance Policy Research Institute (Zaimu Shō Sōgō Seisaku Kenkyūjo), Tokyo. The editors of the published, multivolume collection of archival materials the Matsukata family entrusted to the National Diet Library and Daitō Bunka University—*Matsukata Masayoshi kankei monjo*, ed. Fujimura Tōru (vols. 1–5) and Ōkubo Tatsumasa (vols. 6–20), 20 vols. (Daitō Bunka Daigaku Tōyō Kenkyūjo,

1979–2001)—added a selection of opinion papers and memoranda from the Finance Ministry compilation in vol. 17 (1995) and vol. 18 (1996). That published collection includes, among many other documents, personal histories dictated by Matsukata late in his life; Tokutomi used them as raw material for his official biography.

It is no surprise that historians relying primarily on government records and Matsukata's own papers should subscribe to an inflated view of the man, for he headed the Ministry of Finance for most of the two decades after 1881.

30. On these points, see, for instance, Ericson, "The 'Matsukata Deflation' Reconsidered."

31. "Financial Free-Trade for Japan," *Japan Weekly Mail*, February 27, 1886.

1. FROM "ŌKUMA FINANCE" TO "MATSUKATA FINANCE," 1873–1881

1. Satsuma was a daimyo domain in southwestern Japan, one of the domains that led in the overthrow of the Tokugawa shogunate in 1868. In 1877 disaffected former samurai from Satsuma rose up against the new government their domain had helped establish. Japanese scholars refer to the Satsuma Rebellion as the Southwestern War (Seinan Sensō).

2. Fujimura Tōru, *Meiji zaisei kakuritsu katei no kenkyū* (Chūō Daigaku Shuppanbu, 1968), 440.

3. Itō Hirobumi, "Reasons for Basing the Japanese New Coinage on the Metric System," December 29, 1870, in Matsukata Masayoshi, *Report on the Adoption of the Gold Standard in Japan* (Tokyo: Government Press, 1899), 5. Bimetallism refers to the use of two metals, usually gold and silver, as the monetary standard.

4. Itō, "Reasons," 6–9, 21–22; Masayoshi Takaki, *The History of Japanese Paper Currency (1868–1890)* (Baltimore: Johns Hopkins University Press, 1903), 28–32. The government would complete the retirement of domain notes in 1879.

5. Tamaki, *Japanese Banking*, 31.

6. More precisely, Japan adopted a "gold-exchange standard," as China deposited the ¥374 million in war reparations as pounds sterling in London. On the Bank of Japan's specie reserve held in London, see Simon James Bytheway and Mark Metzler, *Central Banks and Gold: How Tokyo, London, and New York Shaped the Modern World* (Ithaca, NY: Cornell University Press, 2016), 9–16, and Matsukata, *Report on the Adoption of the Gold Standard*, 166–73 (p. 373 for the exchange rate in December 1897 for converting into yen the total Chinese payment to Japan of £37.9 million).

7. Mark Metzler, *Lever of Empire: The International Gold Standard and the Crisis of Liberalism in Prewar Japan* (Berkeley: University of California Press, 2006), 23. On the international move to gold that German and French actions triggered in the early 1870s, see Marc Flandreau, "The French Crime of 1873: An Essay on the Emergence of the International Gold Standard, 1870–1880," *Journal of Economic History* 56, no. 4 (1996): 862–97.

8. *Kindai Nihon keizai shi yōran*, ed. Andō Yoshio, 2nd ed. (Tōkyō Daigaku Shuppankai, 1979), 51–53.

9. *The Currency of Japan: A Reprint of Articles, Letters, and Official Reports, Published at Intervals in the Foreign Newspapers of Japan, together with Translations from Japanese Journals, Relating to the Currency, Paper and Metallic, of the Empire of Japan* (Yokohama: Japan Gazette), 9.

10. Fujimura Tōru, *Matsukata Masayoshi: Nihon zaisei no paionia* (Nihon Keizai Shimbunsha, 1966), 66.

11. Ishii Kanji, "Japan," in *International Banking, 1870–1914*, ed. Rondo Cameron and V. I. Bovykin (New York: Oxford University Press, 1991), 216.

12. Ishii, "Japan," 216.

13. *Meiji zenki zaisei keizai shiryō shūsei*, ed. Ōkura Shō, 21 vols. (Kaizōsha, 1931–1936), vol. 4 (1932), 372–73.

14. Uchida Masahiro, *Meiji Nihon no kokka zaisei kenkyū: kindai Meiji kokka no honshitsu to shoki zaisei no kaimei* (Taga Shuppan, 1992), 351, 362–63, 371.

15. On the Taiwan Expedition, see Robert Eskildsen, "Of Civilization and Savages: The Mimetic Imperialism of Japan's 1874 Expedition to Taiwan," *American Historical Review* 107, no. 2 (April 2002): 388–418. Japan dispatched a force of about thirty-six hundred soldiers to the Chinese province of Taiwan (then known as Formosa) in May 1874 to "chastise" aborigines who had murdered shipwrecked Ryukyu fisherman and, in the end, gained de facto control over the Ryukyu Islands as a result of the British-brokered settlement with the Qing court.

16. *Meiji Taishō oyobi Shōwa zaisei yōran* (Kokusei Kenkyūkai, 1937), 12.

17. Muroyama, *Matsukata Masayoshi*, 117.

18. Muroyama, *Matsukata Masayoshi*, 112–18.

19. Matsukata Masayoshi, "Shihei seiri shimatsu," 1890, in *Nihon kin'yū shi shiryō: Meiji Taishō hen*, ed. Nihon Ginkō Chōsa Kyoku, 26 vols. (Ōkura Shō Insatsu Kyoku, 1956–1961), vol. 16 (1957), 104–7.

20. Muroyama, *Matsukata zaisei kenkyū*, 76; Harada Mikio, *Nihon no kindaika to keizai seisaku* (Tōyō Keizai Shinpōsha, 1972), 224–25, 229.

21. Matsukata, *Report on the Adoption of the Gold Standard*, 108.

22. Motokazu Shindō, "The Inflation in the Early Meiji Era," *Kyoto University Economic Review* 24, no. 2 (1954): 52.

23. Fukuzawa Yukichi, *Fukuzawa Yukichi zenshū*, 2nd ed., 22 vols. (Iwanami Shoten, 1958–1971), vol. 17 (1971), 231; cited in Norio Tamaki, *Yukichi Fukuzawa, 1835–1901: The Spirit of Enterprise in Modern Japan* (Houndmills, Basingstoke, Hampshire: Palgrave, 2001), 112.

24. On Ōkuma's note retirement and silver sell-off, see Muroyama, *Matsukata zaisei kenkyū*, 61–77.

25. *Ōkuma Shigenobu kankei monjo*, ed. Watanabe Ikujirō, 6 vols. (Nihon Shiseki Kyōkai, 1932–1935), vol. 4 (1935), 481–82.

26. Samurai from the Chōshū domain in southwestern Japan had joined samurai from the Satsuma domain in toppling the Tokugawa shogunate and supplying most of the leaders of the new Meiji government.

27. Muroyama, *Matsukata zaisei kenkyū*, 165–66.

28. Duus, *Modern Japan*, 119.

29. Rosovsky, "Japan's Transition," 132.

30. *Segai Inoue Kō den*, ed. Inoue Kaoru Kō Denki Hensankai, 5 vols. (Naigai Shoseki, 1933–1934), vol. 3 (1934), 149–50. The Minister of the Right (Udaijin) was the third highest ranking member of the early Meiji government, whose structure the leaders based on that of the ancient imperial state. In 1885 a modern, Western-style cabinet system replaced that structure, which had centered on a Council of State (Dajōkan).

31. Nishino Kiyosaku, *Rekidai zōshō den* (Tōyō Keizai Shinpōsha, 1930), 42.

32. *Kadokawa Nihon shi jiten*, ed. Takayanagi Mitsutoshi and Takeuchi Rizō, 2nd ed. (Kadokawa Shoten, 1974), 1254.

33. Nakamura Naoyoshi, "Ōkuma Shigenobu to Matsukata Masayoshi," in *Meiji seifu: sono seiken o ninatta hitobito*, ed. Ōkubo Toshiaki (Shin Jinbutsu Ōraisha, 1971), 115.

34. Ozaki Yukio, *The Autobiography of Ozaki Yukio*, trans. Fujiko Hara (Princeton, NJ: Princeton University Press, 2001), 163.

35. On Matsukata's shortcomings as a politician, see Takahashi Makoto, "Matsukata Masayoshi," in Endō Shōkichi, Katō Toshihiko, and Takahashi Makoto, *Nihon no ōkura daijin* (Nihon Hyōronsha, 1964), 71–73.

36. Muroyama, *Matsukata Masayoshi*, 31.

37. Muroyama, *Matsukata Masayoshi*, 58, 66, 96.

38. For more on this proposal, see Inoki Takenori, "Chiso beinō ron to zaisei seiri: 1880 nen 8 gatsu no seisaku ronsō o megutte," in *Matsukata zaisei to shokusan kōgyō seisaku*, 107–26.

39. Muroyama Yoshimasa, "Matsukata *defurēshon* no *mekanizumu*," in *Matsukata zaisei to shokusan kōgyō seisaku*, 144–45. For the continuity argument, which Muroyama disputes, see Ōishi Kaichirō, *Jiyū minken to Ōkuma, Matsukata zaisei* (Tōkyō Daigaku Shuppankai, 1989).

40. Inoue Kiyoshi, for instance, expresses the widely held view that the Matsukata deflation drove a wedge between wealthy farmers and lower-class peasants, sending the opposition Liberal Party to its dissolution in 1884. Inoue Kiyoshi, "Jiyū minken undō," in *Nihon rekishi daijiten*, ed. Nihon Rekishi Daijiten Hensan Iiinkai (Kawade Shobō Shinsha, 1974), vol. 5, 483–84.

41. *Iwakura Kō jikki*, ed. Tada Kōmon, 3 vols. (Iwakura Kōkyūseki hozonkai, 1927), vol. 3, 1595–1600, 1714–16.

42. *Ōkuma monjo*, 6 vols. (Waseda Daigaku Shakai Kagaku Kenkyūjo, 1958–1963), vol. 3 (1960), 444–55.

43. Ōkura Shō, "Kasei kōyō: seifu shihei jireki," vol. 2 (1887), repr. in *Meiji zenki zaisei keizai shiryō shūsei*, vol. 13 (1934), 267–69.

44. *Iwakura Kō jikki*, vol. 3, 1717–19.

45. Muroyama, *Matsukata zaisei kenkyū*, 85.

46. Ōkura Shō, "Kasei kōyō," 267–68.

47. Matsukata Masayoshi, "Zaisei kanki gairyaku," June 1880, in "Matsukata Haku zaisei ronsakushū," 529–35.

48. Ishii Kanji, *Nihon no sangyōka to zaibatsu* (Iwanami Shoten, 1992), 21.

49. *Meiji Tennō ki*, ed. Kunai Chō, 13 vols. (Yoshikawa Kōbunkan, 1968–1977), vol. 5 (1971), 75.

50. Banno Junji, *Kindai Nihon no kokka kōsō* (Iwanami Shoten, 1996), 88–89.

51. *Ōkuma monjo*, vol. 3, 455–62.

52. *Okuma monjo*, vol. 3, 472–74.

53. *Okuma monjo*, vol. 3, 473.

54. *Ōkuma Shigenobu kankei monjo*, vol. 4, 481–82.

55. Matsukata Masayoshi, "Zaisei gi," 1881, in *Meiji zenki zaisei keizai shiryō shūsei*, vol. 1, 331–41.

56. Matsukata, "Zaisei gi," 332, 340.

57. Matsukata Masayoshi, "Matsukata Masayoshi kikigaki *nōto*," in *Matsukata Masayoshi kankei monjo*, vol. 10 (1991), 145.

58. *Meiji Tennō ki*, vol. 5, 555.

59. *Kōshaku Matsukata Masayoshi den*, vol. 1, 842–46; "Kōshaku Matsukata Masayoshi Kyō jikki," ed. Nakamura Tokugorō, in *Matsukata Masayoshi kankei monjo*, vols. 1–5 (1979–1983), vol. 2 (1981), 53.

60. Umemura Mataji, "Matsukata *defure*-ka no shokusan kōgyō seisaku: Nōrin Suisan Shō sōritsu hyaku shūnen o kinen shite," *Keizai kenkyū* 32, no. 4 (October 1981): 347.

61. Muroyama, *Matsukata Masayoshi*, 171–72.

62. Muroyama, *Matsukata zaisei kenkyū*, 166.

63. For a brief discussion of the long-running debate over this issue, see, for instance, Kamiyama, *Meiji keizai seisaku shi no kenkyū*, 3–8.

64. See, for example, Fujimura, *Meiji zaisei kakuritsu katei no kenkyū*, 365.

65. Muroyama, *Matsukata zaisei kenkyū*, 115.

2. ORTHODOX FINANCE AND "THE DICTATES OF PRACTICAL EXPEDIENCY"

1. An early version of this chapter appeared as Steven J. Ericson, "Orthodox Finance and 'The Dictates of Practical Expediency': Influences on Matsukata Masayoshi and the Financial Reform of 1881–1885," *Monumenta Nipponica* 71, no. 1 (2016): 83–117.

2. Matsukata's official biography has played a leading role in advancing this view by asserting that Léon Say, the French finance minister who tutored Matsukata in Paris, had a "deep and lasting" impact on him and influenced every one of the policies in the Matsukata reform. *Kōshaku Matsukata Masayoshi den*, vol. 1, 679; also cited in Harada, *Nihon no kindaika to keizai seisaku*, 180.

3. See, for instance, Komine Yasuei, "Nihon saisho no zaisei gakusha Tajiri Inajirō," *Senshū shōgaku ronshū*, no. 21 (June 1976): 130: "France's conservative, sound financial policy after its defeat in the Franco-Prussian War thus became the model (*moderu*) for the Matsukata deflationary finance." See also Kaida Ikuo, *Seiō zaiseigaku to Meiji zaisei* (Suita, Osaka-fu: Kansai Daigaku Shuppanbu, 1988), 5–6, where the author states that France in the 1870s was an "ideal example" (*kōko no mihon*) for Japan, and French financial studies offered "an extremely good model" (*makoto ni yoki tehon*) for Japanese administrators.

4. John H. Sagers, *Origins of Japanese Wealth and Power: Reconciling Confucianism and Capitalism, 1830–1885* (New York: Palgrave Macmillan, 2006), 3–7 and elsewhere; Katalin Ferber, "Professionalism as Power: Tajiri Inajirō and the Modernisation of Meiji Finance," in *Institutional and Technological Change in Japan's Economy: Past and Present*, ed. Janet Hunter and Cornelia Storz (London: Routledge, 2006), 30, 39. See also Metzler, "The Cosmopolitanism of National Economics," 107–8.

5. Muroyama, *Matsukata Masayoshi*, 399.

6. *Guanzi: Political, Economic, and Philosophical Essays from Early China*, trans. W. Allyn Rickett, 2 vols. (Princeton, NJ: Princeton University Press, 1985–1998).

7. Tokutomi Sohō, "Kaitō rōkō," *Kokumin shinbun*, July 3, 1924, repr. in *Matsukata Masayoshi kankei monjo*, vol. 15 (1994), 359; also cited in Muroyama, *Matsukata Masayoshi*, 420 (which mistakenly gives the page number for the quotation as 358). Tokutomi later edited Matsukata's official biography.

8. Muroyama, *Matsukata Masayoshi*, 403.

9. Muroyama, *Matsukata Masayoshi*, 398, 400–3; Kate Wildman Nakai, *Shogunal Politics: Arai Hakuseki and the Premises of Tokugawa Rule* (Cambridge, MA: Council on East Asian Studies, Harvard University, 1988), 61–62, 97–106.

10. See, for instance, Matsukata's summary of Tokugawa monetary history in his speech to the lower house of the Diet on March 3, 1897, when the government introduced the bill to return Japan to the gold standard, in Matsukata, *Report on the Adoption of the Gold Standard*, 179.

11. Muroyama, *Matsukata Masayoshi*, 403.

12. Nakai, *Shogunal Politics,* 97–98.

13. Tessa Morris-Suzuki, *A History of Japanese Economic Thought* (London: Routledge, 1989), 22.

14. Nakai, *Shogunal Politics*, 105.

15. Matsukata, however, was not unmindful of Western precedents in devising the land tax reform; for instance, as mentioned later, a proposal submitted in 1870 by the Western studies expert Kanda Takahira (1830–1898) based on his translation of an English political economy text appears to have contributed to the program's formulation.

16. Muroyama, *Matsukata Masayoshi*, 398.

17. Muroyama, *Matsukata Masayoshi*, 404.

18. "Financial Free-Trade for Japan." More literally, he declared that the government "must implement [a currency system] after considering its suitability on practical grounds, regardless of theory" (*riron ni towazu shite subekaraku jissai no tokushitsu o kangami sono tekitō o hakarite kore o shikō suru*). Matsukata Masayoshi, "Katō ginkō kyokuchō, Nakamura ittō shuzeikan Ōshū tokō no setsu sōbetsu no ji," January 19, 1886 in "Matsukata Haku zaisei ronsakushū," 659–60.

19. *Kōshaku Matsukata Masayoshi den*, vol. 1, 716–17.

20. Muroyama, *Matsukata Masayoshi*, 1.

21. Muroyama, *Matsukata Masayoshi*, 2, 396.

22. "Kōshaku Matsukata Masayoshi Kyō jikki," in *Matsukata Masayoshi kankei monjo*, vol. 1, 131–32.

23. Takahashi, "Matsukata Masayoshi," 73; Yoshino Toshihiko, *Nihon ginkō shi*, 5 vols. (Shunjūsha, 1975–1979), vol. 1 (1975), 46–47.

24. Yamamoto Kakuma, "Yamamoto Kakuma kenpaku," 1868, fols. 11a–12a, handcopied by Shimazu Hisamitsu, Digital Archive of Rare Materials, Dōshisha University Academic Repository, Kyoto, Japan, accessed August 9, 2015, http://library.doshisha.ac.jp /ir/digital/archive/yamamoto/128/imgidx128.html.

Following the Restoration, Yamamoto became a prominent figure in Kyoto; in 1875 he helped Niijima Jō (1843–1890) found Dōshisha Academy, the predecessor of Dōshisha University, and he was also inaugural speaker of the prefectural assembly in 1879–1880. After Niijima's untimely death in 1890, Yamamoto served as acting president of Dōshisha until his own demise. See the chronology of his life in Yoshimura Yasushi, *Shingan no hito Yamamoto Kakuma* (Kōbunsha, 1986), 399–413. The 2013 NHK television series "Yae no sakura" focused on Yamamoto's sister, who married Niijima.

25. Aoyama Kason, *Yamamoto Kakuma* (Kyoto: Dōshisha, 1928), 205.

26. Fukai Eigo, *Jinbutsu to shisō* (Nihon Hyōronsha, 1939), 356–58; also cited in Yoshino, *Nihon ginkō shi*, vol. 1, 46–47. On Fukai's life and career, see Richard J. Smethurst, "Fukai Eigo and the Development of Japanese Monetary Policy," in *New Directions in the Study of Meiji Japan*, ed. Helen Hardacre (Leiden: Brill, 1997), 125–35.

27. Nishino, *Rekidai zōshō den*, 44.

28. Aoyama, *Yamamoto Kakuma*, 206–10. Matsukata also describes this visit in his "notes," which were compiled between 1898 and 1902: Matsukata, "Matsukata Masayoshi kikigaki nōto," in *Matsukata Masayoshi kankei monjo*, vol. 10, 153.

29. *Meiji kensei keizai shiron* (Kokka Gakkai, 1919), 292; also cited in Yoshino, *Nihon ginkō shi*, vol. 1, 47.

30. In 1868 the Meiji government reorganized the lands formerly controlled by the shogunate and its allies into prefectures and then, after abolishing some 260 daimyo domains in 1871, consolidated the former shogunal and daimyo lands into 75 prefectures. Hita became part of Ōita Prefecture when the regime created that prefecture in December 1871.

31. Hyōdō Tōru, "Matsukata zaisei no genryū ni tsuite: Hita-ken seiki ni okeru kinsatsu, hansatsu mondai o chūshin to shite," *Keizai ronshū* 42 (September 1986): 59–64.

32. Matsukata Masayoshi, "Sho hansatsu dakan no gi," November 20, 1868, and "Kinsatsu tsūyō no kōfu ni tai suru no gi," March 29, 1869, in "Matsukata Haku zaisei ronsakushū," 27–30.

33. Matsukata, "Sho hansatsu dakan no gi," 27.

34. Hyōdō, "Matsukata zaisei no genryū ni tsuite," 70, 72.

35. Muroyama, *Matsukata Masayoshi*, 98, 397.

36. Reischauer, *Samurai and Silk*, 58, 84. Reischauer writes on page 8 that she based her account of Matsukata's life mainly on the two-volume biography *Kōshaku Matsukata Masayoshi den*, edited by Tokutomi Iichirō, which she says was "published by the Matsukata family," as well as "Kōshaku Matsukata Masayoshi Kyō jikki," an extensive manu-

script dictated by Matsukata himself and compiled in 1919–1921; as she provides no citations, however, one can probably assume that parts of her narrative are products of family oral history.

37. See *Dictionnaire des finances*, ed. Léon Say, 2 vols. (Paris: Berger-Levrault, 1889–1894). A translation of the entry on local finance was published by a Japanese commercial press shortly before the Ministry of Finance issued its own translation of the budget section in 1890. See Kaida, *Seiō zaiseigaku to Meiji zaisei*, 35.

38. Kaida, *Seiō zaiseigaku to Meiji zaisei*, 3; Tamotsu Nishizawa, "The Emergence of the Economic Science in Japan and the Evolution of Textbooks, 1860s–1930s," in *The Economic Reader: Textbooks, Manuals and the Dissemination of the Economic Sciences during the Nineteenth and Early Twentieth Centuries*, ed. Massimo M. Augello and Marco E. L. Guidi (London: Routledge, 2012), 306; Yasunori Fukagai, "Political Languages of Land and Taxation: European and American Influences on Japan, 1880s to 1920s," in *The Political Economy of Transnational Tax Reform: The Shoup Mission to Japan in Historical Context*, ed. W. Elliot Brownlee, Eisaku Ide, and Yasunori Fukagai (Cambridge: Cambridge University Press, 2013), 146.

39. Kaida, *Seiō zaiseigaku to Meiji zaisei*, 3–4; Hiroshi Mizuta, "Historical Introduction," in *Enlightenment and Beyond: Political Economy Comes to Japan*, ed. Chūhei Sugiyama and Hiroshi Mizuta (Tokyo: University of Tokyo Press, 1988), 12; Shirō Sugihara, "Economists in Government: Ōkubo Toshimichi, the 'Bismarck of Japan,' and His Times," in *Enlightenment and Beyond*, 212–13. See also *Enlightenment and Beyond*, appendix 2, 293–300, which provides a list of Western economics books translated into Japanese during the period 1867–1912.

40. Umetani Noboru, *Oyatoi gaikokujin: gaisetsu* (Kajima Kenkyūjo Shuppankai, 1968), 69, 71. Among these experts was the Scotsman Alexander Allan Shand (1844–1930), who began teaching courses on public finance for the ministry in 1874 using *Principles of Political Economy* (1848) by John Stuart Mill (1806–1873) and his own work on bank bookkeeping. Tamaki, *Japanese Banking*, 34.

41. Matsukata Masayoshi, "Kaikanzei kaisei gi," December 3, 1874, in "Matsukata Haku zaisei ronsakushū," 190.

42. For details on the two "liberation loans" that France successfully floated in 1871 and 1872—the second of which, at nearly ₣3.5 billion, was "the biggest loan transaction of the nineteenth century"—see Rachel Chrastil, *Organizing for War: France, 1870–1914* (Baton Rouge: Louisiana State University Press, 2010), 61–68.

43. L. C. A. Knowles, *Economic Development in the Nineteenth Century: France, Germany, Russia and the United States* (London: Routledge, 1932), 251. The average net tariff revenue of France as a percentage of net import values rose from 3.8 in 1866–1870 to 5.3 in 1871–1875, continuing to climb over the next two decades. John Vincent Nye, "The Myth of Free-Trade Britain and Fortress France: Tariffs and Trade in the Nineteenth Century," *Journal of Economic History* 51 (March 1991): 26.

44. Matsukata Masayoshi, "Tsūka ryūshutsu o bōshi suru no kengi," September 1875, in "Matsukata Haku zaisei ronsakushū," 30–41.

45. Matsukata, "Tsūka ryūshutsu o bōshi suru no kengi," 36, 38.

46. Unno Fukujū, "Matsukata zaisei to jinushi sei no keisei," in *Iwanami kōza Nihon rekishi*, 26 vols. (Iwanami Shoten, 1975–1977), vol. 15 (1976), 101.

47. Unno, "Matsukata zaisei to jinushi."

48. Matsukata Masayoshi, "Kaikanzei kaisei gi," docs. 1–3, April–December 1874, and "Kaikanzei ken kaifuku no setsu," January 1875, in "Matsukata Haku zaisei ronsakushū," 179–183, 184–87, 190–92, 194; Hyōdō Tōru, "Matsukata Masayoshi no tai-Ō ki ni okeru keika to bunseki: Tani Kin'ichirō 'Meiji jūichi nen tai-Ō nikki' o chūshin to shite," *Tōyō kenkyū*, no. 73 (January 1985): 111–13, 119.

49. Reischauer, *Samurai and Silk*, 84.

50. Wakayama Norikazu, *Hogozei setsu* (Ōkura Shō, 1872); see also Kaida, *Seiō zaisei-gaku to Meiji zaisei*, 31.

51. C. H. Levermore, "Henry Carey and His Social System," *Political Science Quarterly* 5, no. 4 (1890): 559.

52. Sydney Crawcour, "*Kōgyō iken*: Maeda Masana and His View of Meiji Economic Development," *Journal of Japanese Studies* 23, no. 1 (Winter 1997): 104.

53. Rosovsky, "Japan's Transition," 133.

54. Joseph A. Schumpeter, *History of Economic Analysis* (Oxford: Oxford University Press, 1954), 841; also cited in Rosovsky, "Japan's Transition," 133.

55. Sagers, *Origins of Japanese Wealth and Power*, 120; Reischauer, *Samurai and Silk*, 38.

56. "Say, (Jean Baptiste) Léon," in *Encyclopedia Britannica*, 11th ed. (1910–1911).

57. Georges Michel, *Léon Say: sa vie, ses oeuvres* (Paris: Calmann Lévy, 1899), 316.

58. See Marc Flandreau's seminal article on this subject, "The French Crime of 1873."

59. For more on the international monetary conference of 1878 and the Latin Monetary Union, see, for instance, "Paris Monetary Conference," in *Cyclopaedia of Political Science, Political Economy, and the Political History of the United States*, ed. John J. Lalor, 3 vols. (New York: Maynard, Merrill, 1899), vol. 3, 59–63; Henry Parker Willis, *A History of the Latin Monetary Union: A Study of International Monetary Action* (Chicago: University of Chicago Press, 1901); Steven P. Reti, *Silver and Gold: The Political Economy of International Monetary Conferences, 1867–1892* (Westport, CT: Greenwood Press, 1998); Ted Wilson, *Battles for the Standard: Bimetallism and the Spread of the Gold Standard in the Nineteenth Century* (Aldershot, UK: Ashgate, 2000); and Luca Einaudi, *Money and Politics: European Monetary Unification and the International Gold Standard, 1865–1873* (Oxford: Oxford University Press, 2001).

60. Matsukata, "Matsukata Masayoshi kikigaki *nōto*," in *Matsukata Masayoshi kankei monjo*, vol. 10, 133.

61. Rosovsky, "Japan's Transition," 133–34.

62. Jean Garrigues, "Léon Say: un libéral sous la Troisième République (1871–1896)," *Revue historique* 286, no. 1 (July/September 1991): 128.

63. Quoted in Garrigues, "Léon Say," 128.

64. Einaudi, *Money and Politics*, 117.

65. "Paris Monetary Conference," 61.

66. Willis, *History of the Latin Monetary Union*, 179. See also Einaudi, *Money and Politics*, 115.

67. Reti, *Silver and Gold*, 83. See also Einaudi, *Money and Politics*, 136. Both the silver holdings and the arbitrage revenues were products of the "parachute" role France had long played as Europe's bimetallic clearinghouse, which afforded "soft landings" for gold and silver and stabilized the exchange rate between the two metals until the rapid depreciation of silver after 1873. Wilson, *Battles for the Standard*, 53, 127–28, 156.

68. Wilson, *Battles for the Standard*, 148.

69. Matsukata, "Matsukata Masayoshi kikigaki *nōto*," in *Matsukata Masayoshi kankei monjo*, vol. 10, 132. *Harukoganebana* (literally, "spring gold flowers") are bright yellow flowers of the Japanese cornel that bloom in early spring. My thanks to Fabian Drixler for suggesting that Matsukata used a specific floral pun here.

70. Rosovsky, "Japan's Transition," 133–34.

71. "Kōshaku Matsukata Masayoshi Kyō jikki," in *Matsukata Masayoshi kankei monjo*, vol. 2, 269–70.

72. *Kōshaku Matsukata Masayoshi den*, vol. 1, 701.

73. Hyōdō, "Matsukata Masayoshi no tai-Ō ki," 102–4, 114–15. Accompanying Matsukata on his trip to Belgium was a subordinate official, Tani Kin'ichirō (1848–1914), who

kept an intermittent travel diary, the sole extant primary source in Japanese on Matsukata's European tour and the subject of the cited article by Hyōdō. A third member of the party was a translator, Alexander von Siebold (1846–1911), elder son of the famous German physician at the Dutch trading post in Nagasaki in the 1820s, Philipp Franz von Siebold (1796–1866), a pioneer of Japanese studies in Europe. When Philipp returned to Nagasaki in 1859 following the opening of the treaty ports, he brought his teenage son with him. Alexander quickly became fluent in Japanese; and, although his father left Japan for good in 1862, he stayed on as official interpreter for the British legation in Edo and, after the Restoration, began working for the Japanese government, eventually becoming an official interpreter for the Ministry of Finance in 1875. Alexander would serve in the Meiji regime for forty years.

The literature on the elder Siebold is extensive, but apparently no one has yet made use of the Siebold Archive at Ruhr University Bochum and other collections to write about Alexander (see, for instance, Vera Schmidt, ed., *Korrespondenz Alexander von Siebolds: in den Archiven des Japanischen Aussenministeriums und der Tōkyō-Universität, 1859–1895* [Wiesbaden: Harrassowitz, 2000]). Tokyo had ordered Alexander to help the Japanese legation in Berlin with commercial negotiations as well as to interpret for the Paris world's fair delegation; his younger brother, Heinrich, a translator for the Austro-Hungarian legation in Tokyo, likewise did work for the Finance Ministry, according to Tani. Hyōdō "Matsukata Masayoshi no tai-Ō ki," 108, note 4. Besides serving at various Japanese legations in Europe, Alexander also assisted the Foreign Ministry in negotiations to revise the unequal treaties from the abortive attempts in the 1870s and 1880s to the successful conclusion of the 1894 Anglo-Japanese treaty in which Britain agreed to end extraterritoriality in 1899. Charles Lowe, introduction to *Japan's Accession to the Comity of Nations*, by Alexander von Siebold, trans. Charles Lowe (London: Kegan Paul, Trench, Trübner, 1901), viii.

74. Matsukata, *Report on the Adoption of the Gold Standard*, 64.

75. See Michael Schiltz, "An 'Ideal Bank of Issue': The Banque Nationale de Belgique as a Model for the Bank of Japan," *Financial History Review* 13, no. 2 (2006): 179–96, for a critique of the similarities and differences between the two central banks

76. Paul Leroy-Beaulieu, *Traité de la science des finances*, 2 vols. (Paris: Guillaumin, 1877).

77. See, for instance, Fujimura, *Matsukata Masayoshi*, 14; Nishino, *Rekidai zōshō den*, 43.

78. Takahashi, "Matsukata Masayoshi," 73. Matsukata continued to follow Leroy-Beaulieu's later writings; his personal papers, for example, include a translation titled "The Swelling of National Budgets Is the Result of the Growth of Nationalism"—an excerpt from an unidentified work by Leroy-Beaulieu published sometime after 1888. "Kakkoku yosan no bōchō wa kokkashugi hattatsu no kekka," doc. 10:6 of Matsukata ke monjo.

79. For an excellent article on Tajiri's career, see Ferber, "Professionalism as Power." See also Komine, "Nihon saisho no zaisei gakusha"; and Morita Yūichi, *Waga kuni zaisei seido no kindaika: zaimu kanryō no kenkyū* (Kasumigaseki Shuppan, 1990). For a bibliography and chronology relating to Tajiri, see Setoguchi Ryūichi, "Nihon ni okeru zaiseigaku no dōnyū, kōchiku to Tajiri Inajirō," *Senshū Daigaku shi kiyō*, no. 4 (March 2012): 78–79, 81.

80. Ferber, "Professionalism as Power," 32.

81. Harris E. Starr, *William Graham Sumner* (New York: Henry Holt, 1925), 186–87.

82. William Graham Sumner, *A History of American Currency* (New York: Henry Holt, 1874), 323.

83. H. A. Scott Trask, "William Graham Sumner: Monetary Theorist," *Quarterly Journal of Austrian Economics* 8 (Summer 2005): 36, 41.

84. Sumner, *A History of American Currency*, 221 (emphasis in the original).

85. Paul Leroy-Beaulieu, *Boriyū Shi zaisei ron: kanzei no bu*, trans. Tajiri Inajirō, ed. Komai Shigetada (orig. pub. 1880; repr. by Senshū Daigaku Daigaku Shi Shiryōshitsu, 2000), first page of unpaginated preface. Sharif Gernie states that "Leroy-Beaulieu's works marked no great turning-point in economic theory" but "were remarkably successful in presenting the doctrines of laissez-faire capitalism in an accessible form." Sharif Gernie, "Politics, Morality and the Bourgeoisie: The Work of Paul Leroy-Beaulieu (1843–1916)," *Journal of Contemporary History* 27 (April 1992): 345.

86. Marc Flandreau, "Crises and Punishment: Moral Hazard and the Pre-1914 International Financial Architecture," in *Money Doctors: The Experience of International Financial Advising, 1850–2000*, ed. Marc Flandreau (London: Routledge, 2003), 16–17.

87. Paul Leroy-Beaulieu, *Saikei yosan ron*, trans. Komai Shigetada, ed. Tajiri Inajirō (orig. pub. 1883; repr. by Senshū Daigaku Daigaku Shi Shiryōshitsu, 2000), 1. Similar thinking was expressed in *Rizai jiten: yosan no bu*, 2 vols. (Ōkura Shō Shukei Kyoku, 1890)—a translation of articles on budgetary matters from the first volume of *Dictionnaire des finances*, edited by Léon Say; Matsukata ordered the Budget Bureau of the Ministry of Finance to produce the translation, which was made available as a reference for government officials. As a passage from that translation intoned, "The sole principle in forming a budget is to balance revenue and expenditure" (*yosan henseijō yuitsu no gensoku wa shūshi o heikin suru ni ari*). *Rizai jiten: yosan no bu*, vol. 2, 1037.

88. Komai's nearly five-hundred-page translation of the budget section of *Traité*, which Tajiri edited (*Saikei yosan ron*), served as a reference for Inoue Kowashi (1844–1895) while he was drafting parts of the Meiji constitution; it did the same for the Tajiri protégé and future finance minister Sakatani Yoshirō (1863–1941), who oversaw the drafting of an accounting law that became the basis for the "Finance" chapter of the constitution. Uchiyama Hiroshi, *Furansu zaiseigaku no dōnyū to Senshū Gakkō no hitobito: Tajiri Inajirō to Komai Shigetada no seitan 150 nen ni atatte* (Senshū Daigaku Shi Shiryō Kenkyūkai, 2006), 4 and 11, note 3.

Komai reputedly studied at Rutgers College in the middle to late 1870s, but somewhat to the embarrassment of Senshū University, which he and Tajiri and two other returnees from the United States founded in 1880 as Senshū School, as well as of Hitotsubashi University, the predecessor of which Komai would later serve as president, archivists at Rutgers University have found no record of his enrollment, and representatives of the Japanese institutions assume that he simply returned to Japan before graduating; in fact, Komai most likely matriculated at Rutgers Grammar School, the college's preparatory academy.

See Ishizuki Minoru, *Kindai Nihon no kaigai ryūgaku shi* (Kyoto: Minerva Shobō, 1972), 156–58, for an explanation of the marked preference for the United States among Japanese students sent abroad in the early Meiji period (209 of 575 students from 1868 to 1874); many joined Komai in going to New Brunswick, New Jersey, thanks to encouragement from the Japanese government adviser Guido Verbeck and other missionaries of the Dutch Reformed Church, which had founded Rutgers, as well as alumni and instructors of that institution such as the "foreign employees" (*oyatoi*) William Elliot Griffis and David Murray.

89. Tajiri Inajirō, "Hijō junbikin," August 1882, doc. 30:4 of Matsukata-ke monjo; *Hokurai Tajiri sensei denki*, ed. Tsuruoka Isaku, 2 vols. (Tajiri Sensei Denki oyobi Ikō Hensankai, 1933), vol. 2, 730–31. The transmission of Western ideas by Matsukata's eventual subordinates who had traveled or studied abroad and who undertook the details of his policies after 1881 stands in need of further study. Besides Tajiri and Katō Wataru, these finance bureaucrats included Yoshihara Shigetoshi (1845–1887) and Tomita Tetsunosuke (1835–1916), who helped Matsukata draft the founding documents for the Bank of Japan and later became its first two governors. Matsukata's personal papers, Matsukata-ke monjo (held at the Ministry of Finance Policy Research Institute and available on microfilm in

the National Diet Library's Modern Japanese Political History Materials Room), contain numerous proposals and reports from these and other subordinates documenting their contributions to key policies that were carried out under Matsukata; the above-cited 1882 memorandum submitted by Tajiri is just one example.

90. Setoguchi, "Nihon ni okeru zaiseigaku no dōnyū," 63, 69.

91. Helen Herron Taft, *Recollections of Full Years* (New York: Dodd, Mead, 1914), 63.

92. *Meiji Tennō ki*, vol. 5, 75.

93. *Nihon gaikō nenpyō narabi ni shuyō bunsho, 1840–1945*, ed. Gaimu Shō, 2 vols. (Nihon Kokusai Rengō Kyōkai, 1955), vol. 1, 76.

94. "Memo of Conversation between His Majesty and Genl. Grant," in *Guranto shōgun to no gotaiwa hikki* (Kokumin Seishin Bunka Kenkyūjo, 1937), 18–19.

95. J. T. Headley, *The Travels of General Grant* (Philadelphia: New World Publishing, 1881), 514.

96. Donald Keene, *Emperor of Japan: Meiji and His World, 1852–1912* (New York: Columbia University Press, 2002), 332–33.

97. Richard T. Chang, "General Grant's 1879 Visit to Japan," *Monumenta Nipponica* 24, no. 4 (1969): 385.

98. *Kōshaku Matsukata Masayoshi den*, vol. 1, 536.

99. *Kōshaku Matsukata Masayoshi den*, vol. 1, 710.

100. Matsukata, "Kaikanzei kaisei gi."

101. Quoted in Flandreau, "Crises and Punishment," 43, note 21. For the original, see Leroy-Beaulieu, *Traité de la science des finances*, vol. 2, 580.

102. Kamiyama, *Meiji keizai seisaku shi no kenkyū*, 22.

103. "The Sale of Bonds in Exchange for Kinsatsu to English Capitalists," *Japan Weekly Mail*, July 19, 1884; Kamiyama, *Meiji keizai seisaku shi no kenkyū*, 21, 28–29.

104. On foreign borrowing by Japan after the First Sino-Japanese War, see Bytheway, *Investing Japan*, and Toshio Suzuki, *Japanese Government Loan Issues on the London Capital Market, 1870–1913* (London: Athlone Press, 1994).

105. See, for example, Kaida, *Seiō zaiseigaku to Meiji zaisei*, 2–16.

106. In lectures he gave from 1881 to 1883, Tajiri used John J. Lalor's English translation of Roscher's work, which was based on the thirteenth German edition and published, as indicated on the book's title page, "with additional chapters furnished by the author, for this first English and American edition, on paper money, international trade, and the protective system; and a preliminary essay on the historical method in political economy." Wilhelm Roscher, *Principles of Political Economy*, trans. John J. Lalor, 2 vols. (New York: Henry Holt, 1878). Meanwhile, Komai used his own translation of part of the Lalor rendition for his lectures at Senshū. Itani Zen'ichi, "Meiji keizaigaku shi no issetsu: wasurerareta keizai gakusha Tajiri Inajirō Hakushi o chūshin to shite," *Ajia Daigaku shi shogaku kiyō: jinbun, shakai, shizen*, no. 13 (May 1965): 14–15; Komine Yasuei, "Komai Shigetada sensei shōden," *Senshū shōgaku ronshū*, no. 20 (February 1976): 31–32.

107. Uchiyama, *Furansu zaiseigaku no dōnyū*, 55–56; Ferber, "Professionalism as Power," 33. For a summary of Roscher's ideas on the state and socioeconomic development, see Jeffrey E. Hanes, *The City as Subject: Seki Hajime and the Reinvention of Modern Osaka* (Berkeley: University of California Press, 2002), 66–68.

108. Kaneko Masaru, "Nihon no saisho no zaisei gakusha, Tajiri Inajirō," in *Nihon no zaiseigaku: sono senkusha no gunzō*, ed. Satō Susumu (Gyōsei, 1986), 25. For Tajiri's comments on banking models, see *Hokurai Tajiri sensei denki*, vol. 1, 390–91. On the Japanese preference for the German elastic limit system, see Toshihiko Yoshino, "The Creation of the Bank of Japan: Its Western Origin and Adaptation," *Developing Economies* 15 (December 1977): 392–97.

109. Schiltz, "An 'Ideal Bank of Issue,'" 190.

110. Army leaders under Yamagata Aritomo (1838–1922) had already switched from the French to the German model in the late 1870s; in the mid-1880s, Yamagata, as home minister, would also follow the German example in reorganizing the police. Roger Hackett, *Yamagata Aritomo in the Rise of Modern Japan, 1838–1922* (Cambridge, MA: Harvard University Press, 1971), 82, 103.

111. Erik Grimmer-Solem, "German Social Science, Meiji Conservatism, and the Peculiarities of Japanese History," *Journal of World History* 16 (June 2005): 192, 215, 218. For a fascinating look at Japan's disenchantment with economic liberalism toward the end of the 1870s, see Pieter S. de Ganon, "Down the Rabbit Hole: A Study in the Political Economy of Modern Japan," *Past and Present*, no. 213 (November 2011): 237–66.

112. Ōbuchi Toshio, *Meiji shoki seiō zaiseigaku no juyō katei: waga kuni zaiseigaku zenshi ni kansuru ichi shiryō* (Yachiyo Shuppan, 1978), 742–43.

113. Chalmers Johnson, *MITI and the Japanese Miracle* (Stanford, CA: Stanford University Press, 1982), 88.

114. Matsukata, *Report on the Adoption of the Gold Standard*, 54.

115. Cited in Garrigues, "Léon Say," 129.

116. Michel, *Léon Say*, 317–24. Léon Say backed the Freycinet Plan in part because it "appeared to him the only way to boost growth without resorting to protectionism." Garrigues, "Léon Say," 130.

117. Dan Warshaw, *Paul Leroy-Beaulieu and Established Liberalism in France* (Dekalb: Northern Illinois University Press, 1991), 33, 55.

118. Translation from James M. Buchanan, *Public Principles of Public Debt: A Defense and Restatement* (Homewood, IL: R. D. Irwin, 1958), 111. In the 1870s Leroy-Beaulieu began championing another form of state action, namely, empire building, which he argued was vital to the economic well-being of France. He would go on to become a leading imperialist ideologue, supporting policies of colonial expansion that French governments would pursue from the early 1880s.

119. For more on the sale of state enterprises under Matsukata, see chapter 4.

120. Kaneko, "Nihon no saisho no zaisei gakusha," 27 (emphasis in the original).

121. Grimmer-Solem, "German Social Science, Meiji Conservatism," 222.

122. Metzler, "The Cosmopolitanism of National Economics," 117.

3. AUSTERITY AND EXPANSION

1. Yamaguchi Kazuo, *Nihon keizai shi* (Chikuma Shobō, 1968), 147; see *Meiji zaisei shi*, vol. 3, 332, 343, 355, 366, and 377 for data on tax revenue.

2. Inada Masahiro, *Nihon kindai shakai seiritsu ki no minshū undō: konmintō kenkyū josetsu* (Chikuma Shobō, 1990), 49–58.

3. Between 1881 and 1884, proceeds from the sake tax averaged 60 percent of revenue from all central-government taxes exclusive of the land tax: Fukaya Tokujirō, *Meiji seifu zaisei kiban no kakuritsu* (Ochanomizu Shobō, 1995), 178.

4. Muroyama, *Matsukata zaisei kenkyū*, 254. When the government changed the start of the accounting year from July to April beginning with fiscal 1886, it suspended the sake tax for the truncated 1885 fiscal year (from July 1885 to March 1886), though it did collect about ¥1 million in brewery and home-brewing license fees during those months. But by that time Matsukata had essentially completed his currency reform.

5. Kamiyama, *Meiji keizai seisaku shi no kenkyū*, 19; Fukaya, *Meiji seifu zaisei kiban no kakuritsu*, 219. The *koku*, as a unit of weight, equals 330 pounds; it was historically defined as the quantity of rice needed to feed one male samurai for a year.

6. For a list of annual changes in domestic taxes during the 1880s, see Unno, "Matsukata zaisei to jinushi sei no keisei," 131.

7. Personal consumption expenditures for Japan as a whole, which had stood at ¥904 million in 1881, bottomed out in 1884 at ¥691 million. Shinohara Miyohei, *Kojin shōhi shishutsu*, vol. 6 of *Chōki keizai tōkei* (Tōyō Keizai Shinpōsha, 1967), table 1, 132–33.

8. Nakamura, *Meiji Taishō ki no keizai*, 188.

9. Fukaya, *Meiji seifu zaisei kiban no kakuritsu*, 218.

10. Fukaya, *Meiji seifu zaisei kiban no kakuritsu*, 184, 192, 199–200.

11. Fukaya, *Meiji seifu zaisei kiban no kakuritsu*, 199–200.

12. Muroyama, *Matsukata zaisei kenkyū*, 253–54.

13. Muroyama, *Matsukata zaisei kenkyū*, 253; Fukaya, *Meiji seifu zaisei kiban no kakuritsu*, 201, 215.

14. Fukaya, *Meiji seifu zaisei kiban no kakuritsu*, 219, 225–26; Muroyama, *Matsukata zaisei kenkyū*, 204 (for budgeted amounts for sake tax income), 254 (for figures on brewery production).

15. Matsukata Masayoshi, "Meiji jūgo nendo yosan no gi ni tsuki ikensho," February 1882, in "Matsukata Haku zaisei ronsakushū," 417–20.

16. Harada, *Nihon no kindaika to keizai seisaku*, 195–96; Kamiyama, *Meiji keizai seisaku shi no kenkyū*, 18–19.

17. "Kōshaku Matsukata Masayoshi Kyō jikki," in *Matsukata Masayoshi kankei monjo*, vol. 2, 240–41, 321.

18. *Meiji zenki zaisei keizai shiryō shūsei*, vol. 1, 642.

19. For the following discussion of bond issues, I rely heavily on Kamiyama, *Meiji keizai seisaku shi no kenkyū*, 14–30, although a generation earlier Fujimura Tōru actually anticipated much of Kamiyama's argument on Matsukata's resort to these instruments. See by Fujimura: *Matsukata Masayoshi*, 70; and *Meiji zaisei kakuritsu katei no kenkyū*, 390–92.

20. "Kōshaku Matsukata Masayoshi Kyō jikki," in *Matsukata Masayoshi kankei monjo*, vol. 2, 161–62.

21. See, for instance, Kamiyama, *Meiji keizai seisaku shi no kenkyū*, 22, 29.

22. Matsukata, "Zaisei kanki gairyaku," 535.

23. Fukaya, *Meiji seifu zaisei kiban no kakuritsu*, 140–44; Harada, *Nihon no kindaika to keizai seisaku*, 223–24; Matsukata, *Report on the Adoption of the Gold Standard*, 40–41; Muroyama, *Matsukata zaisei kenkyū*, 127 (for Sano's discontinuance of industrial financing out of the reserve fund).

24. Fukaya, *Meiji seifu zaisei kiban no kakuritsu*, 140–41.

25. "The New Public Loan-Bonds," *Japan Weekly Mail*, January 5, 1884; "Notes," *Japan Weekly Mail*, June 6, 1885. The paper quoted the *Jiji shinpō* newspaper as observing in late 1884: "The prosperity which was enjoyed by the agricultural, commercial, and industrial classes was simply the result of the over-issue of paper currency, and their present distress may be said to have virtually arisen from the decrease in its amount. The increase or decrease of paper cannot fail to disturb the tranquility of society; in this respect paper is more formidable than dynamite." "The Stagnation in Trade (Translated from the *Jiji Shimpo*)," *Japan Weekly Mail*, December 27, 1884.

26. Takaki, *The History of Japanese Paper Currency*, 33, 39–43; Matsukata Masayoshi, *The History of National Debts in Japan* (Tokyo: Ōkura Shō, 1890), repr. in *Documents and Studies on 19th C. Monetary History*, ed. Georges Depeyrot and Marina Kovalchuk, no. 173 (Wetteren, Belgium: Moneta, 2014), 93–95; Fujimura, *Meiji zaisei kakuritsu katei no kenkyū*, 440. The government placed orders for the first two batches of the new notes with a German company in 1871–1872 before acquiring the plates used and printing subsequent batches in Japan.

27. Matsukata, *The History of National Debts*, 94.

28. Matsukata, *The History of National Debts*, 95.

29. "Notifications of the Council of State," *Japan Weekly Mail*, January 5, 1884.

30. Kamiyama, *Meiji keizai seisaku shi no kenkyū*, 21. The sale of the redemption bonds to domestic buyers would reduce the quantity of paper money through the destruction of the notes the government would receive in payment. The sale of railway bonds, however, would contract the money supply only for a period of time, but it would be a *long* period, as the government would place notes back in circulation in stages to finance the construction of sections of rail line.

31. "The Sale of Bonds"; Kamiyama, *Meiji keizai seisaku shi no kenkyū*, 28–29.

32. Kamiyama, *Meiji keizai seisaku shi no kenkyū*, 29.

33. Matsukata, *The History of National Debts*, 101.

34. Matsukata, *The History of National Debts*, 116–17.

35. *Meiji zaisei shi*, vol. 8, 490, and vol. 9, 27; Kamiyama, *Meiji keizai seisaku shi no kenkyū*, 21, 23–27; Harada, *Nihon no kindaika to keizai seisaku*, 225–26; Matsukata, *Report on the Adoption of the Gold Standard*, 41.

36. On the significance of the reserve fund, I follow Muroyama, *Kindai Nihon keizai no keisei*, 105–11.

37. Matsukata, *Report on the Adoption of the Gold Standard*, 33, 98.

38. In 1875 the government had changed the fiscal year from a calendar year to July-to-June and in 1885 would change it again to April-to-March.

39. Muroyama, *Kindai Nihon keizai no keisei*, 108–9.

40. Matsukata, *Report on the Adoption of the Gold Standard*, 29.

41. Muroyama, *Kindai Nihon keizai no keisei*, 110.

42. Matsukata, *Report on the Adoption of the Gold Standard*, 98.

43. Kamiyama, *Meiji keizai seisaku shi no kenkyū*, 30.

44. Muroyama, *Kindai Nihon keizai no keisei*, 105; Matsukata, *Report on the Adoption of the Gold Standard*, 41.

45. Muroyama, "Matsukata *defurēshon no mekanizumu*," 149–50; Muroyama, *Kindai Nihon keizai no keisei*, 105.

46. Teranishi Jūrō, "Matsukata *defure no makuro* keizaigaku bunseki (kaitei ban)," in *Matsukata zaisei to shokusan kōgyō seisaku*, 170–72.

47. Muroyama, *Matsukata zaisei kenkyū*, 282.

48. Fukaya, *Meiji seifu zaisei kiban no kakuritsu*, 134–37.

49. For more on this bank, see Norio Tamaki, "The Yokohama Specie Bank: A Multinational in the Japanese Interest, 1879–1931," in *Banks as Multinationals*, ed. Geoffrey Jones (London and New York: Routledge, 1990), 191–216; and Kanji Ishii, "Japanese Foreign Trade and the Yokohama Specie Bank, 1880–1913," in *Pacific Banking, 1859–1959: East Meets West*, ed. Olive Checkland, Shizuya Nishimura, and Norio Tamaki (New York: St. Martin's Press, 1994), 1–23. Specifically on the bank's underwriting of exports, see, for example, Imuta Toshimitsu, "Meiji zenki ni okeru bōeki kin'yū seisaku," in *Nihon keizai seisaku shiron*, ed. Andō Yoshio, vol. 1, 66–80 (Tōkyō Daigaku Shuppankai, 1973).

50. Soda Osamu, *Maeda Masana* (Yoshikawa Kōbunkan, 1973), 68.

51. Matsukata Masayoshi, "Meiji sanjū-nen heisei kaikaku shimatsu gaiyō," May 1899, in *Meiji zenki zaisei keizai shiryō shūsei*, vol. 11, pt. 2, 413–14.

52. Matsukata, *Report on the Adoption of the Gold Standard*, 129.

53. The average monthly price of rice peaked in December 1880 while the value of government notes hit bottom in April 1881. Muroyama, *Matsukata zaisei kenkyū*, 120, 123.

54. "On the Exportation of Rice," November 14, 1882, and "On the Exportation of Kombu," February 13, 1883, in Matsukata, *Report on the Adoption of the Gold Standard*, 137–139; on Sano's suggestion of the rice export program, see *Meiji zaisei shi*, vol. 3, 225.

55. Matsukata, *Report on the Adoption of the Gold Standard*, 135.

56. Hyōdō Tōru, "Matsukata no shihei seiri ki ni okeru bōeki seisaku: Ōkura kyū jidai no kengisho o chūshin to shite," *Tōyō kenkyū*, no. 90 (January 1989): 50, 52; *Meiji zaisei shi*, vol. 13, 990–92. See also Unno, "Matsukata zaisei to jinushi sei no keisei," 113.

57. Fukaya, *Meiji seifu zaisei kiban no kakuritsu*, 141–42; Matsukata, *Report on the Adoption of the Gold Standard*, 83.

58. Matsukata, *Report on the Adoption of the Gold Standard*, 70. In March 1899, by which time the total value of national bank notes in circulation had dropped below ¥2 million, the government declared them no longer legal tender; the last national bank note was redeemed in 1904, the last inconvertible government note in 1899. Matsukata, *Report on the Adoption of the Gold Standard*, 106; Harada, *Nihon no kindaika to keizai seisaku*, 234; G. C. Allen, *A Short Economic History of Japan*, 4th ed. (New York: St. Martin's Press, 1981), 53.

59. Fujimura, *Matsukata Masayoshi*, 70.

4. SPENDING IN A TIME OF "RETRENCHMENT"

1. See by Kobayashi Masaaki, the authority on the divestiture program: *Nihon no kōgyōka to kangyō haraisage: seifu to kigyō* (Tōyō Keizai Shinpōsha, 1977) and "Japan's Early Industrialization and the Transfer of Government Enterprises: Government and Business," *Japanese Yearbook on Business History* 2 (1985): 54–80. A partial version of this chapter appeared as Steven J. Ericson, "Smithian Rhetoric, Listian Practice: The Matsukata 'Retrenchment' and Industrial Policy, 1881–1885," *Japan Forum* 30, no. 4 (2018): 498–520.

2. Matsukata, *Report on the Adoption of the Gold Standard*, 54.

3. The Public Works Ministry disposed of its Nagasaki and Hyogo Shipyards in 1887. On the munitions factories and naval shipyards, see, for instance, Satō Shōichirō, *Rikugun kōshō no kenkyū* (Hassakusha, 1999); Miyake Kōji, *Ōsaka Hōhei Kōshō no kenkyū* (Kyoto: Shibunkaku Shuppan, 1993); and available online at the National Diet Library Digital Collections website (http://dl.ndl.go.jp): *Ōsaka Hōhei Kōshō enkakushi* (Osaka: Ōsaka Heihō Kōshō, 1902); *Kaigun gunbi enkaku* (Kaigun Daijin Kanbō, 1921); and *Yokosuka Kaigun Senshō shi* (Yokosuka: Yokosuka Kaigun Kōshō, 1915), vol. 2.

In December 1881 Itō Hirobumi had in fact proposed the sale of state railroads to "supplement funds for redeeming paper notes" but failed to win Council of State approval; after all, railroads were among the government's biggest moneymakers, returning nearly 9 percent on fixed investment between July 1880 and June 1882. The one exception was the Horonai line, which the government sold in 1889 to the newly established Hokkaido Colliery and Railway in a package deal with the coal mine serviced by that line. Steven J. Ericson, *The Sound of the Whistle: Railroads and the State in Meiji Japan* (Cambridge, MA: Council on East Asian Studies, Harvard University, 1996), 113–14.

4. Kozo Yamamura, "Success Illgotten? The Role of Meiji Militarism in Japan's Technological Progress," *Journal of Economic History* 37, no. 1 (March 1977): 114–15.

5. Peter Ennals, *Opening a Window to the West: The Foreign Concession at Kobe, Japan, 1868–1899* (Toronto: University of Toronto Press, 2014), 165–66.

6. See, for example, Ōishi, *Jiyū minken to Ōkuma, Matsukata zaisei*, chap. 5, based on his article "Matsukata zaisei to jiyū minkenka no zaisei ron: Nihon shihonshugi no genshiteki chikuseki katei no rikai no tame no ichi shiron," *Shōgaku ronshū* 30, no. 2 (January 1962): 380–442; and Satō Shōichirō, "'Matsukata zaisei' to gunkaku zaisei no tenkai," *Shōgaku ronshū* 32, no. 3 (December 1963): 43–89.

7. See especially Muroyama, *Kindai Nihon no gunji to zaisei*.

8. Kobayashi, *Nihon no kōgyōka to kangyō haraisage*, 50–62.

9. The Ministry of Agriculture and Commerce subsequently transferred former Kaitakushi enterprises to Hokkaido Prefecture, which sold most of them to private interests in the latter half of the 1880s. Kobayashi, *Nihon no kōgyōka to kangyō haraisage*, 52, 54. When

the Public Works Ministry closed in December 1885, the administration of state railroads moved briefly to the Home Ministry and that of telegraphs and lighthouses to the newly established Ministry of Communications, which in 1892 assumed management of the government railroads as well. In addition, almost immediately after taking over the Sado gold mine and Ikuno silver mine from the Public Works Ministry, the Ministry of Agriculture and Commerce handed them over to the Ministry of Finance; that ministry, in turn, transferred them to the Imperial Household in 1889. The proposed sale of those mines sparked considerable controversy, but the argument that the Bureau of Imperial Lands would have to make huge investments to raise the profitability of the mines, combined with the "inconvenience" of having to compete with expanding private mines for labor, carried the day in 1896. Kobayashi, *Nihon no kōgyōka to kangyō haraisage*, 337–38, 344–45.

10. To be precise, of the final divestments of state enterprises, the Tomioka filature went to Mitsui in 1893 during the tenure of Finance Minister Watanabe Kunitake, who had replaced Matsukata in 1892, but the oligarch reclaimed the Finance Ministry portfolio in 1896 just before the government finalized the transfer of the Sado gold mine and Ikuno silver mine, together with the Osaka refinery connected to them, to Mitsubishi. Kobayashi, *Nihon no kōgyōka to kangyō haraisage*, 299–301, 357–59; *Kadokawa Nihon shi jiten*, 1257.

11. Thomas Smith, in his classic work on state enterprise in early Meiji, misleadingly asserts that, after defeating Ōkuma's 1880 foreign loan proposal, "the opposition brought forward one of its own," recommending, among other steps, the sale of government enterprises. Thomas C. Smith, *Political Change and Industrial Development in Japan: Government Enterprise, 1868–1880* (Stanford, CA: Stanford University Press, 1955), 98. Smith suggested that Inoue Kaoru in particular introduced the idea of selling off state enterprises at the time, but, as noted below, Ōkuma had actually helped make it part of the discourse as early as 1875. Smith also stated inaccurately that, with the announcement of the divestiture program in November 1880, the government disposed of its mines and factories "just as rapidly as private buyers could be found" and "at bargain prices and on easy terms" and that "most of the enterprises sold were losing money." Smith, *Political Change and Industrial Development in Japan*, 86, 100. He somewhat contradicted himself, however, by noting correctly that "most government enterprises were not sold until 1884" when "terms were relaxed" and the enterprises "generally became marketable." Smith, *Political Change and Industrial Development in Japan*, 92.

12. Following Soda Osamu, Richard Smethurst, for instance, writes that, as finance minister, Matsukata advocated a "top-down" approach to economic development emphasizing "heavy, transplant industries that produced the kinds of goods needed by the military." Richard J. Smethurst, *From Foot Soldier to Finance Minister: Takahashi Korekiyo, Japan's Keynes* (Cambridge, MA: Harvard University Asia Center, 2007), 79, 86.

13. *Ōkuma monjo*, vol. 2 (1959), 1–3.

14. Kobayashi, *Nihon no kōgyōka to kangyō haraisage*, 112.

15. *Kōshaku Matsukata Masayoshi den*, vol. 1, 523–24. The government would indeed privatize the Sakai spinning mill in 1878, but it would not sell the Tomioka filature until fifteen years later. The government did try to unload Tomioka in November 1880 but failed to get any bids on the money-losing operation, which potential buyers also considered excessively large in scale; by 1885 the filature was finally turning a profit, and in the early 1890s, when the state reopened private bidding for Tomioka, Mitsui would come through with the only offer above the minimum asking price. Kobayashi, *Nihon no kōgyōka to kangyō haraisage*, 287–301. (See also note 33 below.) Meanwhile, in 1885, the Ministry of Agriculture and Commerce would transfer the Shimofusa sheep farm to the Imperial Household, which would manage the ranch until its removal to a new site with the construction of Narita International Airport. On the disruption of the closing ceremonies at the Narita site by opponents of the airport in 1969, see David E. Apter and Nagayo Sawa, *Against the*

State: Politics and Social Protest in Japan (Cambridge, MA: Harvard University Press, 1984), 90–92.

16. See, for instance, Muroyama, *Kindai Nihon keizai no keisei*, 41, 83.

17. *Ōkuma Shigenobu kankei monjo*, vol. 4, 110.

18. Kobayashi, *Nihon no kōgyōka to kangyō haraisage*, 109.

19. *Ōkuma Shigenobu kankei monjo*, vol. 4, 112–25; Kobayashi, *Nihon no kōgyōka to kangyō haraisage*, 111.

20. Matsukata, "Zaisei kanki gairyaku," 534.

21. Smith, *Political Change and Industrial Development in Japan*, 99, quoting from Inoue's memorandum in *Segai Inoue Kō den*, vol. 3, 162–73.

22. *Ōkuma monjo*, vol. 3, 455–62. Itō initially refused to cooperate with Ōkuma after discovering that he had sold off silver from the Treasury's reserve fund without authorization, but Ōkuma had the emperor "instruct" Itō to work with him. Muroyama, *Matsukata zaisei kenkyū*, 106.

23. *Ōkuma Shigenobu kankei monjo*, vol. 4, 180–83.

24. Fujimura, *Meiji zaisei kakuritsu katei no kenkyū*, 385–90.

25. Kobayashi, *Nihon no kōgyōka to kangyō haraisage*, 106.

26. Ishizuka Hiromichi, *Nihon shihonshugi seiritsu shi kenkyū: Meiji kokka to shokusan kōgyō seisaku* (Yoshikawa Kōbunkan, 1973), 118. For example, from July 1882 to June 1884 (fiscal 1882 and 1883), the government expended in operating costs alone for the Public Works Ministry's Nagasaki and Hyogo Shipyards close to ¥1 million and for the navy's Yokosuka and Onohama yards ¥2.2 million. From tables in Muroyama, *Kindai Nihon no gunji to zaisei*, 142, 155, 158.

Central government transfers to prefectures fell by half from the years 1879–1880 to the years 1881–1884. Teranishi, "Matsukata *defure*," 170.

27. Kobayashi traces the evolution of industrial policy in the 1870s and early 1880s but discusses only briefly the relationship between the divestiture program and the Matsukata financial reform; he does note that the government sold most of its enterprises in the mid-1880s, when Matsukata completed his deflationary program. Kobayashi's main contributions are to delineate the successive phases of the disposal process and to examine in detail the transfer of individual enterprises.

28. Kobayashi, *Nihon no kōgyōka to kangyō haraisage*, 129–58; Kobayashi, "Japan's Early Industrialization and the Transfer of Government Enterprises," 62–75. The disposal of Miike was the blockbuster sale. Mitsui paid ¥4.56 million for this coal mine, outbidding Mitsubishi by a mere ¥2,300; the final price accounted for nearly half the total cost of all the enterprises the state privatized under the sale program. The hugely profitable Miike mine became the treasure chest or *doru bako* (dollar box) of the nascent Mitsui combine, financing much of its growth and diversification in the ensuing decades. Meanwhile, Mitsubishi compensated for its defeat in the Miike bidding by acquiring a number of private coal mines as well as the lucrative Sado and Ikuno mines. William D. Wray, *Mitsubishi and the N.Y.K.: Business Strategy in the Japanese Shipping Industry* (Cambridge, MA: Council on East Asian Studies, Harvard University, 1984), 252 and 581, note 43.

29. Kobayashi, *Nihon no kōgyōka to kangyō haraisage*, 138–39.

30. Muroyama, *Matsukata zaisei kenkyū*, 282.

31. The only exception was Hiroshima cotton-spinning mill, which the Home Ministry sold in June 1882.

32. "Kōbu Shō enkaku hōkoku," in *Meiji zenki zaisei keizai shiryō shūsei*, vol. 17, pt. 1, 471–72.

33. Gary Saxonhouse, "A Tale of Technological Diffusion in the Meiji Period," *Journal of Economic History* 34, no. 1 (1974), 150–51. As I have noted elsewhere, the problem was just the opposite for silk reeling: "the government's celebrated Tomioka filature was too

large and sophisticated to serve as a model for private silk producers, who, even if they mechanized, tended to adopt smaller-scale, simplified versions of Western technology." Mark Jones and Steven Ericson, "Social and Economic Change in Prewar Japan," in *A Companion to Japanese History*, ed. William M. Tsutsui (Malden, MA: Blackwell, 2006), 182.

34. Table 4.2 includes spending on arsenals and shipyards by the army and navy from 1876 on. Ishizuka, *Nihon shihonshugi seiritsu shi kenkyū*, 131. For example, the navy's capital expenditures (*kōgyō hi*) for the Yokosuka Shipyard rose from ¥164,670 for fiscal 1877–1880 to ¥389,091 for fiscal 1881–1884. Kobayashi, *Nihon no kōgyōka to kangyō haraisage*, 119.

35. Ericson, *The Sound of the Whistle*, 175.

36. See, for instance, Yamamura, "Success Illgotten?"; and Steven J. Ericson, "Taming the Iron Horse: Western Locomotive Makers and Technology Transfer in Japan, 1870–1914," in *Public Spheres, Private Lives in Modern Japan, 1600–1950: Essays in Honor of Albert M. Craig*, ed. Gail Lee Bernstein, Andrew Gordon, and Kate Wildman Nakai, 185–217 (Cambridge, MA: Harvard University Asia Center, 2005).

37. Wray, *Mitsubishi and the N.Y.K.*, 305–6.

38. Wray, *Mitsubishi and the N.Y.K.*, 304.

39. Kamiyama, *Meiji keizai seisaku shi no kenkyū*, 26. On public bonds issued through 1889, see Matsukata, *The History of National Debts*.

40. David Anson Titus, *Palace and Politics in Prewar Japan* (New York: Columbia University Press, 1974), 64–74; Wray, *Mitsubishi and the N.Y.K.*, 235–44. For Matsukata's memoranda of November 18, 1884 ("Teishitsu zaisan setsubi no gi"), and March 24, 1887 ("Nihon Yūsen Kaisha no kabuken o Teishitsu zaisan ni hennyū suru no gi"), recommending these transfers of stock to the Imperial Household, see "Matsukata Haku zaisei ronsakushū," 536–37, 545–46.

41. Kobayashi, *Nihon no kōgyōka to kangyō haraisage*, 102; *Meiji zaizei shi*, vol. 8, 877, 888; Matsukata, *The History of National Debts*, 109–12.

42. Ishizuka, *Nihon shihonshugi seiritsu shi kenkyū*, 141, 149.

43. Soda Osamu, "Matsukata zaisei to 'Kōgyō iken,'" in *Kindai nōgaku ronshū*, ed. Kashiwa Suketaka (Yōkendō, 1971), 222.

44. Crawcour, "*Kōgyō iken*," 96–97.

45. Smethurst, *From Foot Soldier to Finance Minister*, 80. On the "Kōgyō iken" debate, see also Ariizumi Sadao, *Meiji seiji shi no kiso katei: chihō seiji jōkyō shiron* (Yoshikawa Kōbunkan, 1980), 167–200; Soda, *Maeda Masana*, 83–121; and Mikuriya Takashi, *Meiji kokka keisei to chihō keiei, 1881–1890* (Tōkyō Daigaku Shuppankai, 1980), 71–76.

46. Senghaas, "Friedrich List," 460.

47. Sagers, *Origins of Japanese Wealth and Power*, 129.

48. Mikuriya, *Meiji kokka keisei to chihō keiei*, 30–37, 73–75.

49. Itami Masahiro, "Meiji chūki ni okeru chihō nōkō ginkō no seiritsu ni kansuru oboegaki," *Kagawa Daigaku keizai ronsō* 37, no. 4 (October 1964): 70–90.

50. Matsukata was no proponent of "balanced development," but he hardly "[left] agriculture to develop by itself" (Metzler, "The Cosmopolitanism of National Economics," 113). Nor was he unlike Maeda in sharing "with Frederick [*sic*] List and the economists of the German historical school a lifelong scorn for abstract economic theories" (Crawcour, "*Kōgyō iken*," 75), as he indicated at the end of his immersion in European economic theory and practice in 1878 when he remarked that scholarship, "no matter how superior" or "how advanced in logic," was "of no use to the state whatsoever" if it didn't "conform to reality." *Kōshaku Matsukata Masayoshi den*, vol. 1, 716–17.

51. Ishii, *Nihon no sangyōka to zaibatsu*, 13–14. The leader of this association, Hoshino Chōtarō, was the elder brother of Arai Ryōichirō, the U.S.-based silk merchant whom Haru Matsukata Reischauer wrote about in *Samurai and Silk*, her dual biography of her

grandfathers, Matsukata Masayoshi and Arai. The loan forgiveness, however, predated the Matsukata-Arai family connection by three decades.

52. Hyōdō, "Matsukata no shihei seiri ki ni okeru bōeki seisaku," 48–49.

53. Ishizuka, *Nihon shihonshugi seiritsu shi kenkyū*, 130–31, 140.

54. Quasi-banks were financial institutions not formally chartered as banks.

55. "Keihan, Kyūshū ryō chihō sangyō shisatsu hōkoku," doc. 58:6 of Matsukata-ke monjo. The preserved document omits the report on the Kansai region.

56. Ishizuka, *Nihon shihonshugi seiritsu shi kenkyū*, 144.

57. Ishizuka, *Nihon shihonshugi seiritsu shi kenkyū*, 145; Kikkawa Hidezō, *Shizoku jusan no kenkyū* (Yūhikaku, 1935), 534–36. On samurai assistance (*shizoku jusan*) efforts by the Meiji government, see also Andō Seiichi, *Shizoku jusan shi no kenkyū* (Osaka: Seibundō, 1988).

58. Ōishi, *Jiyū minken to Ōkuma, Matsukata zaisei*, 339.

59. *Kaigun gunbi enkaku*, 5–6, accessed August 29, 2018, http://dl.ndl.go.jp/info:ndljp/pid/970713.

60. *Koshaku Matsukata Masayoshi den*, vol. 1, 875–79.

61. *Iwakura Kō jikki*, vol. 3, 897–99.

62. *Iwakura Kō jikki*, vol. 3, 908–13.

63. *Kaigun gunbi enkaku*, 6–7.

64. Japan's trade surpluses from 1882 to 1885 averaged over ¥7 million a year. Calculated from tables in Muroyama, *Matsukata zaisei kenkyū*, 275–76.

65. Matsukata Masayoshi, "Gunbi kōchō hi no gi," December 26, 1882, in "Matsukata Haku zaisei ronsakushū," 145.

66. Satō, "'Matsukata zaisei' to gunkaku zaisei no tenkai," 53.

67. Calculated from figures in Muroyama, *Kindai Nihon no gunji to zaisei*, 130, note 5.

68. Matsukata Masayoshi, "Kaku chihō kan Enryōkan ni shūkai no sekijō ni oite," December 1882, in "Matsukata Haku zaisei ronsakushū," 605–8.

69. Muroyama, *Kindai Nihon keizai no keisei*, 127.

70. Matsukata, *Report on the Adoption of the Gold Standard*, 142.

71. *Meiji zaisei shikō* (Tōyō Keizai Shinpōsha, 1911), 161–63; *Kindai Nihon keizai shi yōran*, 4.

72. From table 15 in Muroyama, *Kindai Nihon no gunji to zaisei*, 98.

73. Muroyama, *Kindai Nihon no gunji to zaisei*, 126.

74. From July 1885 to March 1886, after which the government switched to an April-to-March fiscal year.

75. Matsukata Masayoshi, "Kaigun kōsai jōrei seitei no gi," May 3, 1886, in "Matsukata Haku zaisei ronsakushū," 105–6; Kamiyama, *Meiji keizai seisaku shi no kenkyū*, 26.

76. Muroyama, *Kindai Nihon no gunji to zaisei*, 135–37. Average annual outlays calculated from table 29 in Muroyama, *Kindai Nihon no gunji to zaisei*, 137.

5. FOUNDING A CENTRAL BANK

1. See Andrew Cobbing, *The Satsuma Students in Britain: Japan's Early Search for the "Essence of the West"* (Richmond, Surrey, UK: Japan Library, 2000).

2. Tamaki, *Japanese Banking*, 29–30; *Meiji zaisei shi*, vol. 13, 18.

3. *Nihon Ginkō hyaku-nen shi*, ed. Nihon Ginkō Hyaku-nen Shi Hensan Iinkai, 7 vols. (Nihon Ginkō, 1982–1986), vol. 1 (1982), 17–18, 32 (hereafter *NGHS*). I have converted the cited lunar calendar dates.

4. *NGHS*, vol. 1, 19.

5. Yoshino Toshihiko, *Nihon Ginkō seido kaikaku shi* (Tōkyō Daigaku Shuppankai, 1962), 56.

6. *NGHS*, vol. 1, 19–20, 33.

7. Yoshino, *Nihon Ginkō seido*, 57. For more on Shand's career, see Olive Checkland and Norio Tamaki, "Alexander Allan Shand, 1844–1930—A Banker the Japanese Could Trust," in *Britain and Japan: Biographical Portraits*, ed. Ian Nish, vol. 2, 65–78 (Folkestone, UK: Japan Library, 1997).

8. Ishii Kanji, "Nihon Ginkō seido," in *Nihon Ginkō kin'yū seisaku shi*, ed. Ishii Kanji (Tōkyō Daigaku Shuppankai, 2001), 17. On Tokuno's principal claim to fame—modernizing the printing of Japanese paper money—see, for instance, Nagashima Takeshi, "Tokuno Ryōsuke to Meiji shoki no insatsu jigyō: tokuni shihei seizō ni tsuite," *Shakai kagaku tōkyū* 14, no. 3 (March 1969): 49–66.

9. *NGHS*, vol. 1, 47–49.

10. *NGHS*, vol. 1, 49–50.

11. Ishii, "Nihon Ginkō seido," 18. See also Yoshino, *Nihon Ginkō seido*, 59–60, and *NGHS*, vol. 1, 85–88.

12. *NGHS*, vol. 1, 119; *Ōkura Shō jinmei roku: Meiji, Taishō, Shōwa*, ed. Ōkura Shō Hyaku-nen Shi Henshū Shitsu (Ōkura Zaimu Kyōkai, 1973), 72, 118–19, 194.

13. Matsukata, *Report on the Adoption of the Gold Standard*, 45.

14. Data available for 1897, when the Fifteenth National converted to an ordinary commercial bank, show that ex-daimyo held shares in other national banks such as the 20th, the 30th, the 89th, and the 147th. Sawai Minoru, "Shiryō: Meiji ki no ōkabunushi—*Ginkō kaisha yōroku* no shūkei," *Ōsaka Daigaku keizaigaku* 52, no. 4 (March 2003): 260.

15. Matsukata, *Report on the Adoption of the Gold Standard*, 45.

16. Mark Metzler, *Capital as Will and Imagination: Schumpeter's Guide to the Postwar Japanese Miracle* (Ithaca, NY: Cornell University Press, 2013), and email message to author, February 8, 2017.

17. Matsukata, *Report on the Adoption of the Gold Standard*, 64.

18. Matsukata, *Report on the Adoption of the Gold Standard*, 64.

19. National Bank of Serbia, "Tradition of Central Banking," accessed August 11, 2017, http://www.nbs.rs/internet/english/10/10_8/index.html.

20. Yoshino, *Nihon Ginkō seido*, 86; Yoshino, "The Creation of the Bank of Japan," 387.

21. Yoshino claims that Matsukata's March 1882 memorandum shows that he and his subordinates extensively investigated not only the central banks of Britain, France, and Belgium but also those of Germany, Austria, Hungary, Italy, and the Netherlands. Yoshino, *Nihon ginkō seido*, 116; Yoshino, "The Creation of the Bank of Japan," 389. Yet the memo offers details solely on the British, French, and Belgian national banks and mistakenly states that the Bank of Amsterdam, at the time of its establishment, "closely" followed the "pattern" of Belgium's central bank. Matsukata, *Report on the Adoption of the Gold Standard*, 47, 64. In fact, the Bank of Amsterdam had existed from 1609 to 1819 and given way as the country's central bank to the Nederlandsche Bank, founded in 1814.

22. Yoshino, *Nihon Ginkō seido*, 116; Yoshino, "The Creation of the Bank of Japan," 389; *NGHS*, vol. 1, 175–76.

23. Charles A. Conant, *The National Bank of Belgium* (Washington, DC: Government Printing Office, 1910), 14–16.

The NBB initially went by the name "Banque Nationale" to distinguish it from Banque de Belgique; not until the government renewed the bank's right of note issue in 1900 did it take the name Banque Nationale de Belgique to clarify its status in dealings with other countries. Erik Buyst et al., *The Bank, the Franc and the Euro: A History of the National Bank of Belgium* (Tielt, Belgium: Lannoo, 2005), 40.

24. Schiltz, "An 'Ideal Bank of Issue,'" 190.

25. Conant, *The National Bank of Belgium*, 15; Buyst et al., *The Bank, the Franc and the Euro*, 37.

26. Yoshino, *Nihon Ginkō seido*, 116; Buyst et al., *The Bank, the Franc and the Euro*, 43, for the quote.

27. Yoshino, *Nihon Ginkō seido*, 116.

28. Tamaki, *Japanese Banking*, 62. For a line-by-line comparison of the two sets of regulations, see *NGHS*, vol. 1, 177–182; also, Yoshino, *Nihon Ginkō seido*, 87–92.

29. *NGHS*, vol. 1, 188–207, and Yoshino, *Nihon Ginkō seido*, 93–114, give side-by-side comparisons of the two banks' articles of incorporation.

30. Yoshino, "The Creation of the Bank of Japan," 388.

31. Yoshino, "The Creation of the Bank of Japan," 389; Charles Goodhart, *The Evolution of Central Banks* (Cambridge, MA: MIT Press, 1988), 155; Schiltz, "An 'Ideal Bank of Issue,'" 194; *NGHS*, vol. 1, 185.

As one indicator of the strong authority over the central bank the Meiji regime inherited from the Belgian government—actually suggesting the enlargement of that authority in the Japanese case—the authors of the BoJ's centennial history counted the number of times the words "approval," "authorization," "assent," and "directive" on the part of the state or finance minister appear in the two banks' charters: twelve in the Belgian case, nineteen in the Japanese one. *NGHS*, vol. 1, 187–88.

32. P. Kauch, *La Banque nationale de Belgique, 1850–1918* (Brussels: La Banque nationale de Belgique, 1950), 50. Author's translation.

33. *NGHS*, vol. 1, 175.

34. Buyst et al., *The Bank, the Franc and the Euro*, 37; Conant, *The National Bank of Belgium*, 180.

35. Goodhart, *The Evolution of Central Banks*, 155.

36. *NGHS*, vol. 1, 138, 182; Matsukata Masayoshi, "Nihon Ginkō sōritsu no gi," March 1, 1882, in "Matsukata Haku zaisei ronsakushū," 355; Goodhart, *The Evolution of Central Banks*, 182, note 16, for the suggestion regarding profit-making and the Imperial Household. On a similar note, Kobayashi Masaaki writes that, when the Ministry of Finance transferred the Sado gold mine and Ikuno silver mine to the Imperial Household in 1889, the emphasis shifted from supplying material for coinage to generating high profits for the imperial estate. Kobayashi, *Nihon no kōgyōka to kangyō haraisage*, 338.

37. Hugh T. Patrick, "External Equilibrium and Internal Convertibility: Financial Policy in Meiji Japan," *Journal of Economic History* 25, no. 2 (June 1965): 210.

38. *NGHS*, vol. 1, 184.

39. Yoshino, *Nihon Ginkō seido*, 52.

40. Yoshino, "The Creation of the Bank of Japan," 390.

41. Yagi Yoshikazu, "'Meiji 14-nen seihen' to Nihon Ginkō: Kyōdō Un'yu Kaisha kashidashi o megutte," *Shakai Keizai Shigaku* 53, no. 5 (December 1987): 636–60. For details on the crisis, see the classic articles by Joyce Lebra, "Ōkuma Shigenobu and the 1881 Political Crisis," *Journal of Asian Studies* 18, no. 4 (August 1959): 475–87, and Andrew Fraser, "The Expulsion of Ōkuma from the Government in 1881," *Journal of Asian Studies* 26, no. 2 (February 1967): 213–36.

42. Fraser, "The Expulsion of Ōkuma," 234.

43. *NGHS*, vol. 1, 232–33.

44. For details on the founding of the KUK and its subsequent merger with Mitsubishi's shipping company, see Wray, *Mitsubishi and the N.Y.K.*, 129–225.

45. Yagi, "'Meiji 14-nen seihen' to Nihon Ginkō," 645–48.

46. *NGHS*, vol. 1, 333–34.

47. Yagi, "'Meiji 14-nen seihen' to Nihon Ginkō," 651–52.

48. Yagi, "'Meiji 14-nen seihen' to Nihon Ginkō," 652.

49. *Kōshaku Matsukata Masayoshi den*, vol. 1, 780.

50. Yagi, "'Meiji 14-nen seihen' to Nihon Ginkō," 642; *NGHS*, vol. 1, 101, on the similarities between the two memoranda.

51. Yagi, "'Meiji 14-nen seihen' to Nihon Ginkō," 641; *NGHS*, vol. 1, 105.

52. Yagi, "'Meiji 14-nen seihen' to Nihon Ginkō," 642.

53. *NGHS*, vol. 1, 224–26.

54. Yagi, "'Meiji 14-nen seihen' to Nihon Ginkō," 643.

55. *NGHS*, vol. 1, 234–35.

56. Wray, *Mitsubishi and the NYK*, 26.

57. Wray, *Mitsubishi and the NYK*, 193–98, 206–7.

58. Yagi, "'Meiji 14-nen seihen' to Nihon Ginkō," 657.

59. From Article 12 of the Bank of Japan Regulations, *NGHS*, vol. 1, 179.

60. Yagi, "'Meiji 14-nen seihen' to Nihon Ginkō," 657–58. On the BoJ's stock collateral lending, which it expanded to include ten additional railway companies at the time of the Panic of 1890, see Ericson, *The Sound of the Whistle*, 176–82.

61. Yagi, "'Meiji 14-nen seihen' to Nihon Ginkō," 642.

62. Yagi, "'Meiji 14-nen seihen' to Nihon Ginkō," 638.

63. Matsukata, *Report on the Adoption of the Gold Standard*, 60.

64. *NGHS*, vol. 1, 3; Yoshino, *Nihon Ginkō seido*, 52.

65. Matsukata, *Report on the Adoption of the Gold Standard*, 61.

66. Matsukata, *Report on the Adoption of the Gold Standard*, 47, 57.

67. Wray, *Mitsubishi and the N.Y.K.*, 151–59; the quote is from p. 156.

68. Matsukata, *Report on the Adoption of the Gold Standard*, 67.

69. Matsukata, *Report on the Adoption of the Gold Standard*, 82.

70. Ishii, "Nihon Ginkō seido," 24–25.

71. Matsukata, *Report on the Adoption of the Gold Standard*, 58.

72. Schiltz, "An 'Ideal Bank of Issue,'" 194. On the YSB, see *Yokohama Shōkin Ginkō shi*, 5 vols. (Yokohama Shōkin Ginkō, 1920).

73. Tamaki, *Yukichi Fukuzawa*, 108–19.

74. Raymond W. Goldsmith, *The Financial Development of Japan, 1868–1977* (New Haven, CT: Yale University Press, 1983), 50.

75. Furusawa Kōzō, "Yokohama Shōkin Ginkō jōrei no seitei to kawase seisaku," in *Meiji ki Nihon tokushu kin'yū rippō shi*, ed. Shibuya Ryūichi (Waseda Daigaku Shuppanbu, 1977), 89–90, 96–97.

76. Ishii, "Japan," 93.

77. Tamaki, *Japanese Banking*, 47; Imuta, "Meiji zenki ni okeru bōeki kin'yū seisaku," 67.

78. *NGHS*, vol. 1, 113.

79. Shinya Sugiyama, *Japan's Industrialization in the World Economy, 1859–1899* (London: Athlone Press, 1988), 120–21.

80. *NGHS*, vol. 1, 393.

81. Muroyama, *Matsukata zaisei kenkyū*, 275–76.

82. Kamiyama, *Meiji keizai seisaku shi no kenkyū*, 28–29.

83. Charles White Merrill, *Summarized Data of Silver Production* (Washington, DC: United States Printing Office, 1930), 4; Matsukata, *Report on the Adoption of the Gold Standard*, 147–51.

84. Takahashi Makoto, *Meiji zaisei shi kenkyū* (Aoki Shoten, 1964), 87; Matsukata Masayoshi, "Shihei seiri shimatsu," 67.

85. *NGHS: shiryō hen* (vol. 7, 1986), 332, 414.

86. Beginning in 1883, the Meiji government did authorize a score of "special export ports"—outside the treaty port system—from which it barred Western merchants. From these ports scattered across Japan, local merchants exported coal, rice, and other goods mainly to silver-standard Asian countries, though they had to rely primarily on Western shipping. Catherine L. Phipps, *Empires on the Waterfront: Japan's Ports and Power, 1858–1899* (Cambridge, MA: Harvard University Asia Center, 2015).

87. "Matsukata Masayoshi kankei monjo," in *Nihon kin'yū shi shiryō, Meiji Taishō hen*, ed. Nihon Ginkō Chōsa Kyoku, vol. 4. (Tokyo: Ōkura Shō Insatsu Kyoku, 1958), 1045–47.

88. Herbert M. Bratter, *Silver Market Dictionary* (New York: Commodity Exchange, 1933), 114.

89. Yamamoto Yūzō, *Ryō kara en e: Bakumatsu, Meiji zenki kahei mondai kenkyū* (Minerva Shobō, 1994), 225.

90. Matsukata, *Report on the Adoption of the Gold Standard*, 105, 374–75; *Dai Nihon gaikoku bōeki nenpyō* (*Annual Return of the Foreign Trade of the Empire of Japan*), 1895 (Ōkura Shō, 1896), 5, National Diet Library Digital Collections, Tokyo, Japan, accessed July 8, 2018, http://dl.ndl.go.jp/info:ndljp/pid/804305.

91. Kris James Mitchener, Masato Shizume, and Marc D. Weidenmier, "Why Did Countries Adopt the Gold Standard? Lessons from Japan," *Journal of Economic History* 70, no 1 (March 2010): 49–50.

92. Matsukata, *Report on the Adoption of the Gold Standard*, 105. Fiscal 1894 (April 1894 to March 1895) coincided with the Sino-Japanese War.

93. Metzler, *Lever of Empire*, 27–28.

94. Garrett Droppers, "Monetary Changes in Japan," *Quarterly Journal of Economics* 12, no. 2 (1898): 167. Similarly, Simon Bytheway writes: "Japan's de facto silver standard, in effect, served as a protective tariff . . . and encouraged exports." Bytheway, *Investing Japan*, 38.

By contrast, for gold-bloc importing nations, as U.S. Representative Francis Newlands (1846–1917) of Nevada, a white supremacist and member of the Silver Party, exclaimed in 1896, protective tariffs had done little to stop "the invasion of manufactured products from Oriental countries, particularly Japan." Newlands went on to assert that "the fall in exchange between silver and gold" had "resulted in doubling the efficiency of the cheap labor of silver standard countries in its competition with the labor of gold standard countries. . . . No tariff wall can be made sufficiently high to keep out the products of silver standard countries which, measured in gold, cost only one-half of what they used to." "Competition of Japanese Labor," *San Francisco Chronicle*, February 19, 1896.

95. Matsukata, "Shihei seiri shimatsu," 68.

96. Okada Shunpei, "Meiji ki no keizai hatten to gin hon'i sei," *Seikei Daigaku keizai kenkyū* 30 (December 1969): 35.

97. Matsukata, "Shihei seiri shimatsu," 67–68.

98. Harada, *Nihon no kindaika to keizai seisaku*, 229; *NGHS: shiryō hen*, 332.

99. Harada, *Nihon no kindaika to keizai seisaku*, 146–47.

100. *NGHS*, vol. 1, 281.

101. Buyst et al., *The Bank, the Franc and the Euro*, 39.

102. Matsukata, *Report on the Adoption of the Gold Standard*, 71.

103. *NGHS*, vol. 1, 287.

104. *NGHS*, vol. 1, 288.

105. *NGHS*, vol. 1, 288.

106. Harada, *Nihon no kindaika to keizai seisaku*, 146–47, for the paper-silver yen ratio; *NGHS: shiryō hen*, 414, for government, national bank, and BoJ notes in circulation.

107. *NGHS*, vol. 1, 290–91.

108. *Meiji zaisei shi*, vol. 13, 236.

109. *NGHS*, vol. 1, 305, *shiryō hen*, 414–16; Allen, *A Short Economic History of Japan*, 53. Tamaki notes that, of the 153 national banks, 122 reorganized as ordinary banks, 16 merged with other banks, 9 voluntarily liquidated, and 6 closed by order of the government. Tamaki, *Japanese Banking*, 75.

110. Tajiri Inajirō, "Shihei hakkō hōhō," August 1882, doc. 46:5 of Matsukata-ke monjo.

111. Komine, "Nihon saisho no zaisei gakusha," 101–02. The full text of Tajiri's opinion paper is reproduced in *Hokurai Tajiri sensei denki*, vol. 1, 386–402; see also pp. 484–485 for the section in which Tajiri brings up the elastic limit method.

112. Charles Lanmam, *Leading Men of Japan, with an Historical Summary of the Empire* (Boston: D. Lothrop, 1883), 147, 249.

113. *NGHS*, vol. 1, 318.

114. *NGHS: shiryō hen*, 414.

115. *NGHS*, vol. 1, 351.

116. Calculated from tables in Kamiyama, *Meiji keizai seisaku shi no kenkyū*, 21, 26, 97; for a list of the bond issues, see p. 26. During the Panic of 1890, however, stock collateral lending as a relief measure figured more prominently than lending on the security of public bonds.

117. At the end of 1886, for example, the BoJ held ¥11.6 million in public bonds. *NGHS: shiryō hen*, 272.

118. Fujimura, *Matsukata Masayoshi*, 79.

119. Kamiyama, *Meiji keizai seisaku shi no kenkyū*, 103–4.

6. "POOR PEASANT, POOR COUNTRY"?

1. P. Mayet, *Agricultural Insurance in Organic Connection with Savings-Banks, Land-Credit, and the Commutation of Debts: Proposals for the Amelioration of the Condition of the Japanese Agriculturalist*, trans. Arthur Lloyd (London: Swan Sonnenschein, 1893), 1. This chapter draws on Steven J. Ericson, "'Poor Peasant, Poor Country!' The Matsukata Deflation and Rural Distress in Mid-Meiji Japan," in *New Directions in the Study of Meiji Japan*, ed. Helen Hardacre, 387–96 (Leiden: E. J. Brill, 1997).

2. Yagi Haruo, *Nihon kindai keizai shi* (Nihon Hyōronsha, 1981), 101, 109.

3. Rosovsky, "Japan's Transition," 138–39.

4. Gordon, *A History of Modern Japan*, 95.

5. See especially the volume of essays edited by Umemura and Nakamura, *Matsukata zaisei to shokusan kōgyō seisaku*.

6. Nishikawa Shunsaku, *Nihon keizai no seichō shi* (Tōyō Keizai Shinpōsha, 1985), 201; Yamamoto Yūzō, "Meiji ishin ki no zaisei to tsūka," in *Kaikō to ishin*, ed. Umemura Mataji and Yamamoto Yūzō, vol. 3 of *Nihon keizai shi* (Iwanami Shoten, 1989), 167.

7. For data on the contraction of the paper money supply and on the decline in wholesale prices, see Harada, *Nihon no kindaika to keizai seisaku*, 227; *Kindai Nihon keizai shi yōran*, 60; and Muroyama, *Matsukata zaisei kenkyū*, 242.

8. See, for instance, Ōishi, *Jiyū minken to Ōkuma, Matsukata zaisei*, 215–19.

9. Yamamoto, "Meiji ishin ki no zaisei to tsūka," 162, 167.

10. Teranishi, "Matsukata *defure*," 176; Muroyama, "Matsukata *defurēshon*," 149–51.

11. Yamamoto, "Meiji ishin ki no zaisei to tsūka," 167; Ishii Kanji, *Nihon keizai shi*, 2nd ed. (Tōkyō Daigaku Shuppankai, 1991), 168.

12. Teranishi, "Matsukata *defure*," 178.

13. For more on official responses to the 1890 Panic, see my "Railroads in Crisis: The Financing and Management of Japanese Railway Companies During the Panic of 1890," in *Managing Industrial Enterprise: Cases from Japan's Prewar Experience*, ed. William D.

Wray (Cambridge, MA: Council on East Asian Studies, Harvard University, 1989), especially 166–70.

14. Teranishi, "Matsukata *defure*," 172–73, 179.

15. Muroyama, "Matsukata *defurēshon*," 146–49, 152.

16. Matsukata, "Matsukata Masayoshi kikigaki *nōto*," 153.

17. "Kōshaku Matsukata Masayoshi Kyō jikki," in *Matsukata Masayoshi kankei monjo*, vol. 2, 161–62.

18. "Kōshaku Matsukata Masayoshi Kyō jikki," 284.

19. Muroyama, *Matsukata zaisei kenkyū*, 243, 245.

20. Translation of "Notification No. 20 of the Department of Agriculture and Commerce," May 30, 1885, in "Agricultural Depression," *Japan Weekly Mail*, June 6, 1885.

21. Ōhama Tetsuya, "Matsukata zaisei-ka no mura to gōnō: Aichi ken Kitashidara gun ni okeru 'saikyū shuisho' juyō katei," in *Kindai Nihon keisei katei no kenkyū*, ed. Fukuchi Shigetaka Sensei Kanreki Kinen Ronbun Shū Kankō Iinkai (Yūzankaku, 1978), 284.

22. Harada, *Nihon no kindaika to keizai seisaku*, 217.

23. On the 1878 law, see Ōhama, "Matsukata zaisei-ka no mura to gōnō," 279, 283. On the land tax extension, see "Weekly Notes," *Japan Weekly Mail*, November 17, 1883, and Ōta Kasaku, *Meiji, Taishō, Shōwa beika seisaku shi* (Kokusho Kankōkai, 1977), 171.

24. "The Rice Harvest of 1883 (Translated from the *Bukka Shimpo*)," *Japan Weekly Mail*, April 12, 1884.

25. Ōhama, "Matsukata zaisei-ka no mura to gōnō," 293, note 12.

26. See, for instance, Sakairi Chōtarō, *Meiji zenki zaisei shi* (Sakai Shoten, 1988), 386.

27. Mayet, *Agricultural Insurance*, 66–67.

28. *Chiba ken nōchi seido shi*, ed. Tanabe Katsumasa and Makino Michihiko, vol. 1 (Chiba Ken Nōchi Seido Shi Kankōkai, 1949), 490. According to Kerry Smith, the dispossession of the *kama* (iron pot or kettle) was a standard trope in Japan during the depression in the 1930s. Personal communication to author, March 1994.

29. Muroyama, *Matsukata zaisei kenkyū*, 245, 247–50. With a two-year lag, the marked rise in bankruptcies between 1881 and 1884—from about 8,000 to over 27,000—correlates closely with the jump in suicides officially attributed to "distress over livelihood or despairing over misfortune" (*kakkei no konkyū mata wa hakumei o nagekite*) between 1883 and 1886—from 956 to 2,171. Both trends reversed dramatically the year after those periods, with recorded bankruptcies dropping to some 12,500 in 1885 and suicides to around 1,200 in 1887. The Home Ministry clarified the phrase "despairing over misfortune" by changing it to "owing to poverty" (*hinkon ni yori*) in 1928. Annaka Susumu, "Matsukata zaisei ki ni okeru dō-fu-ken betsu jisatsu ritsu" (paper presented at the annual conference of the Shakai Keizai Shi Gakkai, Tokyo, Japan, May, 2017), citing data on suicides from *Dai Nihon Teikoku Naimu Shō tōkei hōkoku*, nos. 1–2 (Naimu Shō, 1886–1887). The figures on bankruptcies are from Muroyama, *Matsukata zaisei kenkyū*, 248.

30. Miwa Ryōichi, *Gaisetsu Nihon keizai shi: kin-gendai*, 2nd ed. (Tōkyō Daigaku Shuppankai, 2002), 53, notes that the number of farm households edged down slightly from 5.5 million in 1880 to 5.48 million in 1885 and then to 5.45 million in 1890, a trend one might expect irrespective of economic cycles for a country in the early stages of industrialization.

31. Yamaguchi, *Nihon keizai shi*, 151; Takafusa Nakamura, *Economic Growth in Prewar Japan*, trans. Robert A. Feldman (New Haven, CT: Yale University Press, 1983), 56.

32. William Wray suggested this point about the land tax reform in commenting on a paper I wrote in my first year of graduate study and subsequently expanded into the entry "Matsukata Fiscal Policy" in *Kodansha Encyclopedia of Japan* (Tokyo: Kodansha, 1983).

33. Kai Hideo, "Meiji jūnendai no keizai kōzō to sono henka: Shiga ken no jirei o tōshite," *Shigaku kenkyū*, no. 106 (1968): 10–11, 15–16.

34. Richard J. Smethurst, *Agricultural Development and Tenancy Disputes in Japan, 1870–1940* (Princeton, NJ: Princeton University Press, 1986), 61–65.

35. Smethurst, *Agricultural Development and Tenancy Disputes in Japan*, 59, note 34.

36. Miwa, *Gaisetsu Nihon keizai shi*, 53.

37. Mayet, *Agricultural Insurance*, 5, 66–67.

38. Nakamura, *Economic Growth in Prewar Japan*, 55–57. Among others, Thomas Smith also cited Mayet's estimate. Smith, *Political Change and Industrial Development*, 82–83.

39. "Kōgyō iken," vol. 15, in *Meiji zenki zaisei keizai shiryō shūsei*, vol. 18, pt. 2, 816, 841, 847; Soda, "Matsukata zaisei to *Kōgyō iken*," 221–22.

40. Smethurst, *Agricultural Development and Tenancy Disputes*, 281–82.

41. Goldsmith, *The Financial Development of Japan*, 31.

42. Inada, *Nihon kindai shakai seiritsu ki no minshū undō*, 49–58.

43. Mayet, *Agricultural Insurance*, 68.

44. See, for instance, Ike, *The Beginnings of Political Democracy in Japan*, 138, 148.

45. Irokawa Daikichi, *Konmintō to Jiyūtō* (Yōransha, 1984), 22–25; Tsurumaki Takao, "Konmintō jiken: kaisetsu," in *Santama jiyū minken shiryō shū*, ed. Irokawa Daikichi (Yamato Shobō, 1979), vol. 2, 554–60; Neil L. Waters, *Japan's Local Pragmatists: The Transition from Bakumatsu to Meiji in the Kawasaki Region* (Cambridge, MA: Council on East Asian Studies, Harvard University, 1983), 119, 125–28.

46. Muroyama, *Matsukata zaisei kenkyū*, 248, 254.

47. Michael Lewis, *Becoming Apart: National Power and Local Politics in Toyama, 1868–1945* (Cambridge, MA: Harvard University Asia Center, 2000), 33–35.

48. Fukaya, *Meiji seifu zaisei kiban no kakuritsu*, 230.

49. "Fukui ken junsatsu hōkoku," November 1883, cited in Fukaya, *Meiji seifu zaisei kiban no kakuritsu*, 231.

50. "Ishikawa ken, Toyama ken junsatsu hōkoku," November 1883, cited in Fukaya, *Meiji seifu zaisei kiban no kakuritsu*, 233.

51. Muroyama, *Matsukata zaisei kenkyū*, 252, 254.

52. In 1881–1885, of over 22 million gainfully employed Japanese, workers in modern industries accounted for less than 2 percent of the total, workers in traditional industries for 27 percent, and farmers and forestry workers for the remaining 71 percent. Nakamura, *Meiji Taishō ki no keizai*, 188.

53. Matsukata, *Report on the Adoption of the Gold Standard*, 35, 99–100.

54. Kajinishi Mitsuhaya et al., *Nihon shihonshugi no seiritsu*, 2 vols. (Tōkyō Daigaku Shuppankai, 1955–1965), vol. 2 (1965), 452; *Kindai Nihon keizai shi yōran*, 64.

55. "On the Violent Fluctuations in the Prices of Commodities (Translated from the *Mainichi Shimbun*)," *Japan Weekly Mail*, February 10, 1883.

56. Not until 1894 would Japan's total output of filature silk surpass that of the hand-reeled type. Ishii, *Nihon keizai shi*, 161.

57. Matsukata, *Report on the Adoption of the Gold Standard*, 103, for the cotton fiber prices; Muroyama, *Matsukata zaisei kenkyū*, 240, 254, 276, for the annual total values of textiles produced, total amounts of sake brewed, and total values of raw silk exported; *Dai Nihon Teikoku tōkei nenkan*, vol. 7 (Naikaku Tōkei Kyoku, 1888), 184, for average annual prices of sake for seventeen localities stretching across Japan from Sapporo to Kagoshima. I estimated the total values of raw silk produced assuming Japan exported roughly 70 percent of raw silk output in the early to middle 1880s.

58. Muroyama, *Matsukata zaisei kenkyū*, 240, 266, and 291–92, note 24.

59. Shigeto Tsuru, "Economic Fluctuations in Japan, 1868–1893," *Review of Economics and Statistics* 23, no. 4 (November 1941): 180. Tsuru cited Takizawa Naoshichi, *Kōhon Nihon kin'yū shi ron* (Yūhikaku Shobō, 1912), 186–87.

In 1900, exports of cotton yarn and cloth and of silk fabrics, which had shot up over the previous decade, together trailed only those of raw silk, accounting for 20 percent of all Japanese exports in value; by then, raw cotton had become by far Japan's single biggest import item, making up one fifth of total imports in value that year as well. Steven J. Ericson, "*Japonica, Indica*: Rice and Foreign Trade in Meiji Japan," *Journal of Japanese Studies* 41, no. 2 (Summer 2015): 319, 322.

60. The Meiji government had floated two small loans totaling £3.4 million on the London market in 1870 and 1873 to cover railroad building and the commutation of samurai stipends but eschewed further borrowing from abroad until 1898–1899. In addition, private Japanese companies quietly borrowed foreign money: for example, Mitsui narrowly avoided bankruptcy in 1874 by obtaining a large loan from the Yokohama branch of Britain's Oriental Bank, and a company Gotō Shōjirō founded with Osaka merchants in 1873 relied on financing from the Yokohama branch of Jardine, Matheson. See by Ishii Kanji: "Ginkō sōsetsu zengo no Mitsui-gumi: kiki to sono kokufuku," *Mitsui Bunko ronsō*, no. 17 (1983): 1–55, and *Kindai Nihon to Igirisu shihon: Jādin Maseson Shōkai o chūshin ni* (Tōkyō Daigaku Shuppankai, 1984), 261–351.

61. Nakamura, *Economic Growth in Prewar Japan*, 5–6; *Historical Statistics of the United States, Colonial Times to 1970* (Washington, DC: U.S. Bureau of the Census, 1975), 224, 885; B. R. Mitchell, *International Historical Statistics: Europe, 1750–2005*, 6th ed. (Basingstoke, UK: Palgrave Macmillan, 2007), 621, 623, 1010–11. Those three Western countries and China took 89 percent of Japanese exports in 1885. Muroyama, *Matsukata zaisei kenkyū*, 276.

62. Metzler, "Japan's Matsukata Deflation," 3–4.

63. "Crippled Trade," *Japan Weekly Mail*, December 20, 1884.

64. *Dai Nihon teikoku tōkei nenkan*, vol. 5 (Tōkei Kyōkai, 1886), 237, 244, 253; Nakamura Takafusa, "Meiji ishin ki zaisei kin'yū seisaku tenbō: Matsukata *defurēshon* zenshi," in *Matsukata zaisei to shokusan kōgyō seisaku*, 22. If one adds to coal exports the bunker coal sold to foreign vessels, then rice alternated with coal as Japan's fourth- or fifth-biggest export item from 1882 to 1884 and trailed coal and copper in 1885. *Dai Nihon gaikoku bōeki nenpyō*, 1882, 59, and 1885, 273–74, 278, accessed June 20, 2013, http://dl.ndl.go.jp /info:ndljp/pid/804293, http://dl.ndl.go.jp/info:ndljp/pid/804295; table II-23 in Sumiya Mikio, *Nihon sekitan sangyō bunseki* (Iwanami Shoten, 1968), 184–85. As Sumiya points out, after the government removed the tariff on bunker coal in 1869, foreign steamers took on coal under that rubric not just for their own use but, to a considerable extent, for "export" as well; by the same token, as the Ministry of Agriculture and Commerce observed in 1886, a portion of the coal Japan sent to factories on the continent ended up as bunker coal in Asian ports. Sumiya, *Nihon sekitan sangyō bunseki*, 184–85. Hence, one should perhaps combine the somewhat overlapping official statistics on coal for "export" and coal for foreign "ship's use."

65. Nakamura, *Meiji Taishō ki no keizai*, 53. See also by Nakamura: "19-seiki Nihon keizai no seichō to kokusai kankyō—1870–1900 (Meiji 3–33) nen," in *Matsukata zaisei to shokusan kōgyō seisaku*, 213–38.

Telecommunication also played a role in magnifying downswings in Japan; cables laid by a Danish company between Nagasaki and Vladivostok as well as Shanghai connected Japan to Europe by telegraph from the surprisingly early date of January 1, 1872. Daniel R. Headrick, *The Invisible Weapon: Telecommunications and International Politics, 1851–1945* (New York: Oxford University Press, 1991), 44. As Barry Eichengreen and Marc Flandreau observe, in the late nineteenth and early twentieth centuries "panics spread contagiously across borders, transmitting at the speed of the international telegraph, provoking global financial crises," such as the panics that broke out in the West in 1884 and 1890, both of which contributed to severe downturns in Japan. Barry Eichengreen and Marc Flandreau, introduction to *The Gold Standard in Theory and History*, ed. Eichengreen and Flandreau, 2nd ed. (London: Routledge, 1997), 10.

66. *Ōsaka keizai shiryō shūsei* (Osaka: Ōsaka Shōkō Kaigisho, 1971), vol. 1, 416–17.

67. Ōmameuda Minoru, *Kindai Nihon no shokuryō seisaku* (Kyoto: Minerva Shobō, 1993), 18–25.

68. "The Payment of Land-Tax in Rice (Translated from the *Hochi Shimbun*)," *Japan Weekly Mail*, October 27, 1883. After farmers initially took advantage of this program in 1877, no one applied for partial payment in kind until 1883, when plummeting rice prices drove land tax payers to once again turn to it; the government discontinued the program in 1889. Ōta, *Meiji, Taishō, Shōwa beika seisaku shi*, 117, 168.

69. Ōmameuda, *Kindai Nihon no shokuryō seisaku*, 29–30.

70. Calculated from tables in *Dai Nihon gaikoku bōeki nenpyō*, 1882, 60, and 1885, 272, accessed June 25, 2013, http://dl.ndl.go.jp/info:ndljp/pid/804293, http://dl.ndl.go.jp /info:ndljp/pid/804295. For more on Japan's foreign trade in rice during the Meiji period, see Ericson, "*Japonica, Indica*," 317–45.

71. Muroyama argues that foreign, and particularly U.S., demand for Japanese raw silk and tea mitigated the severity of the depression in Japan, while Ōmameuda claims that European demand for Japanese rice helped to stabilize its price from the middle to late 1880s. Muroyama, *Matsukata zaisei kenkyū*, 276–78; Ōmameuda, *Kindai Nihon no shokuryō seisaku*, 38, and table 1.5 for European rice imports, 30.

72. Inada, *Nihon kindai shakai seiritsu ki no minshū undō*, 108; Muroyama, *Matsukata zaisei kenkyū*, 242.

73. Data for tea calculated from table 1 in the introduction to Teramoto Yasuhide, *Senzenki Nihon chagyō shi kenkyū* (Yūhikaku, 1999), 16–17, and for raw silk from table 4.23 in Muroyama, *Matsukata zaisei kenkyū*, 277. After briefly surpassing China in tea exports to the United States in 1876–77, Japan remained behind China in every year until 1906. Table 5.2 in Teramoto, *Senzenki Nihon chagyō shi*, 150–51. In raw silk exports to the United States, however, Japan pulled ahead of China in 1882 and held on to its lead over both China and Italy into the early twentieth century, substantially widening that lead from the mid-1900s. Sugiyama Shin'ya, "Kokusai kankyō to gaikoku bōeki," in *Kaikō to ishin*, 207–8. For data from 1890 on, see table 5 in Ishii Kanji, *Nihon sanshigyō shi bunseki* (Tōkyō Daigaku Shuppankai, 1972), 43. From 1881 to 1885, raw silk on average accounted in value for 38.1 per cent of Japan's total exports per year and tea for 18.6 percent. Calculated from table 2 in the introduction to Teramoto, *Senzenki Nihon chagyō shi*, 22–23. I wish to thank Robert Hellyer for recommending the Teramoto book.

74. "Depression of 1882–1885," in *Business Cycles and Depressions: An Encyclopedia*, ed. David Glasner (New York: Garland, 1997), 149–51. For data on U.S., French, and British imports of Japanese raw silk, see Muroyama, *Matsukata zaisei kenkyū*, 277.

75. On Gunma silk prices, see "Official Trading," *Japan Weekly Mail*, January 10, 1885. Sugiyama writes that a steady deterioration in the quality of Japanese silk also contributed to the decline in its price. Sugiyama, *Japan's Industrialization in the World Economy*, 96. On Japanese tea prices, see table 5.2 in Teramoto, *Senzenki Nihon chagyō shi*, 150.

76. "The Silk Trade of the Half Year Ending 30th June, 1882," *Japan Weekly Mail*, July 22, 1882.

77. "The Silk Trade of the Half Year Ending 31st December, 1882," *Japan Weekly Mail*, February 3, 1883.

78. "The Silk Trade in Japan," *Japan Weekly Mail*, July 26, 1884; "Silk and Tea Prospects in 1885," *Japan Weekly Mail*, June 6, 1885.

79. "The Tea Trade—Cause and Effect," *Japan Weekly Mail*, February 10, 1883; "The Tea Trade of Japan," *Japan Weekly Mail*, March 10, 1883.

80. "The Silk Trade of the Half Year Ending 31st December, 1881," *Japan Weekly Mail*, February 4, 1882; "The Silk Trade of the Half Year Ending 31st December, 1882."

81. "The Silk Trade of the Half Year Ending 30th June, 1882."

82. "Review of the Tea Trade in 1884," *Japan Weekly Mail*, March 7, 1885.

83. "The Silk Trade of the Half Year Ending 30th June, 1882."

84. "Silk and Tea Prospects in 1885."

85. Sugiyama, *Japan's Industrialization in the World Economy*, 150–51.

86. Citing a 1912 government study, Teramoto notes that Japanese tea was popular especially in states on the West Coast, in the western half of the northern tier, and to some extent on the East Coast. Teramoto, *Senzenki Nihon chagyō shi*, 147.

87. For data on U.S. consumption of coffee and imports of Japanese tea, see table 5.2 in Teramoto, *Senzenki Nihon chagyō shi*, 152; on changing U.S. and Canadian shares of Japanese tea exports, see Sugiyama, *Japan's Industrialization in the World Economy*, 143, 147, 151, 159.

88. Nakamura, "19-seiki Nihon keizai no seichō to kokusai kankyō," 234–35. Scholars have tended to treat the enterprise boom of the late 1880s, as they have the Matsukata deflation, almost entirely as a domestic phenomenon. Similarly, historians have been apt to attribute the Panic of 1890—Japan's first "general overproduction" crisis (Nakamura, "19-seiki Nihon keizai no seichō to kokusai kankyō," 232)—to internal factors such as the poor rice harvest that year or excessive promotion accompanying the enterprise boom, without mentioning passage of the Sherman Silver Purchase Act in the United States and the global financial panic of 1890.

89. For data on tea exports and prices, see table 1 of the introduction and table 5.2 in Teramoto, *Senzenki Nihon chagyō shi*, 16, 150; on rice exports, see Ōmameuda Minoru, "Beikoku seisan no kakudai to tai-Yōroppa yushutsu no tenkai," in *Kigyō bokkō: Nihon shihonshugi no keisei*, ed. Takamura Naosuke (Kyoto: Minerva Shobō, 1992), 295, 304.

90. Nakamura, "19-seiki Nihon keizai no seichō to kokusai kankyō," 233; Nakamura, *Meiji Taishō ki no keizai*, 56–58.

91. Alan H. Gleason, "Economic Growth and Consumption in Japan," in *The State and Economic Enterprise in Japan*, ed. William W. Lockwood (Princeton, NJ: Princeton University Press, 1965), 411, 414.

92. Smethurst, *Agricultural Development and Tenancy Disputes*, 60.

93. Ōmameuda, *Kindai Nihon no shokuryō seisaku*, 48, for the rising trend in the price of rice. On the 1920–1922 and 1927–1932 deflations, see Metzler, *Lever of Empire*, 161.

94. Nakamura, *Economic Growth in Prewar Japan*, 56.

95. Ronald Dore, *Land Reform in Japan* (London: Oxford University Press, 1959), 23.

96. Yamaguchi, *Nihon keizai shi*, 151, for percentages of pure tenants and part-owner, part-tenant farmers.

97. P. K. Hall, "Harvest Fluctuations in an Industrializing Economy: Japan, 1887–1912," *Agricultural History Review* 33, no. 2 (1985): 162–63.

98. Kazushi Ohkawa and Miyohei Shinohara, eds., *Patterns of Japanese Economic Development: A Quantitative Appraisal* (New Haven, CT: Yale University Press, 1979), 87, for the rate of growth of rice production; Kayō Nobufumi, ed., *Nihon nōgyō kiso tōkei* (Nōrin Suisangyō Seisan Seikōjō Kaigi, 1958), 338, for data on per capita consumption and total domestic output of rice. For more on trends in grain consumption during the Meiji period, see Ericson, "*Japonica, Indica*."

99. Metzler, *Lever of Empire*, 217–39; Metzler, email message to author, March 31, 2012.

100. Mutian Liu, "The Matsukata Financial Reform in Global Perspective," unpublished paper, Dartmouth College, 2009, 7, 14.

101. Metzler, *Lever of Empire*, 27–28.

102. Nakamura, *Meiji Taishō ki no keizai*, 58–59. "The 'Johnny Appleseed' of Meiji business" is Peter Duus's felicitous description of a man who helped establish hundreds of private companies during his career. Duus, *Modern Japan*, 2nd ed., 98.

In contrast to Japan in the late nineteenth century, in the United States at that time, support for gold monometallism came from "those strongly tied to international commercial and financial activities"—Northeastern traders, bankers, investors, and "most export-oriented manufacturers"—presumably reflecting those Americans' greater affinity with the British-dominated gold bloc. Jeffrey A. Frieden, "The Dynamics of International Monetary Systems: International and Domestic Factors in the Rise, Reign, and Demise of the Classical Gold Standard," in *Coping with Complexity in the International System*, ed. Jack Snyder and Robert Jervis (Boulder, CO: Westview Press, 1993), 148–49.

103. Droppers, "Monetary Changes in Japan," 169.

104. B. R. Mitchell, *International Historical Statistics: Africa, Asia and Oceania, 1750–2005*, 5th ed. (Basingstoke, UK: Palgrave Macmillan, 2007), 563, 566.

105. On rice imports, see Ōmameuda, "Beikoku seisan no kakudai," 318; on silk and tea exports, see Sugiyama, *Japan's Industrialization in the World Economy*, 80, and table 1 in the introduction to Teramoto, *Senzenki Nihon chagyō shi*, 16.

106. By 1900 the total export value of each of those three commodities had risen to more than double that of tea, but each of them still trailed raw silk in total export value by greater than half that year. *Dai Nihon gaikoku bōeki nenpyō*, 1900, accessed July 2, 2013, http://dl.ndl.go.jp/info:ndljp/pid/804310.

107. On foreign borrowing after 1897 and the central bank's extensive program of lending on the security of corporate stock during the Panic of 1890 and beyond, see Ericson, *The Sound of the Whistle*, 286 and 176–82, respectively.

CONCLUSION

1. Rodrik, *The Globalization Paradox*, 164.

2. Teranishi, "Matsukata *defure*," 157.

3. Jeffrey Sachs, "What I Did in Russia," accessed August 27, 2018, http://jeffsachs.org/2012/03/what-i-did-in-russia/.

4. Fukaya, *Meiji seifu zaisei kiban no kakuritsu*, 141.

5. Muroyama, *Matsukata Masayoshi kenkyū*, 114–15, 167–68.

6. Steven Bryan, "Interwar Japan, Institutional Change, and the Choice of Austerity," *Asiatische Studien—Études Asiatiques* 69, no. 2 (2015): 470.

7. See, for instance, by Alberto Alesina and Silvia Ardagna: "Large Changes in Fiscal Policy: Taxes Versus Spending," *Tax Policy and the Economy* 24, no. 1 (2010): 35–68, and "Tales of Fiscal Adjustment," *Economic Policy* 13, no. 27 (October 1998): 487–545. As Steven Bryan points out, however, Alesina and Ardagna, who exemplify the orthodox IMF-style "rules over discretion" literature of the 1990s, basically argue that austerity itself is expansionary because it increases confidence, whereas exchange rate devaluation, which accompanied austerity in most of the cases they studied, is what kept austerity from inducing a depression in each of those cases: "austerity is only expansionary if accompanied by currency devaluation. Without devaluation, austerity is simply austerity." Bryan, "Interwar Japan," 465. Also, Steven Bryan, email message to author, January 29, 2018.

8. Metzler, *Lever of Empire*, 67.

9. Kamiyama, *Meiji keizai seisaku shi no kenkyū*, 26.

10. In 1879, for instance, only 11 percent of Japan's population lived in urban locations with more than 10,000 people. Takeo Yazaki, *Social Change and the City in Japan: From Earliest Times through the Industrial Revolution* (Tokyo: Japan Publications, 1968), 391.

11. Sake brewing, the biggest manufacturing industry of the early to middle Meiji period, stands out as a subject in need of monographic study in English, offering a valuable site for investigating not only business and fiscal trends but also political developments, as seen in the growing division between large and small brewers within the tax reduction movement of the opposition parties. See, for example, *Shakai keizai shigaku* 55, no. 2 (1989), which features seven articles on the development of the Japanese sake-brewing industry from the Tokugawa period to the early Shōwa era ("Nihon ni okeru shuzō gyō no tenkai: kinsei kara kindai e"), including Ikegami Kazuo, "Meiji ki no shuzei seisaku," 189–212, and Nakamura Takafusa, "Shuzō gyō no sūryō shi: Meiji-Shōwa shoki," 213–41.

12. See, for example, Carl Mosk, *Japanese Economic Development: Markets, Norms, Structures* (London: Routledge, 2008), 238: "Ironically the Dodge Line program echoes the one carried out under Matsukata in the aftermath of the Satsuma Rebellion. Both programs were designed to fight inflation generated by war; both programs involved bringing the government's fiscal and monetary house in order; both programs involved running a surplus." Also, in "Treatment of Foreign Capital—A Case Study for Japan," in *Capital Movements and Economic Development*, ed. John H. Adler (New York: Stockton Press, 1967), 158, Saburo Okita and Takeo Miki write: "The enforcement of the 'Dodge Line' was as drastic a step as that of the deflationary policy adopted by Matsukata during the Meiji era. The successful enforcement of the Dodge Line laid the foundation for the subsequent development of the Japanese economy."

13. Koichi Hamada and Munehisa Kasaya, "The Reconstruction and Stabilization of the Postwar Japanese Economy: Possible Lessons for Eastern Europe?" Economic Growth Center, Yale University, September 1992, 1, accessed August 25, 2017, http://aida.wss.yale.edu/growth_pdf/cdp672.pdf.

14. Hamada and Kasaya, "The Reconstruction and Stabilization of the Postwar Japanese Economy," 24, 30, 45 (table 3).

15. Metzler, *Capital as Will and Imagination*, 72, 148–55.

16. See Bryan, "Interwar Japan," 463, on Matsukata's devaluation of the gold exchange rate by 50 percent in 1897.

Works Cited

The place of publication for all Japanese-language works is Tokyo unless otherwise noted.

"Agricultural Depression." *Japan Weekly Mail*, June 6, 1885.

Alesina, Alberto, and Silvia Ardagna. "Large Changes in Fiscal Policy: Taxes Versus Spending." *Tax Policy and the Economy* 24, no. 1 (2010): 35–68.

——. "Tales of Fiscal Adjustment." *Economic Policy* 13, no. 27 (October 1998): 487–545.

Allen, G. C. *A Short Economic History of Japan*, 4th ed. New York: St. Martin's Press, 1981.

Andō Seiichi. *Shizoku jusan shi no kenkyū*. Osaka: Seibundō, 1988.

Annaka Susumu. "Matsukata zaisei ki ni okeru dō-fu-ken betsu jisatsu ritsu." Paper presented at the annual conference of the Shakai Keizai Shi Gakkai, Tokyo, May 27, 2017.

Aoyama Kason. *Yamamoto Kakuma*. Kyoto: Dōshisha, 1928.

Apter, David E., and Nagayo Sawa. *Against the State: Politics and Social Protest in Japan*. Cambridge, MA: Harvard University Press, 1984.

Ariizumi Sadao. *Meiji seiji shi no kiso katei: chihō seiji jōkyō shiron*. Yoshikawa Kōbunkan, 1980.

Austin, James E. "Teaching Note: Japan (A) Supplements I & II." "Business, Government and the International Economy" course, Harvard Business School, Boston, 1987–1990.

Banno Junji. *Kindai Nihon no kokka kōsō*. Iwanami Shoten, 1996.

Bratter, Herbert M. *Silver Market Dictionary*. New York: Commodity Exchange, 1933.

Bryan, Steven. *The Gold Standard at the Turn of the Twentieth Century: Rising Powers, Global Money, and the Age of Empire*. New York: Columbia University Press, 2010.

——. "Interwar Japan, Institutional Change, and the Choice of Austerity." *Asiatische Studien—Études Asiatiques* 69, no. 2 (2015): 451–76.

Buchanan, James M. *Public Principles of Public Debt: A Defense and Restatement*. Homewood, IL: R. D. Irwin, 1958.

Buyst, Erik, Ivo Maes, Walter Pluym, and Marianne Danneel. *The Bank, the Franc and the Euro: A History of the National Bank of Belgium*. Tielt, Belgium: Lannoo, 2005.

Bytheway, Simon James. *Investing Japan: Foreign Capital, Monetary Standards, and Economic Development, 1859–2011*. Cambridge, MA: Harvard University Asia Center, 2014.

Bytheway, Simon James, and Mark Metzler. *Central Banks and Gold: How Tokyo, London, and New York Shaped the Modern World*. Ithaca, NY: Cornell University Press, 2016.

Chang, Ha-Joon. *Kicking Away the Ladder: Development Strategy in Historical Perspective*. London: Anthem Press, 2002.

Chang, Richard T. "General Grant's 1879 Visit to Japan." *Monumenta Nipponica* 24, no. 4 (1969): 373–92.

Checkland, Olive, and Norio Tamaki. "Alexander Allan Shand, 1844–1930—A Banker the Japanese Could Trust." In *Britain and Japan: Biographical Portraits*, edited by Ian Nish, vol. 2, 65–78. Folkestone, UK: Japan Library, 1997.

Chiba Ken nōchi seido shi, edited by Tanabe Katsumasa and Makino Michihiko, vol. 1. Chiba Ken Nōchi Seido Shi Kankōkai, 1949.

Chrastil, Rachel. *Organizing for War: France, 1870–1914*. Baton Rouge: Louisiana State University Press, 2010.

Cobbing, Andrew. *The Satsuma Students in Britain: Japan's Early Search for the "Essence of the West."* Richmond, Surrey, UK: Japan Library, 2000.

"Competition of Japanese Labor." *San Francisco Chronicle*, February 19, 1896.

Conant, Charles A. *The National Bank of Belgium.* Washington, DC: Government Printing Office, 1910.

Crane, George T. "Economic Nationalism: Bringing the Nation Back In." *Millennium: Journal of International Studies* 27, no. 1 (March 1998): 55–75.

Crawcour, Sydney. "*Kōgyō iken*: Maeda Masana and His View of Meiji Economic Development." *Journal of Japanese Studies* 23, no. 1 (Winter 1997): 69–104.

"Crippled Trade." *Japan Weekly Mail*, December 20, 1884.

The Currency of Japan: A Reprint of Articles, Letters, and Official Reports, Published at Intervals in the Foreign Newspapers of Japan, together with Translations from Japanese Journals, Relating to the Currency, Paper and Metallic, of the Empire of Japan. Yokohama: Japan Gazette, 1882.

Dai Nihon gaikoku bōeki nenpyō (*Annual Return of the Foreign Trade of the Empire of Japan*), 1882–1887, 1896, 1900. Ōkura Shō, 1883–1888, 1897, 1901. National Diet Library Digital Collections, Tokyo. Accessed June 20, 2013, June 25, 2013, July 2, 2013, and July 8, 2018. http://dl.ndl.go.jp.

Dai Nihon Teikoku Naimu Shō tōkei hōkoku, nos. 1–2. Naimu Shō, 1886–1887.

Dai Nihon Teikoku tōkei nenkan, vols. 5 and 7. Tōkei Kyōkai, 1886, and Naikaku Tōkei Kyoku, 1888.

de Ganon, Pieter S. "Down the Rabbit Hole: A Study in the Political Economy of Modern Japan." *Past and Present*, no. 213 (November 2011): 237–66.

"Depression of 1882–1885." In *Business Cycles and Depressions: An Encyclopedia*, edited by David Glasner, 149–51. New York: Garland, 1997.

Dictionnaire des finances, edited by Léon Say, 2 vols. Paris: Berger-Levrault, 1889–1894.

Dore, Ronald. *Land Reform in Japan.* London: Oxford University Press, 1959.

Droppers, Garrett. "Monetary Changes in Japan." *Quarterly Journal of Economics* 12, no. 2 (1898): 153–85.

Duus, Peter. *Modern Japan*, 2nd ed. Boston: Houghton Mifflin, 1998.

Eichengreen, Barry, and Marc Flandreau. "The Geography of the Gold Standard." In *Currency Convertibility: The Gold Standard and Beyond*, edited by Jorge Braga de Macedo, Barry Eichengreen, and Jaime Reis, 113–43. London: Routledge, 1996.

——. Introduction to *The Gold Standard in Theory and History*, edited by Barry Eichengreen and Marc Flandreau, 2nd ed., 1–30. London: Routledge, 1997.

Einaudi, Luca. *Money and Politics: European Monetary Unification and the International Gold Standard, 1865–1873.* Oxford: Oxford University Press, 2001.

Enlightenment and Beyond: Political Economy Comes to Japan, edited by Chūhei Sugiyama and Hiroshi Mizuta. Tokyo: University of Tokyo Press, 1988.

Ennals, Peter. *Opening a Window to the West: The Foreign Concession at Kobe, Japan, 1868–1899.* Toronto: University of Toronto Press, 2014.

Ericson, Steven J. "*Japonica, Indica*: Rice and Foreign Trade in Meiji Japan." *Journal of Japanese Studies* 41, no. 2 (Summer 2015): 317–45.

——. "The 'Matsukata Deflation' Reconsidered: Financial Stabilization and Japanese Exports in a Global Depression, 1881–85." *Journal of Japanese Studies* 40, no. 1 (2014): 1–28.

——. "Matsukata Fiscal Policy." In *Kodansha Encyclopedia of Japan*. Tokyo: Kodansha, 1983.

——. "Orthodox Finance and 'The Dictates of Practical Expediency': Influences on Matsukata Masayoshi and the Financial Reform of 1881–1885." *Monumenta Nipponica* 71, no. 1 (2016): 83–117.

——. "'Poor Peasant, Poor Country!' The Matsukata Deflation and Rural Distress in Mid-Meiji Japan." In *New Directions in the Study of Meiji Japan*, edited by Helen Hardacre, 387–96. Leiden: E. J. Brill, 1997.

——. "Railroads in Crisis: The Financing and Management of Japanese Railway Companies during the Panic of 1890." In *Managing Industrial Enterprise: Cases from Japan's Prewar Experience*, edited by William D. Wray, 121–82. Cambridge, MA: Council on East Asian Studies, Harvard University, 1989.

——. "Smithian Rhetoric, Listian Practice: The Matsukata 'Retrenchment' and Industrial Policy, 1881–1885," *Japan Forum* 30, no. 4 (2018): 498–520.

——. *The Sound of the Whistle: Railroads and the State in Meiji Japan*. Cambridge, MA: Council on East Asian Studies, Harvard University, 1996.

——. "Taming the Iron Horse: Western Locomotive Makers and Technology Transfer in Japan, 1870–1914." In *Public Spheres, Private Lives in Modern Japan, 1600–1950: Essays in Honor of Albert M. Craig*, edited by Gail Lee Bernstein, Andrew Gordon, and Kate Wildman Nakai, 185–217. Cambridge, MA: Harvard University Asia Center, 2005.

Eskildsen, Robert. "Of Civilization and Savages: The Mimetic Imperialism of Japan's 1874 Expedition to Taiwan." *American Historical Review* 107, no. 2 (April 2002): 388–418.

Ferber, Katalin. "Professionalism as Power: Tajiri Inajirō and the Modernisation of Meiji Finance." In *Institutional and Technological Change in Japan's Economy: Past and Present*, edited by Janet Hunter and Cornelia Storz, 27–42. London: Routledge, 2006.

"Financial Free-Trade for Japan." *Japan Weekly Mail*, February 27, 1886.

Flandreau, Marc. "Crises and Punishment: Moral Hazard and the Pre-1914 International Financial Architecture." In *Money Doctors: The Experience of International Financial Advising, 1850–2000*, edited by Marc Flandreau, 13–48. London: Routledge, 2003.

——. "The French Crime of 1873: An Essay on the Emergence of the International Gold Standard, 1870–1880." *Journal of Economic History* 56, no. 4 (1996): 862–97.

Fraser, Andrew. "The Expulsion of Ōkuma from the Government in 1881." *Journal of Asian Studies* 26, no. 2 (February 1967): 213–36.

Frieden, Jeffrey A. "The Dynamics of International Monetary Systems: International and Domestic Factors in the Rise, Reign, and Demise of the Classical Gold Standard." In *Coping with Complexity in the International System*, edited by Jack Snyder and Robert Jervis, 137–62. Boulder, CO: Westview Press, 1993.

Fujimura Tōru. *Matsukata Masayoshi: Nihon zaisei no paionia*. Nihon Keizai Shinbunsha, 1966.

——. *Meiji zaisei kakuritsu katei no kenkyū*. Chūō Daigaku Shuppanbu, 1968.

Fukagai, Yasunori. "Political Languages of Land and Taxation: European and American Influences on Japan, 1880s to 1920s." In *The Political Economy of Transnational Tax Reform: The Shoup Mission to Japan in Historical Context*, edited by W. Elliot Brownlee, Eisaku Ide, and Yasunori Fukagai, 143–66. Cambridge: Cambridge University Press, 2013.

Fukai Eigo. *Jinbutsu to shisō*. Nihon Hyōronsha, 1939.

Fukaya Tokujirō. *Meiji seifu zaisei kiban no kakuritsu*. Ochanomizu Shobō, 1995.

Fukuzawa Yukichi. *Fukuzawa Yukichi zenshū*, 2nd ed., 22 vols. Iwanami Shoten, 1958–1971.

Furusawa Kōzō. "Yokohama Shōkin Ginkō jōrei no seitei to kawase seisaku." In *Meiji ki Nihon tokushu kin'yū rippō shi*, edited by Shibuya Ryūichi, 67–140. Waseda Daigaku Shuppanbu, 1977.

Garrigues, Jean. "Léon Say: un libéral sous la Troisième République (1871–1896)." *Revue historique* 286, no. 1 (July/September 1991): 119–41.

Gernie, Sharif. "Politics, Morality and the Bourgeoisie: The Work of Paul Leroy-Beaulieu (1843–1916)." *Journal of Contemporary History* 27 (April 1992): 345–62.

Gleason, Alan H. "Economic Growth and Consumption in Japan." In *The State and Economic Enterprise in Japan*, edited by William W. Lockwood, 391–444. Princeton, NJ: Princeton University Press, 1965.

Goldsmith, Raymond W. *The Financial Development of Japan, 1868–1977*. New Haven, CT: Yale University Press, 1983.

Goodhart, Charles. *The Evolution of Central Banks*. Cambridge, MA: MIT Press, 1988.

Gordon, Andrew. *A History of Modern Japan: From Tokugawa Times to the Present*, 3rd ed. Oxford: Oxford University Press, 2013.

Grimmer-Solem, Erik. "German Social Science, Meiji Conservatism, and the Peculiarities of Japanese History." *Journal of World History* 16 (June 2005): 187–222.

Guanzi: Political, Economic, and Philosophical Essays from Early China, translated by W. Allyn Rickett, 2 vols. Princeton, NJ: Princeton University Press, 1985–1998.

Hackett, Roger. *Yamagata Aritomo in the Rise of Modern Japan, 1838–1922*. Cambridge, MA: Harvard University Press, 1971.

Hall, P. K. "Harvest Fluctuations in an Industrializing Economy: Japan, 1887–1912." *Agricultural History Review* 33, no. 2 (1985): 158–72.

Hamada, Koichi, and Munehisa Kasaya. "The Reconstruction and Stabilization of the Postwar Japanese Economy: Possible Lessons for Eastern Europe?" Economic Growth Center, Yale University, September 1992. Accessed August 25, 2017. http://aida.wss.yale.edu/growth_pdf/cdp672.pdf.

Hanes, Jeffrey E. *The City as Subject: Seki Hajime and the Reinvention of Modern Osaka*. Berkeley: University of California Press, 2002.

Harada Mikio. *Nihon no kindaika to keizai seisaku*. Tōyō Keizai Shinpōsha, 1972.

Harlen, Christine Margerum. "A Reappraisal of Classical Economic Nationalism and Economic Liberalism." *International Studies Quarterly* 43, no. 4 (December 1999): 733–44.

He, Wenkai. *Paths toward the Modern Fiscal State: England, Japan, and China*. Cambridge, MA: Harvard University Press, 2013.

Headley, J. T. *The Travels of General Grant*. Philadelphia: New World Publishing, 1881.

Headrick, Daniel R. *The Invisible Weapon: Telecommunications and International Politics, 1851–1945*. New York: Oxford University Press, 1991.

Helleiner, Eric. "Economic Nationalism as a Challenge to Economic Liberalism? Lessons from the 19th Century." *International Studies Quarterly* 46, no. 3 (September 2002): 307–29.

——. *The Making of National Money: Territorial Currencies in Historical Perspective*. Ithaca, NY: Cornell University Press, 2003.

Historical Statistics of the United States, Colonial Times to 1970. Washington, DC: U.S. Bureau of the Census, 1975.

Hokurai Tajiri sensei denki, edited by Tsuruoka Isaku, 2 vols. Tajiri Sensei Denki oyobi Ikō Hensankai, 1933.

Hyōdō Tōru. "Matsukata Masayoshi no tai-Ō ki ni okeru keika to bunseki: Tani Kin'ichirō 'Meiji jūichi nen tai-Ō nikki' o chūshin to shite." *Tōyō kenkyū*, no. 73 (January 1985): 93–120.

——. "Matsukata no shihei seiri ki ni okeru bōeki seisaku: Ōkura kyū jidai no kengisho o chūshin to shite." *Tōyō kenkyū*, no. 90 (January 1989): 33–58.

——. "Matsukata zaisei no genryū ni tsuite: Hita-ken seiki ni okeru kinsatsu, hansatsu mondai o chūshin to shite." *Keizai ronshū* 42 (September 1986): 49–72.

Ike, Nobutaka. *The Beginnings of Political Democracy in Japan*. Baltimore: Johns Hopkins University Press, 1950.

Ikegami Kazuo. "Meiji ki no shuzei seisaku." *Shakai keizai shigaku* 55, no. 2 (1989): 189–212.

Imuta Toshimitsu. "Meiji zenki ni okeru bōeki kin'yū seisaku." In *Nihon keizai seisaku shiron*, edited by Andō Yoshio, vol. 1, 66–80. Tōkyō Daigaku Shuppankai, 1973.

Inada Masahiro. *Nihon kindai shakai seiritsu ki no minshū undō: konmintō kenkyū josetsu.* Chikuma Shobō, 1990.

Inoki Takenori. "Chiso beinō ron to zaisei seiri: 1880 nen 8 gatsu no seisaku ronsō o megutte." In *Matsukata zaisei to shokusan kōgyō seisaku*, 107–26.

Inoue Kiyoshi. "Jiyū minken undo." In *Nihon rekishi daijiten*, edited by Nihon Rekishi Daijiten Hensan Iiinkai, vol. 5, 483–84. Kawade Shobō Shinsha, 1974.

Irokawa Daikichi. *Konmintō to Jiyūtō.* Yōransha, 1984.

Ishii Kanji. "Ginkō sōsetsu zengo no Mitsui-gumi: kiki to sono kokufuku." *Mitsui Bunko ronsō*, no. 17 (1983): 1–55.

——. "Japan." In *International Banking, 1870–1914*, edited by Rondo Cameron and V. I. Bovykin, 214–30. New York: Oxford University Press, 1991.

——. "Japanese Foreign Trade and the Yokohama Specie Bank, 1880–1913." In *Pacific Banking, 1859–1959: East Meets West*, edited by Olive Checkland, Shizuya Nishimura, and Norio Tamaki, 1–23. New York: St. Martin's Press, 1994.

——. *Kindai Nihon to Igirisu shihon: Jādin Maseson Shōkai o chūshin ni.* Tōkyō Daigaku Shuppankai, 1984.

——. "Nihon Ginkō seido." In *Nihon Ginkō kin'yū seisaku shi*, edited by Ishii Kanji, 17–26. Tōkyō Daigaku Shuppankai, 2001.

——. *Nihon keizai shi*, 2nd ed. Tōkyō Daigaku Shuppankai, 1991.

——. *Nihon no sangyōka to zaibatsu.* Iwanami Shoten, 1992.

——. *Nihon sanshigyō shi bunseki.* Tōkyō Daigaku Shuppankai, 1972.

Ishizuka Hiromichi. *Nihon shihonshugi seiritsu shi kenkyū: Meiji kokka to shokusan kōgyō seisaku.* Yoshikawa Kōbunkan, 1973.

Ishizuki Minoru. *Kindai Nihon no kaigai ryūgaku shi.* Kyoto: Minerva Shobō, 1972.

Itami Masahiro. "Meiji chūki ni okeru chihō nōkō ginkō no seiritsu ni kansuru oboegaki." *Kagawa Daigaku keizai ronsō* 37, no. 4 (October 1964): 70–90.

Itani Zen'ichi. "Meiji keizaigaku shi no issetsu: wasurerareta keizai gakusha Tajiri Inajirō Hakushi o chūshin to shite." *Ajia Daigaku shi shogaku kiyō: jinbun, shakai, shizen*, no. 13 (May 1965): 1–21.

Itō Hirobumi. "Reasons for Basing the Japanese New Coinage on the Metric System," December 29, 1870. In Matsukata, *Report on the Adoption of the Gold Standard*, 2–5.

Iwakura Kō jikki, edited by Tada Kōmon, 3 vols. Iwakura Kōkyūseki hozonkai, 1927.

James, Harold. *The End of Globalization: Lessons from the Great Depression.* Cambridge, MA: Harvard University Press, 2001.

Johnson, Chalmers. *MITI and the Japanese Miracle.* Stanford, CA: Stanford University Press, 1982.

Jones, Mark, and Steven Ericson. "Social and Economic Change in Prewar Japan." In *A Companion to Japanese History*, edited by William M. Tsutsui, 172–88. Malden, MA: Blackwell, 2006.

Kadokawa Nihon shi jiten, edited by Takayanagi Mitsutoshi and Takeuchi Rizō, 2nd ed. Kadokawa Shoten, 1974.

Kai Hideo. "Meiji jūnendai no keizai kōzō to sono henka: Shiga ken no jirei o tōshite." *Shigaku kenkyū*, no. 106 (1968): 1–20.

Kaida Ikuo. *Seiō zaiseigaku to Meiji zaisei.* Suita, Osaka-fu: Kansai Daigaku Shuppanbu, 1988.

Kaigun gunbi enkaku. Kaigun Daijin Kanbō, 1922. National Diet Library Digital Collections. Accessed August 29, 2018. http://dl.ndl.go.jp/info:ndljp/pid/970713.

Kaikō to ishin, edited by Umemura Mataji and Yamamoto Yūzō. Vol. 3 of *Nihon keizai shi*. Iwanami Shoten, 1989.

Kajinishi Mitsuhaya, Katō Toshihiko, Ōshima Kiyoshi, and Ōuchi Tsutomu. *Nihon shihonshugi no seiritsu*, 2 vols. Tōkyō Daigaku Shuppankai, 1955–1965.

Kamiyama Tsuneo. *Meiji keizai seisaku shi no kenkyū*. Hanawa Shobō, 1995.

Kaneko Masaru. "Nihon no saisho no zaisei gakusha, Tajiri Inajirō." In *Nihon no zaiseigaku: sono senkusha no gunzō*, edited by Satō Susumu, 16–28. Gyōsei, 1986.

Kauch, P. *La Banque nationale de Belgique, 1850–1918*. Brussels: La Banque nationale de Belgique, 1950.

Kayō Nobufumi, ed. *Nihon nōgyō kiso tōkei*. Nōrin Suisangyō Seisan Seikōjō Kaigi, 1958.

Keene, Donald. *Emperor of Japan: Meiji and His World, 1852–1912*. New York: Columbia University Press, 2002.

"Keihan, Kyūshū ryō chihō sangyō shisatsu hōkoku." Document 58:6 of Matsukata-ke monjo.

Kikkawa Hidezō. *Shizoku jusan no kenkyū*. Yūhikaku, 1935.

Kindai Nihon keizai shi yōran, edited by Andō Yoshio, 2nd ed. Tōkyō Daigaku Shuppankai, 1979.

Knowles, L. C. A. *Economic Development in the Nineteenth Century: France, Germany, Russia and the United States*. London: Routledge, 1932.

Kobayashi Masaaki. "Japan's Early Industrialization and the Transfer of Government Enterprises: Government and Business," *Japanese Yearbook on Business History* 2 (1985): 54–80.

———. *Nihon no kōgyōka to kangyō haraisage: seifu to kigyō*. Tōyō Keizai Shinpōsha, 1977.

"Kōbu Shō enkaku hōkoku." In *Meiji zenki zaisei keizai shiryō shūsei*, vol. 17, pt. 1.

"Kōgyō iken," vol. 15. In *Meiji zenki zaisei keizai shiryō shūsei*, vol. 18, pt. 2, 811–70.

Komine Yasuei. "Komai Shigetada sensei shōden." *Senshū shōgaku ronshū*, no. 20 (February 1976): 27–80.

———. "Nihon saisho no zaisei gakusha Tajiri Inajirō." *Senshū shōgaku ronshū*, no. 21 (June 1976): 97–146.

"Kōshaku Matsukata Masayoshi Kyō jikki," edited by Nakamura Tokugorō. In *Matsukata Masayoshi kankei monjo*, vols. 1–5 (1979–1983).

Kōshaku Matsukata Masayoshi den, edited by Tokutomi Ichirō, 2 vols. Kōshaku Matsukata Masayoshi Denki Hakkōjo, 1935.

Laidler, David. "British Monetary Orthodoxy in the 1870s." *Oxford Economic Papers*, n.s., 40, no. 1 (March 1988): 74–109.

Lanmam, Charles. *Leading Men of Japan, with an Historical Summary of the Empire*. Boston: D. Lothrop, 1883.

Lebra, Joyce. "Ōkuma Shigenobu and the 1881 Political Crisis." *Journal of Asian Studies* 18, no. 4 (August 1959): 475–87.

Leroy-Beaulieu, Paul. *Boriyū Shi zaisei ron: kanzei no bu*, translated by Tajiri Inajirō, edited by Komai Shigetada. Originally published in 1880. Reprinted by Senshū Daigaku Daigaku Shi Shiryōshitsu, 2000.

———. "Kakkoku yosan no bōchō wa kokkashugi hattatsu no kekka." Document 10:6 of Matsukata ke monjo.

———. *Saikei yosan ron*, translated by Komai Shigetada, edited by Tajiri Inajirō. Originally published in 1883. Reprinted by Senshū Daigaku Daigaku Shi Shiryōshitsu, 2000.

———. *Traité de la science des finances*, 2 vols. Paris: Guillaumin, 1877.

Levermore, C. H. "Henry Carey and His Social System." *Political Science Quarterly* 5, no. 4 (1890): 553–82.

Lewis, Michael. *Becoming Apart: National Power and Local Politics in Toyama, 1868–1945*. Cambridge, MA: Harvard University Asia Center, 2000.

Liu, Mutian. "The Matsukata Financial Reform in Global Perspective." Unpublished paper, Dartmouth College, 2009.

Lowe, Charles. Introduction to *Japan's Accession to the Comity of Nations*, by Alexander von Siebold, translated by Charles Lowe, vii-xiii. London: Kegan Paul, Trench, Trübner, 1901.

Marvin, George. "The Alexander Hamilton of Japan: Prince Masayoshi Matsukata, the Valedictorian of the Elder Statesmen." *Asia* 25 (January 1925): 54–57, 81–83.

"Matsukata Haku zaisei ronsakushū," compiled by Sakatani Yoshirō, 1893. Originally published in *Meiji zenki zaisei keizai shiryō shūsei*, vol. 1 (1931). Reprinted in *Matsukata Masayoshi kankei monjo*, suppl. vol. (2001).

Matsukata ke monjo, 67 vols. Ministry of Finance Policy Research Institute (Zaimu Shō Sōgō Seisaku Kenkyūjo), Tokyo. Available on microfilm from Yumani Shobō, 1987.

Matsukata Masayoshi. "Gunbi kōchō hi no gi," December 26, 1882. In "Matsukata Haku zaisei ronsakushū," 144–47.

——. *The History of National Debts in Japan*. Tokyo: Ōkura Shō, 1890. Reprinted in *Documents and Studies on 19th C. Monetary History*, edited by Georges Depeyrot and Marina Kovalchuk, no. 173. Wetteren, Belgium: Moneta, 2014.

——. "Kaigun kōsai jōrei seitei no gi," May 3, 1886. In "Matsukata Haku zaisei ronsakushū," 105–6.

——. "Kaikanzei kaisei gi," documents 1–3, April–December 1874. In "Matsukata Haku zaisei ronsakushū," 179–83, 184–87, 190–92.

——. "Kaikanzei ken kaifuku no setsu," January 1875. In "Matsukata Haku zaisei ronsakushū," 194.

——. "Kaku chihō kan Enryōkan ni shūkai no sekijō ni oite," December 1882. In "Matsukata Haku zaisei ronsakushū," 605–8.

——. "Katō ginkō kyokuchō, Nakamura ittō shuzeikan Ōshū tokō no setsu sōbetsu no ji," January 19, 1886. In "Matsukata Haku zaisei ronsakushū," 658–65.

——. "Kinsatsu tsūyō no kōfu ni tai suru no gi," March 29, 1869. In "Matsukata Haku zaisei ronsakushū," 29–30.

——. "Matsukata Masayoshi kikigaki *nōto*." In *Matsukata Masayoshi kankei monjo*, vol. 10 (1991), 116–82.

——. "Meiji jūgo nendo yosan no gi ni tsuki ikensho," February 1882. In "Matsukata Haku zaisei ronsakushū," 417–20.

——. "Meiji sanjū-nen heisei kaikaku shimatsu gaiyō," May 1899. In *Meiji zenki zaisei keizai shiryō shūsei*, vol. 11, pt. 2, 313–593.

——. "Nihon Ginkō sōritsu no gi," March 1, 1882. In "Matsukata Haku zaisei ronsakushū," 341–57.

——. "Nihon Yūsen Kaisha no kabuken o Teishitsu zaisan ni hennyū suru no gi," March 24, 1887. In "Matsukata Haku zaisei ronsakushū," 545–46.

——. "On the Exportation of Rice," November 14, 1882, and "On the Exportation of Kombu," February 13, 1883. In Matsukata, *Report on the Adoption of the Gold Standard*, 137–39.

——. *Report on the Adoption of the Gold Standard in Japan*. Tokyo: Government Press, 1899.

——. "Shihei seiri shimatsu," 1890. In *Nihon kin'yū shi shiryō: Meiji Taishō hen*, edited by Nihon Ginkō Chōsa Kyoku, vol. 16, 1–143. Ōkura Shō Insatsu Kyoku, 1957.

——. "Sho hansatsu dakan no gi," November 20, 1868. In "Matsukata Haku zaisei ronsakushū," 27–29.

——. "Teishitsu zaisan setsubi no gi," November 18, 1884. In "Matsukata Haku zaisei ronsakushū," 536–37.

——. "Tsūka ryūshutsu o bōshi suru no kengi," September 1875. In "Matsukata Haku zaisei ronsakushū," 30–41.

——. "Zaisei gi," 1881. In *Meiji zenki zaisei keizai shiryō shūsei*, vol. 1, 331–41.

——. "Zaisei kanki gairyaku," June 1880. In "Matsukata Haku zaisei ronsakushū," 529–35.

Matsukata Masayoshi kankei monjo, edited by Fujimura Tōru (vols. 1–5) and Ōkubo Tatsumasa (vols. 6–20), 20 vols. Daitō Bunka Daigaku Tōyō Kenkyūjo, 1979–2001.

"Matsukata Masayoshi kankei monjo." In *Nihon kin'yū shi shiryō, Meiji Taishō hen*, edited by Nihon Ginkō Chōsa Kyoku, vol. 4. Ōkura Shō Insatsu Kyoku, 1958.

Matsukata zaisei to shokusan kōgyō seisaku, edited by Umemura Mataji and Nakamura Takafusa. Kokusai Rengō Daigaku, 1983.

Mayet, P. *Agricultural Insurance in Organic Connection with Savings-Banks, Land-Credit, and the Commutation of Debts: Proposals for the Amelioration of the Condition of the Japanese Agriculturalist*, translated by Arthur Lloyd. London: Swan Sonnenschein, 1893.

McClain, James L. *A Modern History of Japan*. New York: W. W. Norton, 2002.

Meiji kensei keizai shiron. Kokka Gakkai, 1919.

Meiji Taishō oyobi Shōwa zaisei yōran. Kokusei Kenkyūkai, 1937.

Meiji Tennō ki, edited by Kunai Chō, 13 vols. Yoshikawa Kōbunkan, 1968–1977.

Meiji zaisei shi: Matsukata Haku zaisei jireki, edited by Meiji Zaisei Shi Hensankai, 15 vols. Maruzen, 1904–1905.

Meiji zaisei shikō. Tōyō Keizai Shinpōsha, 1911.

Meiji zenki zaisei keizai shiryō shūsei, edited by Ōkura Shō, 21 vols. Kaizōsha, 1931–1936.

"Memo of Conversation between His Majesty and Genl. Grant." In *Guranto shōgun to no gotaiwa hikki*, 13–27. Kokumin Seishin Bunka Kenkyūjo, 1937.

Merrill, Charles White. *Summarized Data of Silver Production*. Washington, DC: United States Printing Office, 1930.

Metzler, Mark. *Capital as Will and Imagination: Schumpeter's Guide to the Postwar Japanese Miracle*. Ithaca, NY: Cornell University Press, 2013.

——. "The Cosmopolitanism of National Economics: Friedrich List in a Japanese Mirror." In *Global History: Interactions between the Universal and the Local*, edited by Anthony G. Hopkins, 98–130. Basingstoke, UK: Palgrave Macmillan, 2006.

——. "Japan's Matsukata Deflation in Transnational and Cross-Temporal Perspective." Paper presented at the annual conference of the Association for Asian Studies, Chicago, IL, March 27, 2009.

——. *Lever of Empire: The International Gold Standard and the Crisis of Liberalism in Prewar Japan*. Berkeley: University of California Press, 2006.

Michel, Georges. *Léon Say: sa vie, ses oeuvres*. Paris: Calmann Lévy, 1899.

Mikuriya Takashi. *Meiji kokka keisei to chihō keiei, 1881–1890*. Tōkyō Daigaku Shuppankai, 1980.

Mitchell, B. R. *International Historical Statistics: Africa, Asia and Oceania, 1750–2005*, 5th ed. Basingstoke, UK: Palgrave Macmillan, 2007.

——. *International Historical Statistics: Europe, 1750–2005*, 6th ed. Basingstoke, UK: Palgrave Macmillan, 2007.

Mitchener, Kris James, Masato Shizume, and Marc D. Weidenmier. "Why Did Countries Adopt the Gold Standard? Lessons from Japan." *Journal of Economic History* 70, no. 1 (March 2010): 27–56.

Miwa Ryōichi. *Gaisetsu Nihon keizai shi: kin-gendai*, 2nd ed. Tōkyō Daigaku Shuppankai, 2002.

Miyajima, Shigeki, and Warren E. Weber. "A Comparison of National Banks in Japan and the United States between 1872 and 1885." *Monetary and Economic Studies* 19, no. 1 (February 2001): 31–48.

Miyake Kōji. *Ōsaka Hōhei Kōshō no kenkyū.* Kyoto: Shibunkaku Shuppan, 1993.

Mizuta, Hiroshi. "Historical Introduction." In *Enlightenment and Beyond*, 3–35.

Morita Yūichi. *Waga kuni zaisei seido no kindaika: zaimu kanryō no kenkyū.* Kasumigaseki Shuppan, 1990.

Morris-Suzuki, Tessa. *A History of Japanese Economic Thought.* London: Routledge, 1989.

Mosk, Carl. *Japanese Economic Development: Markets, Norms, Structures.* London: Routledge, 2008.

Muroyama Yoshimasa. *Kindai Nihon keizai no keisei: Matsukata zaisei to Meiji no kokka kōsō.* Chikura Shobō, 2014.

——. *Kindai Nihon no gunji to zaisei: gunji kakuchō o meguru seisaku keisei katei.* Tōkyō Daigaku Shuppankai, 1984.

——. "Matsukata *defurēshon* no *mekanizumu.*" In *Matsukata zaisei to shokusan kōgyō seisaku*, 127–55.

——. *Matsukata Masayoshi: ware ni kisaku aru ni arazu, tada shōjiki aru nomi.* Kyoto: Minerva Shobō, 2005.

——. *Matsukata zaisei kenkyū: futaiten no seisaku kōdō to keizai kiki kokufuku no jissō.* Kyoto: Minerva Shobō, 2004.

Mussa, Michael, and Miguel Savastano. "The IMF Approach to Economic Stabilization." *NBER Macroeconomics Annual* 14 (1990): 79–122.

Nagashima Takeshi. "Tokuno Ryōsuke to Meiji shoki no insatsu jigyō: tokuni shihei seizō ni tsuite." *Shakai kagaku tōkyū* 14, no. 3 (March 1969): 49–66.

Nakai, Kate Wildman. *Shogunal Politics: Arai Hakuseki and the Premises of Tokugawa Rule.* Cambridge, MA: Council on East Asian Studies, Harvard University, 1988.

Nakamura Naoyoshi. "Ōkuma Shigenobu to Matsukata Masayoshi." In *Meiji seifu: sono seiken o ninatta hitobito*, edited by Ōkubo Toshiaki, 91–116. Shin Jinbutsu Ōraisha, 1971.

Nakamura, Takafusa. *Economic Growth in Prewar Japan*, translated by Robert A. Feldman. New Haven, CT: Yale University Press, 1983.

——. "19-seiki Nihon keizai no seichō to kokusai kankyō—1870–1900 (Meiji 3–33) nen." In *Matsukata zaisei to shokusan kōgyō seisaku*, 213–38.

——. "Meiji ishin ki zaisei kin'yū seisaku tenbō: Matsukata *defurēshon* zenshi." In *Matsukata zaisei to shokusan kōgyō seisaku*, 3–34.

——. *Meiji Taishō ki no keizai.* Tōkyō Daigaku Shuppankai, 1985.

——. "Shuzō gyō no sūryō shi: Meiji-Shōwa shoki." *Shakai keizai shigaku* 55, no. 2 (1989): 213–41.

National Bank of Serbia. "Tradition of Central Banking." Accessed August 11, 2017. http://www.nbs.rs/internet/english/10/10_8/index.html.

"The New Public Loan-Bonds." *Japan Weekly Mail*, January 5, 1884.

Nihon gaikō nenpyō narabi ni shuyō bunsho, 1840–1945, edited by Gaimu Shō, 2 vols. Nihon Kokusai Rengō Kyōkai, 1955.

Nihon Ginkō hyaku-nen shi, edited by Nihon Ginkō Hyaku-nen Shi Hensan Iinkai, 7 vols. Nihon Ginkō, 1982–1986.

Nishikawa Shunsaku. *Nihon keizai no seichō shi.* Tōyō Keizai shinpōsha, 1985.

Nishino Kiyosaku. *Rekidai zōshō den.* Tōyō Keizai Shinpōsha, 1930.

Nishizawa, Tamotsu. "The Emergence of the Economic Science in Japan and the Evolution of Textbooks, 1860s–1930s." In *The Economic Reader: Textbooks, Manuals and the Dissemination of the Economic Sciences during the Nineteenth and Early Twentieth Centuries*, edited by Massimo M. Augello and Marco E. L. Guidi, 305–23. London: Routledge, 2012.

"Notes." *Japan Weekly Mail*, June 6, 1885.

"Notifications of the Council of State." *Japan Weekly Mail*, January 5, 1884.

Nye, John Vincent. "The Myth of Free-Trade Britain and Fortress France: Tariffs and Trade in the Nineteenth Century." *Journal of Economic History* 51 (March 1991): 23–46.

Ōbuchi Toshio. *Meiji shoki seiō zaiseigaku no juyō katei: waga kuni zaiseigaku zenshi ni kansuru ichi shiryō.* Yachiyo Shuppan, 1978.

"Official Trading." *Japan Weekly Mail*, January 10, 1885.

Ōhama Tetsuya. "Matsukata zaisei-ka no mura to gōnō: Aichi ken Kitashidara gun ni okeru 'saikyū shuisho' juyō katei." In *Kindai Nihon keisei katei no kenkyū*, edited by Fukuchi Shigetaka Sensei Kanreki Kinen Ronbun Shū Kankō Iinkai, 277–94. Yūzankaku, 1978.

Ohkawa, Kazushi, and Miyohei Shinohara, eds. *Patterns of Japanese Economic Development: A Quantitative Appraisal.* New Haven, CT: Yale University Press, 1979.

Ōishi Kaichirō. *Jiyū minken to Ōkuma, Matsukata zaisei.* Tōkyō Daigaku Shuppankai, 1989.

——. "Matsukata zaisei to jiyū minkenka no zaisei ron: Nihon shihonshugi no genshiteki chikuseki katei no rikai no tame no ichi shiron." *Shōgaku ronshū* 30, no. 2 (January 1962): 380–442.

Okada Shunpei. "Meiji ki no keizai hatten to gin hon'i sei." *Seikei Daigaku keizai kenkyū* 30 (December 1969): 29–52.

Okita, Saburo, and Takeo Miki. "Treatment of Foreign Capital—A Case Study for Japan." In *Capital Movements and Economic Development*, edited by John H. Adler, 139–74. New York: Stockton Press, 1967.

Ōkuma monjo, 6 vols. Waseda Daigaku Shakai Kagaku Kenkyūjo, 1958–1963.

Ōkuma Shigenobu kankei monjo, edited by Watanabe Ikujirō, 6 vols. Nihon Shiseki Kyōkai, 1932–1935.

Ōkura Shō. "Kasei kōyō: seifu shihei jireki," vol. 2, 1887. Reprinted in *Meiji zenki zaisei keizai shiryō shūsei*, vol. 13 (1934), 141–278.

Ōkura Shō jinmei roku: Meiji, Taishō, Shōwa, edited by Ōkura Shō Hyaku-nen Shi Henshū Shitsu. Ōkura Zaimu Kyōkai, 1973.

Ōmameuda Minoru. "Beikoku seisan no kakudai to tai-Yōroppa yushutsu no tenkai." In *Kigyō bokkō: Nihon shihonshugi no keisei*, edited by Takamura Naosuke, 295–324. Kyoto: Minerva Shobō, 1992.

——. *Kindai Nihon no shokuryō seisaku.* Kyoto: Minerva Shobō, 1993.

"On the Violent Fluctuations in the Prices of Commodities (Translated from the *Mainichi Shimbun*)." *Japan Weekly Mail*, February 10, 1883.

Ōsaka Hōhei Kōshō enkakushi. Osaka: Ōsaka Heihō Kōshō, 1902.

Ōsaka keizai shiryō shūsei, vol. 1. Osaka: Ōsaka Shōkō Kaigisho, 1971.

Ōta Kasaku. *Meiji, Taishō, Shōwa beika seisaku shi.* Kokusho Kankōkai, 1977.

Ozaki Yukio. *The Autobiography of Ozaki Yukio*, translated by Fujiko Hara. Princeton, NJ: Princeton University Press, 2001.

"Paris Monetary Conference." In *Cyclopaedia of Political Science, Political Economy, and the Political History of the United States*, edited by John J. Lalor, vol. 3, 59–63. New York: Maynard, Merrill, 1899.

Patrick, Hugh T. "External Equilibrium and Internal Convertibility: Financial Policy in Meiji Japan." *Journal of Economic History* 25, no. 2 (June 1965): 187–213.

"The Payment of Land-Tax in Rice (Translated from the *Hochi Shimbun*)." *Japan Weekly Mail*, October 27, 1883.

Phipps, Catherine L. *Empires on the Waterfront: Japan's Ports and Power, 1858–1899.* Cambridge, MA: Harvard University Asia Center, 2015.

Pierson, John D. *Tokutomi Sohō, 1863–1957: A Journalist for Modern Japan.* Princeton, NJ: Princeton University Press, 1980.

Reischauer, Haru Matsukata. *Samurai and Silk: A Japanese and American Heritage.* Cambridge, MA: Harvard University Press, 1986.

Reti, Steven P. *Silver and Gold: The Political Economy of International Monetary Conferences, 1867–1892.* Westport, CT: Greenwood Press, 1998.

"Review of the Tea Trade in 1884." *Japan Weekly Mail,* March 7, 1885.

"The Rice Harvest of 1883 (Translated from the *Bukka Shimpo*)." *Japan Weekly Mail,* April 12, 1884.

Rizai jiten: yosan no bu, 2 vols. Ōkura Shō Shukei Kyoku, 1890.

Rodrik, Dani. *The Globalization Paradox: Democracy and the Future of the World Economy.* New York: W. W. Norton, 2011.

Roscher, Wilhelm. *Principles of Political Economy,* translated by John J. Lalor, 2 vols. New York: Henry Holt, 1878.

Rosovsky, Henry. "Japan's Transition to Modern Economic Growth, 1868–1885." In *Industrialization in Two Systems,* edited by Henry Rosovsky, 91–139. New York: John Wiley & Sons, 1966.

Sachs, Jeffrey. "What I Did in Russia." Accessed August 27, 2018. http://jeffsachs.org/2012/03/what-i-did-in-russia/.

Sagers, John H. *Origins of Japanese Wealth and Power: Reconciling Confucianism and Capitalism, 1830–1885.* New York: Palgrave Macmillan, 2006.

Sakairi Chōtarō. *Meiji zenki zaisei shi.* Sakai Shoten, 1988.

"The Sale of Bonds in Exchange for Kinsatsu to English Capitalists." *Japan Weekly Mail,* July 19, 1884.

Satō Shōichirō. "'Matsukata zaisei' to gunkaku zaisei no tenkai." *Shōgaku ronshū* 32, no. 3 (December 1963): 43–89.

——. *Rikugun kōshō no kenkyū.* Hassakusha, 1999.

Sawai Minoru. "Shiryō: Meiji ki no ōkabunushi—*Ginkō kaisha yōroku* no shūkei." *Ōsaka Daigaku keizaigaku* 52, no. 4 (March 2003): 251–80.

Saxonhouse, Gary. "A Tale of Technological Diffusion in the Meiji Period." *Journal of Economic History* 34, no. 1 (1974): 149–65.

"Say, (Jean Baptiste) Léon." In *Encyclopedia Britannica,* 11th ed., 1910–1911.

Schiltz, Michael. "An 'Ideal Bank of Issue': The Banque Nationale de Belgique as a Model for the Bank of Japan." *Financial History Review* 13, no. 2 (2006): 179–96.

——. "Money on the Road to Empire: Japan's Adoption of Gold Monometallism, 1873–97." *Economic History Review* 65, no. 3 (2012): 1147–68.

Schmidt, Vera, ed. *Korrespondenz Alexander von Siebolds: in den Archiven des Japanischen Aussenministeriums und der Tōkyō-Universität, 1859–1895.* Wiesbaden, Germany: Harrassowitz, 2000.

Schumpeter, Joseph A. *History of Economic Analysis.* Oxford: Oxford University Press, 1954.

Segai Inoue Kō den, edited by Inoue Kaoru Kō Denki Hensankai, 5 vols. Naigai Shoseki, 1933.

Senghaas, Dieter. "Friedrich List and the Basic Problems of Modern Development." *Review* (Fernand Braudel Center) 14, no. 3 (1991): 451–67.

Setoguchi Ryūichi. "Nihon ni okeru zaiseigaku no dōnyū, kōchiku to Tajiri Inajirō." *Senshū Daigaku shi kiyō,* no. 4 (March 2012): 51–81.

Shindō, Motokazu. "The Inflation in the Early Meiji Era." *Kyoto University Economic Review* 24, no. 2 (1954): 39–59.

Shinohara Miyohei. *Kojin shōhi shishutsu,* vol. 6 of *Chōki keizai tōkei.* Tōyō Keizai Shinpōsha, 1967.

"Silk and Tea Prospects in 1885." *Japan Weekly Mail,* June 6, 1885.

"The Silk Trade in Japan." *Japan Weekly Mail,* July 26, 1884.

"The Silk Trade of the Half Year Ending 30th June, 1882." *Japan Weekly Mail,* July 22, 1882.

"The Silk Trade of the Half Year Ending 31st December, 1881." *Japan Weekly Mail,* February 4, 1882.

"The Silk Trade of the Half Year Ending 31st December, 1882." *Japan Weekly Mail*, February 3, 1883.

Smethurst, Richard J. *Agricultural Development and Tenancy Disputes in Japan, 1870–1940*. Princeton, NJ: Princeton University Press, 1986.

———. *From Foot Soldier to Finance Minister: Takahashi Korekiyo, Japan's Keynes*. Cambridge, MA: Harvard University Asia Center, 2007.

———. "Fukai Eigo and the Development of Japanese Monetary Policy." In *New Directions in the Study of Meiji Japan*, edited by Helen Hardacre, 125–35. Leiden: Brill, 1997.

Smith, Thomas C. *Political Change and Industrial Development in Japan: Government Enterprise, 1868–1880*. Stanford, CA: Stanford University Press, 1955.

Soda Osamu. *Maeda Masana*. Yoshikawa Kōbunkan, 1973.

———. "Matsukata zaisei to 'Kōgyō iken.'" In *Kindai nōgaku ronshū*, edited by Kashiwa Suketaka, 221–38. Yōkendō, 1971.

Sproat, Audrey T. "Japan (A) Supplement I" and "Japan (A) Supplement II." Cambridge, MA: President and Fellows of Harvard College, 1975.

"The Stagnation in Trade (Translated from the *Jiji Shimpo*)." *Japan Weekly Mail*, December 27, 1884.

Starr, Harris E. *William Graham Sumner*. New York: Henry Holt, 1925.

Stiglitz, Joseph. *Globalization and Its Discontents*. New York: W. W. Norton, 2003.

Sugihara, Shirō. "Economists in Government: Ōkubo Toshimichi, the 'Bismarck of Japan,' and His Times." In *Enlightenment and Beyond*, 211–21.

Sugiyama, Shinya. *Japan's Industrialization in the World Economy, 1859–1899*. London: Athlone Press, 1988.

———. "Kokusai kankyō to gaikoku bōeki." In *Kaikō to ishin*, 173–221.

Sumiya Mikio. *Nihon sekitan sangyō bunseki*. Iwanami Shoten, 1968.

Sumner, William Graham. *A History of American Currency*. New York: Henry Holt, 1874.

Suzuki, Toshio. *Japanese Government Loan Issues on the London Capital Market, 1870–1913*. London: Athlone Press, 1994.

Sylla, Richard. "Financial Systems and Economic Modernization." *Journal of Economic History* 62 (June 2002): 277–92.

Taft, Helen Herron. *Recollections of Full Years*. New York: Dodd, Mead, 1914.

Tajiri Inajirō. "Hijō junbikin," August 1882. Document 30:4 of Matsukata-ke monjo.

———. "Shihei hakkō hōhō," August 1882. Document 46:5 of Matsukata-ke monjo.

Takahashi Makoto. "Matsukata Masayoshi." In Endō Shōkichi, Katō Toshihiko, and Takahashi Makoto, *Nihon no ōkura daijin*, 53–74. Nihon Hyōronsha, 1964.

———. *Meiji zaisei shi kenkyū*. Aoki Shoten, 1964.

Takaki, Masayoshi. *The History of Japanese Paper Currency (1868–1890)*. Baltimore: Johns Hopkins University Press, 1903.

Takizawa Naoshichi. *Kōhon Nihon kin'yū shi ron*. Yūhikaku Shobō, 1912.

Tamaki, Norio. *Japanese Banking: A History, 1859–1959*. Cambridge: Cambridge University Press, 1995.

———. "The Yokohama Specie Bank: A Multinational in the Japanese Interest, 1879–1931." In *Banks as Multinationals*, edited by Geoffrey Jones, 191–216. London: Routledge, 1990.

———. *Yukichi Fukuzawa, 1835–1901: The Spirit of Enterprise in Modern Japan*. Houndmills, Basingstoke, Hampshire, UK: Palgrave, 2001.

"The Tea Trade—Cause and Effect." *Japan Weekly Mail*, February 10, 1883.

"The Tea Trade of Japan." *Japan Weekly Mail*, March 10, 1883.

Teramoto Yasuhide. *Senzenki Nihon chagyō shi kenkyū*. Yūhikaku, 1999.

Teranishi Jūrō. "Matsukata *defure* no *makuro* keizaigaku bunseki (kaitei ban)." In *Matsukata zaisei to shokusan kōgyō seisaku*, 157–85.

Titus, David Anson. *Palace and Politics in Prewar Japan*. New York: Columbia University Press, 1974.

Tokutomi Sohō. "Kaitō rōkō." *Kokumin shinbun*, July 3, 1924. Reprinted in *Matsukata Masayoshi kankei monjo*, vol. 15 (1994), 351–59.

Tooze, Adam. *Crashed: How a Decade of Financial Crises Changed the World*. New York: Viking, 2018.

Trask, H. A. Scott. "William Graham Sumner: Monetary Theorist." *Quarterly Journal of Austrian Economics* 8 (Summer 2005): 35–54.

Tsuru, Shigeto. "Economic Fluctuations in Japan, 1868–1893." *Review of Economics and Statistics* 23, no. 4 (November 1941): 176–89.

Tsurumaki Takao. "Konmintō jiken: kaisetsu." In *Santama jiyū minken shiryō shū*, edited by Irokawa Daikichi, vol. 2, 554–60. Yamato Shobō, 1979.

Uchida Masahiro. *Meiji Nihon no kokka zaisei kenkyū: kindai Meiji kokka no honshitsu to shoki zaisei no kaimei*. Taga Shuppan, 1992.

Uchiyama Hiroshi. *Furansu zaiseigaku no dōnyū to Senshū Gakkō no hitobito: Tajiri Inajirō to Komai Shigetada no seitan 150 nen ni atatte*. Senshū Daigaku Shi Shiryō Kenkyūkai, 2006.

Umemura Mataji. "Matsukata *defure*-ka no shokusan kōgyō seisaku: Nōrin Suisan Shō sōritsu hyaku shūnen o kinen shite." *Keizai kenkyū* 32, no. 4 (October 1981): 347–57.

Umetani Noboru. *Oyatoi gaikokujin: gaisetsu*. Kajima Kenkyūjo Shuppankai, 1968.

Unno Fukujū. "Matsukata zaisei to jinushi sei no keisei." In *Iwanami kōza Nihon rekishi*, vol. 15, 91–133. Iwanami Shoten, 1976.

Vurpillat, J. Taylor. "Empire, Industry, and Globalization: Rethinking the Emergence of the Gold Standard in the 19th-century World." *History Compass* 12, no. 6 (2014): 531–40.

Wakayama Norikazu. *Hogozei setsu*. Ōkura Shō, 1872.

Warshaw, Dan. *Paul Leroy-Beaulieu and Established Liberalism in France*. Dekalb, IL: Northern Illinois University Press, 1991.

Waters, Neil L. *Japan's Local Pragmatists: The Transition from Bakumatsu to Meiji in the Kawasaki Region*. Cambridge, MA: Council on East Asian Studies, Harvard University, 1983.

"Weekly Notes." *Japan Weekly Mail*, November 17, 1883.

Williamson, John. "The Washington Consensus as Policy Prescription for Development." Lecture delivered at the World Bank, New York, January 13, 2004. Accessed August 19, 2018. https://piie.com/publications/papers/williamson0204.pdf.

Willis, Henry Parker. *A History of the Latin Monetary Union: A Study of International Monetary Action*. Chicago: University of Chicago Press, 1901.

Wilson, Ted. *Battles for the Standard: Bimetallism and the Spread of the Gold Standard in the Nineteenth Century*. Aldershot, UK: Ashgate, 2000.

Wray, William D. *Mitsubishi and the N.Y.K.: Business Strategy in the Japanese Shipping Industry*. Cambridge, MA: Council on East Asian Studies, Harvard University, 1984.

Wright, Robert E. *Hamilton Unbound: Finance and the Creation of the American Republic*. Westport, CT: Greenwood Press, 2002.

Yagi Haruo. *Nihon kindai keizai shi*. Nihon Hyōronsha, 1981.

Yagi Yoshikazu. "'Meiji 14-nen seihen' to Nihon Ginkō: Kyōdō Un'yu Kaisha kashidashi o megutte." *Shakai Keizai Shigaku* 53, no. 5 (December 1987): 636–60.

Yamaguchi Kazuo. *Nihon keizai shi*. Chikuma Shobō, 1968.

Yamamoto Kakuma. "Yamamoto Kakuma kenpaku," 1868. Handcopied by Shimazu Hisamitsu. Digital Archive of Rare Materials, Dōshisha University Academic Repository, Kyoto. Accessed August 9, 2015. http://library.doshisha.ac.jp/ir/digital/archive/yamamoto/128/imgidx128.html.

Yamamoto Yūzō. "Meiji ishin ki no zaisei to tsūka." In *Kaikō to ishin*, pp. 111–72.

——. *Ryō kara en e: Bakumatsu, Meiji zenki kahei mondai kenkyū*. Minerva Shobō, 1994.

Yamamura, Kozo. "Success Illgotten? The Role of Meiji Militarism in Japan's Technological Progress." *Journal of Economic History* 37, no. 1 (March 1977): 113–35.

Yazaki, Takeo. *Social Change and the City in Japan: From Earliest Times through the Industrial Revolution*. Tokyo: Japan Publications, 1968.

Yokohama Shōkin Ginkō shi, 5 vols. Yokohama Shōkin Ginkō, 1920.

Yokosuka Kaigun Senshō shi, vol. 2. Yokosuka: Yokosuka Kaigun Kōshō, 1915.

Yoshimura Yasushi. *Shingan no hito Yamamoto Kakuma*. Kōbunsha, 1986.

Yoshino, Toshihiko. "The Creation of the Bank of Japan: Its Western Origin and Adaptation." *Developing Economies* 15 (December 1977): 381–401.

——. *Nihon Ginkō seido kaikaku shi*. Tōkyō Daigaku Shuppankai, 1962.

——. *Nihon ginkō shi*, 5 vols. Shunjūsha, 1975–1979.

Index

Page numbers followed by n or nn indicate notes; page numbers followed by *t* indicate tables; page numbers followed by *f* indicate figures.

Printed in the USA
CPSIA information can be obtained
at www.ICGtesting.com
CBHW030146270424
7638CB00012B/131/J

THE CLOSED PARTISAN MIND

THE CLOSED
PARTISAN
MIND

A New Psychology of American
Polarization

Matthew D. Luttig

CORNELL UNIVERSITY PRESS   **ITHACA AND LONDON**

First published 2023 by Cornell University Press

Library of Congress Cataloging-in-Publication Data

Names: Luttig, Matthew D., 1984– author.
Title: The closed partisan mind : a new psychology of American polarization / Matthew D. Luttig.
Description: Ithaca [New York] : Cornell University Press, 2023. | Includes bibliographical references and index.
Identifiers: LCCN 2022034150 (print) | LCCN 2022034151 (ebook) | ISBN 9781501768897 (hardcover) | ISBN 9781501768903 (epub) | ISBN 9781501768910 (pdf)
Subjects: LCSH: Political psychology—United States. | Polarization (Social sciences)—Political aspects—United States. | Right and left (Political science)—United States—Psychological aspects. | Party affiliation—United States—Psychological aspects. | Political culture—United States. | Group identity—Political aspects—United States.
Classification: LCC JA74.5 .L88 2023 (print) | LCC JA74.5 (ebook) | DDC 320.01/9—dc23/eng/20220915
LC record available at https://lccn.loc.gov/2022034150
LC ebook record available at https://lccn.loc.gov/2022034151

To Karen, Estelle, and Cecilia

The thing about democracy, beloveds, is that it is not neat, orderly, or quiet. It requires a certain relish for confusion.

—Molly Ivins

Contents

Acknowledgments

Many people have helped with this work over the years. I would like to thank, first and foremost, my family. Karen, Estelle, Cecilia, my parents, in-laws, and siblings, thank you all. My former advisers at the University of Minnesota (Howard Lavine, Chris Federico, and Paul Goren, especially) inspired my interest in political psychology and gave many helpful comments on this scholarship. John Bullock was beyond generous in agreeing to serve on my dissertation committee, and his comments were instrumental in my thinking about this topic. My current colleagues at Colgate University welcomed me into their department, and many of them have offered valuable commentary on various drafts of this book. In the fall of 2019, Thomas Edsall, Chris Johnston, and Jon Rogowski kindly agreed to participate in a book conference; I am grateful for their many useful suggestions and ideas. Finally, I would like to thank editors Emily Andrew and Bethany Wasik at Cornell University Press for their assistance throughout the publication process. This material is based on work supported by the National Science Foundation under Grant no. 1424049.

THE RIGIDITY OF THE RIGHT *AND* THE RIGIDITY OF THE EXTREMES

In November 2016, immediately following the election of President Donald Trump, *Saturday Night Live* ran a comedy sketch in the form of an advertisement in which "the unthinkable didn't happen." A liberal paradise called "the bubble" was proposed. The bubble was a place where the internet was restricted to show only "the good sites": HuffPo, DailyKos, YouTube videos about sushi rice, and "the explosive comedy of McSweeney's." The bubble promised to be a utopia for open-minded free thinkers to close themselves in and avoid the then-imminent America of President Trump. The implication of this sketch, of course, is that strong Democrats with the most negative reaction toward Trump were—despite espousing openness—actually rather closed-minded.[1]

Republicans, meanwhile, seem to like their bubbles just as much as *SNL*'s hypothetical Democrats. For instance, many Republicans express a host of factually erroneous beliefs: that the 2020 presidential election was stolen, that Trump's presidential inauguration drew more attendees than any other inauguration in US history, and that global warming is a hoax. These and other attitudes suggest that Republicans, like the aforementioned parodied Democrats, are closed and feel secure only when ensconced inside their own bubble.

These parodies, anecdotes, and data points about public opinion in the modern United States suggest that Democrats and Republicans alike may be more closed than open. Many people, in fact, would agree with this description. For instance, a 2016 report published by the Pew Research Center indicated that majorities of both Democrats and Republicans thought that members of the other party were more closed-minded than their fellow copartisans.[2] Are these

1

characterizations fair? What, precisely, is the relationship between closed minds and partisan identity? Is it accurate to say that modern partisans are, in some sense, psychologically closed?

This book investigates these questions. Specifically, I examine whether people who are psychologically closed are more intensely partisan than people who are psychologically open. By "partisan," I mean something specific: the extent to which people feel an identification with, an emotional connection to, and a sense of personal relevance for supporting the Democratic and Republican Parties. I focus on the construct of partisanship for two reasons. First, partisanship is one of the primary ways in which Americans today are politically divided (e.g., Iyengar, Sood, and Lelkes 2012; Mason 2015). There may also be some amount of ideological polarization in society, depending on which political scientist you ask (e.g., Fiorina, Abrams, and Pope 2011 versus Abramowitz 2010). But while the debate over the ideological climate continues, the partisan environment is fairly settled: according to Mason (2018, 77), "Political scientists can disagree until we are blue in the face over the extent of America's policy polarization, but are citizens prejudiced in their evaluations of political opponents? Absolutely."

The second reason I focus on partisanship in particular is that many political scientists (though not all) conceive of partisanship as a social identity rather than a reflection of ideological orientations or policy preferences. This conception has profound implications for our expectations about the association between closed minds and the intensity of an individual's partisanship. Indeed, since I derive my hypotheses about the link between closed minds and intense partisan identities from psychological literature closely associated with the social identity paradigm, this book can be viewed as a type of test of the social identity conception of partisanship.

I label the type of partisanship that I investigate in the following pages *group-centric partisanship*. As I define it, this is a way of expressing one's social identification with the political parties, and it reflects the multiple components of social identity theory as defined by Henri Tajfel (1972, 292) as "the individual's knowledge that he belongs to certain social groups together with some emotional and value significance to him of this group membership." This definition incorporates both cognitive self-categorization (knowledge of belonging) and emotional and value significance (feelings and judgments). The term therefore builds on past understandings of partisanship within the expressive or social identity perspective as a "psychological attachment" (Campbell et al. 1960) and an enduring identity signifying emotional connection (Green, Palmquist, and Schickler 2002). The concept of group-centric partisanship also incorporates a number of the concepts and measures that political scientists have developed to capture differences in the intensity of partisanship, including partisan strength and affective partisan polarization.

Yet none of the concepts or measures of variation across people in the intensity of their partisanship currently in use in the field of political science (including partisan strength or affective polarization) achieves the goal of capturing the multifaceted definition of social identity. Both the traditional and newer, revised measures of partisan identity strength (e.g., Huddy, Mason, and Aarøe 2015) primarily reflect cognitive self-categorization but neglect feelings and values as well as views of the outgroup. Similarly, Iyengar, Sood, and Lelkes's (2012, 406) theory of affective polarization seeks to utilize a "definitional test of social identity theory" by deploying a measure of the difference in the feelings people have toward their own party relative to the opposition. This incorporates the emotional dimension of social identity, and the crucial importance of outgroup as well as ingroup sentiment, but it does not measure the cognitive or value components of the theory. I believe that a more complete understanding of the social identity theory of partisanship can be achieved by incorporating all of these attributes of partisanship into a single conception. From this perspective, the concepts of partisan strength and affective polarization should be thought of as expressions of being a group-centric partisan. This book, therefore, will examine the relationship between psychological closure and group-centric partisanship, by which I mean strong partisan identification, affectively polarized feelings about the parties, and the extent to which one incorporates the parties' perceived values into their own worldview.

In conducting this inquiry, I build on and engage with a great deal of scholarship from political psychologists, many of whom have previously examined whether and how psychological closure (and related variables) may be associated with political preferences. For example, rigidity, dogmatism, and fear of threat and uncertainty were traits that earlier researchers associated with Nazism and fascism, and more recently with right-wing authoritarianism (Adorno et al. 1950; Altemeyer 1988). Others, however, have argued that a rigid or closed cognitive style is associated with extremism on both the left and the right (e.g., Rokeach 1960; Greenberg and Jonas 2003). These two hypotheses—the rigidity of the right versus the rigidity of the extremes—constitute the primary claims that both earlier and modern researchers have investigated with respect to the relationship between psychological closure and political preferences.

Today the rigidity-of-the-Right hypothesis has many more supporters than the alternative, particularly among scholars who study US politics. Ariel Malka and colleagues (2017, 126) reflect this when they write that "people who are intolerant of uncertainty and sensitive to threat tend to have a cognitive-motivational affinity for right-wing ideology. It is fair to say that this viewpoint has become conventional wisdom." One of my aims in this book is to push back—slightly—and release some tension from this reigning view of the relationship between psychological closure and political preferences that exists among many political psychologists. To do so, I argue that psychological closure is a construct that leads toward group-centric partisanship among both Republicans and Democrats.

Nevertheless, it is fair to assert that people who are closed tend to identify more with Republicans, while people who are open tend to be found more among Democrats. While this claim may not hold up in all eras or all contexts, it does seem to be valid in the contemporary United States (e.g., Johnston, Lavine, and Federico 2017). My own data even bear this out. For instance, in a survey I commissioned in 2014 through the organization YouGov, I found that 58 percent of Republicans, compared to 46 percent of Democrats, scored in the top half of a measure known as the need for cognitive closure (NFCC), a well-validated measure of psychological closure that I will elaborate on shortly. One point, therefore, for the rigidity-of-the-Right hypothesis.

The conventional view, however, often ends at this finding: that closure is more common among those on the right than it is among those on the left. But this finding does not eliminate the possibility that psychological closure may lead people, regardless of whether they are Democrat or Republican, to exhibit characteristics of group-centric partisanship: identifying strongly with their party, displaying negative feelings toward the political outgroup, and conforming to the views of party leaders. The conventional view, in other words, risks oversimplifying the relationship between closed minds and political preferences. A more accurate summary of the relationship between closed minds and political attitudes needs to incorporate an alternative perspective labeled "the rigidity of the extremes."

Indeed, there are strong theoretical reasons to think that this rigidity-of-the-extremes hypothesis may also have some validity. As I will explain in detail in chapter 1, there is a correspondence between psychological theories of cognitive closure and social identity theories of partisanship that leads to the alternative expectation that closed minds may be attracted to extreme political preferences on both the left and the right. Crucially, however, the "extremes" that these theories suggest will be appealing to the psychologically closed are not ideological in nature. Rather, psychological research on cognitive closure suggests that it is an attribute that predisposes an individual to be "group-centric": motivated to identify strongly with their own group, incorporate the group's values into their own, and distance themselves from their opponents. Hence, I suggest that political psychologists revise their understanding of the rigidity-of-the-extremes hypothesis away from ideological values and toward a group-centric understanding, with partisanship reconceived as a social identity rather than an expression of ideology. Based on these theoretical premises, I hypothesize that psychological closure could lead both Democrats and Republicans toward a more group-centric expression of partisanship. Therefore, the closing of the partisan mind, I suggest, may be a bipartisan process.

The Open and Closed Mind

The distinction between "open" and "closed" is at the heart of this book. Throughout, the conception and measure of closure or closed-mindedness that I employ are based on the philosophy and psychology of the need for cognitive closure (NFCC). NFCC is a widely used variable in the psychological literature that, crucially, provides a very clear theory about, and measure of, the concept of closed-mindedness. Arie Kruglanski (2004, 14)—who pioneered the study of the need for cognitive closure—describes those with a strong need for cognitive closure as desiring to "seize" and "freeze" on beliefs and information. People with a strong need for cognitive closure are more likely to "seize" on readily available information to reach a quick conclusion, as that is more closure providing than maintaining an open mind, and to "freeze" on that conclusion—to maintain their closure—once a judgment has been formed. Federico and Deason (2012, 201) provide another helpful definition of the concept: "In general, individuals with a high need for closure tend to find uncertainty highly unsettling, and they try to eliminate it as quickly and definitely as possible."

Most of us can recall times when a period of uncertainty or strife temporarily made us anxious and eager to resolve a particular challenge or situation. Individuals with a high level of need for cognitive closure experience this discomfort on a chronic basis. Hence, the closed-minded thinking that individuals with a strong need for cognitive closure engage in is driven not by malice but by a deeper psychological need to avoid and/or eliminate psychic stress. Such individuals are motivated to avoid the painful experience of uncertainty or confusion, and as a result they exhibit a cognitive style that leads them to quickly form judgments and to hold on dogmatically to those judgments once formed. Quickly forming judgments and holding those judgments dogmatically are characteristic of the closed mind, and the value of the NFCC construct is that it seeks to capture those two aspects of information processing directly.

The measures of NFCC that I rely on most in this book are scales based on a series of questions (fifteen, in the case of the YouGov study mentioned above). Appendix A presents the full set of questions that make up these NFCC scales. The questions ask respondents to agree or disagree with a variety of statements, including (1) "I don't like situations that are uncertain," (2) "I feel irritated when one person disagrees with what everyone else in a group believes," (3) "When I am confronted with a problem, I'm dying to reach a solution very quickly," (4) "I find that establishing a consistent routine enables me to enjoy life more," and (5) "I prefer things that I am used to over things I am unfamiliar with."

One benefit of these questions is their face validity in assessing the extent to which someone is open- or closed-minded. The closed prefer situations that are certain, feel irritated by a lack of conformity within a group, feel real relief when they can reach a solution quickly, prefer living within a highly consistent routine, and favor the familiar over the unfamiliar. The open, by contrast, exhibit the opposite tendencies: they revel in ambiguity, enjoy discussions within groups of dissimilar people, are capable of withholding judgment on a difficult problem, prefer having diverse days where the unexpected can happen, and enjoy exposing themselves to new people, things, and ideas rather than what they already know and feel comfortable with.

Another benefit of these questions is the absence of any explicit political content. Unlike widely used measures in political psychology, such as the Big Five personality traits of openness to experience and some measures of authoritarianism, such as the right-wing authoritarianism (RWA) scale, the NFCC questionnaire completely avoids anything related to political disputes.[3] This is a major but potentially overlooked benefit of the NFCC scale in comparison to other widely used measures in the field. At a minimum, it implies that associations between the need for cognitive closure and political outcome variables will not be tautological. The absence of political content should also protect against respondents giving "false" answers to the questions, a possibility for questions such as those on child-rearing preferences—the basis for the modern measure of authoritarianism—which may have become implicitly partisan and therefore incentivize people to provide a politically "correct" response (see Luttig 2021).[4]

The origin of open and closed minds is multifaceted. Like many psychological variables, individual differences in the NFCC construct appear to be a product of both nature and nurture, genetics and environment. Research has established that individual differences in the NFCC scale are partly heritable (e.g., Ksiazkiewicz, Ludeke, and Krueger 2016). But genes alone do not determine an individual's need for cognitive closure. In fact, recent research suggests that we have some degree of control over how open or closed we are—for example, that activities such as reading fiction (Djikic, Oatley, and Moldoveanu 2013), practicing mindfulness and meditation (Pokorski and Suchorzynska 2017) and cognitive behavioral training (Jackson et al. 2012) can make someone more open-minded (i.e., decrease their need for cognitive closure and/or increase their openness to new experiences). Thus, while this book treats NFCC largely as a predisposition, a precursor to outcome variables such as political beliefs, this should in no way be interpreted to imply that an individual's score on NFCC is unalterable. An individual's degree of open- or closed-mindedness, like most other aspects of individual psychology, can and does change.

How do the open and closed differ from each other? Research suggests that people at the poles of the NFCC construct differ in a variety of ways. For example, studies show that people high in the need for cognitive closure score lower on the openness-to-experience dimension of the Big Five personality traits (e.g., Neuberg, Judice, and West 1997), are less creative (Chirumbolo et al. 2004), are more prejudiced against outgroups (e.g., Roets and Van Hiel 2011a), consider less information when forming opinions (Choi et al. 2008), are less supportive of proenvironmental policies and behaviors (Panno et al. 2018), are more likely to be religious fundamentalists (Brandt and Reyna 2010; Saroglou 2002) and to endorse conspiracy beliefs (Marchlewska, Cichocka, and Kossowska 2018), are sometimes more militaristic (Federico, Golec, and Dial 2005), and are groupcentric, a mindset characterized by attitudes such as favoritism toward ingroups and the denigration of outgroups (Kruglanski et al. 2006).

The Ideological and Partisan Beliefs of Open and Closed Minds

Several researchers have also investigated how people with open and closed minds differ in terms of their Left-versus-Right political views. Studies show that people with high levels of the need for cognitive closure are more conservative and more likely to identify as Republicans, whereas those who are more open-minded tend to be more common among self-identified liberals and Democrats. In a meta-analysis of over eighty studies, John Jost and colleagues (2003) concluded that political conservatism has its roots in the psychological need to protect against threat and uncertainty, and NFCC was used as one of the primary indicators of the motivation to avoid uncertainty, which predicts embracing a conservative political orientation. This paradigm about the psychological underpinnings of conservative ideology is sometimes described as the "rigidity-of-the-Right" hypothesis: individuals who are politically aligned with the Right are characterized by psychological traits, such as the need for cognitive closure, associated with a rigid cognitive style. The originator of the NFCC scale describes why those high in the need for cognitive closure are less common on the left side of the political spectrum: "Because left-wing ideologies espouse egalitarianism, democracy, and openness to new ideas, their contents are *incompatible* with need-for-closure-based psychological strivings for stability and inequality" (Kruglanski 2004, 148; emphasis added).

But despite the consensus within the field that people who are cognitively closed are more likely to identify with right-wing ideologies and political parties, recent scholarship has identified limitations and qualifications to this general claim. For example, one point of growing consensus is that psychological closure has a natural affinity with conservatism in the domain of social and cultural politics (regarding, for instance, immigration, gay marriage, and abortion), but not for economic issues (e.g., the minimum wage and the marginal tax rate) (e.g., Johnston, Lavine, and Federico 2017; Malka et al. 2014).

Another common finding in the field is that the association between psychological needs (like the need for cognitive closure) and political attitudes is concentrated among individuals who are highly "attentive" to politics (that is, they know and care about politics and spend at least some of their limited time following current events), and among those who are the most highly educated (Federico and Tagar 2014; Jost, Federico, and Napier 2009; Johnston, Lavine, and Federico 2017; Malka et al. 2014). The attentive and the educated possess two characteristics that enhance the link between their psychology and their politics. First, they are more knowledgeable about politics, and so they have greater ability to choose political attitudes that serve the purposes they desire (such as reaching cognitive closure). Second, the attentive are more likely than the indifferent to think that their political attitudes reflect who they are (Johnston, Lavine, and Federico 2017). Those individuals who pay attention to politics, then, have greater motivation to use politics for self-serving purposes. People who spend time following politics therefore have both a greater ability and more of a motivation to bring their psychological goals into alignment with their political beliefs.

Another set of emerging findings is that the psychological need for closure is sometimes associated with particular policy preferences, more among self-identified liberals than conservatives. For example, Federico, Deason, and Fisher (2012) show, in the domain of specific policy preferences (or what political scientists call *operational ideology*—that is, one's attitudes about issues being debated at a specific time and place), that NFCC has stronger effects among those who identify symbolically as liberal than among those who identify as conservative. Similarly, Baldner et al. (2018) have shown that the effect of NFCC on the endorsement of binding moral foundations (moral values emphasizing ingroup loyalty, respect for authority, and religious or spiritual sanctity) is greater for liberals than it is for conservatives.[5] Findings like these complicate a blanket rigidity-of-the-Right narrative, and they suggest that there is value in investigating how the NFCC construct is related to political attitudes separately among individuals on the left and on the right. Thus, even though prior scholarship has shown that Republicans are more closed than Democrats, we should not make presumptions about how this correlation maps onto or can explain levels of group-centric partisanship *within* a party.

Theoretical considerations also suggest a need to complicate a simplistic rigidity-of-the-Right hypothesis as an explanation for the intensity of partisanship. In particular, the rigidity-of-the-Right model developed in political psychology was originally based on differences between liberals and conservatives, not Democrats and Republicans. But partisanship, according to many political scientists, is not simply a reflection of a person's ideological perspective. Instead many political scientists argue that partisan identity is a type of social identity in its own right, a product of socialization and emotional connection rather than a rational reflection of political values (e.g., Campbell et al. 1960; Green, Palmquist, and Schickler 2002; Greene 2004; Huddy, Mason, and Aarøe 2015). Indeed, the theory of affective polarization—the growing divide between people's feelings toward their own party and their feelings toward the opposite party—itself originates in this distinction between ideology and affect. As Iyengar, Sood, and Lelkes (2012, 406) put it, "To the extent that party identification represents a meaningful group affiliation, the more appropriate test of polarization is affective, not ideological."

It is based on this perspective that Iyengar, Sood, and Lelkes (2012) identified a previously overlooked amount of polarization in US society. Prior to their work, most research on polarization in public opinion focused on ideology (e.g., Abramowitz 2010; Fiorina, Abrams, and Pope 2011). From an ideological perspective, it was clear that people were "sorting"—that is, bringing their political preferences and ideology into alignment with their partisanship (e.g., Levendusky 2009), but it was not clear that people were polarizing. Yet when Iyengar, Sood, and Lelkes (2012) shifted the frame of reference to partisan affect (that is, positive affect toward one's own group and negative affect toward the outgroup), the evidence for polarization became clear. They showed that more Americans had become opposed to interparty marriage and had developed a wider gap in their feelings toward the two parties: they liked their own party more and the opposite party much less.

One of the widely known consequences of the need for cognitive closure is that it creates a pressure for people to like their own group more than outgroups, a pattern reflected in the argument that people with a strong NFCC are "group-centric" (Kruglanski et al. 2006). The pattern and kind of mass polarization that emerged in the United States in the latter decades of the twentieth century and that persist into the present are therefore reminiscent of this broader psychological pattern, whereby people with a strong need for closure develop strong ties to their own group and become hostile toward outgroups. Could this psychological dynamic provide insight into the rise of affective polarization—and other characteristics of group-centric partisanship, such as partisan strength—in US society?

To date, a few studies have investigated this possibility. Zmigrod, Rentfrow, and Robbins (2019), for example, have found that extreme partisans—regardless of whether they are Democrat or Republican—exhibit a cognitive style indicative of closed-mindedness and inflexibility. I too have reported, in two publications, a similar set of findings: that strong Democrats and Republicans, as well as Democrats and Republicans with the most affectively polarized feelings about the parties, are more authoritarian (Luttig 2017) and score higher in their need for cognitive closure (Luttig 2018). Findings like these suggest that even while there are more closed-minded individuals in the Republican camp than in the Democratic one, the closed-minded, regardless of party, are also most common among strong partisans and the affectively polarized than among weakly identified partisans and those with more moderate feelings about the parties. The strongest and most divided partisans—those who, in other words, exhibit a group-centric type of partisanship—on both sides of the aisle appear to be characterized by a shared tendency for psychological closure.

The Closing of the Partisan Mind as a Bipartisan Phenomenon

In the chapters that follow, I expand on these findings by unpacking the theoretical link between partisanship as a social identity and group-centric partisanship rooted in the need for cognitive closure, assessing whether group-centric partisans are more likely to be closed- than open-minded, explaining why this pattern exists, and illuminating how this relationship has come about and given rise to the resurgence of partisan thinking in the US electorate. I want to emphasize that the association between closed minds and group-centric partisanship depends fundamentally on the political environment. It is only because politics has recently become a sphere in which it is easy to reach closure that the closed-minded have been turned into group-centric partisans; in previous eras where politics was confusing and difficult, the closed were turned off from expressing this type of extreme partisanship. The upshot of this transition is that the nature of partisanship in the United States has changed. For people who are closed, partisanship has become less about emotional goodwill than about cognitive certainty regarding who is one of "us" and who is one of "them." Partisanship for the closed has, in turn, become akin to a religious identity, a place of comfort and solace where party leaders can act like a pastor leading a sermon, telling voters that to be a member of this party means endorsing certain positions and believing in certain truths.

Implications of Partisan Closure

Subsequent chapters unpack the psychological theory and historical dynamics that have given rise to group-centric partisanship rooted in the need for cognitive closure and assess various hypotheses that I derive from these theoretical premises. Some of the highlights of the findings include the following. In chapter 3, I show that there is a consistent and substantively strong relationship between the need for cognitive closure and indicators of group-centric partisanship, including measures such as partisan strength and affective polarization, among attentive supporters of both parties. In chapter 4, I show that the relationship between NFCC and group-centric partisanship has gotten stronger over time in the United States in response to polarization among political elites. And in chapter 5, I illustrate how political campaigns increase group-centric partisanship in part by making the public more politically attentive. Collectively, these chapters demonstrate that various indicators of group-centric partisanship are rooted in the need for cognitive closure, that this dynamic is evident among both Republicans and Democrats, and that this relationship is a variable one, across people, time, and events such as political campaigns.

These findings have both theoretical and normative implications. Theoretically, they suggest that political psychologists would be well served to revise their thinking about the relationship between psychological closure and political preferences. It is true that closure, or rigidity, is more common on the right than on the left. But it is also true that closure is more common at the extremes than among the moderates or independents—at least, that is, when partisanship rather than ideology is the dependent variable. These findings also, then, bolster the perspective in political science that partisanship represents something distinct from ideology and is a type of group identity rather than a running tally of policy preferences. As I elaborate further in the conclusion, however, these analyses also suggest a way to reconcile previously incompatible perspectives about partisanship. In particular, I suggest that the social identity framework may be most applicable to the closed, while for the psychologically open, partisanship may be a more substantive reflection of political perspectives. Theoretically, then, these findings have implications for enduring debates in political psychology and political science about the politics of the closed-minded and about the nature of partisanship.

But these findings, I suggest, also have normative implications. As Molly Ivins tells us, democracies are not neat and orderly. But neatness and order are precisely what the closed mind seeks. An increasing number of strong Democrats and strong Republicans therefore have a psychological mindset that is hard to reconcile with the always fluid politics of democracy. The increasing numbers of closed or group-centric partisans that this book documents and describes help to illuminate why US politics has become increasingly toxic and even dangerous. In the conclusion, I offer some possible strategies for opening the closed partisan mind.

THE CLOSING OF THE PARTISAN MIND

> **All movements, however different in doctrine and aspiration, draw their early adherents from the same types of humanity; they all appeal to the same types of mind.**
>
> —Eric Hoffer, *The True Believer*

Eric Hoffer, a San Francisco longshoreman and philosopher, observed in his book *The True Believer* that social movements from both the Left and the Right appeal to people with a similar type of mind. That type of mind, Hoffer (1951, 59) claimed, was one that was "frustrated." The frustrated individual seeks an escape from the self in some larger collective. The purpose of joining a political movement, Hoffer argued, is not for the instrumental goals the group claims to be seeking, but for psychological benefits such as "drown[ing] the voice of guilt within us" (95). The self-righteousness of the politically mobilized reflects deeply personal psychological motivations rather than instrumental policy goals.

Hoffer's account of social movements mirrors the explanation discussed here for the origins of group-centric partisanship in contemporary US politics. Like Hoffer, I argue that people who exhibit the characteristics of group-centric partisans, including being strong partisans and being affectively polarized, are motivated in part by deeper psychological needs, and are not simply the strongest supporters of their party's policy platform. Furthermore, in another echo of Hoffer, I argue that group-centric Republicans and Democrats, however different in label and doctrine they appear to be, appeal to a similar type of mind. Unlike Hoffer, though, I argue that the type of mind that leads one toward becoming a group-centric partisan is a closed mind rather than a frustrated one.

As I discussed in the introduction, the need-for-cognitive-closure scale provides a useful means of distinguishing people who are open- and closed-minded. An abundance of research, including my own, suggests that individuals who score higher on the NFCC scale tend to be more Republican than Democratic. This finding is consistent with the rigidity-of-the-Right hypothesis and the idea that right-wing parties and beliefs advance policies that resonate or match with individuals who dislike uncertainty (e.g., Jost et al. 2003).

But it is not self-evident that this perspective illuminates the nature and origins of the intense type of partisan conflict that the United States is currently experiencing. Is partisan conflict in the US a battle between parties that are psychologically different? Or are analysts like Hoffer on to something in asserting that extremists of all types are similar in some way? This chapter provides a theoretical framework for addressing this question, using the construct of the need for cognitive closure.

The upshot of the theoretical framework I describe is a revised formulation of the rigidity-of-the-extremes hypothesis, in which I state that the need for cognitive closure may lead people, regardless of their party, to express a more intense type of partisanship that I label *group-centric*. To unpack the basis of this argument, I describe the theory of *groups as epistemic providers* and *uncertainty-identity theory*. Both of these theories provide the rationale for my central contention that the contemporary closing of the partisan mind is a bipartisan phenomenon.

Collectively, the ideas expressed in this chapter allow for an integrative statement about the political psychology of closed minds and partisan group-centrism in US politics. The three major variables identified in the theory are (1) individual differences in the need for cognitive closure, (2) variation in the internal cohesiveness and polarization of the political parties (i.e., how effectively the parties provide closure or a "shared reality" to their supporters), and (3) individual and contextual differences in political attention. The major empirical hypothesis of this book is that the confluence of these three variables creates a group-centric form of partisanship that is reflected in measures such as partisan strength and affective partisan polarization.

Groups as Epistemic Providers

One of the characteristics of people who have a strong need for cognitive closure is that they tend to be group-centric. This theoretical claim is articulated in a review essay by Arie Kruglanski and colleagues (2006). Kruglanski et al. (2006, 88) develop their theory of the link between the need for cognitive closure and group-centrism through a set of logical deductions. They first define the need for cognitive closure as a psychological state or trait in which an individual is driven by a desire for firm knowledge. This desire originates from a motivation rooted in the perceived costs and benefits of possessing or not possessing cognitive closure, and may derive, Kruglanski (2004, 2) writes, from "Mother Nature (probably via the evolutionary process). . . . [T]he capacity to occasionally shut our minds, that is, develop the sense of secure knowledge that obviates our felt need for further agonizing deliberation" can spur us to action and help us "get on with our lives."

Take, for example, the issue of abortion. Many people may be comfortable not having a firm opinion on this issue. These individuals can recognize the complexities of the issue and see the strengths and weaknesses of both the pro-choice and the pro-life position. They can live their lives without concluding whether abortion is right or wrong. But other people need to have an answer to this question and a need for closure on this issue. They would be motivated to stop the agonizing deliberation they feel when thinking about abortion and would want instead to "seize" and "freeze" on an opinion. But what opinion should they form?

Kruglanski et al.'s (2006, 88) second proposition provides an answer: "Firm individual [or subjective] knowledge is grounded in the shared reality of one's reference groups." In other words, our knowledge about the world, how it works, what is true and false, right or wrong, and our opinions about issues like abortion, can be made certain, or "frozen," when such beliefs are shared with fellow group members. Embedded in this second proposition is a claim that may seem somewhat unusual at first glance. The claim, in short, is that our opinions about the world, including our preferences about public policy debates, do not solely emerge from within, through self-reflection or because of internal attributes, but are also heavily affected by the views of those in our social milieu. This dimension of public opinion has been somewhat neglected by political psychologists, who often point to internal characteristics, whether they be personality traits, moral foundations, or broad values, as the source of policy preferences. But however strongly internal psychological forces may push us in one or another direction on a controversial topic, Kruglanski et al.'s second proposition asserts that our confidence in this assessment hinges on that belief being shared with like-minded others. Absent a reference group to cement that belief, our preferences will be uncertain, fluid, and subject to change.

A number of other psychologists have made similar claims worth noting. For instance, Leon Festinger (1950, 272) argues that "an opinion, a belief, an attitude is 'correct,' 'valid,' and 'proper' to the extent that it is anchored in a group of people with similar beliefs, opinions, and attitudes." Hardin and Higgins (1996, 28) make a similar observation when they write that "in the absence of social verification, experience is transitory, random, and ephemeral; once acknowledged by others and shared in a continuing process of social verification termed 'shared reality,' experience is no longer mere capricious subjectivity, but instead achieves the phenomenological status of objective reality."

In other words, then, firm subjective knowledge about the world, and certainty in our political opinions about issues like abortion, can be achieved only when that knowledge is shared and agreed on by others. Absent a shared reality that is provided by a group, firm knowledge will be difficult to acquire. Hence, individuals with a need for firm knowledge—those who score highly in the need for cognitive closure—will naturally find groups more appealing than those who have less of a need for firm knowledge and who instead can tolerate their subjective knowledge being held with greater levels of doubt and uncertainty.

Many classic experiments in social psychology illustrate the importance of group dynamics for individual beliefs and behavior. For example, Muzafer Sherif's (1936) experiments on the autokinetic effect—a visual illusion of light moving in a dark room even though it is still—illustrates the tendency of individuals to conform to group norms. In these experiments, Sherif had individuals first estimate on their own how much the light moved. Then Sherif created groups of three individuals; each group included one member who had a different perception of how much the light moved than the other two. Sherif observed a tendency for those with outlying perceptions to bring their views into line with the perception of the two other group members. This example illustrates the general tendency of human beings to bring their individual subjective beliefs into line with others when the group believes something different from them. It is hard for individuals to stand alone in their beliefs, particularly when they stand opposed to others they consider to be similar to themselves or part of the same group. As Jamil Zaki (2020, 119) summarizes some findings from the research on conformity, "People find foods tastier, faces more attractive, and songs catchier when others like them. We litter and vote more often after learning that others have. The extent to which a scandal outrages us, a political candidate invigorates us, or climate change frightens us depends on how people around us feel." One upshot of this proposition is that political cognition is often social; the views and reactions of others around us influence our own thoughts and opinions.

Kruglanski et al. (2006, 85) build on these and other findings in social psychology. What the second proposition of their theory asserts is that individual knowledge about anything, even our own direct perceptions, as in the Sherif experiments, let alone our beliefs about an issue as complex as abortion, becomes stronger and more certain when those beliefs are shared with others. Furthermore, once a group has formed a view of "reality," regardless of how arbitrary it may be, it will exert pressure on fellow group members to conform to the group's belief, particularly if that individual is motivated to seize and freeze on a viewpoint. Cognitive closure, therefore, is achieved when individual knowledge is socially supported by the beliefs of one's reference groups. Hence, if one wants to seize and freeze on an attitude about abortion policy, the views of one's reference groups (such as a political party) would provide a viable solution to an otherwise agonizing conundrum as to which opinion one should hold. Note here, too, that there is no requirement that an opinion about abortion be extreme in order to offer someone cognitive closure. One can achieve cognitive closure from—that is, can seize and freeze on—an abortion perspective that is "moderate," as long as that position is provided in the shared reality of a reference group.

The third assertion that Kruglanski et al. (2006) make in their theory of groups as epistemic providers is that the ability of a group to provide a shared reality is variable, and varies as a function of a group's entitativity, or groupness. What makes a group entitative or groupy? Kruglanski et al. (2006, 85) write that "a central aspect of groupness resides in the coherence and consistency of the shared reality a group provides for its members, different groups in the same situation and the same group across situations may well differ in their degree of groupness or 'entitativity.'" "Coherence" and "consistency" are the two operable words above that define variation across groups in their degree of entitativity. When groups are coherent (or uniform, homogenous, unanimous, and constrained), and when they are consistent in those beliefs across situations and over time, they are more effective providers of a shared reality compared to groups that are diverse or heterogenous and whose beliefs are known to vary.

I believe that this proposition is key to understanding the rise in partisan strength and affective polarization over time in the United States, as both parties have changed in ways that have made them more coherent and consistent over the past few decades. This is evident in the case of abortion. In the 1970s and 1980s, the parties' positions were not nearly as opposed as they are today. Joe Biden, for example, cast a vote in 1982 for a constitutional amendment that would have allowed states to overturn *Roe v. Wade*, which proved problematic in the 2020 Democratic primaries. Anyone desiring cognitive closure on the abortion issue could not have found it from the political parties in the previous century. But today the parties provide a more consistent abortion opinion than in the past, allowing supporters to easily seize and freeze on a position.

The last proposition that Kruglanski et al. (2006, 88) assert is simply a logically derived extension of the points raised above: "The need for cognitive closure should foster the emergence of group-centrism in its varied manifestations." Manifestations of group-centrism include pressure to have a uniform opinion, endorsement of autocratic leadership, intolerance of diversity in group composition, rejection of opinion deviates, ingroup favoritism and outgroup derogation, attraction to groups possessing strongly shared realities, adherence to group norms, and loyalty to one's ingroup, qualified by the degree to which it is a "good" shared reality provider. All of these manifestations help to foster and maintain a shared sense of reality and firm knowledge. The theory that the need for cognitive closure promotes group-centrism therefore follows from a logical set of deductions based on claims about the interaction between individual motivations (for firm knowledge) and social relations (groups as epistemic or shared reality providers). Hence, Kruglanski et al. (2006, 85) write, "because persons construct their beliefs in concert with their fellow members, individual knowledge is inevitably grounded in a shared reality, and a desire for shared reality is tantamount to the quest for a firm individual knowledge."

This theory has clear empirical implications for the study of partisanship, especially if we conceive of partisanship as another type of group identity (e.g., Campbell et al. 1960; Green, Palmquist, and Schickler 2002; Huddy, Mason, and Aarøe 2015; Mason 2015). In particular, the manifestations of NFCC-based group-centrism, such as ingroup favoritism, outgroup derogation, and loyalty to one's ingroup, have clear empirical resonances with concepts and measures in political science, such as partisan strength and affective polarization. Hence, this theory suggests that NFCC may be associated with a group-centric type of partisanship that is expressed through signs like stronger partisan identities and more extreme levels of affective polarization. Furthermore, this theory suggests that the relationship between NFCC and group-centric partisanship may vary as a function of the perceived polarization of the parties. In environments where the parties are perceived as more divided and internally coherent, the relationship between NFCC and group-centric expressions of partisanship should grow stronger.

Uncertainty-Identity Theory

Michael Hogg's research on uncertainty-identity theory leads to the same expectations but is derived from the traditions of social identity and self-categorization theories (Tajfel 1969, 1974; Tajfel et al. 1979). Both social identity theory and self-categorization theory were influenced by Muzafer Sherif and colleagues' (1954) famous Robbers Cave experiment. In this experiment, young boys at a camp were divided into two teams (the Rattlers and the Eagles) and, after a week spent with just their own team members, were subsequently made aware of the other group's existence. Despite the boys in both groups having much in common, Sherif and other researchers at the camp observed that the two groups quickly engaged in competition with each other. They called each other names, showed a clear bias favoring ingroup members, and started fighting with members of the opposite group.

Henri Tajfel, inspired by these studies, wanted to examine the minimal conditions that would spur people toward the ingroup favoritism and outgroup discrimination observed in the Robbers Cave experiment. Tajfel designed the "minimal group paradigm" experiments as a baseline on which he could build in greater conditions for intergroup competition, based on the assumption that the "minimal" condition of simply assigning individuals to a group (with no meaning or value associated with that group) would be insufficient to create said competition. This assumption turned out to be wrong. On the basis of simply categorizing an individual as a member of a group, Tajfel and colleagues observed substantial levels of intergroup competition. For example, one experiment classified people as preferring paintings by Klee, others as preferring Kandinsky; in another, people were told that they were "overestimators" while others were "underestimators" of the number of dots on a screen. Note that people were randomly assigned to these conditions; they did not reflect their actual artistic preferences or dot-estimating capabilities. From this act of mere categorization, Tajfel and colleagues observed that people exhibited a clear tendency to favor members of their ingroup at the expense of the outgroup.

One of the explanations offered for this phenomenon was that group identities provide us with a sense of self-esteem; ingroup bias has the effect of bolstering our own self-image and providing a sense of positive distinctiveness (Turner 1975). But the empirical basis for self-enhancement as a motivational root of social identity processes such as ingroup bias and outgroup discrimination became "muddy" based on research conducted during the 1990s (Hogg 2007, 71). The ambiguity of the self-esteem hypothesis drove Michael Hogg and colleagues to formulate an alternative hypothesis about the motivations underlying social identity processes: uncertainty reduction (Mullin and Hogg 1998; Grieve and Hogg 1999).

As Hogg (2007, 71) summarizes in an essay reviewing his research on uncertainty-identity theory, "An epistemic motivation related to uncertainty was implicit in Tajfel's early discussion of social categorization (Tajfel 1972, 1974). Tajfel (1969, 92) believed that people engage in a 'search for coherence' to preserve the integrity of the self-image. . . . Tajfel and Billig (1974) suggested that one reason why people identify with minimal groups might be to impose structure on intrinsically uncertain circumstances. This idea was not pursued further—the motivational focus shifted to positive distinctiveness." That is, the motivational focus stayed on the theory of positive distinctiveness until Hogg and colleagues began their exploration of the role of uncertainty reduction in processes of social identification.

Uncertainty-identity theory has many similarities with Kruglanski et al.'s (2006) theory of groups as epistemic providers. It starts with the assumption that uncertainty is a generally uncomfortable state of mind. Uncertainty is mentally painful, and when we experience it, we want to get over it. We are especially motivated to reduce uncertainty when we are uncertain about something we care about, and particularly when we are uncertain about some aspect about our self and our relations with others. Human beings are incredibly social creatures. We want to know who we are and where we fit in. "Ultimately," Hogg (2007, 73) observes, "people like to know who they are and how to behave and what to think, and who others are and how they might behave and what they might think."

Hogg argues that social identities provide one of the most effective and accessible tools for alleviating feelings of uncertainty about the self and others. Our identities reduce uncertainty by providing prototypes of typical group members. Beliefs about prototypical characteristics of groups (e.g., Republicans are pro-life; Democrats are pro-choice) can *prescribe* perceptions, beliefs, feelings, values, and so on, that one can adopt if they choose to identify with that group. According to Hogg,

> When we categorize someone as a member of a specific group, we assign the group's attributes to varying degree to that person. We view them through the lens of the prototype of that group; seeing them not as unique individuals but as more or less prototypical group members—a process called *depersonalization*. When we categorize others, ingroup or outgroup members, we stereotype them and have expectations of what they think and feel and how they will behave. When we categorize ourselves, self-categorization, exactly the same process occurs—we assign prescriptive ingroup attributes to ourselves, we autostereotype, conform to group norms, and transform our self-conception. In this way, group identification very effectively reduces self-related uncertainty. It provides us with a sense of who we are that prescribes what we should think, feel, and do. (2007, 80)

Group identification can therefore reduce uncertainty about the self through the provision of group prototypes. The hypothesis that Hogg derives from this is that uncertainty (and the motivation to reduce uncertainty, which arises when we feel uncertain) will drive social identification processes, including ingroup loyalty and outgroup derogation. In one particularly telling demonstration of the centrality of uncertainty reduction to social identity processes, Hogg and Grieve (1999) showed that the minimal group paradigm effect is *eliminated* under conditions of high subjective certainty about the self. By reducing their participants' need for certainty about who they were, Hogg and Grieve (1999) ameliorated their need to identify with a group in the context of the minimal group paradigm. By contrast, in a state of high subjective uncertainty, Hogg and Grieve (1999) observed substantial amounts of ingroup bias in the minimal group context. Like Kruglanski et al. (2006), this theory thus places the psychological need for certainty at the core of social identity processes such as ingroup love and outgroup hatred.

Also like Kruglanski et al. (2006), Hogg and colleagues identify group-level entitativity as a key factor in the ability of groups to function as certainty providers. Groups that are highly entitative (that is, groups that have clear boundaries and have common cohesive goals) are better at providing certainty than less entitative groups. In Hogg's words, "An unclearly structured low-entitativity group that has indistinct boundaries, ambiguous membership criteria, limited shared goals, and little agreement on group attributes will do a poor job of reducing or fending off self or self-related uncertainty. In contrast, a clearly structured high-entitativity group with sharp boundaries, unambiguous membership criteria, highly shared goals, and consensus on group attributes will do an excellent job" (2007, 88). More plainly, social groups vary in their ability to provide prototypical traits and characteristics that can provide self-related certainty. Highly entitative groups are more effective at this role than less entitative groups. Thus, when people are uncertain, they will identify and identify more strongly with highly entitative groups that have clear group attributes than with less entitative groups that do not.

Like the theory of groups as epistemic providers, uncertainty-identity theory, combined with the well-established theory in political science that partisanship is a social identity, leads to the expectation that the desire to avoid uncertainty—a desire that is more strongly felt by individuals with a strong need for cognitive closure—will lead to stronger partisan identities and more extreme levels of affective polarization. Uncertainty-identity theory's emphasis on entitativity, and the importance it places on the capacity of groups to reduce uncertainty through the provision of group prototypes, also coheres with the theory of groups of epistemic providers in the implication that the relationship between uncertainty-reduction motives and group-centric partisanship will be stronger in eras of highly polarized parties than in eras of more diffuse parties.

Importantly, both the theory of groups as epistemic providers and uncertainty-identity theory postulate that only certain groups provide closure and/or reduce uncertainty. In particular, groups that provide a unified shared reality and/or a clear set of prototypes that their supporters can adopt are especially effective at providing this psychological benefit. Individuals with a strong need for closure, therefore, become group-centric only toward groups that they perceive as capable of providing these needs: groups that tell their supporters who is one of "us" and who is one of "them," what that means, and what beliefs accompany those group identifications. Over the past fifty years, the political parties in the United States have changed in ways that have made them more appealing to individuals with a strong need for closure. Today, the parties prescribe both self- and other-related prototypes to make it easier for supporters to think about the political landscape (e.g., Ted Cruz calling the Democrats the party of Lisa Simpson and

Republicans the party of Homer, Bart, Maggie, and Marge), and they provide a shared reality that offers partisans a script about what political positions they should embrace. Below I document how some of the changes in the political landscape have made partisanship more effective at reducing uncertainty and providing firm knowledge.

Changes in the Political Environment and the Unfolding of Partisan Group-Centrism

Over the past several decades, a number of changes have transformed partisanship in the US into an effective epistemic provider. I focus on three in particular. The first is the ideological polarization of political elites, which changed the parties from "big tent" parties lacking coherent goals and having substantial overlap into ideologically coherent parties with clearly distinct agendas. The second is the fragmentation of the media environment, which facilitated the creation of distinct partisan shared realities. Finally, the third is the realignment of the parties on the basis of various social identities, such as symbolic ideology, race/ethnicity, and religion (e.g., Mason 2018), which created clearer prototypes of both Democratic and Republican partisans. These three changes in the political environment have increased the ability for partisanship to provide a shared reality and reduce self-related uncertainty. The parties today, aided and abetted by sympathetic media outlets, provide a coherent shared reality that allows their supporters to seize and freeze on beliefs about the political world, themselves, and their opponents.

Polarization of political elites

The first change that has contributed to making partisanship a more effective provider of cognitive closure is polarization among elites, by which I mean elected officials and highly engaged political activists. It is widely acknowledged by political scientists that Republican and Democratic elites have polarized ideologically and have also become more divided over issues that cannot easily be classified as ideological. The result of this change is that the parties are now more effective at providing their supporters with a shared reality; they prescribe a set of beliefs that their supporters can adopt with confidence and certainty.

The polarization of political elites can be illustrated with quantitative indicators based on congressional roll call votes such as DW-Nominate and party unity scores, both of which track changes in the voting behavior of members of Congress over time (McCarty, Poole, and Rosenthal 2016). DW-Nominate scores allow researchers to place individual members of Congress in a one-dimensional ideological space from liberal to conservative. Based on this measure, which tracks the ideologies of every member of Congress throughout history, McCarty, Poole, and Rosenthal (2016, 3) identify two recent changes in the ideological mapping of members of Congress: "First, at the level of individual members of Congress, moderates are vanishing. Second, the two parties have pulled apart. *Conservative* and *liberal* have become almost perfect synonyms for *Republican* and *Democrat*." In other words, the parties no longer overlap in Congress (moderates are vanishing) and there are thus clear boundaries between the parties at the elite level. The two parties have also drifted further apart (the median Democrat has shifted left and the median Republican has shifted right). This ideological polarization of the two parties in Congress started during the mid-1970s and has steadily increased since.

Party unity scores provide another quantitative indicator of voting patterns in Congress, and by this measure, too, party elites have undoubtedly polarized over time. A vote in Congress is considered a party unity vote when a roll call vote divides at least 50 percent of Democrats against at least 50 percent of Republicans. Based on this indicator, there has been a clear rise over time in the number of votes that divide the parties. In 1970, for example, only about one-third of votes in the Senate divided Democrats and Republicans in this way. In 2010, nearly three-quarters of votes in the Senate divided a majority of Democrats against a majority of Republicans. In other words, as recently as 1970, most votes did not divide Democrats from Republicans in the Senate. By 2010, by comparison, most Senate votes split fairly neatly across partisan lines.

David Rohde (1991) and Sam Rosenfeld (2018) describe the process by which the political parties were transformed from big-tent parties of various factions in the middle of the twentieth century to vehicles for competing ideological agendas by the turn of the twenty-first century. Rohde emphasizes institutional changes in Congress (particularly the House) that empowered majority party leaders to push issues favored by a "majority of the majority," a philosophy that continues to shape the structure and behavior of the House and its members today. Rohde observes that these institutional changes began in the 1970s after conservative southern Democrats started being replaced by conservative Republicans and liberal Democrats, leading both parties to become more ideologically cohesive. The reduction in ideological cross-pressures within the parties incentivized "party government," whereby the majority party empowered their leaders to push items favored by a majority of the majority, away from the median preference of the legislative body as a whole. In the 1970s it was Democrats who had a majority in Congress and who, by virtue of changes in their southern delegation and the election of "new-breed northerners," had become a more ideologically cohesive party and changed the structure of Congress to advance issues on which the Democratic Party was unified. This process was accelerated under Newt Gingrich's leadership in the 1990s and continued through Nancy Pelosi's first speakership in the 2000s (Aldrich and Rohde 2019). The result of these changes was increased party unity in Congress, and issues that might bring the parties together are often kept off the agenda altogether.

Rosenfeld (2018) attributes the marriage of ideology and partisanship among political elites to the efforts of various actors who believed that parties *should* represent distinct ideological agendas. The American Political Science Association (1950) was one actor that advocated this change, believing that clearly defined parties would invigorate partisan competition and stimulate greater ideological thought among the public. Political activists also believed that the parties should be vehicles for advancing particular ideological beliefs, and they were crucial in changing the parties to become more ideological. Phyllis Schlafly's *A Choice Not an Echo*, published in 1964 and used in support of the staunchly conservative Barry Goldwater campaign, provides a prominent example of political activists in the middle of the century working to forge a new type of ideologically motivated party. The McGovern-Fraser reforms initiated after the fraught 1968 Democratic convention, in which the traditional factions within the Democratic coalition reached a crisis, also helps to illustrate the beliefs that would eventually shift power within both parties toward ideologically driven activists and away from traditional power brokers. Rosenfeld (2018, 151) cites one contributor to these reforms, James MacGregor Burns, as saying that his remade party "would welcome and recruit members on the basis of one test and one test alone—belief in the principles and goals of the party as defined in the national platform" and that "those who do not share its goals would see no point in joining it, or staying in it." These two examples, one from the GOP and one from the Democratic Party, illustrate how ideologically driven activists helped shift power within both parties away from those who could dole out patronage and make compromises between competing interest groups and toward issue-driven activists. The result was that the two parties, especially at the elite level, came to represent only those members who could pass an ideological litmus test. By the end of the twentieth century, the parties were no longer loose coalitions with indistinct boundaries, ambiguous membership criteria, and limited shared goals; instead they had become distinct groups defined by competing ideological interests.

But while the parties have become divided by ideology, political conflict among elites cannot be reduced to ideological disagreements. Frances Lee (2009, 18) argues that a lot of partisan conflict in Congress reflects the "inherent zero-sum conflicts between the two parties' political interests as they seek to win elections and wield political power." Thus, the parties often vote against each other not necessarily because of real disagreements, but because they want to weaken support for the other party or their initiatives. For example, votes on the debt ceiling used to be a routine matter; every president since Harry Truman has had to sign at least one bill raising it (Lee 2017). But recently, especially during Barack Obama's presidency and again during Joe Biden's, debt ceiling votes have become grist for the partisan mill as Republican legislators have used these votes as tools to (1) try to convince the electorate of the Democratic president's profligacy, and (2) exert concessions in other matters of public policy. Despite being an issue that Republican and Democratic presidents and legislators alike have supported in the past, and not being an issue that can be categorized as liberal or conservative since the vote on the debt ceiling does not actually change spending priorities, the debt ceiling has come to be seen as a tool for partisans to paint the party holding the presidency as irresponsible.

Illustrating the nonideological nature of some partisan conflict in Congress are those instances in which partisans vote for (or against) issues that they should be ideologically opposed to (or supportive of). Lee (2009, 76–77) provides as an example the partisan switch on the issue of federal sponsoring of testing in public schools. In 1993, this was an initiative proposed by President Clinton and supported by Democrats in Congress but opposed by congressional Republicans. In 2001, however, President Bush proposed a similar policy. This time, federal school testing was supported by Republicans and opposed by congressional Democrats. Ideology cannot readily explain this shift in voting patterns. A better explanation is that when presidents get behind an issue, their copartisans in the legislature have a political incentive to offer their support, and the president's political opponents have an incentive to oppose the presidential initiative and hope that the president can be weakened in the process. Lavine, Johnston, and Steenbergen (2012, xi) recount a similar example based on a 2003 vote to expand Medicare, "the most significant piece of social welfare legislation since the Great Society." One might assume this legislation was supported mostly by liberal Democrats. In fact, however, this was a proposal offered by Republican president George W. Bush and supported almost exclusively by congressional Republicans. Republicans supported, and Democrats opposed, a liberal policy initiative in order to rally behind their partisan interests in bolstering (or weakening) the incumbent president.

These persistent political conflicts separating elite Democrats from elite Republicans signal to voters that the parties are fundamentally distinct from each other. Most issues that garner political attention end up enmeshed in the web of partisan conflict, even if the issue is not ideological. The result is that on any salient issue, Democratic and Republican elites communicate to their followers different interpretations and sometimes even different facts. They communicate, in other words, a distinct but shared reality. It is easy for members of the public today to know what to think about an issue simply by looking to the leaders of their party. Since there is typically little disagreement within a party on any given issue, people do not need to think hard or question the validity of the information their leaders provide to them. They also do not need an ideological worldview to guide their political preferences. In fact, such an ideology would have led people astray from their party in the cases of federal school testing and Medicare expansion. It is far easier for people to simply look toward and adopt the positions of their political leaders. When those leaders are all unified in their position on an issue, their partisan supporters can acquire their "own" opinion on that issue with confidence.

The upshot is that today people can easily seize and freeze on a political opinion; the parties allow their supporters to readily acquire political closure. Compare this environment to the environment fifty years ago, when the parties were not often unified on issues. In that environment, forming a political opinion required considerably more cognitive effort, and one could be never certain one's belief was the "right" one, since it lacked the permanence that is obtained by a consensual shared reality. It is perhaps not surprising that in this earlier environment, political opinions were shown to be highly unstable over time (Converse 2006). But today, because the parties have become so ideologically cohesive, people can be confident that their beliefs are the "right" ones.

These changes in the political parties have not gone unnoticed by the public. Research has demonstrated that, in response to the polarization of political elites, the public has come to perceive the parties as increasingly distinct. No longer do most people see the parties as an echo; they see a clear choice when they think of differences between Republicans and Democrats. For example, Marc Hetherington (2001) reported a fairly dramatic spike in the percentage of American respondents perceiving "important differences between the parties" starting in 1980. Corwin Smidt (2017) updates this time series on perceptions of party differences and observes a continuing rise in the number of Americans who recognize the parties as different from each other throughout the 1990s and into the 2000s. By 2008, nearly 90 percent of those with high levels of political awareness were reported as believing that there are important differences between the parties (compared to only about 66 percent of those with low levels of political awareness). In short, the public now sees the two parties as separate groups with important differences.

As a result, the parties today are much are more highly *entitative* groups than the parties of the past. Party elites now have coherent goals, clear boundaries, and unambiguous membership criteria, and are consistent in these characteristics across issues and over time. The parties provide a shared reality to their supporters by communicating a relatively uniform position on almost all issues, a position that in almost every case is opposed by the other political party. From the perspective of potential voters, it is now much simpler to know which position they should take on an issue; it is easier for them to seize and freeze on their political opinions than in the past, when the parties represented a diverse group of interests with varying opinions on any given issue. As a result, partisanship today should be more appealing to individuals with a strong need for cognitive closure than partisanship was in the past. Individuals with a strong need for closure should be more likely to identify as strong partisans and exhibit dislike toward the opposite party in this environment, as these manifestations of group-centrism help to cement the shared reality of their party.

But political elites did not provide for this shared reality on their own. They have been aided and abetted by media entrepreneurs navigating an environment transformed by new technologies such as cable and the internet. These technological innovations, too, have been critical for the creation of partisan shared realities and, thus, for the emergence of group-centric partisanship rooted in the need for cognitive closure.

The Fragmentation of the Media Environment and the Rise of Partisan Media

For much of the twentieth century, Americans of both Republican and Democratic persuasions had a common source of shared reality: the television news media. In 1972, Walter Cronkite was the most trusted man in the United States. Lacking alternative choices, in the evenings many Americans tuned in to the major broadcast networks, all of which aired news programming at similar times (e.g., Prior 2007, 16). Without the intense competitive pressures that would soon overtake the news media, these news organizations could offer relatively "hard" journalistic coverage and take an objective or neutral stance. The result was that, regardless of partisan affiliation, Americans turned to the same few news sources and thus had a common basis for their beliefs about what was happening in the world, the consequences of policy proposals, and interpretations of events. And it was precisely in this period that political partisanship was in the throes of dealignment: partisan strength reached its lowest point in 1978, split-ticket voting was at record highs throughout this period, and many Republicans in Congress (and among the public) turned against Richard Nixon following the Watergate scandal.

But with the introduction of cable television, news organizations faced increased competitive pressures. In response to the changed environment, the mainstream news aired more "soft" coverage to try to attract viewers, a shift that seems to have directly contributed to the rapid decline in trust in the media that has occurred since the mid-1970s (Ladd 2012, chap. 5). Today, only 41 percent of Americans express trust in the news.[1]

As Americans turned away from traditional news organizations, an opportunity was created for entrepreneurs to capitalize on their discontent. Niche news organizations presenting an explicitly ideological view of the news found their footing in this new setting. Technological changes opened the space for these entrepreneurs, and Americans' growing distrust of traditional news organizations helped provide willing viewers.

Thus came the emergence of conservative talk radio, represented by such figures as Rush Limbaugh and Glenn Beck, and ideological programs on cable channels such as Fox News and MSNBC. These outlets, or at least segments presented on them, present their viewers with an explicitly ideological take on current events. Democrats and Republicans no longer share common "pictures in their heads," to paraphrase Walter Lippmann. Instead, Democrats and Republicans can tune in to like-minded media sources that offer an explicitly one-sided perspective. This shift was instrumental in the creation of separate partisan realities. As such, this change in the media environment also made politics and partisanship more appealing to those individuals who desire firm knowledge—that is, individuals with a strong need for cognitive closure. In today's environment, the media make it much easier for people to seize and freeze on political views by presenting information in an ideologically biased manner that reinforces the messages people are hearing from their political leaders.

The internet furthered this development by creating echo chambers in which people are protected from encountering viewpoints, arguments, and perspectives that might puncture the shared reality offered by their partisan group (Sunstein 2018). Research suggests that most people consume a more diverse media diet than is implied by the term "echo chambers" (e.g., Eady et al. 2019; Guess 2021), but the internet and social media, like cable television, give people more choice over their news sources. Given the natural psychological impulse to avoid cognitive dissonance, the introduction of choice often leads people to selectively consult media sources that bolster their preexisting opinions (Stroud 2011). The internet offers people a space where their beliefs can be, if they so choose, continually and willfully verified, helping those beliefs achieve the status of truth or objective reality. People's beliefs about the political world, their shared reality, become more easily "frozen" when they are not presented with contrasting viewpoints.

While the polarization of the parties around competing ideological goals set the stage for partisanship to be an epistemic provider of cognitive closure, it is unlikely that this change alone would have effectively created the separate realities that are so appealing to individuals seeking firm knowledge. The parties also needed to burst the power of mainstream news organizations, which in the middle of the twentieth century worked to forge a set of factual beliefs that Democrats and Republicans among the public held in common. To this end, party leaders and media entrepreneurs worked to vilify the mainstream media, weakening trust in those institutions and shifting viewers' attention toward explicitly partisan media that articulated party doctrine (Ladd 2012). Eric Hoffer (1951, 79) describes this process as a strategy typical of extremist political movements: "All active mass movements strive, therefore, to interpose a fact-proof screen between the faithful and the realities of the world." By creating a "screen"—in this case a partisan perceptual screen, to use the phrase coined by Campbell et al. (1960, 133)—through which followers can interpret the world, belief systems become immune to objective reality. What makes for an effective screen? To Hoffer (1951, 80), "the effectiveness of a doctrine does not come from its meaning but from its certitude. No doctrine however profound and sublime will be effective unless it is presented as the embodiment of the one and only truth."

The emergence of like-minded media outlets is a central part of the story of how partisanship has become a more effective provider of a shared reality. For those who dislike uncertainty and crave cognitive closure, tuning in to their side's nightly broadcasts provides reassurance that their beliefs are valid. A tightly bound social network, where like-minded news articles are shared and opposing views are vilified, similarly provides the certainty and solace that individuals with a strong need for closure desire. Prior to the introduction of these technologies, it would have been much harder for separate shared realities differentiating the parties to emerge. Therefore, we should view the new media environment as a key contributor to reforming the nature of partisanship into a place where those seeking firm knowledge and cognitive closure find their certainty.

Social Sorting and Partisan Prototypes

A third important change in the political environment is the social sorting of the party system. Social sorting refers to the fact that the political parties today are divided on the basis of other social identities, such as race, religion, class, and geography (Mason 2018). This separation of the parties along the lines of these social identities provides the parties with more explicit prototypes that provide greater certainty to people about who typical Democrats and Republicans are and what they are like. Democrats are highly educated, racially and ethnically diverse, and atheist or agnostic. Republicans are less educated, white, and Christian. These prototypes exist more in our minds than in reality (e.g., Ahler and

Sood 2018), but because so many people think of Democrats and Republicans in these prototypical ways, identifying someone (including oneself) as a partisan provides "knowledge" about who that person is and what he or she is like. This change in the party system, much like the ideological separation of the parties, has the potential to alleviate psychological uncertainty about the self and others (Hogg 2007).

A number of scholars have documented this recent sorting of the party system. In fact, this social sorting, and its contributions to partisan polarization, is the primary focus of Lilliana Mason's (2018) book. She writes, "We have gone from two parties that are a little bit different in a lot of ways to two parties that are very different in a few powerful ways" (43). Specifically, she shows that the two parties, over the past six decades, have become more distinct from each other in terms of their ideological identity (i.e., liberal or conservative), their religious beliefs, and their racial and ethnic identities. These social distinctions between the parties allow partisanship to become an identity that prescribes prototypes of ingroup and outgroup members. By categorizing oneself as a Democrat or a Republican, one can readily assign prototypical characteristics of that group to oneself, reducing self-related uncertainty.

Indeed, much of the ideological and religious sorting that has occurred over this time period has taken place as partisans have changed their ideological and religious identities to match the increasingly clear prototypes of fellow partisans on these dimensions (Levendusky 2009; Margolis 2018). And while racial and ethnic identities are less subject to partisan-driven change (but not entirely devoid of it either; see, e.g., Egan 2020), racial *attitudes* have increasingly moved in response to beliefs about the prototypical racial attitudes of one's partisan ingroup (Engelhardt 2018). Thus, the social sorting of the two parties has made partisanship a more effective provider of certainty about the self and others and therefore more appealing to those individuals with a strong need for cognitive closure. Social sorting has in fact caused individuals to change some of their own identities to bring them into closer alignment with the perceived identities of their party. This is precisely the type of pattern that social psychologists like Hogg (2007, 80) would anticipate: "When we categorize ourselves, self-categorization, exactly the same process occurs—we assign prescriptive ingroup attributes to ourselves, we autostereotype, conform to group norms, and transform our self-conception."

Another perspective on social sorting is that it varies between the two parties. Grossmann and Hopkins (2016, 67) develop this "asymmetrical perspective" when they write that Democrats "attract voters who endorse specific parts of their policy agenda, who identify with a social group within their coalition, or who sympathize with the party claiming to fight the powerful on behalf of the downtrodden. In contrast, the Republican Party's potential attractiveness rests on symbolic conservativism and a shared general perspective on the proper role of government in society." This claim that Democrats and Republicans differ qualitatively, with the former emphasizing the social groups in the party's coalition and the latter its ideological worldview, is not necessarily irreconcilable with the group-centric perspective on partisanship that I am offering here. The group-centric perspective, notably, is silent about the *type* of shared reality or group prototypes that parties offer their supporters. Thus, a party in the "groups as epistemic providers" framework could offer prototypes that reduce self-related uncertainty and provide cognitive closure about social groups within the coalition or about the symbolic goals that the party stands for. The key in the group-centric perspective is not the content, but the *manner* in which that content is communicated. As long as the content, whatever it is, is shared within the group, provides clear markers of group identity, and creates boundaries between "us" and "them," it can serve to reduce uncertainty and appeal to individuals with a strong need for cognitive closure. Thus, both the Democratic and Republican Parties can function as epistemic providers despite this asymmetry in the type of goals that they advocate.

This theoretical perspective may also illuminate patterns of group-centric partisanship among supporters of Donald Trump, despite the oft-noted lack of a consistent ideological reality presented to them. Barber and Pope (2019), for instance, have shown that strong Trump supporters willingly follow him regardless of whether the position he takes on an issue is a liberal or conservative one. What characterizes the shared reality from Trump, therefore, is not his ideological positions. Ideological commitments *could* provide a basis for constructing a shared reality, but it is not necessary. In the case of Trump, supporters are not getting ideological closure in the classic sense, but they are getting closure about who the "good guys" and "bad guys" are in the ongoing drama of US politics, about where they should get their news and whom they can trust. Trump supporters also get closure about specific political issues, particularly those (like the Robert Mueller investigation into the 2016 Trump campaign's relations with Russia, or the 2020 election) that directly challenge Trump himself. The content of the shared reality—the precise offerings made available by the group—is endlessly variable. What matters is not the content of that reality, but how it is communicated. As long as a group has a high degree of internal unification in some salient domains, and those domains create sharp boundaries between "us" and "them," that group will be entitative and will be able to help its supporters seize and freeze on their beliefs and their sense of self and where they fit in.

The Crucial Role of Political Attention

The two psychological theories reviewed above state that the desire for cognitive closure causes people to become group-centric because our beliefs about the world and the self are given greater permanence and certainty when those beliefs are shared with like-minded others. But neither theory specifies which groups people will turn to for closure. Both theories state that highly entitative and cohesive groups are more effective at providing closure than internally diverse groups. But a lot of group identities can provide a shared reality and offer comfort to individuals with a strong need for cognitive closure. Why and when, then, would people turn to political parties to fulfill this need?

One condition, discussed above, is the extent to which partisanship offers firm knowledge. As I have argued, the ability of parties to provide seizing and freezing on political beliefs has substantially strengthened over the past fifty years as political elites have polarized, explicitly partisan media have reemerged, and the social/demographic characteristics of Democratic and Republican partisans have become more distinct. But another, perhaps necessary condition is that political identity must be important to people in order for them to use their partisan affiliation for psychological closure. Someone who does not care about politics is unlikely to rely on political identity for psychological closure, and will instead look elsewhere—for instance, to religious identity.

This insight leads to my third theoretical claim: the relationship between the need for cognitive closure and being a group-centric partisan should be concentrated among individuals who are highly knowledgeable about and interested in politics. The concept that I label *political attention*—which I measure with various indicators, including general knowledge of political facts, self-described interest in politics, a preference for partisan media over traditional news sources, and, in one case where these other measures are absent, an individual's level of education—is indicative of two key aspects of an individual that should strengthen the relationship between the need for cognitive closure and the strength of the person's partisan identity. First, those individuals who are more attentive to politics and more highly educated should have greater exposure to elite discourse and partisan media (e.g., Zaller 1992), and thereby be more enmeshed in their parties' "realities." For example, research suggests that political knowledge, rather than promoting more "correct" attitudes, enhances conspiracy beliefs among conservatives—beliefs that are frequently mentioned by Republican Party leaders and in right-wing partisan media (Miller, Saunders, and Farhart 2016)—and polarizes Democrats and Republicans in their views about climate change (Tesler 2018). As one's political attention increases, one becomes more exposed to the separate realities constructed by the two parties, not necessarily to more accurate opinions. Corwin Smidt's (2017) research on perceptions of party differences, too, shows a clear difference between individuals with high and low levels of political attention in terms of their recognition of stark differences between the parties. Those who are highly attentive are much more likely to see the parties as representing a clear choice, not an echo.

The second characteristic of being highly attentive to politics is that it signals that one's political identity is important to one personally, to one's self-image. This perspective of political attention borrows from that developed by Johnston, Lavine, and Federico (2017, 47), who write that paying attention to politics is partly "rooted in a desire to express core aspects of the self through politics. In this view, people do not expect to change public policy by placing bumper stickers on their cars, by posting political messages on social media, or by arguing with their relatives at Thanksgiving dinner. They engage in these behaviors because they reinforce and signal an important component of their self-image." Consistent with this perspective, Johnston, Lavine, and Federico (2017) show that there is a strong correlation between measures of political interest and general political knowledge, with survey questions asking respondents whether their political attitudes are "an important reflection of who I am" and whether their political preferences "are an important part of my self-image."[2] High levels of political attention, therefore, signal both exposure to the epistemic communities constructed by both parties and that political identity is important to the individual.

Hypothesis

The sections above allow for an integrative statement about the political psychology of the need for cognitive closure and partisan group-centrism in US politics. The three major variables from the theory are (1) individual differences in the need for cognitive closure, (2) variation in the entitativity or polarization of the political parties (i.e., how effectively the parties provide a shared reality to their supporters, which increases as a function of ideological polarization and partisan conflict among elected officials, media fragmentation along partisan or ideological lines, and the extent to which partisanship is associated in the public's mind with clear stereotypes), and (3) individual and contextual differences in political attention. The major empirical hypothesis to be evaluated in subsequent chapters is that the confluence of these three variables creates a group-centric form of partisanship that is reflected in measures such as partisan strength and affective partisan polarization.

The Mueller Investigation as a Case Study of Partisans' Distinct Shared Realities

One case that illustrates the separate realities of the Democratic and Republican Parties is the Robert Mueller investigation of 2017–19, which was charged with investigating accusations that the 2016 Trump presidential campaign had colluded with Russia throughout the 2016 election and that President Trump had obstructed justice during his presidency. As with many contemporaneous controversies, public opinion about this issue was sharply divided by partisanship. For example, a CBS News poll conducted after Attorney General William Barr released his controversial summary of the Mueller report found that while 68 percent of Republicans thought that the report exonerated Trump, only 9 percent of Democrats thought similarly.[3] And like many preceding disputes, this issue is one that—at least for some time—was characterized fundamentally by uncertainty about what really happened. In the face of this uncertainty, political leaders and their media allies were able to craft favorable narratives that provided their viewers with firm knowledge.

The conclusion of the Mueller investigation offered an opportunity for information to be provided with the weight of authority that lay outside the he said–she said battle lines that had been drawn between Democrats and Republicans on the issue. It was for this reason that Donald Trump—back when he still had access to Twitter—tried to paint the Mueller team as simply "13 Angry Democrats." From this perspective, any information Mueller provided in his report could be simply interpreted from this well-established, us-versus-them, partisan frame. Yet the Mueller report never provided the unambiguous certainty that could potentially have punctured the closure that Democratic and Republican partisans had already reached on the issue. Thus, while Mueller concluded that there was insufficient evidence to charge the Trump campaign with a conspiracy to work with Russia during the 2016 campaign, he also detailed numerous interactions between the Trump team and Russia that may have been considered inappropriate. On the obstruction issue, Mueller's report was even more ambiguous. Mueller and his team described several episodes that they considered potential cases of obstruction of justice, but they failed to offer a firm conclusion.

Partisan opinion leaders and talking heads in the media filled this uncertainty with their own conclusions. Trump tweeted, "No Collusion! No Obstruction!" following the release of the report. And on Fox News there were ample opportunities for viewers to come away certain in their belief that Trump had done no wrong. For example, Sean Hannity remarked on May 29, 2019, following Mueller's press conference after the release of his report, "At this hour, what you are hearing from the Democrats [and] their, well, pet parrots in the media mob? Is nothing more than dumb, idiotic noise. Only noise, per usual, ongoing hysteria. Not about truth, not about facts. You've had two years of lies and hoaxes and conspiracy theories peddled every second, every minute of every hour of every day. And it's just one more round of lying, tinfoil hat conspiracy theories, Trump-bashing over a narrative that is totally dead and buried" (Bump 2019).

As Hannity's remarks indicate, Democrats and Democratic-aligned media offered very different interpretations. Indeed, the response from many Democrats was to call for Trump's impeachment. Kamala Harris, for example, tweeted on May 29, 2019, that "we need to start impeachment proceedings." Rachel Maddow on MSNBC responded to the conclusion of the Mueller report with skepticism about the conclusions that had been reached. To this day, Democrats and Republicans remain divided over the report, its conclusions, and what actions (if any) it warranted. There is not, and likely never will be, a shared consensus on the nature of the 2016 Trump campaign's relations with Russia and Trump's actions while in office. Beliefs about these questions are formed within partisan echo chambers that convey separate realities to their supporters.

Zack Beauchamp (2019), writing for Vox ahead of the Mueller report's release, had anticipated these reactions. He wrote that he was "profoundly pessimistic about the future of the Mueller investigation. Even if Mueller's full report is released in a timely fashion—and that's still an 'if' at this point, not a 'when'—people will read it differently, in each case trying to vindicate their narrative of events. There will never be a *shared sense of reality* about what really happened in 2016 or whether Trump obstructed justice during the investigation. No authoritative document could overcome the deep systemic forces that produced this dispute" (emphasis added). The Mueller investigation, and the partisan reactions to it, reveals the separate realities in which Democrats and Republicans now reside. To return to Kruglanski et al. (2006), the provision of a shared reality is one core function of a social group. When groups provide a shared reality, they work as epistemic providers, turning our subjective beliefs into objective truths. "The sharing of realities has been repeatedly highlighted as a definitional aspect of groupness," Kruglanski et al. (2006, 85) write. As the two parties have divided in the realities they provide to their supporters, they have become more "groupy," or entitative, and thus more appealing, especially to those individuals with a strong psychological need for cognitive closure.

In sum, this dispute reveals the deeply divided realities in which Democrats and Republicans reside in the present era when highly controversial partisan challenges arise. As is evident in this case, both party elites and partisan media entrepreneurs play an important role in conveying these separate realities to partisan supporters. If party elites did not divide so sharply in their reactions to this and similar cases, and if there was no partisan media offering opposing interpretations to politically engaged supporters, it is hard to imagine that the Mueller report would have divided mass Democrats and Republicans as sharply as it did.

The Rise of the Group-Centric Partisan

To integrate psychological research on group-centrism with broad patterns of historical change in US politics, I have argued that the political environment has increased the appeal of partisanship to those individuals with a psychological need for cognitive closure, particularly those who pay a lot of attention to politics. As a result, highly attentive individuals with a strong need for cognitive closure should exhibit a more group-centric form of partisanship: identifying more strongly with their party, expressing higher levels of affective polarization, and incorporating the parties' perceived values into their own worldview. One implication here is that it is incomplete to explain the rise of group-centric partisanship solely as a product of elite polarization, changes in the media environment, or social sorting. If most people were highly comfortable with doubt and uncertainty, they would be capable of navigating this new environment without becoming group-centric in their partisanship. It is primarily those people *uncomfortable* with doubt and uncertainty, who desire firm knowledge, for whom these structural changes in the political environment have meaningfully altered their partisan identities.

Thus, I hypothesize that those individuals high in the need for cognitive closure have become group-centric partisans precisely because the party system has changed in ways that they find appealing. Similarly, absent these changes in the political environment, those individuals with a strong need for cognitive closure would likely remain ambivalent about politics. When the two parties overlap, and lack internally coherent goals and inconsistent membership criteria, they are perceived as too ambiguous to offer firm knowledge or cognitive closure. In short, the rise of group-centric partisanship can be accounted for only by recognizing how the changes in the political environment have created parties that fulfill the psychological needs of the cognitively closed. In the remaining chapters, I set about assessing these hypotheses, starting first with an empirical assessment of the relationship between psychological closure and group-centric partisanship.

THE NEED FOR COGNITIVE CLOSURE AND PARTISAN GROUP-CENTRISM

One of the dominant trends over the past few decades of US politics has been the increasing partisanship of the US electorate. Studies have reported that strength of party identification is on the rise (Mason 2015), that the most engaged partisans are motivated more by the emotional stakes of winning and losing than by the policy consequences of election returns (Huddy, Mason, and Aarøe 2015), that feelings about the parties have become more intense and divided (Iyengar, Sood, and Lelkes 2012), and that more partisans are intolerant toward the idea of interparty marriage (Iyengar, Sood, and Lelkes 2012). All of these outcomes are expressions of what I label group-centric partisanship, and from the perspective of viewing each of these variables as expressions of the same underlying trait, it is not particularly surprising that they have all risen in tandem. Here, I provide an empirical assessment that examines and analyzes the relationship between the need for cognitive closure and each of these outcomes—partisan strength, intensity of partisan social identity, difference in feelings about the two parties, and attitudes toward interparty marriage—among both Republicans and Democrats. Researchers have found rising responses to all four of these measures, ushering in a wave of scholarship on the concept of affective polarization. The findings reported in this chapter therefore are relevant for those interested in the causes of affective polarization in US society. To the extent that the partisan group-centrism hypothesis is valid, I expect to find that NFCC increases each of these outcomes among politically attentive Republicans and Democrats.

Data and Methodological Details

Data for the subsequent analyses come from three separate sources: a nationally representative 2008 survey collected by Christopher Federico through GfK networks, a representative survey from 2014 that I collected through YouGov, and a 2018 SSI study that I collected. Each of these surveys contains unique indicators of group-centric partisanship. For instance, the GfK study, which also has the best claim to being nationally representative given that firm's subject recruitment methodology, contains a traditional measure of strong partisanship. The YouGov study captured the partisan social identity scale and feeling thermometers toward both parties. And the SSI survey was administered to ask respondents a revised measure of attitudes regarding interparty marriage (Klar, Krupnikov, and Ryan 2018). All three of these surveys were administered in an environment of high political polarization or party entitativity. Therefore, the second variable of the model is constant in these analyses, and what varies are individual differences in the need for cognitive closure and political attention. The hypothesis for this chapter, therefore, is that the interaction of NFCC and political attention will be positively associated with these various indicators of group-centric partisanship.[1]

In all of the models presented in this chapter, I control for standard demographic characteristics often used in political behavior research: age, education, income, sex, and race/ethnicity. I also include a control variable for *ideological self-identification*, a measure that seems to mostly reflect a social identification as either liberal or conservative (Mason 2018). This measure in all surveys is derived from a question asking respondents to categorize themselves on a seven-point scale from extremely liberal to extremely conservative. As Mason (2015) shows, partisans who share their party's ideological identity also exhibit the most partisan polarization. The second substantive control variable I include in the analysis is an index of respondents' extremism in response to questions about their issue attitudes (ranging from moderate on all issues to extreme on all issues). One theory is that partisan strength and affective polarization reflect different substantive disagreements between Democrats and Republicans over policy issues (e.g., Sniderman and Stiglitz 2012; Webster and Abramowitz 2017). The policy extremism variable controls for the likelihood that some people are driven to express a group-centric form of partisanship because they feel very strongly about policy issues.

One common strategy in past research on some of these outcome variables, the feeling thermometer difference variable in particular (what political scientists have taken to calling affective polarization), is to control for partisan strength. That is, many researchers will examine the relationship between partisan strength and affective polarization, modeling an assumption that the former precedes or causes the latter. For both theoretical and empirical reasons, I do not take that approach here. Part of my rationale for this decision is my conception of these outcomes as expressions of the same underlying latent variable of group-centric partisanship. Theoretically, therefore, modeling any one of these variables as a function of another is at least partly tautological. Empirically, it is not clear that partisan self-categorization precedes feelings about the parties, the assumption made in models in which partisan strength is included as a predictor of affective polarization. Affect, in fact, is widely theorized to precede cognition (e.g., Zajonc 1980), a notion that would suggest modeling partisan strength as a function of affective feelings toward the parties, rather than vice versa. My goal, however, is not to tease out the relations among different components of the group-centric conception of partisanship. Rather, my agenda is to assess whether psychological closure increases the expression of group-centric partisanship (and whether it does so among members of both parties). The clearest way to pursue this agenda is to model the relationship between NFCC and the various indicators of group-centric partisanship, conditional only on demographic variables and variables capturing alternative theories of these outcomes (e.g., ideological identity and policy preferences). That is the approach that the models below are designed to follow.

In presenting the findings, I focus on communicating the most central results about the relationship between NFCC, political attention, and partisan group-centrism. Interested readers can see the full tables in appendix B.

Study 1: Partisan Strength

In the first set of analyses, I examine the relationship between NFCC and the probability of a respondent identifying as a strong partisan. Partisan strength, I have claimed, is one expression of group-centric partisanship. Being a strong partisan captures the knowledge-of-group-identification dimension mentioned by Tajfel (1972), as well as the loyalty component of group-centrism identified by Kruglanski et al. (2006). Strength of partisan identification, therefore, is one component of the social identity theory of partisanship, and being a strong partisan is one way for an individual to express a group-centric form of partisanship.

Partisan strength is also widely acknowledged to be an important variable in political science, though more scholarship has investigated its effects than its causes. For instance, researchers have shown that strong partisans are more politically engaged and more biased in favor of their party (e.g., Bartels 2002; Fowler and Kam 2007), and are the least supportive of bipartisanship (Harbridge and Malhotra 2011). To the extent that strong partisanship reflects strong social identification with a political party and group-centric impulses, it should be rooted in the same motivation that drives group-centrism generally: the need for cognitive closure. This section presents a test of this possibility.

For this analysis, I utilize the 2008 GfK study, which contains a fourteen-item measure of the need-for-cognitive-closure scale (Pierro and Kruglanski 2006). Consistent with previous scholars, I find in this data set that more Republicans than Democrats score high on NFCC. Twenty-four percent of Republicans score in the top quartile of NFCC, compared to 20 percent of Democrats, while 36 percent of Democrats reside in the bottom quartile of the variable, compared to only 23 percent of Republicans. The remainder of respondents score somewhere in between. The data set also includes three indicators of political attention: self-described *political interest*, an eight-item measure of *general political knowledge*, and a two-item measure of *political-identity centrality*, which measures how important respondents say their political beliefs are to their self-concept.

The dependent variable is a traditional measure of partisan strength based on a measure of partisanship with seven response options: strong Democrat (18 percent), not-so-strong Democrat (16 percent), lean Democrat (10 percent), independent (13 percent), lean Republican (9 percent), not-so-strong Republican (14 percent), and strong Republican (19 percent).[2] Using this measure, I examine, using a binary logistic regression model, whether the need for cognitive closure predicts identification as a strong partisan (vs. a not-so-strong partisan or a partisan leaner) at high levels of political attention, and among Democrats and Republicans separately. Appendix A includes a list of the survey questions that go into the measurement of these key variables.[3] For ease of interpretation, each variable in the following analysis is rescored to range from 0 to 1, except for age, which is kept in its natural metric.

According to my hypothesis, I predict that the probability of a respondent identifying strongly with his or her party should rise as the need for cognitive closure rises, among respondents who are highly attentive to politics. Indeed, I find no significant direct relationship between NFCC and partisan strength among either Democrats ($b = 0.38$, $p < n.s.$) or Republicans ($b = 0.60$, $p < n.s.$) in this study. This is not surprising, however, as I anticipate that the relationship between NFCC and being a strong partisan will be concentrated among people who know and care about politics. The best way to test this prediction is with an analysis that models partisan strength as a function of an interaction between NFCC and political attention.

Table 2.1 presents the results of models estimating the probability of a Republican respondent identifying strongly with the Republican Party as an interactive function of NFCC and three measures of political attention (for full results, including control variables, see appendix B). As indicated in the table, the coefficient estimate for the interaction between NFCC and political attention is in the expected (positive) direction for all three indicators of political attention, but attains statistical significance in only one case (with the political-identity centrality variable). These findings suggest that, among highly attentive respondents, going from a low to a high value of NFCC increases the probability of a Republican respondent identifying strongly with the Republican Party, but in only one case can we make that inference with a high degree of statistical certainty.

In that latter case, the findings suggest a strong relationship between partisan strength and the psychological need for cognitive closure, among those Republican respondents who say that their political beliefs are an important reflection of their identity. Approximately 40 percent of Republican respondents score highly on the political-identity centrality scale. Fifty percent of Republican respondents in the survey agree or strongly agree with the statement that their political attitudes and beliefs are an important reflection of who they are, while 32 percent agree or strongly agree that their political attitudes are a part of their self-image. The political-identity centrality variable combines responses to these two questions. For respondents who score highly on this variable, the results in model 3 of table 2.1 suggest that NFCC plays a powerful role indeed in predicting the strength of Republican partisanship.

Specifically, among Republican respondents who score in the highest quintile of the political-identity centrality variable, the average marginal effect (AME) of going from the lowest to the highest value of NFCC is to increase

TABLE 2.1 NFCC, political attention, and partisan strength—Republicans

VARIABLES	(1)	(2)	(3)
	STRONG PARTISANSHIP	STRONG PARTISANSHIP	STRONG PARTISANSHIP
NFCC	−2.05	−0.17	−7.10**
	(3.181)	(4.916)	(2.224)
NFCC × Political interest	3.24 (4.043)		
NFCC × Political knowledge		1.03 (5.815)	
NFCC × Political-identity centrality			12.39** (3.218)
N	626	626	626

Logistic regression model coefficients; standard errors in parentheses. Control variables include income, education, age, white, Black, female, ideology, and policy extremism.

** $p < 0.05$, * $p < 0.10$

the probability of a respondent being a strong partisan by 0.66. The average marginal effect can be interpreted in this and the following studies as the effect of moving from the lowest to the highest value on the NFCC measure on the outcome variable, as averaged across each observation in the sample. A 0.66 increase in the probability of strong Republican identification as a function of moving from the lowest to the highest value of NFCC is, to put it bluntly, a huge effect. Not all Republicans who say that their political beliefs are important to them are equally likely to be strong Republicans. Those who score highly on the NFCC scale are much more likely to be strong than weak partisans, while those with a weak need for closure are significantly less likely to be strong partisans. Among the large and politically significant subgroup of Republican respondents who say that their political attitudes are personally relevant to them, therefore, NFCC has a very powerful ability to predict who is and who is not a strong Republican partisan.

Next, I run the same analyses but among Democrats instead of Republicans. This is the critical analysis for assessing the group-centric partisanship hypothesis. Is the closing of the partisan mind limited to Republicans, or is it bipartisan? If it is bipartisan, we should again observe a positive and statistically significant interaction between NFCC and political attention in predicting the strength of partisanship among self-identified Democrats.

Table 2.2 presents the results. Here we again see a consistent positive interaction between NFCC, political attention, and partisan strength. In this case, however, the key interaction term is statistically significant in each case. Therefore, we have here even more dispositive evidence in support of the partisan group-centrism thesis. At high levels of political attention, as measured by political interest, general political knowledge, and political-identity centrality, the need for cognitive closure is strongly predictive of partisan strength among self-identified Democrats. Thus, even though it is true that more Republicans than Democrats have a strong need for closure, it is also true that, at high levels of political attention, high-NFCC Democrats are more likely to be strong supporters of their party than low-NFCC Democrats.

To better illustrate these findings, I will unpack the relationship between NFCC, political knowledge, and strong Democratic partisanship. The political knowledge scale in this survey is based on eight factual questions about US political institutions and leaders (e.g., How long is the term of office for a US senator?). Twenty percent of Democrats in the 2008 GfK survey answered all eight questions correctly. My findings suggest that it is among these most knowledgeable respondents that the need for cognitive closure leads to stronger partisan identity. Specifically, for these "political experts," the average marginal effect of going from the lowest to the highest value in the need for cognitive closure is associated

TABLE 2.2   NFCC, political attention, and partisan strength—Democrats

VARIABLES	(1)	(2)	(3)
	STRONG PARTISANSHIP	STRONG PARTISANSHIP	STRONG PARTISANSHIP
NFCC	−3.86*	−3.75*	−3.67*
	(2.138)	(2.151)	(2.027)
NFCC × Political interest	5.85**		
	(2.672)		
NFCC × Political knowledge		5.80**	
		(2.871)	
NFCC × Political-identity centrality			6.57**
			(2.941)
N	650	650	650

Logistic regression model coefficients; standard errors in parentheses. Control variables include income, education, age, white, Black, female, ideology, and policy extremism.

** $p < 0.05$, * $p < 0.10$

with an increase of 0.29 in the predicted probability of a respondent identifying as a strong Democrat.

Strong partisans are some of the most politically active Americans. They vote at high rates and are among the most eager to have their voices heard. What makes someone a strong partisan? These findings suggest that the need for cognitive closure is part of the answer. For people who crave certainty and a shared reality, becoming a strong partisan appears to be a viable means for achieving cognitive closure. This, however, is true in these surveys only for people who, for whatever reason, care about and are interested in politics. This makes sense, as politics can be confusing, complicated, and difficult—precisely what people with a strong need for closure dislike. Yet having a strong need for closure is likely to push those who are interested in and knowledgeable about politics toward becoming strong partisans, and this is true regardless of whether they identify as Republicans or Democrats.

Study 2: Partisan Social Identity Strength

In this next study, I examine the relationship between the need for cognitive closure, political attention, and a variable labeled partisan social identity strength. The partisan social identity strength measure was created by Huddy, Mason, and Aarøe (2015) to provide an indicator of partisan strength that better matches with social identity theory, and that better captures variation in the intensity of one's partisan commitments. This measure is intended to reflect the expressive, identity-based theory of partisanship. Questions in the scale ask people how important their partisan identity is to them, how well the term "Democrat" or "Republican" applies to them, whether they use the word "we" instead of "they" when talking about their partisan ingroup, and the extent to which they think about themselves as being members of the party they say they support. Huddy, Mason, and Aarøe (2015) validate the expressive dimension of this measure by showing that people with strong partisan social identities respond more to threats to their group's political standing than to threats to the group's policy positions.

But while this measure is surely an improvement over the traditional indicator of partisan strength that I assessed in the previous section, it does not fully capture all dimensions of social identity theory. In particular, the measure seems to prioritize cognitive self-categorization over the emotional and value significance of group membership. Moreover, the measure does not incorporate attitudes about the partisan outgroup, a component that Iyengar, Sood, and Lelkes (2012) remind us is key to the social identity definition. Therefore, this measure, too, I suggest, should be viewed as another expression of group-centric partisanship. It greatly improves on previous measures of partisan self-categorization, and especially the intensity of that identity, but alone the measure does not fully reflect the social identity of partisanship. I hypothesize that NFCC will increase partisan social identity strength, particularly among those who are highly attentive to politics, and for both Republicans and Democrats.

To assess these predictions, I administered a survey in 2014 using the research firm YouGov (N = 1,200).[4] The survey included a fifteen-item measure of the need for cognitive closure (Roets and Van Hiel 2011b), two measures of political attention (a political knowledge questionnaire and a measure of self-described political interest), and the partisan social identity scale, as provided in Huddy, Mason, and Aarøe (2015). The specific survey questions for these main items are provided in appendix A. As in the previous analysis, the NFCC and political attention measures are here rescored to range from 0 to 1.

Unlike the partisan strength measure in the previous analysis, this measure of partisan social identity strength is a continuous variable (which, again, I rescore to range from 0 to 1), with 0 indicating the weakest possible social identification with one's party and 1 the strongest identification. The mean rating on the scale is 0.63 for self-identified Democrats and 0.62 for Republicans. Twenty-one percent of Democrats, and 15 percent of Republicans, say that their partisanship is "extremely" important to them. Seventeen percent of Democrats, and 11 percent of Republicans, say that the term "Democrat" (or "Republican") describes them "extremely well." Eleven percent of Democrats, and 6 percent of Republicans, report using the word "we" instead of "they" when talking about the party they support. And finally, 38 percent of Democrats, compared to 33 percent of Republicans, say that they think of themselves as being a Democrat (or Republican) "a great deal" of the time. Scoring a 1 on the combined variable, as 6 percent of Democrats and 3 percent of Republicans do, indicates the strongest response to all four of the partisan social identity questions.

With respect to the need for cognitive closure, this survey confirmed the general rigidity-of-the-Right pattern (as described in chapter 1): there tend to be slightly more Republicans than Democrats at high values of the need-for-closure scale, and more Democrats at low values of NFCC. But this pattern does not rule out the prediction of group-centric partisanship that NFCC will increase strength of partisanship among politically attentive individuals regardless of whether they identify with Republicans or Democrats. Here I test that prediction with a similar analysis, as reported above: interacting NFCC with measures of political attention in the prediction of partisan social identity strength. The results of an analysis modeling the direct relationship between NFCC and partisan social identity strength reveal again an insignificant pattern among Democrats ($b = 0.04, p < n.s.$) and Republicans ($b = -0.00, p < n.s.$). Does NFCC increase partisan social identity strength at high levels of political attentiveness?

The results in table 2.3 are generally consistent with theoretical expectations. In three of four analyses, the interaction term between NFCC and political attention (here measured with an indicator of political knowledge and political interest) reaches statistical significance, and in all four cases the relationship is in the anticipated positive direction. Thus, these findings indicate that, at high levels of political attention, going from a low to a high value on the need-for-cognitive-closure scale increases the strength of an individual's partisan social identity.

TABLE 2.3   NFCC, political attention, and partisan social identity strength

VARIABLES	REPUBLICANS		DEMOCRATS	
	(1)	(2)	(3)	(4)
	PARTISAN SOCIAL IDENTITY STRENGTH	PARTISAN SOCIAL IDENTITY STRENGTH	PARTISAN SOCIAL IDENTITY STRENGTH	PARTISAN SOCIAL IDENTITY STRENGTH
NFCC	−0.51*	−0.34**	−0.40*	−0.17
	(0.278)	(0.146)	(0.227)	(0.183)
NFCC × Political knowledge	0.65*		0.68**	
	(0.335)		(0.283)	
NFCC × Political interest		0.50**		0.43
		(0.200)		(0.263)
N	373	373	508	508

OLS coefficients; standard errors in parentheses. Control variables include income, education, age, white, Black, female, ideology, and policy extremism.

** $p < 0.05$, * $p < 0.10$

In this data set, approximately 40 percent of Republicans scored at the highest level of political knowledge, as did approximately 34 percent of Democrats. It is among these most knowledgeable respondents that a strong need for closure produces the strongest increase in partisan social identity strength. For knowledgeable Republicans, the average marginal effect of going from a low to a high value of NFCC increases the predicted level of partisan social identity strength by 0.14, on the 0–1 scale. For Democrats, the AME of NFCC on partisan social identity strength among the most knowledgeable is even more pronounced: going from the lowest to the highest value of NFCC is estimated to lead to an increase in partisan social identity strength of 0.28 on the 0–1 scale, or an increase of 28 percentage points. These are by no means trivial effects. For the most knowledgeable respondents, these findings once again suggest that the need for cognitive closure is a pronounced predictor of being a group-centric partisan.

Study 3: Party Feeling Thermometers

In this section I examine the relationship between the need for cognitive closure and a measure of party feeling thermometers. The party feeling thermometers ask people to rate both the Democratic and Republican Parties on a "feeling thermometer" that ranges from 0 to 100, where scores below 50 indicate "cold" feelings and scores above 50 indicate "warm" feelings (50, therefore, serves as a neutral point). Recently, these feeling thermometers have gained increasing attention by political scientists, as it has been shown that the gap between the ratings people give to their own party and the ratings given to the outparty has grown (e.g., Iyengar, Sood, and Lelkes 2012). This trend has become indicative of a phenomenon that Iyengar, Sood, and Lelkes (2012) label "affective polarization."

Affective polarization refers to the increasingly divided feelings that people have toward their own party compared to the opposite party. In the past, people liked their own party slightly more than the opposite party; today they like their own party much more. To capture this phenomenon, researchers like Iyengar, Sood, and Lelkes (2012) subtract respondents' feelings toward the opposite party from their feelings toward their own party. Positive scores on this feeling thermometer difference variable indicate that the respondents express more warmth toward their own party than toward the opposition. As I have stated, I believe that affective polarization provides a valid measure of the emotional dimension of partisan social identity. For that reason, I include the measure as another indicator of group-centric partisanship.

Here I examine the extent to which NFCC is associated with more positive values on the feeling thermometer difference variable. As in the previous sections, I estimate scores on the feeling thermometer difference variable as a function of the interaction between NFCC and measures of political attention. I include the same set of control variables mentioned in the above analyses. As in the previous two studies, all variables except age have been rescored to range from 0 to 1.

The data for this analysis come again from the 2014 YouGov study described in the previous section. The dependent variable is derived from subtracting respondents' ratings of the opposite party from their ratings of their own party on the feeling thermometer. In its natural metric, this feeling thermometer difference variable ranges, in theory, from +100 to −100, where +100 indicates the warmest feelings for one's own party and the coldest feelings for the opposite party, 0 indicates an equal rating for each party, and −100 signals a rating for the opposite party at the warmest level and one's own party at the coldest level. In practice, most people score positively on the feeling thermometer scale, indicating warmer feelings for the party they identify with than for the opposition. In the current data set, values on the feeling thermometer difference variable range from +100 to −74. Most respondents (85 percent), however, score above 0, indicating a relative preference for their own party; another 11 percent score at 0, rating both parties equally; the remainder indicate having warmer feelings for the opposite party than for their own. In the analyses below, I rescore the variable to range from 0 to 1 to ease interpretation. The results of an analysis modeling the direct relationship between NFCC and the party feeling thermometer variable reveal once again an insignificant pattern among both Democrats ($b = 0.02$, $p < n.s.$) and Republicans ($b = 0.08$, $p < n.s.$). Table 2.4 presents the results of the critical interaction model between NFCC, political attention, and party feeling thermometer differences.

In three of four tests in table 2.4, the interaction between NFCC and political attention is positive and statistically significant in predicting party feeling thermometer levels. Those who score high in both the need for cognitive closure and political attention are more likely to have more extreme ratings on the party feeling thermometer difference variable, indicating more positive feelings toward their own party than toward the opposition. Thus, among the politically attentive, and for both Republicans and Democrats, higher levels of cognitive closure are associated with higher levels of affective partisan polarization.

For example, approximately 27 percent of Republicans and 20 percent of Democrats indicated in the survey that they "always" pay attention to politics and elections (the highest value on the variable I labeled "political interest"). For these individuals, highly attuned to political affairs, the need for cognitive closure plays a strong role in differentiating those with a high degree of affective

TABLE 2.4   NFCC, political attention, and party feeling thermometer differences

VARIABLES	REPUBLICANS		DEMOCRATS	
	(1)	(2)	(3)	(4)
	PARTY FEELING THERMOMETER DIFFERENCE	PARTY FEELING THERMOMETER DIFFERENCE	PARTY FEELING THERMOMETER DIFFERENCE	PARTY FEELING THERMOMETER DIFFERENCE
NFCC	0.03	−0.15	−0.53**	−0.17
	(0.244)	(0.150)	(0.134)	(0.142)
NFCC × Political knowledge	0.07		0.90**	
	(0.288)		(0.180)	
NFCC × Political interest		0.35*		0.42**
		(0.201)		(0.196)
$\underline{N}$	373	373	508	508

OLS coefficients; standard errors in parentheses. Control variables include income, education, age, white, Black, female, ideology, and policy extremism.

** $p < 0.05$, * $p < 0.10$

polarization from those with more moderate attitudes toward the parties. Among the most attentive Republicans, the average marginal effect of going from the lowest to the highest value of NFCC is associated with a 35-point increase in the feeling thermometer difference score (using the variable's natural metric). Among the most attentive Democrats, by comparison, the AME of going from the lowest to the highest value of NFCC is associated with a 44-point increase. In short, among those who are most frequently tuning in to politics, those with a strong need for closure are much more polarized by this metric than those with a weak need for closure. The closed exhibit much more extreme and divided feelings about the parties than the open.

Study 4: Attitudes about Interparty Marriage

The final analysis I will report on in this chapter is of the relationship between the need for cognitive closure and attitudes about interparty marriage. Marital attitudes are frequent indicators of social distance and prejudice. In the United States, for example, opposition toward interracial marriage has been used as an indicator of racism (e.g., Bonilla-Silva 2006). Research has also shown that attitudes about marriage across ethnic lines in Africa are indicative of the degree to which ethnic groups are socially and politically divided (e.g., Posner 2004). Marital attitudes therefore reflect an enduring indicator of the extent to which groups see themselves as divided and their willingness to tolerate, intermingle with, and live among other members of their community.

Thus, it was somewhat shocking to many when Iyengar, Sood, and Lelkes (2012) showed in their article on the rise of affective polarization that large and increasing numbers of Democrats and Republicans expressed opposition or unease at the prospect of having a son or daughter marry someone across party lines. According to them, in 1960, when survey researchers asked partisans to express thoughts about interparty marriage, few people (approximately 5 percent) expressed any intolerance toward the idea. But they find that in more recent years, a large number of both Democrats and Republicans state that they would feel unhappy if a son or daughter of theirs married someone from the opposite party. The authors report, based on a 2010 survey, that approximately one out of every four partisans would be "somewhat upset" or "very upset" about the possibility of interparty marriage. Since the publication of that article, attitudes toward interparty marriage have become another indicator of affective partisan polarization. I believe that the interparty marriage item also reflects core dimensions of the social identity concept. It reflects a sense of loyalty to the ingroup and a visceral, emotional rejection of the outgroup. Hence, this item, too, I suggest, provides another way of assessing the extent to which a respondent is a group-centric partisan.

In an article published in 2018, and using the same YouGov data set analyzed in the two previous sections of this chapter, I showed that the need for cognitive closure is associated with a higher probability of a respondent—at least, a politically attentive respondent—indicating an opposition to interparty marriage (Luttig 2018). Like the findings reported above, this association was positive and statistically significant for both Republicans and Democrats. Hence, using this indicator of social distance or affective polarization, I reported another piece of evidence consistent with the rigidity-of-the-(partisan)-extremes hypothesis.

But research has subsequently emerged that challenges the validity of the traditional measure of attitudes toward interparty marriage. Klar, Krupnikov, and Ryan (2018) convincingly argue that the original survey questions measuring attitudes about interparty marriage potentially conflated negative attitudes toward the outparty specifically with negative attitudes toward both parties. As Klar and Krupnikov (2016) show, a number of people have gone "undercover" in their partisanship—not expressing their partisan identities or engaging in expressive partisan behavior—because they believe it is no longer socially desirable to identify with the parties. As a result, individuals who are opposed to having their children marry someone from the opposite political party may also be opposed to having their children marry someone from their own party. To quote Klar, Krupnikov, and Ryan (2018, 381), "In order to measure affective *polarization* properly, one must identify those who both *dislike the outparty* and *like their inparty*. When researchers ask only about dislike for the other party, they run the risk of overestimating affective polarization" (emphasis in the original).

Past measures of attitudes toward interparty marriage, including those I have published, do not sufficiently distinguish dislike of members from the opposite party specifically from dislike of partisanship generally. My purpose in this section is to attempt to remedy this shortcoming of my prior publication and to assess whether, using a revised measure of attitudes toward interparty marriage proposed by Klar, Krupnikov, and Ryan (2018), the need for cognitive closure is predictive of a preference for having offspring marry a member of their own party rather than a supporter of the political opposition.

In 2018 I commissioned a survey with the research firm SSI to address this concern by including questions that ask respondents how they would feel if one of their children married someone from both the Democratic and Republican Parties, capturing sentiment toward both inparty and outparty marriage and, therefore, better capturing the concept of affective polarization. The dependent variable here is a measure of *relative* preference for intraparty versus interparty marriage. If the need for cognitive closure increases opposition toward marriage of members of both parties, then it should be unrelated to this measure of social distance that incorporates feelings toward both inparty and outparty marriage. On the other hand, if NFCC contributes to group-centric partisanship, it should lead to a greater preference for inparty marriage relative to outparty marriage, and among supporters of both the Republican and Democratic Parties.[5]

Another feature of the 2018 SSI survey is that I included a measure of media preference as another indicator of political attention. Recall that the attentive are characterized by both their cognitive ability and their motivations. But the political interest variable used above potentially conflates two distinct motives: to be better informed and to have one's preexisting views validated. News choice provides a way to distinguish between these two motivations. Those who say they prefer like-minded media sources (Fox News for Republicans, MSNBC for Democrats) rather than a news show from a more neutral place such as PBS are, arguably, revealing their motivation for confirming their views rather than for obtaining neutral information. Thus, I hypothesize that the need for cognitive closure will be associated with group-centric partisanship (in this case, opposition to interparty marriage) more among those who use the media for affirmation (like-minded news) than among those who use the media to become informed (PBS). The political attention and NFCC variables are all, for the sake of interpretation, rescored to range from 0 to 1 in the following analysis.

The dependent variable in the following study takes values ranging from −3 to +4 (and is kept in that metric in the analyses below). Negative numbers indicate a greater preference for outparty marriage, while positive numbers indicate a preference for inparty marriage (0 indicates that respondents answered identically in their attitudes about inparty and outparty marriage). Approximately 58 percent of respondents indicated no preference for inparty or outparty marriage, 5 percent indicated a preference for outparty marriage, and the remaining 37 percent indicated a relative preference for inparty marriage and thus a group-centric form of partisanship. Does the psychological need for cognitive closure continue to explain variation in partisan marital attitudes using this measure?

The answer is unequivocally yes. First, note that I find in this study a significant *direct* effect of NFCC on affective polarization. Going from a low to a high level of the need for cognitive closure is associated with greater bias in favor of inparty marriage among both Republicans ($b = 0.76$, $p < 0.05$) and Democrats ($b = 0.74$, $p < 0.05$). As anticipated by my theory and hypotheses, however, this effect is concentrated among highly attentive respondents and among those who indicate a preference for like-minded over neutral news. Figures 2.1 and 2.2 provide a look at the relationship between the need for cognitive closure and partisan polarization across low and high levels of political attention among Republicans (figure 2.1) and Democrats (figure 2.2). Thus, figure 2.1 shows that the need for closure is associated with partisan group-centrism (as indicated by a greater preference for inparty relative to outparty marriage) among Republicans, but only for those who are interested in politics, say that their political identities are important to their self-image, prefer like-minded news, and are high in general political knowledge. For Republicans who do not follow politics, the need for cognitive closure is unrelated to this expression of group-centric partisanship.

Figure 2.2 shows a similar pattern among Democrats. At low levels of political attention, the need for cognitive closure is inconsistently related to group-centric partisanship. But at high attention levels (interest in politics, identity centrality, preference for like-minded news, and general political knowledge), NFCC increases the extent to which Democrats express a preference for inparty relative to outparty marriage. But the interaction term between NFCC and political attention on marital attitudes among Democrats is statistically significant only for the attention variables of interest in politics ($p < 0.05$) and political knowledge ($p < 0.05$). In short, the 2018 SSI survey provides consistent support for the partisan group-centrism hypothesis: the need for cognitive closure is associated with opposition to interparty marriage among both Democrats and Republicans, especially those who pay a lot of attention to the political environment.

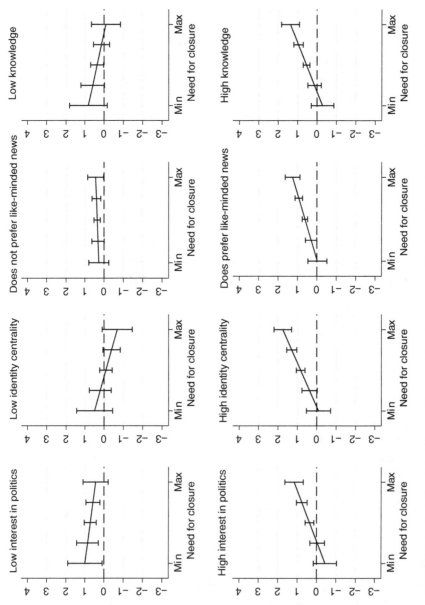

FIGURE 2.1 Relationship between the need for closure and affective polarization at low and high levels of political attention—Republicans. Note: Bars represent 95 percent confidence intervals.

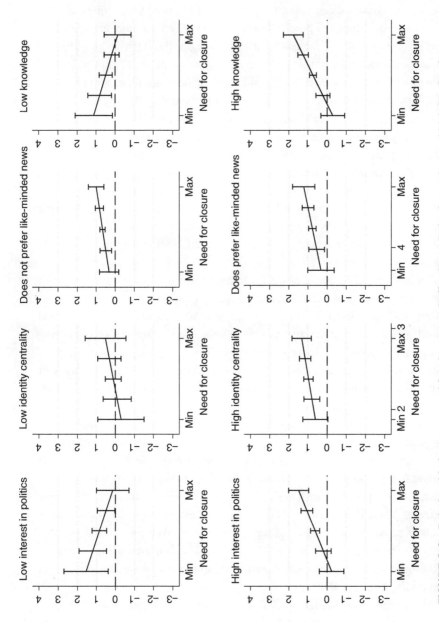

FIGURE 2.2 Relationship between need for closure and affective polarization at low and high levels of political attention—Democrats. Note: Bars represent 95 percent confidence intervals.

The Need for Cognitive Closure and Political Independence

The studies above suggest that stronger levels of the need for cognitive closure are associated, among the politically attentive, with being a more group-centric type of partisan: NFCC increases partisan strength, the intensity of partisans' social identification with their party, levels of affective polarization, and intolerance of interparty marriage. The flip side of these findings is that lower levels of NFCC are associated with a *weakened* form of partisanship. Among respondents who indicate a partisan affiliation, the findings above suggest, individuals with greater cognitive openness are more likely to "lean" toward their party or be a "not strong" partisan, have weaker social identifications with their party, be less affectively polarized, and be more tolerant of interparty marriage. Furthermore, my data also suggest that individuals with a weak need for cognitive closure are more likely to shun partisanship altogether, compared to individuals with a strong need for cognitive closure. NFCC, therefore, provides some insight into today's "pure" independents, but the results of these analyses are more suggestive than definitive.

For instance, in the 2008 Knowledge Networks survey, the interaction between NFCC and political knowledge is a statistically significant predictor of identification as a "pure" independent ($b = -7.29$, $p < 0.05$). At high levels of political knowledge, as the need for cognitive closure rises, the probability of identifying as a pure independent falls. This is what the theory of groups as epistemic providers would anticipate. As parties become perceived as effective providers of cognitive closure, they appeal more to individuals with a strong need for closure, and people with a weak need for closure become turned off from partisanship.[6]

An analysis of the relationship between NFCC and "pure" Independence from the political parties from the 2014 YouGov study presents similar findings. In that study, I find a significant main effect between NFCC and identification as a "pure Independent" ($b = -1.27$, $p < 0.10$). This finding suggests that as NFCC *weakens* (and openness rises), the likelihood of shunning partisanship altogether increases. There is also evidence suggesting that this finding strengthens at high levels of political knowledge, replicating the finding from the 2008 Knowledge Networks data ($b = -2.98$, $p = 0.144$). This finding, however, while suggestive, falls short of conventional levels of statistical significance, so we should interpret that finding with caution.

These results suggest that NFCC can be used to identify both sides of the partisanship spectrum: strong partisans and those abandoning their partisan identities altogether. At one end are concentrated individuals with a strong need for closure. Politically attentive strong Democrats and strong Republicans alike share a similar psychological need for cognitive closure. Their polar opposite in terms of psychology is not the other side, therefore, but those who are less partisan or completely independent. This divide, I suggest, is as important as the Left-Right divide. Individuals who are more open appear, in the present context of US politics, to find partisanship unappealing, as neither party embraces a complicated and ambivalent stance on, or approach to, pressing political questions.

Summary and Implications

The analyses reported in the four studies provide the first support for the rigidity-of-the-extremes hypothesis. I examined the relationship between the need for cognitive closure and partisan group-centrism using four dependent variables: partisan strength, partisan social identity strength, party feeling thermometer differences, and attitudes toward interparty marriage. The results have been consistent: the need for closure is a strong predictor of each outcome variable for both Republicans and Democrats at high levels of political attention. These results provide support for the theory of group-centric partisanship. The conflict between Democrats and Republicans does not appear to originate in a clash between rigid right-wingers and open-minded leftists; instead, strong partisans on both sides are characterized by a psychological characteristic—the need for cognitive closure—associated with group-centrism and psychological rigidity.

It is also noteworthy that NFCC is positively associated with each of these outcome variables. That consistency across these dependent variables supports the conception of each of these variables as separate indicators of a group-centric form of partisanship characterized by a strong sense of belonging, an affective divide in feelings toward the ingroup relative to the outgroup, and a willingness to conform to the parties' perceived values. Therefore, the growth in both the number of strong partisans and affective partisan polarization in US politics can be viewed as a simultaneous expression of a group-centric form of partisanship rooted in the need for cognitive closure.

A second empirical conclusion from this chapter is that the relationship between NFCC and group-centric partisanship is conditional on political attention. In particular, the relationship between being closed and being a group-centric partisan is concentrated among the most attentive. This finding potentially challenges an assumption in much of the political science literature that paying attention to politics translates into "good" democratic citizenship. Thus, attentive respondents, others have found, tend to participate the most in politics and appear the most capable of constructing their political beliefs along the same ideological lines as political elites. Many scholars, therefore, treat politically knowl-edgeable and interested respondents as ideal citizens: the bedrock foundation on which our democratic system depends (e.g., Delli Carpini and Keeter 1996). The inattentive, by comparison, are often portrayed as politically incompetent: rarely participating in public affairs and, when they do, making decisions in haphazard ways and on the basis of superfluous criteria.

This portrait of differences between the attentive and inattentive is not sup-ported in the analyses above. Instead, it is those who are paying attention who are the most affected by nonideological motives for psychological closure. Given the limited instrumental value of following public affairs, most people follow poli-tics because it provides certain expressive benefits, such as conveying who one is as a person (e.g., Somin 2006). Thus, for the attentive respondents—those who know about and express an interest in public affairs—partisanship is important to their self-image, a part of their self-conception and social identity. Apathetic respondents, by comparison, rarely think of themselves as members of a political party, outside, perhaps, of the hustle and bustle of a presidential campaign (as I will discuss more in chapter 4).

This underappreciated difference between the attentive and inattentive leads to different expectations about the psychology of partisanship. For the former, partisanship may be more like a social identity: an affective group attachment rooted in the need for psychological certainty. For the latter, those who do not closely follow politics, by contrast, partisanship is likely to be less stable over time, less important to political decision-making, and less a source of psycho-logical solace. The upshot of this empirical difference should be a shift in the way we evaluate the political competence of the attentive and apathetic. While political apathy may fall short on some indicators of political competence (civic knowledge, participation rates), the attentive are more psychologically invested in their partisan commitments and therefore may be less willing to take the steps necessary for democratic accountability—for example, voting their party out of office for bad performance, scandalous behavior, violating the party's ideological commitments, or disrespecting the rule of law.

It is precisely because the politically attentive are the most active in partici-pating in elections and communicating with elected officials that their cognitive closed-mindedness is problematic. These findings suggest a fundamental tension between, on the one hand, a lack of attention and the problems associated with low participation rates and political attention, and, on the other hand, political attention coupled with dogmatism. As Johnston, Lavine, and Federico (2017, 14) describe this "real democratic dilemma," the inattentive "do not participate at high rates, and thus people who do participate are typically more concerned with gratifying their identities than achieving good policy outcomes."

But the results here—which, in general, are consistent with this description of the democratic dilemma—also suggest a solution, or at least a crucial caveat in the form of high attention to politics in combination with a weak psychological need for firm knowledge. I find that when NFCC is weak, an increase in political attention often leads toward a decrease in partisan strength, intensity of partisan social identity, party feeling thermometer differences, and intolerance toward interparty marriage. These individuals—attentive but not cognitively closed—represent one solution to the democratic dilemma. Attention to politics does not inherently promote political dogmatism. When the need for closure is weak, the informed and politically interested appear to be quite capable of sustaining a political open mind and tolerating those who identify with their political opponents.

Therefore, I have uncovered new support for an old hypothesis: psychological closure contributes to political extremism (of a particular, partisan, and group-centric kind). This finding bolsters contemporary concerns about the politically aware population by showing that these individuals—who are the most influential in our politics—are most affected by their psychological characteristics. A necessary next step in evaluating the theory of partisan group-centrism is to unpack the broader social and political context in which individuals with a strong need for cognitive closure become group-centric partisans. This goal is achieved in the next chapter, where I assess the extent to which polarized political parties (i.e., those that prescribe clear beliefs to their supporters) attract the psychologically closed better than parties that are diffuse and fail to prescribe clear ideas. Elite polarization, the fragmentation of the media, and social sorting have contributed to changing perceptions of the political parties. The undoing of these perceptions, therefore, may have some potential to weaken the partisan commitments of those who crave cognitive closure.

CLEAR CHOICES, GROUP-CENTRIC PARTISANS

As I described in chapter 1, US politics has undergone a dramatic change over the past few decades. Political elites have polarized, the media environment has fragmented, and supporters of the two parties have become more demographically distinct. The parties are no longer echoes of each other; they give voters clear choices. I argued that these changes may be vital to understanding why individuals with a strong need for cognitive closure are, today, group-centric partisans. In the psychological literature, for example, the theory of groups as epistemic providers (Kruglanski et al. 2006) states that the relationship between the psychological need for cognitive closure and group-centrism varies based on the context and nature of the groups in question. It depends, in particular, on a group being perceived as a unified whole and sharply distinct from relevant outgroups (i.e., entitativity). A group must be capable of providing firm knowledge—about the world or the self—in order to attract those individuals motivated by a desire to achieve cognitive closure.

Thus, the strong association between NFCC and being a group-centric partisan documented in the previous chapter should, I hypothesized, represent a relatively recent phenomenon. This chapter assesses this claim in two studies. First, I examine whether the relationship between psychological closure and group-centric partisanship has changed over time. To do so, I assess the extent to which NFCC predicts strength of partisanship in the present era compared to the past. Second, I report the results of an experiment I conducted that manipulated subjects' perceptions about the polarization of the two parties. Here, I examine whether the power of party leaders to influence public opinion among their followers with high levels of NFCC increases when those elites are perceived to be politically polarized. This study, therefore, models the effect of NFCC and political attention on partisan group-centrism at different levels of party entitativity or polarization. In both cases, the studies converge on the finding that conditions of party polarization create the link between closed minds and group-centric expressions of partisanship.

Overall, the results support the argument that changes in the party system and the broader social and political environment appear to be causing respondents with a strong need for cognitive closure to become group-centric partisans. The link between NFCC and partisan group-centrism among highly attentive members of the population (1) exists in the present but not the past, and (2) is strengthened when political elites are perceived to be polarized.

Study 1: The Link between NFCC and Partisan Group-Centrism in the Past and Present

One empirical way of assessing the theory that polarized parties caused the link between closed minds and group-centric partisanship is simply to examine whether the relationship between the need for cognitive closure and partisan group-centrism is constant across time. I hypothesize that the link should be stronger in contemporary years than in the past, as a result of changes that have taken place over time in US politics and society.

To assess this claim, I draw on data collected by the General Social Survey (GSS), a nationally representative survey done on a regular basis by the National Opinion Research Center at the University of Chicago.[1] In 1988, the GSS first asked respondents to express their approval or disapproval of a statement that can be used as an indicator of individual differences in the need for cognitive closure: "Right and wrong are not usually a simple matter of black and white; there are many shades of gray." Stronger agreement with this statement indicates a low need for cognitive closure, while disagreement indicates a strong need for closure. As this has been used as a proxy for NFCC in previous research (e.g., Brandt and Reyna 2010; Peterson et al. 2009), the measurement of this item in distinct time periods—1988, 2006, 2008, and 2010—provides an opportunity for assessing whether the link between the need for closure and expressions of partisanship are stronger in today's era of polarized parties than in the past.

The GSS also includes a measure of partisanship and partisan strength in the years 1988, 2006, 2008, and 2010, which I use as dependent variables. Unfortunately, the GSS does not include a traditional measure of political knowledge or political interest consistently throughout these years. It does, however, include a measure of respondents' level of education, which I rely on as a proxy for political attention. While this is not ideal, education is commonly used as a substitute for political knowledge and attention (e.g., Converse 2006), and previous scholarship in political psychology suggests that, like other indicators of political attention, education increases the association between personality characteristics and political attitudes (e.g., Federico and Tagar 2014).

This data set, therefore, provides the crucial ingredients for assessing my hypotheses. It includes a measure of the need for cognitive closure in 1988, before partisan polarization and media fragmentation turned partisanship into a potential source of psychological certainty, and does so again in 2006, 2008, and 2010, after the political environment had undergone the profound changes that made the parties more "groupy," or entitative, and therefore more appealing to individuals seeking cognitive closure. The data set also includes an indicator of group-centric partisanship with the partisan strength variable, and a widely used proxy for political attention (education). Therefore, this study allows for an assessment of whether the expression of group-centric partisanship, the relationship between the need for closure and a more intense variety of partisan identification, can be tied to contemporaneous changes in the political environment. The key test is whether, at high levels of education, people with a strong need for cognitive closure are more likely to identify with, and identify strongly with, a political party in recent years, but not in 1988.[2]

Identifying as a Partisan

In the first analysis, I examine whether individuals with a strong need for cognitive closure are more likely to identify with a party, rather than as independents, in recent years than in the past. That is, when respondents are asked about their partisanship, the GSS first asks them, "Generally speaking, do you usually think of yourself as a Republican, Democrat, Independent, or what?" The first analysis assesses the extent to which NFCC is related to people responding "Democrat" or "Republican," rather than "Independent," in response to this first question.[3] As indicated in the previous chapter, those who are more psychologically open may increasingly shun partisanship, while those who are closed gravitate toward it, in light of changes in the party system. This section tests that claim.

Given that the transformation of the party system should have made the contemporary parties more appealing to those seeking closure than the parties of the late 1980s were, I expect that individuals today with a strong need for closure would be more likely to be partisans than individuals with a weak need for closure. By contrast, I expect that in 1988, before the polarization of the party system had reached its apex, individuals with a strong need for closure would not be any more likely than individuals with a weak need for closure to find partisan identification gratifying. Figure 3.1 presents the results of the analysis assessing whether, at high levels of education, NFCC's association with being a partisan rather than an independent varies across these two periods of time.

As figure 3.1 illustrates, there is clear support for the theoretical expectation that, at high levels of education, individuals with a strong need for closure will, in the present period but not in the past, find the parties attractive and therefore be more likely to identify as partisans than individuals with a weak need for closure. In 1988, the need for cognitive closure appears, if anything, to decrease the likelihood that an individual will identify with a political party, though this negative relationship is not statistically significant ($b = -0.29$, $p = n.s.$). There is no relationship between NFCC and partisanship in this earlier time period because partisanship at the time did not function well as an epistemic or shared reality provider that gave a party's supporters clear prototypes about what it meant to support that party.

From 2006 to 2010, however, the need for cognitive closure does have a pronounced effect on the likelihood of an educated respondent choosing to identify with a party rather than identifying as an independent ($b = 0.40$, $p < 0.05$). In other words, figure 3.1 shows that in 1988 the relationship between NFCC and being a partisan is negative but not significantly so, while in 2006–10 the relationship between NFCC and being a partisan is positive and statistically significant. In 2006–10, people who are highly educated and have a strong need for closure are more likely to say they identify with one of the two major parties than people who are educated and have a weak need for closure. In the contemporary era of US politics, individuals who view right and wrong as black and white rather than as shades of gray are more likely to identify as partisans than individuals who see ambiguity in matters of right and wrong. Partisanship has become a source for firm knowledge and cognitive closure.

Another way to see figure 3.1 is to look at the likelihood of an individual identifying with a political party at the same level of NFCC across these two time periods. For example, figure 3.1 shows that for people with a low need for cognitive closure, the predicted probability of identifying with a party is about 0.63 in 1988 and approximately 0.62 in 2006–10. In other words, individuals with low scores of NFCC are just as likely to be partisans in the contemporary period as in the past. But at the highest level of NFCC, the predicted probability of identifying as a partisan was just 0.56 in 1988, compared to 0.71 in the more recent period, a jump of 15 percentage points. This difference in the effect of NFCC across these

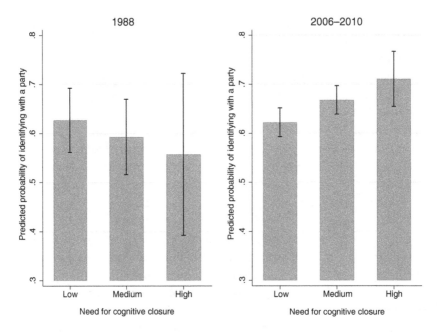

FIGURE 3.1 The effect of NFCC on being a partisan (vs. an independent) in 1988 and 2006–10. Note: Bars represent 95 percent confidence intervals. Results limited to those with more than a high school degree.

two time periods just misses statistical significance using a conservative two-tailed hypothesis test ($p = 0.137$). As the parties have polarized and the political environment has changed more generally, it appears that only individuals with a strong need for closure have responded by becoming more likely to identify as partisans.

Identifying as a Strong Partisan

In the next analysis, I assess the extent to which the need for cognitive closure predicts strong partisanship (among partisan identifiers but not leaners) across these time periods, one of the indicators of a group-centric type of partisanship. For those respondents who answered "Democrat" or "Republican" in response to the first question posed to them by the GSS, the GSS then follows up with a second question that asks, "Would you call yourself a strong [Democrat/Republican] or a not very strong [Democrat/Republican]?" Figure 3.2 presents the results of an analysis examining whether NFCC increases the probability that a respondent chooses strong partisanship as opposed to not-very-strong partisanship.

Figure 3.2 shows a dynamic similar to that observed in figure 3.1. In 1988, there is a slight but statistically insignificant negative relationship between NFCC and the predicted probability of a partisan identifying as a strong partisan ($b = -0.12$, $p < n.s.$). By contrast, in 2006–10, the relationship between NFCC and strong partisanship is positive and statistically significant ($b = 0.38$, $p < 0.10$). The need for cognitive closure causes highly educated respondents to be strong partisans in the present period of time, but not in the past.

Similarly, a look across the two time periods reveals how the rise of strong partisanship in the United States over the past few decades has been driven largely by individuals with a strong need for cognitive closure. Thus, the predicted probability of an individual with the lowest value on the NFCC scale identifying strongly with a political party was just 0.37 in 1988 and 0.44 in 2006–10, a 7-percentage-point increase. By comparison, the predicted probability of an individual with the highest value on the NFCC scale identifying strongly with a political party was 0.34 in 1988 and 0.54 in 2006–10, a 20-percentage-point increase. As in the previous analysis, this difference in the effect of NFCC across the two time periods is just shy of statistical significance using the more stringent two-tailed hypothesis test ($p = 0.144$). Some caution, therefore, is warranted in

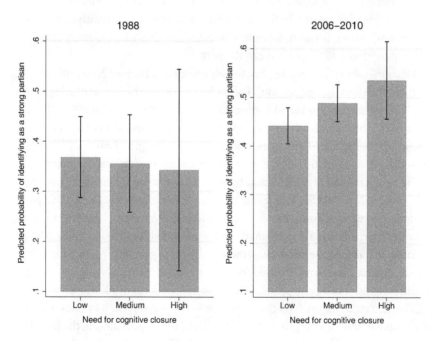

FIGURE 3.2 The effect of NFCC on being a strong partisan (vs. a not-very-strong partisan) in 1988 and 2010. Note: Bars represent 95 percent confidence intervals. Results limited to those with more than a high school degree.

these findings. Nevertheless, I believe that the findings are at least highly suggestive, especially in light of the less-than-ideal measure of NFCC included in the study.

Summary

These two analyses illustrate the dynamic and variable relationship between the psychological need for cognitive closure and partisanship across time in US politics. In the past, before the parties were polarized, individuals with strong and weak needs for cognitive closure were similarly likely to identify with a party and to identify strongly with a party. But today, individuals with a strong need for closure are significantly more likely than those with a weak need for closure to be partisans and to be strong partisans. Consistent with the theory that modern parties function as epistemic providers of a shared reality, the increase in group-centric partisanship over time in the United States can be partly accounted for by the increasing tendency of individuals with a strong psychological need for cognitive closure to become strong partisans in response to changes in the political environment. Partisanship is no longer just an emotional identity akin to a sports affiliation; it is now an identity that provides cognitive closure, a way of making sense of the world. Individuals who can handle more cognitive complexity, by comparison, are no more or less likely to identify with or identify strongly with a party today than they were in the past.

Of course, these findings are, like those presented in chapter 2, conditional on political attention (qua education). For individuals with a high level of education, NFCC leads to partisan identification and strong partisanship in 2006–10, but not in 1988. Indeed, this difference between the highly and less engaged is itself statistically significant. Thus, in a model predicting strength of partisanship from 2006 to 2010 as a function of the need for closure, education, and an interaction of the two variables, the interaction term of this equation is statistically significant ($b = 0.17$, $p < 0.05$). This indicates that for the highly educated, their psychological need for closure drives their partisan commitment, while for the less educated, partisanship remains unaffected by an individual's score on the NFCC variable. It is among the educated—those individuals generally praised for being knowledgeable about and involved in politics—where the psychological need to acquire cognitive certainty produces a group-centric form of partisanship.

The next study expands on these findings in two ways. First, it isolates the role of elite polarization by specifically manipulating that aspect among the broader set of changes that have taken place in US society. Second, it extends the analysis to the process of opinion formation and the last dimension of the social identity conception of partisanship: the incorporation of the group's views into one's own worldview. Together, these two aspects of the next study illustrate how the polarization of political elites has fostered a stronger sense of partisan group-centrism.

Study 2: The Effect of Polarization on Elite Opinion Leadership

Fanatics of all kinds are actually crowded together at one end. It is the fanatic and the moderate who are poles apart and never meet. . . . It is easier for a fanatic Communist to be converted to fascism, chauvinism or Catholicism than to become a sober liberal.

—Eric Hoffer, *The True Believer*

The theory of groups as epistemic providers developed by Kruglanski et al. (2006) postulates that, in addition to ingroup love and outgroup hatred, group-centrism grounded in the epistemic need for cognitive closure will also foster pressure for members to conform their beliefs about the world to the beliefs of their group. This, indeed, is also a key dimension of the social identity concept (Tajfel 1972). In this section I assess this claim in the context of political opinion formation. I build on the finding, documented in the political science literature, that the polarization of political elites has strengthened the extent to which partisans in the electorate, when forming opinions, follow partisan cues rather than alternative sources of information such as the arguments used in support of a policy position. For example, Druckman, Peterson, and Slothuus (2013) show that when political elites are polarized over policy issues, partisans will follow their party leaders even when the position of those party leaders is contradicted by a "strong argument." By contrast, when elites are not polarized in their position over an issue, the position with a strong argument supporting it receives much greater support. As Druckman, Peterson, and Slothuus (2013, 75) summarize their conclusion, "In polarized conditions citizens turn to partisan biases and ignore arguments that they otherwise consider to be 'strong.'"

This finding is consistent with the theory of group-centric partisanship developed in this book. The polarization of political elites increases the entitativity of partisanship, or the sense that a party represents a coherent and distinct group. The result of this change is that partisanship becomes a viable source for a shared reality and firm knowledge. Once this change in the nature of partisan groups occurs, the psychological theory of groups as epistemic providers predicts that partisan groups will have greater authority over the opinions and beliefs of their members—particularly, of course, over the opinions and beliefs of members with a strong need for cognitive closure, who are motivated to achieve a shared reality in order to attain confidence in their beliefs about the world. Thus, one extension of Druckman, Peterson, and Slothuus's theory and findings that I would add, based on the theory developed in this book, is that the power of polarized elites over the opinion formation of partisans should be greatest among individuals with a strong need for cognitive closure.

Finally, I predict that this interaction between elite polarization and the need for cognitive closure on conformity to elite positions in matters of opinion formation will be greatest among respondents who are highly attentive to politics. The attentive, recall, know and care about politics, and are therefore personally invested in their partisan identity. It is on these individuals, then, that the psychological need for group-centrism should exert its strongest effect.

Research Design

To assess these expectations, I added an opinion formation experiment to the 2014 YouGov study described in chapter 2. This study, like Druckman, Peterson, and Slothuus (2013), attempted to give participants two competing considerations to choose from when forming an opinion about a public policy issue. In this case, the two considerations were (1) support from party elites, and (2) the ideological stance typically associated with a policy position. Thus, each issue that partisans were asked to express an opinion about was associated with both partisan signals and long-standing ideological implications, and these two pieces of information were designed to push partisan respondents in opposing directions.

The study assessed opinion formation about four public policy issues: (1) Medicaid expansion, (2) affirmative action, (3) global warming, and (4) environmental regulation of iron mining. Each of these issues has clear associations with ideological liberalism and conservatism in US politics. Thus, Medicaid expansion is a clearly liberal issue, as is support for affirmative action, for policies that address global warming, and for environmental regulation. Therefore, if partisans are thinking about these issues ideologically, they should know these ideological associations and choose the "correct" policy position accordingly, with Republicans choosing the conservative stance on an issue and Democrats the stereotypically liberal option. In each case, however, respondents were given information that their party elites were taking an ideologically inconsistent position on the issue: Democrats were opposing Medicaid expansion, while Republicans were supporting it, for example. The key question, therefore, is whether partisans align their own position on an issue with the position of their party, even though this position is inconsistent with the general ideological outlook of the party. Furthermore, how do variables such as elite polarization, the need for cognitive closure, and political attention condition how people respond to this information environment?

The key manipulation in the experiment is the polarization of the parties. Following Druckman, Peterson, and Slothuus (2013), as well as Matthew Levendusky's (2009) work on the role of political polarization in the increasing levels of constraint between partisan identity and policy attitudes, respondents were randomly assigned to either a high- or a low-polarization treatment condition.[4] In the low-polarization condition, respondents were told, "As you can see, the partisan divide is not stark on this issue, as the parties are not very far apart. [Party A] tend to support [the issue]; [Party B] tend to oppose [the issue]. However, members of each party can be found on both sides of the issue." In addition to this information, respondents were shown an image of the positions of hypothetical partisans in Congress on the issue. In the low-polarization treatment condition, respondents saw an image with significant overlap between the parties, and though one party was clearly presented as supporting the issue and the other party as opposing it, there was also some overlap between the parties.

In the high-polarization condition, respondents were told, "As you can see, the partisan divide is stark on this issue, as the parties are very far apart. [Party A] strongly support [the issue]; [Party B] strongly oppose [the issue]. Also, most members of each party are on the same side as the rest of their party on this issue." As in the low-polarization condition, this verbal description of the parties' positions was complemented by a graphical image showing hypothetical partisans in Congress. In the high-polarization graphic, the parties were very far apart, and there was a large gap between them.[5]

These manipulations capture differences between a low- and high-polarization political environment. In the less polarized environment, the parties do not provide respondents with a shared reality or firm knowledge, whereas in the highly polarized environment the parties are much more entitative and therefore capable of providing closure. Thus, I hypothesized that this manipulation should strengthen the power of party leaders to persuade their supporters to adopt their positions, even, as was the case here, when the position of party leaders is contrary to that party's ideological reputation.

After exposure to this information, respondents were asked to report their own position on the issue: whether they supported or opposed Medicaid expansion, efforts to combat global warming, affirmative action, and environmental regulations, on a seven-point Likert scale. This study, as discussed in previous chapters, also included a fifteen-item measure of the need for cognitive closure and a multi-item index of political-knowledge and interest-in-politics questions, which, to simplify the presentation here, are combined to form a scale for political attention (alpha = 0.62).[6] To test my hypotheses, I assessed the likelihood of a respondent taking the same side on an issue as his or her party (e.g., Democratic partisans adopting a conservative policy position, and Republicans adopting a liberal position), as a function of elite polarization, the need for cognitive closure, political attention, and the interaction between these three variables. This allowed for a direct assessment of the theory of parties as epistemic providers: when parties are polarized, an individual psychologically craves closure, and that individual knows and cares about politics, the conditions for partisan group-centrism should be strongest.

Figure 3.3 displays the results of a model estimating the likelihood of a respondent choosing the same (ideologically incorrect) position presented as being supported by the respondent's party leaders, averaged across all four issues, as a function of the three variables central to my theory and analysis. Thus, on the left-hand side of the figure, when respondents were exposed to the low-polarization treatment condition, the likelihood of their choosing their party's position on the issue appears to be unaffected by the need for cognitive closure. By contrast, in the high-polarization treatment condition, individuals with a strong need for cognitive closure are—at high levels of political attention—significantly and substantially more likely than those with a weak need for cognitive closure to choose the same side of the policy issue as their party leaders. Indeed, in this right-hand side of figure 3.3, I observe that the likelihood of an individual bringing his or her attitudes into uniformity with party leaders increases by over 50 percentage points when moving from a weak to a strong need for cognitive closure in the condition of high elite polarization and at high levels of political knowledge and interest.

The upshot of this experiment is that it shows how the impact of NFCC on partisan group-centrism—captured here with opinion formation and bringing one's own opinions into alignment with group leaders—varies as a function of the political environment. It is only in the condition of high elite polarization that the interaction between political attention and NFCC significantly affects this manifestation of partisan group-centrism. The polarization of political elites has been central to making the parties shared reality providers that appeal to individuals with a strong need for cognitive closure. As a result of this shift in the political environment, high-NFCC respondents, particularly those who are invested in politics, have reacted by becoming more partisan, even to the point where they are willing to adopt policy positions that diverge from the ideological reputations of their partisanship. These partisans are group-centric partisans, not ideologues, and while they may exhibit more constraint between their partisan identities and issue attitudes, this is not necessarily a reflection of their growing

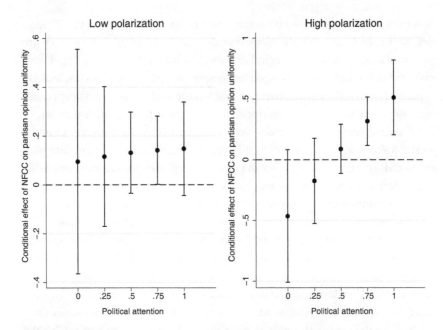

FIGURE 3.3 The effect of NFCC on partisan opinion uniformity across low and high levels of elite polarization. Note: Bars represent 95 percent confidence intervals.

capacity for ideological thinking. Instead this increasing constraint reflects the growing power that party leaders, who now are unified and offer firm knowledge, have over the opinions of their followers.

Polarization Changed the Nature of Partisanship

Together, these two studies establish the important temporal dynamic driving the association between the psychological need for cognitive closure and partisan polarization. This relationship is a recent phenomenon; it did not exist in 1988, as demonstrated in the GSS study. And the experimental section of this chapter established that manipulating perceptions of elite polarization similarly "activated" the relation between NFCC and manifestations of partisan group-centrism among the politically attentive.

As the parties have changed, as Democratic and Republican elites have become more divided and more cohesive unto themselves, and as the media environment has fragmented, the psychology of partisanship has changed. Politics has become simplified. Are you pro-life or pro-choice? Defund the police, or LAW & ORDER!?

Policy choices like these are no longer presented to the public with the difficulties, ambiguities, and complications that they naturally entail. Instead they are presented as simple, obvious, logical decisions. In turn, it has become cognitively easier for one to know one's position on complex issues, as it involves just looking to party leaders—all of whom today are much more likely to agree with each other than they were in the past—to derive an attitude one can feel confident about.

Of course, trends in the parties have not been a constant movement toward greater uniformity from the past to the present. The electoral cycle, in particular, exerts change on the parties. For example, during primaries, candidates seeking their party's nomination emphasize the differences between themselves and their competitors. Following the primary, then, parties unify around their general election candidate as the dynamics switch to competition between the two parties. This dynamic, too, has implications for the theory of partisanship as epistemic provider. Specifically, it suggests that general election campaigns should—like elite polarization more generally—cause individuals with a strong need for cognitive closure to gravitate especially strongly toward their party. Elections, in other words, should be among the most polarizing of events in our politics because they create the conditions in which the two parties best exhibit the characteristics most appealing to the cognitively closed. Thus, while this chapter focused squarely on the historical polarization of the two major political parties responsible for creating the link between closed minds and the intense kind of partisanship currently rampant in US politics, the next chapter focuses on the results of this polarization over the course of a contentious political campaign: the 2016 presidential contest between Hillary Clinton and Donald Trump.

THE DYNAMICS OF PARTISAN CLOSURE AND THE 2016 PRESIDENTIAL CAMPAIGN

During presidential campaigns, two critical things happen that should affect the relationship between psychological closure and political preferences. First, as campaigns shift from the primary to the general election, the messages being communicated to the public change. During the primary, political communication emphasizes differences within the parties, a state of affairs that should inhibit the ability for political parties to clearly prescribe beliefs and offer cognitive closure. By contrast, as the primary ends and the two parties settle on their general election nominee, political communication shifts to emphasize the unity of each party and its differences with the opposition. Hence, in this latter stage of campaigns, the closure-providing capacities of political parties should be at their height. The second key dynamic of political campaigns, and presidential campaigns in particular, is that they represent a moment when most Americans pay some attention to politics. Political campaigns, therefore, represent a case in which two of the three major variables in the psychological theory undergo important change.

The upshot of these two dimensions of presidential campaigns is that they should provide events that "trigger" the theoretical link between NFCC and group-centric partisanship. Recall the concept of entitativity described in chapter 1 and its connection to the theories of groups as epistemic providers and uncertainty-identity theory. Both theories state that the link between the need for cognitive closure (or the motive to reduce uncertainty, in the case of the latter theory), and group-centric outcomes such as strong ingroup identification and outgroup derogation is strengthened in environments where groups are internally unified and sharply differentiated from the outgroup. This is when groups are effective at providing a shared reality or self-related prototypes that effectively reduce uncertainty and provide cognitive closure.

Therefore, as the internal conflicts made apparent during primary elections wane and as the walls differentiating the parties wax as the general election unfolds, individuals who crave firm knowledge should be the most likely to strengthen their partisan allegiances and exhibit dislike of the partisan outgroup. Furthermore, this association should be strengthened during presidential campaigns *regardless* of an individual's general level of political attention. In this environment, almost everyone is exposed to some political discourse, and many people who otherwise do not pay much attention to politics take an interest when the White House is at stake. It is for these reasons, I believe, that campaigns have been shown to be one of the forces driving the rising tide of partisan antagonism in our society (Iyengar, Sood, and Lelkes 2012).

This chapter assesses these claims in the context of the 2016 presidential campaign, one of the most vicious political campaigns in recent memory. The two candidates vying for the presidency that year, Hillary Clinton and Donald Trump, were polar opposites in many respects. Clinton, a longtime staple of US politics, former first lady, senator, and secretary of state, and first female major-party nominee for the presidency, appealed to many traditional Democrats but came to be viewed unfavorably by the rest of the electorate. Donald Trump, by contrast, had never held political office before in his life. His appeal was rooted partly in his promise to "drain the swamp" and remake US politics. The two candidates differed not only in their political history but in their style, manners, and character as well. And both candidates became, over the course of the campaign, more disliked than liked.

Thus, the stage was set for 2016 to be a highly acrimonious election. And it was. Clinton and Trump raised vicious attacks against each other. Clinton's commercials showing Trump mimicking reporters with disabilities and bragging about sexual assault left a deep impression on many Americans, who widely viewed Trump as not having the personality or temperament to hold office.[1] Similarly, Trump's attacks on Clinton for her email scandal and for forcing Americans to relive former president Bill Clinton's sexual escapades contributed to a widespread sense that Clinton could not be trusted.[2] In the face of these biting personal attacks, 2016 held the potential to increase the already polarized state of US politics.

Capturing Campaign Effects

While the 2016 campaign seems to have been almost designed to foster greater partisanship in the electorate, actually identifying campaign effects has always been a challenge for the social sciences. Larry Bartels (2006) wrote about the challenges of identifying campaign effects in a 2006 book chapter titled "Three Virtues of Panel Data for the Analysis of Campaign Effects." The second and the third of these virtues are of the most relevance here, as they directly address issues of causal inference in the context of political campaigns.[3] Bartels's second virtue of panel data—data that interview the same people at multiple points over time—is that they "permit analyses of opinion change in which prior opinions appear as explanatory variables" (2006, 136). The third virtue is that "panel data facilitate analyses in which relevant explanatory variables are measured outside the immediate campaign setting" (136). The upshot of these two virtues is that panel data provide a better basis for causal inference, as temporal priority is a necessary condition for an independent variable to cause a dependent variable.

The use of panel data, therefore, allows for an assessment of whether psychological NFCC precedes partisan polarization. By including a lagged measure of partisan polarization as an explanatory variable, I can investigate whether high NFCC was associated with changes in levels of partisan polarization over the course of the 2016 campaign. In sum, the use of panel data in this context provides further evidence about (1) the nature of the temporal relationship between NFCC and partisan polarization, and (2) whether the 2016 presidential campaign facilitated change toward greater partisan polarization particularly among individuals with a strong need for cognitive closure.

Data and Analysis

Fortunately, researchers at the University of Minnesota carried out just such a panel survey in order to allow for an investigation into the unfolding of partisan polarization over the course of the 2016 campaign. This survey allows me to assess whether individual differences in the need for cognitive closure contributed to that dynamic. Beginning in July 2016, before the campaigns had held their nominating conventions, and over four separate waves concluding after the election, these researchers tracked respondents recruited by Survey Sampling International and measured their attitudes toward the parties, among many other attitudes people held about politics at the time.[4] In addition, the July wave included a six-item measure of the need-for-cognitive-closure scale, based on the highest-performing items identified by me in the 2014 YouGov study used throughout earlier chapters of this book. Given this rich source of data, I can assess my hypotheses in the context of one of the most consequential elections of modern US history, and leverage the panel data to assess (1) whether

NFCC is temporally prior to measures of partisan polarization, and (2) whether elections provide a moment of high party entitativity that causes high-NFCC respondents to become even more group-centric in their partisan attitudes and identities.

This study includes three of the measures of group-centric partisanship analyzed in previous chapters of this book: (1) the traditional measure of partisan strength, (2) a measure of partisanship as a social identity (Huddy, Mason, and Aarøe 2015), and (3) feeling thermometers of both parties. The study also includes three additional measures, each of which reflects different components of Tajfel's (1972) definition of social identity as composed of knowledge of belonging to a social group together with emotional and value significance of group membership. The alternative partisanship measure (4) asks respondents how strongly they "identify" with their party (an alternative way of assessing knowledge of belonging compared to the traditional partisan strength measure, which asks whether respondents "think of themselves" as partisan). The partisan certainty dependent variable (5) further captures the cognitive categorization dimension of partisan strength in asking respondents about how certain they are in their Democratic or Republican outlook. And finally, the partisan morality variable (6) reflects the value significance of partisan group membership in asking respondents a set of questions about the extent to which their partisanship informs their ethics. In conceiving of partisan strength as a latent variable composed of multiple cognitive, affective, and value dimensions, I believe that it is a strength to include analyses for each of these dependent variables.[5] Question wording for all key variables is included in appendix A.

In discussing the results from this and the next survey, I present the simple main effect of the need for cognitive closure on partisan polarization (averaged across all levels of political attention). I do not find in these analyses support for the expectation that the effect of NFCC on partisan group-centrism is concentrated among individuals with high levels of political attention. I believe, however, that the lack of this interaction effect in this case does not invalidate the attention-interaction hypothesis. Instead I believe that this set of null findings tells us something important about political campaigns. Campaigns, I believe these results suggest, heighten levels of political attention broadly throughout the population. Especially with social media so prominent in our lives, everyone (or nearly everyone) gets exposed to political discourse regardless of whether they seek it out, and regardless of whether they live in a battleground state. During presidential campaigns, politics becomes essentially unavoidable. Furthermore, people take more of an active interest in politics during presidential campaigns. During these contests, it is hard not to feel like politics is important to one's own life, and therefore people give politics more of their limited attention. As a result, most people during presidential campaigns exhibit the two characteristics of individuals who, at other times, I characterize as being highly attuned to politics: (1) they are exposed to political discussion, and (2) they are motivated to pay greater attention to the sound and fury of political contestation.

Before making use of the panel data, I wanted to assess whether, in July of 2016, before the general election campaign really heated up, individuals with a strong need for cognitive closure were more group-centric in their partisanship than individuals with a weak need for closure.[6] Figures 4.1 and 4.2 offer a simple conclusion to this question: on the eve of the 2016 campaign, individuals with a strong need for cognitive closure already expressed higher levels of group-centric partisanship than those who were more cognitively open (full results of these analyses are available in appendix B).

In July of 2016, on the eve of the contest between Clinton and Trump, I find across numerous indicators that individuals with a strong need for closure were already more group-centric in their partisanship than individuals with a weak need for closure. Specifically, for Republicans, I find a positive and statistically significant ($p < 0.05$) association between NFCC and group-centrism among five of the dependent variables. The only insignificant relationship among Republicans is with the feeling thermometer dependent variable. Aside from this one finding, however, we can conclude, based on these findings, that among Republicans, those individuals with a strong need for cognitive closure were more strongly Republican in their cognitive categorization (across two distinct measures), more likely to say that their Republican partisanship was important to their social identity, more certain about their partisanship, and more likely to report that their Republican identity was important to their sense of morality and right and wrong.

The results for Democrats are nearly identical. Across the same five measures of partisan group-centrism, I find statistically significant ($p < 0.05$) support for the expectation that individuals with a strong need for cognitive closure were more likely to express a group-centric form of partisanship than individuals with a weak need for cognitive closure. Democrats who scored higher on NFCC expressed a greater likelihood of cognitively identifying strongly with the Democratic Party (across two ways of measuring self-categorization), a stronger Democratic social identity, greater certainty about their Democratic partisanship, and a greater feeling that their Democratic partisanship was connected to their moral beliefs and reflections. Once again, the only clear null effect that emerges in this analysis is with the feeling thermometer dependent variable, where individuals with a strong need for closure were no different than individuals with a weak need for closure.

This lack of an effect of NFCC on the feeling thermometer variable could reflect in part the highly negative associations that many voters had with both Clinton and Trump throughout the 2016 campaign. Thus, the real effect of

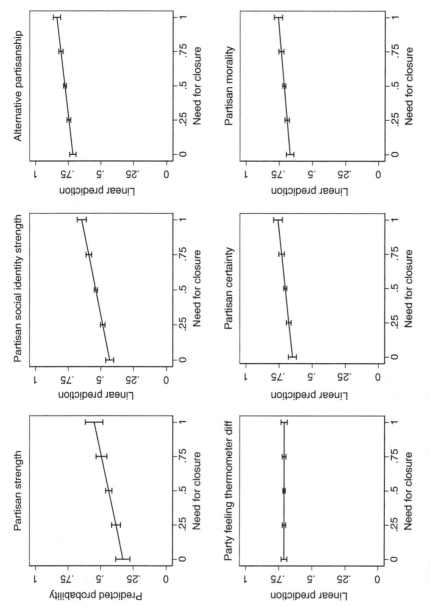

FIGURE 4.1 Relationship between NFCC and partisan polarization—Republicans. Note: Bars represent 95 percent confidence intervals.

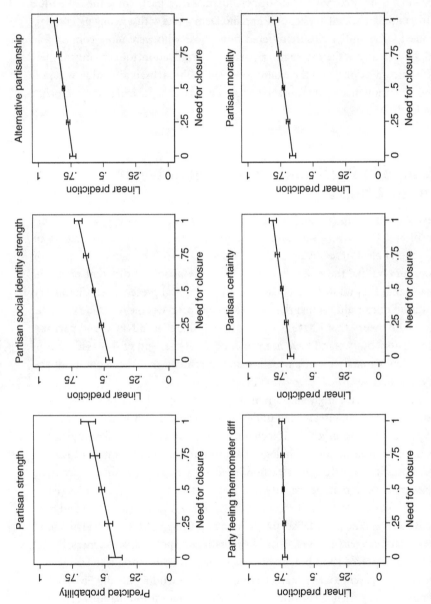

FIGURE 4.2 Relationship between NFCC and partisan polarization—Democrats. Note: Bars represent 95 percent confidence intervals.

NFCC on the eve of the 2016 general election campaign was not in fueling hatred toward the opposite party (which was strong enough without it), but in keeping partisans strongly committed to supporting their own party come the fall. As the 2016 campaign heated up, Republicans and Democrats with a strong psychological need for cognitive closure differed from those who were more comfortable with uncertainty in their strength of partisan identification, the certainty of their partisan convictions, and the extent to which their partisan affiliation was said to be a component of their moral belief system. What happened as the campaign unfolded?

Change in Partisan Polarization between Waves 1 and 2

Wave 2 of the 2016 Minnesota panel study was in the field between September 10 and 16, 2016, while wave 3 was in the field during the conclusion of the general election campaign: October 20–29, 2016. The main advantage of panel surveys like these, which survey the same people at different points in time, is that they allow for an assessment of temporal precedence. A necessary condition of causality is that the causal variable precedes the outcome variable. This is the theory that I have posited for the link between NFCC and partisan polarization, but so far, I have not provided an assessment of this assumption. The following analyses, in part, allow me to remedy that shortcoming of the previous analyses.

This is an increasingly important assessment for political psychologists to undertake, as recent research has undermined the previously long-standing presumption that most psychological characteristics precede political attitudes. For instance, the measure of psychological authoritarianism based on child-rearing preferences was constructed in the hope of identifying an exogenous indicator of this element of human personality that would precede political attitudes (Feldman and Stenner 1997). But recent research of my own (Luttig 2021) and others (Bakker, Lelkes, and Malka 2021; Goren and Chapp 2019; Smith et al. 2021) shows that this variable is in fact *endogenous* to many political preferences. Political attitudes precede and potentially cause changes in authoritarianism. This is true of other psychological characteristics as well, including the Big Five trait of openness to experience (Boston et al. 2018) and moral foundations (Hatemi, Crabtree, and Smith 2019). Hence, it is increasingly important that political psychologists abandon assumptions about the temporal relationship between psychological variables and political ones. In my case, this recent research demands that I at least assess whether NFCC does in fact precede and lead to increases in expressions of partisan group-centrism, rather than the alternative, that being a group-centric partisan increases an individual's need for cognitive closure.

The need for cognitive closure, measured in July, is clearly prior in time to the partisanship measures from September and October (that is, there is no logical way for partisan polarization at a later time period to cause levels of need for closure measured in an earlier period). By including a control variable for a respondent's level of partisan polarization in July (per Bartels 2006), before the nominating conventions even began, I track how the need for closure—measured in July—contributes to changes in partisan polarization between this relatively subdued period and September, when the campaign was in full swing (wave 2), and between September and when the campaign reached its pinnacle at the end of October (wave 3). As in the previous analyses, I include the same set of control variables (also measured in wave 1).

In addition to testing the assumption that NFCC is temporally prior to levels of partisan polarization, these panel studies also allow for an examination of the psychology of partisanship in the midst of an ongoing political campaign. The 2016 campaign is particularly notable in light of the fact that it brought to the fore two very different candidates offering opposed messages to the American people. As such, it was a context in which perceptions of the parties' entitativity should have grown. The parties, in this and other recent campaigns, tried to present a unified front, rallying around their respective nominees, and to clearly differentiate themselves from their partisan opponent. Because of this dynamic within political campaigns, as campaigns progress from the summer into the fall, identification as a strong partisan should become increasingly attractive to respondents with a strong psychological need for cognitive closure, who are attracted to cohesive groups that present themselves as a solid source for a comforting shared reality.

Partisanship, however, is among the most stable of variables over time in the study of American political behavior (e.g., Converse 2006; Green, Palmquist, and Schickler 2002). It is therefore difficult to imagine widespread changes occurring in levels of partisan strength or affective polarization over these few months. Any detectable movement, in fact, may be unexpected over this relatively short time frame and when considering past research on the stability of partisan identification. Indeed, there are very strong correlations between each of the measures of partisan polarization across survey waves in this study. For example, the correlation between the wave 1 and wave 2 partisan social identity measures was greater than 0.75 for both Democrats and Republicans. This was among the most stable of the measures of partisanship used in this study.

But despite the stability of partisanship, I do find some evidence that NFCC led to increases in partisan group-centrism over this time period, though it was limited to only a few of the dependent variables. Tables 1 and 2 present the results.

As shown in tables 4.1 and 4.2, between wave 1 in July and wave 2 in September, I find a sizeable and significant effect of the need for closure on increases in partisan social identity strength for both Republicans and Democrats, as well as a significant effect of NFCC on the traditional partisan strength measure for Democrats. Between July and September of the 2016 presidential campaign, Democrats and Republicans with a high need for closure increased the strength of their

TABLE 4.1 The effect of NFCC (wave 1) on change in partisan strength (wave 1–wave 2), Republicans

VARIABLES	(1)	(2)	(3)	(4)	(5)
	PARTISAN STRENGTH, W2	PARTY FEELING THERMOMETER DIFFERENCE, W2	PARTISAN CERTAINTY, W2	PARTISAN MORALITY, W2	PARTISAN SOCIAL IDENTITY, W2
Lagged DV	4.29**	0.60**	0.42**	0.41**	0.70**
	(0.284)	(0.033)	(0.047)	(0.045)	(0.027)
NFCC, W1	0.72	0.00	−0.01	−0.01	0.09**
	(0.706)	(0.025)	(0.051)	(0.046)	(0.031)
Observations	668	690	651	645	668

Standard errors in parentheses; column 1 contains logistic regression coefficient estimates. Remaining columns present OLS regression coefficient estimates. Control variables include political interest, political knowledge, education, income, age, white, Black, ideology, policy extremism.

** $p < 0.05$, * $p < 0.10$

TABLE 4.2 The effect of NFCC (wave 1) on change in partisan strength (wave 1–wave 2), Democrats

VARIABLES	(1)	(2)	(3)	(4)	(5)
	PARTISAN STRENGTH, W2	PARTY FEELING THERMOMETER DIFFERENCE, W2	PARTISAN CERTAINTY, W2	PARTISAN MORALITY, W2	PARTISAN SOCIAL IDENTITY, W2
Lagged DV	4.27**	0.44**	0.44**	0.43**	0.74**
	(0.240)	(0.031)	(0.051)	(0.053)	(0.024)
NFCC, W1	2.17**	0.03	−0.00	−0.03	0.07**
	(0.578)	(0.025)	(0.053)	(0.051)	(0.027)
Observations	908	890	870	865	904

Standard errors in parentheses; column 1 contains logistic regression coefficient estimates. Remaining columns present OLS regression coefficient estimates. Control variables include political interest, political knowledge, education, income, age, white, Black, ideology, policy extremism.

** $p < 0.05$, * $p < 0.10$

identification with their party. Figure 4.3 presents the results of this analysis, and shows the effect of NFCC on changes in partisan social identity strength. To put this finding into context, I also show the effect of policy extremism, ideological identity, political interest, and the stability estimate of partisan social identity strength from wave 1 to wave 2.

Figure 4.3 shows the effect of NFCC on partisan social identity strength in wave 2, conditional on partisan social identity strength in wave 1 and relative to other variables that may be associated with increases in partisan strength over the course of a presidential campaign, such as political interest, ideology, and policy extremism. As the figure shows, there is a very strong correlation between partisan social identity strength in wave 1 and partisan social identity strength in wave 2. The only two variables associated with increases in partisan social identity strength are the need for cognitive closure and political interest (neither ideology nor policy extremism increased or decreased partisan social identity strength between waves 1 and 2). These findings lend support to one of the primary hypotheses of this book: the need for cognitive closure leads to increases in partisan polarization for both Republicans and Democrats.

One reason this finding in particular is important is that the dependent variable, partisan social identity strength, is central to understanding political participation

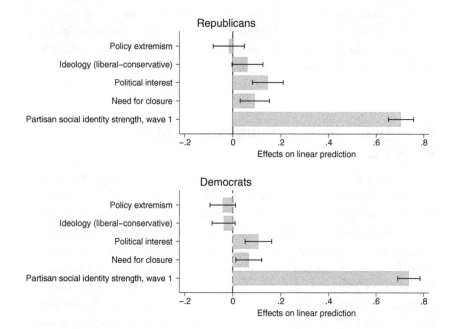

FIGURE 4.3 Predictors of partisan social identity strength, wave 2. Note: Bars represent 95 percent confidence intervals.

and partisan activism. As Huddy, Mason, and Aarøe (2015) show, this measure of partisan strength outperforms variables such as ideological self-placement and policy preferences in predicting campaign activity. Strong partisans, as indicated by this measure, are also more emotionally reactive to election outcomes: angry when they believe their party will lose and uplifted when they believe their side is poised to win. Yet we know less about what makes someone a strong partisan over the course of a presidential campaign. The results here suggest that the need for closure is one variable that causes partisans of both persuasions to commit more strongly to, and therefore be more active on behalf of, their party during presidential campaigns. Individuals with a psychological predisposition to group-centrism, more so than ideology or policy preferences, strengthen their commitment to the partisan team over the course of a presidential campaign.

These findings therefore support the theoretical argument that I have made in this book: that the need for cognitive closure precedes and causes increases in expressions of group-centric partisanship. But it is also possible that the relationship between partisan group-centrism and NFCC is reciprocal. Unfortunately, I do not have the data to assess that possibility. Furthermore, it is also the case that the evidence for the temporal primacy of NFCC is limited here to the few instances when its relationship to group-centric partisanship is statistically significant. The majority of the tests above show no significant relationship between NFCC and changes in expression of partisanship. Therefore, I view these findings as suggestive evidence for my theoretical expectations, but not definitive or certainly capable of ruling out the possibility that political attitudes influence an individual's degree of cognitive closure.

Change in Partisan Polarization between Waves 2 and 3

Did the need for cognitive closure lead to further increases in partisan group-centrism between September (wave 2) and October (wave 3) of the 2016 presidential campaign? The answer is yes but, once again, inconsistently so. Republicans with a strong need for cognitive closure increased their level of affective polarization, as indicated by the party feeling thermometer difference scale ($b = 0.08$, $p < 0.05$). In other words, as the campaign shifted from September to October, Republicans with a strong need for cognitive closure became 8 percentage points more group-centric in terms of their emotional feelings toward the two parties than Republicans with a weak need for closure. But the relationship between NFCC and increases in partisan strength ($b = 0.36$, $p = n.s.$), partisan certainty ($b = 0.03$, $p = n.s$), partisan morality ($b = -0.03$, $p = n.s.$), and partisan social identity strength ($b = -0.02$, $p = n.s.$) were all statistically insignificant.

Among Democrats, meanwhile, individuals who are psychologically averse to uncertainty became more certain in their partisan identity ($b = 0.08$, $p < 0.10$) and increased the extent to which they believed their partisanship to be central to their moral belief system ($b = 0.13$, $p < 0.05$). But the relationship between NFCC and increases in partisan strength ($b = -0.59$, p=$n.s$), party feeling thermometer differences ($b = -0.03$, $p = n.s$), and partisan social identity strength ($b = 0.05$, $p = n.s$) were all insignificant. The full set of results is provided for each dependent variable in appendix B.

Together, these panel findings suggest two important details. First, they suggest that the NFCC variable is temporally prior to, and can explain changes in, levels of partisan group-centrism over time. Again, the findings are inconsistent across the dependent variable measures, for reasons that defy easy explanation, so there is some warrant for caution in interpreting the findings. Nevertheless, it is still important that the data did uncover some evidence consistent with the notion that the need for cognitive closure precedes and gives rise to a group-centric form of partisanship. Given the relative lack of panel studies with regard to the relationship between personality characteristics and political attitudes in the field, these inconsistent findings on their own are not inconsiderable.

These findings also suggest that we can rule out the alternative as the *sole* explanation for the relationship between NFCC and group-centric partisanship: that being a group-centric partisan causes an individual to become more closed. I do not have the ability to test that hypothesis, and I am certainly open to future studies investigating the possibility of a reciprocal relationship between the need for cognitive closure and indicators of partisan group-centrism. Nevertheless, these findings do, I believe, suggest that the correlation between the need for cognitive closure and group-centric partisanship that I have uncovered throughout this book arises at least to some degree as a function of closed personalities becoming more group-centric in the expression of their partisan identification.

How Presidential Campaigns Polarize the US Electorate

The findings reported in this chapter indicate that general election campaigns for the US presidency provide a context in which partisanship becomes especially attractive to individuals with a strong psychological need for cognitive closure. Campaigns are when the entitativity, or groupiness, of the parties reaches its zenith. The boundary lines are drawn, distinctions are made, the two groups unify around their chosen nominee, and the disagreements revealed during the primary are papered over. When this happens, people who crave the certainty that can be provided only by a closed community and shared reality network find in the parties a welcome source for the firm knowledge they seek. Clear choices create rigid partisans by providing a welcome home for the cognitively rigid, who see the world in stark, black-and-white terms. Election campaigns can seem so polarizing, these findings suggest, because they provide the perfect breeding ground for the type of partisan group-centrism that has become increasingly commonplace in US politics. Political campaigns tap into the type of messaging most appealing to the psychologically closed, and unlike most other periods, they attract most people's attention. It is because campaigns tap into the underlying sources of strong partisanship and affective polarization that they become moments of intense partisan enthusiasm and anger.

Furthermore, the results reported here illustrate that psychological closure causes both Republicans and Democrats to embrace their chosen party more strongly, a pattern of results that contradicts the conventional narrative about the psychological characteristics of Trump's and Clinton's supporters. The 2016 campaign is conventionally perceived as a culmination of a longer-term process of psychological sorting within the party system. The psychologically closed found in Donald Trump, the conventional story goes, a candidate whose very worldview matched their own. Any remaining Democrats predisposed to authoritarianism or dogmatism should, in this case, have defected from their party. Meanwhile, those who were open should have seen their psychological worldview best reflected by the Democrats and the Clinton campaign. As the 2016 campaign unfolded, these psychological distinctions should have been made crystal clear to American voters, allowing people to more easily align their partisan identities with their psychological worldviews.

In this analysis, I do not find any evidence for this story. In no case did I find the closed abandoning the Democratic Party, for instance. Instead I found numerous instances of closed Democrats becoming stronger supporters of their party as the election unfolded. As the 2016 campaign progressed, the psychologically closed became, if anything, more attached to whichever party they identified with at the beginning of the campaign. Closed Republicans became more Republican, and closed Democrats became more Democratic. The psychological composition of the parties was not shaken by Donald Trump's emergence onto the partisan playing field. Instead, as the battle lines became clearer, the rigid and the closed became further entrenched in the camp they already belonged to. The story of the 2016 campaign, therefore, does not appear to be one of a psychological realignment of the parties on the basis of psychological openness versus closure. Rather, the 2016 campaign seems to have accelerated a longer-term process of making the closed more group-centric in their expression of partisanship.

Conclusion

OPENING THE CLOSED MIND?

The spirit of liberty is the spirit which is not too sure that it is right.
—Learned Hand

The American polity of today is troubled. Signs of decay are everywhere: from Freedom House scores to attacks on the Capitol in front of our very eyes. The informal norms of mutual toleration and respect for the institutional rules of the game that helped cement the world's most established democracy are coming undone. Steven Levitsky and Daniel Ziblatt (2018) describe the erosion of these norms over decades and argue that their loss may portend a looming authoritarian crisis in this country. We may in fact be in the midst of such a crisis, as Republican politicians continue to question the legitimacy of the 2020 presidential election and sow doubts in the minds of their supporters about the validity of Joe Biden's presidency. In order to work our way through this politically fraught period of our history, it is important to understand from whence it came.

Political scientists and other commentators widely agree that both political polarization and partisanship are key parts of the problem. The nation's politicians have become more divided, and more ideologically extreme, and this has been a crucial factor behind the bruising hardball politics of the past few decades. And voters, meanwhile, have become more partisan, encouraging the brinksmanship of elected officials. Why has polarization been linked to more intense degrees of partisanship among the masses? What consequences does this resurgence of mass partisanship have for our evaluations of the public's political competence? And what can be done to stem the rising tide of group-centric partisanship?

By reviewing the major theoretical claims and summarizing the most important findings, I connect observations in this book to enduring topics in political science and political psychology: debates over the nature and origins of partisanship, the consequences of political engagement, asymmetries between the two parties, the pros and cons of different types of party systems, and what it means to be a good citizen. All of these important topics, in turn, have implications for future research that can investigate ways in which group-centric partisanship might be diminished.

Summary of Major Claims and Findings

I approached this study with a fairly straightforward question: what is the relationship between closed minds and the partisan divide between Democrats and Republicans? Some scholarship in the political psychology literature may be read to imply a ready answer: Republicans are closed, Democrats are open. Yet I found this answer unsatisfying for two reasons. First, many recent publications by political psychologists have suggested that the relationship between closure and political preferences is more nuanced than the straightforward rigidity-of-the-Right hypothesis would anticipate. In particular, the relationship between closure and political attitudes has been shown to be moderated by (1) variables related to political attention (e.g., Federico and Malka 2018; Federico 2021), (2) the domain of politics under consideration (e.g., economic versus social issues) (e.g., Federico and Malka 2018; Johnston, Lavine, and Federico 2017;), and (3) the symbolic ideological identities of respondents (e.g., Baldner et al. 2018; De Zavala, Cislak, and Wesolowska 2010; Federico, Deason, and Fisher 2012). All of these findings suggest a complex set of patterns by which psychological closure becomes associated with political beliefs, opening up the possibility that closure may lead to left-wing extremism in some domains or among some subgroups.

The second reason why the traditional rigidity-of-the-Right narrative left me unsatisfied had to do with the disjuncture I perceived between the conception of "Left versus Right" in much of the political psychology literature and its treatment in political science. Among many political psychologists, the concept of ideology has reigned supreme (e.g., Jost 2006). But as Nathan Kalmoe (2020) recounts, this prioritization of ideology does not mesh particularly well with the views of many political scientists who study public opinion, who instead tend to prioritize the concept of partisanship and view it not just as an expression of ideology but as an identity in its own regard. Kalmoe concludes his article by stating that "the sound and fury of *mass* politics is real, but it expresses partisan identities and ethnocentric prejudices, signifying nothing ideological for most" (2020, 789; emphasis in the original).

Hence, I ventured toward assessing the relationship between psychological closure and partisanship as well as indicators of the intensity with which people were attached to partisanship. A few contemporaneous articles reinforced this effort to prioritize partisanship over ideology. Iyengar, Sood, and Lelkes's (2012) influential work on affective polarization, defined in social identity terms as the feelings people hold about both their own party and the opposition, illuminated both the extent of the partisan divide in US society and the value of shifting our reference toward partisanship rather than ideology. And Huddy, Mason, and Aarøe's (2015) effort to improve our measure of partisanship from the social identity perspective, along with their demonstration that strong partisans valued expressive goals over instrumental ones, further cemented this approach. Both of these important papers would also improve the empirical indicators I would ultimately embrace as measures of what I came to call "partisan group-centrism."

In addition to these efforts by political scientists, I also found in the psychological literature a set of theoretical paradigms anticipating a strong relationship between the psychological need for closure and group-centrism, a psychological term that encompasses ingroup loyalty, outgroup derogation, and a tendency to conform to group norms. Both Arie Kruglanski and colleagues' (2006) theory of groups as epistemic providers and Michael Hogg's (2007) theory of uncertainty-identity theory therefore provided a framework that led directly to the hypothesis that the desire for psychological closure will increase the intensity of partisanship, *if* we conceive of partisanship as a group identity rather than an ideology. In chapter 1, I reviewed both of these theoretical paradigms and discussed their explanation for why groups provide closure or certainty and why, therefore, individuals with a strong need for closure tend to be more group-centric than individuals who are more cognitively open.

These paradigms also provided key insight into the conditions under which closure leads to group-centrism. It happens, both Kruglanski et al. (2006) and Hogg (2007) theorize, under conditions of high group entitativity, a concept that refers to the cohesiveness or unity of the groups in question. Only entitative, cohesive groups, with shared goals and clear boundaries, are effective providers of psychological closure. Kruglanski et al. and Hogg have slightly different explanations for what it is that groups provide closure about. For Kruglanski et al., it is a "shared reality" generally—perceptions and beliefs about the world that encompass any number of potential considerations. For Hogg, the main benefit of groups is the certainty they provide about the social world, the prototypes that we attach to ourselves and others. This is an important distinction that may have some relevance to future research building on these theoretical premises. But for my purposes, what was most beneficial was the twin insights that (1) people with a strong need for closure or certainty become group-centric, and (2) this process happens under conditions in which groups are perceived to be more internally unified and distinct from related outgroups.

Increasing internal unification and a growing distance from each other are precisely how US political parties have changed over the past decades. This is evident both from quantitative indicators like DW-Nominate and party unity scores and via qualitative and historical records of the transformation of the party system from echoes to clear choices. Thus, I theorized that any increase in the relationship between the need for cognitive closure and partisan group-centrism (1) would be a relatively recent phenomenon rather than an enduring one in US politics, and (2) would increase under perceptions of high rather than low elite polarization.

The final theoretical building block for my analyses was to incorporate recent research within political psychology on the importance of political attention (and, where necessary, related variables such as education) as a moderator of the link between personality and politics. Simply put, paying attention to politics, a concept that is measured primarily by indicators such as knowledge about factual political issues and self-described interest in politics, reflects that someone both understands the current political climate and cares about it. The highly attentive, therefore, are more aware of the growing divide between party elites (Smidt 2017). In addition, the attentive, by virtue of the fact that they are paying attention to a realm that offers little instrumental rewards (Somin 2006), are signaling that they care about politics—that politics, in other words, is a realm that is important to them. Based on these considerations, a number of political psychologists have shown that paying attention *strengthens* the link between indicators of psychological closure and political beliefs (e.g., Federico and Tagar 2014; Federico 2021). Building from this scholarship, I posited the same dynamic: that closure would increase expressions of partisan group-centrism more among the politically interested than among the detached.

The empirical chapters set out to assess these hypotheses. I conceptualized partisan group-centrism as a social identity, and used Tajfel's (1972) definition of social identity as composed of cognitive self-categorization, emotions, and values to guide my identification of measures of the group-centric partisanship construct. In chapter 2, I described the results of the relationship between the psychological need for closure, political attention, and various indicators of partisan group-centrism, including partisan strength, the intensity of partisan social identities, a measure of differences in reported feelings toward the two parties, and a measure of attitudes toward interparty marriage. Across each of these dependent variables, which encompassed different data sources, I found a consistent pattern of positive associations between the need for closure and group-centric partisanship among the most highly attentive supporters of both the Republican and Democratic Parties. And in most cases, this association far surpassed conventional levels of statistical significance. Thus, chapter 2 reports consistent evidence that NFCC leads to stronger expressions of group-centric partisanship, and that it does so for both Republicans and Democrats.

In chapter 3, I assessed whether this relationship has recently emerged as a function of changes in the US party system. First, I assessed whether the linkage between NFCC and group-centric partisanship is a present-day phenomenon or an enduring one. I found that in 1988 there was absolutely no association between NFCC and being a strong partisan, while in more recent years there was one. Second, in a survey experiment on partisan opinion formation, which reflects the values dimension of social identity theory, in which people endorse the group's position as their own, I manipulated the perception of elite polarization. I found in that study that highly attentive, high-NFCC respondents were much more likely to endorse the party's perceived position under conditions of high elite polarization than under conditions of low elite polarization. Collectively, these two studies indicate that elite polarization is a contextual condition that works to strengthen the association between closed minds and group-centric partisanship.

Chapter 4, finally, examined these dynamics during the 2016 presidential campaign. Three findings stand out from this chapter. First, the association between NFCC and group-centric partisanship throughout 2016 was evident for both Republicans and Democrats. Thus, rather than representing a partisan realignment on the basis of psychological closure, the 2016 campaign appears instead to have accelerated the bipartisan closing of the partisan mind. Second, there was no evidence from this chapter for the attention-interaction hypothesis. I conclude from this that during campaigns, most people pay some attention to politics and care to some degree about it. Hence, during campaigns, I suggest, we may see a weaker moderating effect of attention in political psychology than we do during less robust political periods. Third and perhaps most importantly, I found some evidence for the argument that the need for closure precedes and thus gives rise to group-centric partisanship. In light of recent studies in political psychology indicating that politics can lead to changes in psychological orientation rather than, or perhaps in addition to, the reverse dynamic, this evidence is reassuring for the claim that closed minds become attracted to partisanship under certain conditions, and not simply that being partisan causes someone to develop a closed personality.

Collectively, these analyses provide an abundance of evidence supporting a revised rigidity-of-the-extremes thesis, as long as the dependent variables reflect extremity of partisanship and we reconceive of partisanship as a social identity rather than a reflection of ideology. Based on this collection of findings, I suggest that a reconsideration of the relationship between closed minds and the partisan divide in US society is in order. The closed, it is true, are slightly more common among Republicans than among Democrats. But it is also true, I hope to have demonstrated, that being closed predisposes one to becoming a more group-centric partisan, regardless of whether one identifies with the party of the Right or of the Left. The closing of the partisan mind, these findings indicate, is a recent and bipartisan phenomenon.

Theoretical Implications

Partisanship

One implication of the above findings is about the value we gain by thinking about partisanship as a social identity rather than an ideology. The premise of this entire work, in fact, derives from this conception of partisanship, and the proof for this conception rests on the consistent empirical evidence. This is particularly true of the findings among Democrats. The need for cognitive closure, recall, is consistently related to symbolic conservatism and conservative positions on social issues. So even though I control for both symbolic ideology and issue attitudes in the empirical models, there may be some unmeasured ideological component of the NFCC construct that could explain the finding that NFCC increases the intensity of Republican partisanship. But there is no corresponding explanation, at least that I can think of, for making sense of these findings among Democrats *other than* the social identity explanation. These findings, therefore, lend themselves to an enduring debate within political science about the nature and foundations of mass partisanship and provide evidence in favor of the expressive or social identity point of view.

But while I firmly believe that these findings provide evidence for the social identity conception of partisanship, I do not think it is valuable to dismiss entirely the instrumental perspective. Indeed, some of the findings here suggest that the need for closure may in fact help to differentiate people for whom partisanship is group-centric from those for whom partisanship is a more instrumental expression of policy goals. For people with a weak need for cognitive closure, in particular, partisanship may reflect more of a rational "summary judgment" of ideological beliefs and political perceptions than an enduring psychological attachment. In that respect, this work resonates with others that make distinctions between types of partisanship (e.g., Groenendyk 2013; Lavine, Johnston, and Steenbergen 2012).

The work most closely resembling my own in identifying individual difference variables in psychology that help differentiate between different forms of partisanship is Arceneaux and Vander Wielen (2017), which theorizes and tests the roles of the need for cognition and the need for affect in partisan reasoning. Using these two variables, Arceneaux and Vander Wielen (2017) distinguish between reflective and intuitive reasoners, and show that those who are reflective (those who have a high need for cognition and low need for affect) are much more ideological than partisan in the way they reason, while more intuitive reasoners (who have a low need for cognition and a high need for affect) are more emotional and partisan in their reasoning. Thus, these authors suggest, the social identity perspective of partisanship may be more applicable to intuitive reasoners, while the instrumental view may be more appropriate for describing individuals capable of greater reflection.

While there are therefore clear similarities in the implications derived from both Arceneaux and Vander Wielen's (2017) research and my own, the two works are distinct in the nature of the motivations they posit as underlying partisan reasoning. For Arceneaux and Vander Wielen (2017), the motivations for partisanship are primarily emotional or affective in nature (high need for affect), while the benefit of having a high need for cognition is that it allows individuals to overcome their intuitive emotional response due to the enjoyment of thinking that characterizes individuals who score highly on this psychological construct. By contrast, individuals with a strong need for cognitive closure are motivated not by affect but by a particular cognitive goal: to reduce uncertainty. This motivation coincides with a dislike of thinking, but is not synonymous with the need for cognition.[1]

Thus, unlike Arceneaux and Vander Wielen's (2017) perspective that emotion drives partisan reasoning, the motivation underlying the form of group-centric partisanship featured in this book is cognitive in nature. Perhaps these different models of partisanship lend themselves to an integrative effort. While it is beyond the reach of this book to fully theorize such a framework, let alone test it, some speculation is in order.

One possibility is that the nature of partisanship is more diverse than political scientists have previously conceived. In particular, it may be worth differentiating within the social identity paradigm between an emotional type of partisanship rooted in a high need for affect and a cognitive form of group-centric partisanship rooted in a high need for cognitive closure. The corresponding metaphor for the former may be that of a sports fan, while the latter would best be thought of as a type of religious identity and the group-centric partisan a kind of "true believer."

Indeed, I think that this metaphorical distinction between partisans as sports fans versus partisans as religious true believers is a useful one and may help us to distinguish distinct forms of partisanship, even if both categories can be broadly placed within the social identity paradigm. Partisans who are akin to sports fans may feel an emotional bond with their party, stick with their party through good times and bad, and receive a boost in their self-esteem when their party succeeds. But unlike religious true believers, sports fans are often quite capable of criticizing their team, recommending personnel changes, and adjusting their level of commitment to the team in response to its performance. But for the true believer, these responses are unlikely because the organization has become so central not only to their self-esteem but to their very construction of reality. The true believer is a partisan not just because it feels good, but because the parties provide a shared reality and a set of self-related prototypes that give people a sense of order and structure about how the world works and where they fit within it.

Bolstering this perspective, social psychologists have long noted an association between the need for cognitive closure and religious commitments. Like the modern political parties in the United States, religions can reduce uncertainties by prescribing beliefs about right and wrong, ideas about what is true and false, and notions of what typical members of their group are like. Vassilis Saroglou (2002, 185), for example, writes that religion can ameliorate a number of psychologically aversive states for those with a strong need for cognitive closure, such as "disorder among ideas, the chaos in the inner world, the simultaneous presence of incompatible elements, and the lack of integration-subordination of everything to what constitutes the fundamental, essential body of their belief system." Mark J. Brandt and Christine Reyna (2010, 715) similarly write about religion, and particularly about being a religious extremist, that "from a psychological perspective, religious fundamentalism represents an adherence to a set of religious teachings that are believed to contain the inerrant truth. . . . It is this cluster of beliefs surrounding a presumptive inerrant truth that makes fundamentalism a firm knowledge structure." Finally, Michael Hogg, Janice Adelman, and Robert Blagg (2010, 76) write that religions "provide an explanatory ideology and worldview that relates to both the sacred and the secular and shared rituals, behavioral conventions, and normative values and beliefs. Identification with such a group reduces uncertainty in precisely the way described by uncertainty-identity theory." All three of these articles show that individuals who have a strong need for cognitive closure or who are temporarily made to feel uncertain about themselves become stronger religious identifiers.

The group-centric partisanship described in this text, therefore, may require a broadening of the partisanship concept. People may be partisan because of an emotional bond that bolsters their self-esteem (rooted in a high need for affect and low need for cognition), because they rely on the parties to provide a sense of certainty and closure about the world and themselves (rooted in a high need for cognitive closure), or because the parties reflect their values (as in the instrumental perspective).

Indeed, aggregate trends in mass partisanship call perhaps for a more diverse set of frameworks for understanding its manifestations and consequences. For instance, the electorate has experienced a resurgence in mass partisanship as indicated by variables such as partisan strength and affective polarization, but it has also simultaneously observed a rise in partisan "leaners" (Klar and Krupnikov 2016). These leaners, as I discussed earlier, are characterized by a weaker need for cognitive closure compared to group-centric partisans, but Klar and Krupnikov (2016) show that they also have unique concerns related to impression management. Similarly, research has suggested that outparty negativity is more extreme in contemporary US politics than inparty positivity (e.g., Iyengar, Sood, and Lelkes 2012), with issue attitudes having a stronger influence on the former than the latter (e.g., Bougher 2017). People certainly can dislike parties because of what they stand for without relying on a partisan identity for cognitive closure.

The need for cognitive closure, therefore, should be not be seen as necessary for the production of any of the outcome variables examined in this book. There are various pathways through which an individual can become a strong partisan, have negative views of the outgroup, or dislike the thought of interparty marriage. What characterizes group-centric partisanship is a pattern exhibited by multiple symptoms, including having a strong partisan identity, polarized feelings, and a willingness to conform to the party's worldview. It is this pattern, in which the need for cognitive closure gives rise to multiple and diverse indicators of the intensity of partisanship, that I hope to have illuminated in this text.

Political Attention

Another important implication of this work is that political attention is a double-edged sword. On the one hand, interest in politics is crucial in the development of political participation, which any democracy requires. On the other hand, as I demonstrate, political attention can also foster partisan rigidity, which prohibits the reflection and deliberation that good citizenship depends on. In particular, attention when coupled with a strong need for cognitive closure breeds the closed type of group-centric partisanship described in this book.

This finding may help to make sense of what is otherwise a puzzling set of conflicting findings in political science about those who pay attention to politics. Some find that the attentive are more partisan in the way they reason (e.g., Taber and Lodge 2006), while others find the opposite (e.g., Kam 2005). Perhaps attention to politics alone is insufficient for differentiating those who are likely to engage in partisan reasoning from those who can avoid it. Instead, attention to politics should be thought of as an indicator of both having awareness about and taking an interest in the political realm. But this alone will not distinguish between partisan and nonpartisan reasoners. We also need to identify the underlying psychological motivations of respondents. When the motivation is to achieve cognitive closure, attention is likely to enhance partisan reasoning. But when the need for cognitive closure is weak or absent, attention may coincide with a more reflective type of reasoning in which partisan cues are ignored.

Partisan Asymmetries

This work puts forward a straightforward thesis: the closing of the partisan mind is a bipartisan phenomenon. Yet this conclusion should not be read to imply that the closing of the partisan mind—and the nefarious consequences that may result—is symmetrical across the two parties. There are two complications that render such a reading incomplete. The first is simply that there are more closed Republicans than closed Democrats. Thus, group-centric partisanship is an outcome we should see more of on the right side of the political spectrum than on the left (holding all else constant).

A second complication is a product of the theory itself and the implications it has for the types of beliefs that citizens will hold. In particular, the theory of groups as epistemic providers is more or less silent about the types of shared reality that groups can or will construct for their supporters. That "reality," for instance, could emphasize the concerns of social identity groups within the coalition, or symbolic ideological goals (cf. Grossmann and Hopkins 2016). Alternatively, the shared reality constructed within a party could have some fidelity to reality or be removed from it. Here, the messages and views of elites within the parties—including by partisan media outlets—will be instrumental to the opinions that will be expressed by the parties' supporters. Hence, evidence of asymmetries between the parties in terms of the reality of their beliefs should not automatically be interpreted as evidence for psychological differences between the parties. The need for cognitive closure leads partisans, as the experiment in chapter 3 most clearly illustrates, to adopt the opinions of their leaders. Therefore, many of the asymmetries between Democrats and Republicans in factual beliefs may result not from enduring psychological differences but from different messages emanating from party leaders and ideological media outlets.

Polarization and Voter Competence

Another implication of these findings has to do with the consequences of different types of party systems for the competence of voters. As I briefly mentioned at various points in this book, both political scientists and political advocates have long argued in favor of party polarization as a boon to democratic forms of governance. One problem, at least from the perspective of political science, was that most citizens did not think about politics in the same way that their elected officials did. This disjuncture implied a lack of attention among citizens and an incapacity to use the criterion of ideology to make their political decisions. This argument was forcefully put forward by Philip Converse (2006), who showed that Americans lacked constraint in their political belief systems: they held a mix of liberal opinions with conservative ones. By differentiating the parties, political scientists proposed, people would have greater ability and motivation to develop more constrained belief systems and therefore come closer to meeting their ideal of good citizenship.

Indeed, research indicates that elite polarization has increased constraint among the masses (Levendusky 2009). But I would contend that constraint among belief elements may be an insufficient criterion for evaluating voter competence. The growing constraint we have observed in US politics over the past few decades appears to be largely a product of group-centric motivations rather than a greater capacity among the public for ideological reasoning. Americans' increasing constraint therefore reflects the growing power that party leaders, who now are unified and offer firm knowledge, have over the opinions of their followers. In light of these findings, I suggest we shift the criteria we use to evaluate public competence, away from outcome (constrained versus unconstrained) and toward process (partisan versus open-minded). What matters is not the structure of mass opinion, but the way in which people reason. Closed-minded partisan thinking is not, from this perspective, politically beneficial, even if it leads to an appearance of greater ideological constraint. What should be valued, I propose, is open-minded thinking that shuns the motivation to conform to the position of party leaders and instead relies on a greater variety of information as well as more fully cultivated internal values. An open-minded perspective would be one that, to echo Learned Hand, is never too sure that it is right, and that is therefore always capable of change.

Opening the Closed Mind?

Can people be made more open-minded, or are our psychological characteristics fixed and unalterable? Fortunately, research suggests that an individual's degree of open- or closed-mindedness can be changed. Political psychologists are starting to recognize this possibility and are showing that many of the correlations between political preferences and psychological variables arise because our political views influence our personalities (e.g., Bakker, Lelkes, and Malka 2021; Boston et al. 2018; Hatemi, Crabtree, and Smith 2019; Luttig 2021; Smith et al. 2021). The Stanford psychologist Jamil Zaki (2020, 21) reinforces this perspective when he writes, "Our personalities also change more than we might realize. After leaving home, new adults grow more neurotic. After getting married, they become more introverted; after starting their first job, they become more conscientious. We can, of course, also change intentionally. Psychotherapy leaves people less neurotic, more extroverted, and more conscientious than they were before—and these changes last at least a year after therapy ends. Personality doesn't lock us into a particular life path; it also reflects the choices we make." Zaki calls the idea that human personalities are fixed and beyond our control the "Roddenberry hypothesis," referencing Gene Roddenberry, the creator of *Star Trek: The Next Generation*, which embodied this hypothesis in the fixed nature of many of the characters on the show. But Zaki informs us that this hypothesis is wrong. Citing numerous works from neuroscience on the plasticity of the brain, as well as work by psychologists like Carol Dweck (2008), whose research on mindset illustrates the power of our beliefs and actions over our own psychological characteristics, Zaki (2020, 21) claims that "we're not static or frozen; our brains and minds shift throughout our lives." Based on these new findings about the malleability of personality, it is now possible to examine those factors that create more open-mindedness.

What, then, has the potential to foster open minds and, with them, politically healthier forms of citizenship? Fortunately, psychological research has already identified some candidates that may help promote greater psychological and therefore political openness. In particular, research suggests that psychological openness can be enhanced by strategies such as reading literary fiction, practicing cognitive behavioral therapy, and practicing mindfulness and meditation (Djikic, Oatley, and Moldoveanu 2013; Jackson et al. 2012; Pokorski and Suchorzynska 2017). While the mechanisms for these effects are not definitively understood, some research suggests that these types of "treatments" work by changing neural connections in the brain, which undermines our default modes of thinking about ourselves and others. In a more open state of mind brought about by meditation, fiction, or cognitive behavioral training, people are given the opportunity to literally rewrite aspects of their personality, such as the need for cognitive closure.

For instance, Mieczyslaw Pokorski and Anna Suchorzynska (2017) find that meditation practices significantly increase scores on the openness-to-experience dimension of the Big Five personality traits, a dimension that is highly related to the need for cognitive closure (with more openness on the Big Five trait corresponding closely to lower levels of the need for cognitive closure) (see also Crescentini and Capurso 2015; van den Hurk et al. 2011). This result may occur as a function of reduced activity in the default mode network of the brain, a state of mind associated with increased neural plasticity, and a component of the brain that appears to be less active in the midst of meditation and among experienced meditators (e.g., Brewer et al. 2011; Garrison et al. 2015; Pollan 2019, 305).

In fact, researchers have connected heightened activity in the default mode network with the type of closed or group-centric partisan thinking described in this book. Specifically, Jonas T. Kaplan, Sarah I. Gimbel, and Sam Harris (2016) of USC conducted a neuroimaging study in which self-identified liberals were presented with information that contradicted their personal political beliefs. In response, participants showed increased activity precisely in the default mode network. The default mode network, in other words, became activated when people's political identities were threatened. It follows that reducing activity in the default mode network may facilitate greater open-mindedness, not just in terms of personality but also in terms of political judgment. Practices like meditation, therefore, which reduce activity in the default mode network, may help to foster more political open-mindedness.

Another viable option for reducing the psychological need for closure is the reading of literary fiction. Literary texts are by their very nature ambiguous and lacking in closure with respect to interpretation. Cognitively, literature provides access to another's consciousness, a function that may draw on and expand the default mode network, suppressing the overbearing and rigid ego characteristic of those with closed minds. Virginia Woolf pointed toward this function of literature when she wrote that "the state of reading consists in the complete elimination of the ego."[2] Consistent with this hypothesis, numerous neuroimaging studies have found that reading fiction does serve to exercise the default mode network (e.g., Mar 2004; Tamir et al. 2016). For these reasons, the reading of literature has the potential to change minds, reduce the need for closure, make people more open, allow them to empathize more with those who disagree with them politically, and therefore become less polarized. While no studies as yet have assessed these hypotheses directly, there is an abundance of suggestive research that implies their plausibility.

First, an experimental study by Maja Djikic, Keith Oatley, and Mihnea C. Moldoveanu (2013) from the University of Toronto discovered that exposure to literary short stories (as compared to a nonfiction essay) reduced participants' need for cognitive closure. The variable that I have identified in this book as the primary psychological source of partisan polarization appears to be changeable in response to a relatively innocuous exposure to literary fiction. Fiction, it appears, may not only offer an alternative sense of belonging and identity, but may also directly make people more open-minded. This is the means by which good fiction can disturb the comfortable, with potentially profound psychological and sociological effects.

These lessons have been applied by Elizabeth Levy Paluck and Donald Green (2009) in a second suggestive study assessing the efficacy of a fictional radio program, *New Dawn*, in changing the political culture in Rwanda. The *New Dawn* program exposed Rwandans to a narrative of a Romeo-and-Juliet story in which star-crossed lovers become entangled in the conflict between Hutus and Tutsis (a situation that could very well take place in the current United States, where there is a rising tide of opposition to interparty marriage). Exposure to this storyline, in which the two lovers attempt to bring about a unification of the two opposed communities, seems to have had lasting and meaningful effects on the political culture in Rwanda. Specifically, the program seemed to cultivate in listeners a greater sense of independence from authority figures and changed the ways listeners sought to resolve community problems. A fictional narrative, exposing people to the lives of others, had meaningful consequences for important attitudinal and behavioral indicators of societal conflict and polarization.

Literature has the potential to increase political open-mindedness by undermining the default predictions and categorizations that our brains are designed to make in the most efficient way possible. This is what the Norwegian writer Karl Ove Knausgaard (2015) suggests is the defining characteristic of literature in a *New Yorker* article titled "Vanishing Point." As he writes, "The indefinite human, faceless and devoid of character, the mass human, lives its life in patterns by which it is bound and is the material of statistics." This is the realm of cognition exhibited by the default mode network, where we seek to make quick judgments and generalizable inferences from a limited amount of information. But as Knausgaard observes, "The instant a novel is opened and a reader begins to read, the remoteness between writer and reader dissolves. The *other* that thereby emerges does so in the reader's imagination, assimilating at once into his or her mind. This establishing of proximity to another self is characteristic of the novel." The ego, and the default mode network, may subsequently expand on this assimilation of minds. The mind in the hands of a powerful storyteller lets go of its assumptions, its default mode, and opens to the mind of the writer and the actions of the characters.

Knausgaard (2015) goes on to note that the novel is a space where reality is "idiosyncratic, particular, and singular: in other words, it represents the exact opposite of the media, which strives toward the universal and general." By undermining the general, the regular patterns of life, and exposing us instead to the idiosyncratic and the particular, literature teaches us that the predictions our brains were designed to make efficiently, on the basis of limited data, are often wrong or incomplete. This may cause uncertainty to rise in the brain, neural connections to become unglued, and the default mode network to shut down or expand, much like what happens when we meditate. The result of such an experience may be more openness and, as a result, reduced group-centrism in the realm of politics.

The suggestion made here that literary fiction can reduce group-centric partisanship is of course speculative and awaits future research. But the existing literature does identify important theoretical mechanisms warranting this research. Fiction increases openness to new experiences (Djikic, Oatley, and Moldoveanu 2013), increases empathy (Mar, Oatley, and Peterson 2009), interacts in suggestive ways with the default mode network of the brain (Mar 2004; Tamir et al. 2016), and has been shown to decrease other types of group-based social conflict (Paluck and Green 2009). Perhaps John Adams was on to something when he included a section titled "The Encouragement of Literature" in the constitution for the Commonwealth of Massachusetts.

The final possibility with some demonstrated potential for changing minds toward greater psychological openness is cognitive training. Jackson et al. (2012) conducted a study in which participants were assigned to complete various mental tasks meant to increase their cognitive ability. These tasks included activities like crossword and sudoku puzzles as well as inductive reasoning exercises aimed at fostering the recognition of novel patterns. These interventions, through a period of sixteen weeks, had a demonstrable effect on the personality trait of openness to experience. This study, conducted primarily among older adults, both illustrates the malleability of personality—that human beings are psychologically fluid—and also identifies a fairly benign set of tasks that can mitigate against the psychological closed-mindedness driving our currently polarized society.

In short, research suggests a variety of ways in which the psychological foundations of group-centric partisanship can be ameliorated. In this last section I hope to have offered some suggestions and identified plausible mechanisms for changing partisan minds. A number of political scientists, concerned about polarization in US politics, have argued for institutional changes to the party system or to the US Constitution. While we should continue these conversations, this last discussion suggests there may be alternative remedies to the type of polarization in our society, in the form of psychological interventions. Some part of human nature may indeed be inimical to life in a liberal democracy, especially one as vast and diverse as ours. Institutions can be designed to protect us from our worst impulses, as the Constitution sought to do. But we—those of us who study political psychology and those who cherish the values of liberty and democracy—should avail ourselves of all the tools at our disposal to create a more perfect union. Opening minds, I suggest, should become another focus of our investigations into how to overcome the problems of toxic partisanship and polarization in US politics.

SURVEY QUESTIONNAIRES FOR KEY VARIABLES

15-Item Measure of the Need for Cognitive Closure (NFCC), 2014 YouGov Survey (alpha = 0.89) and 2018 SSI Survey (alpha = 0.83)

Please rate how much you agree or disagree with these statements. (Strongly disagree—Strongly agree)

1. I don't like situations that are uncertain.
2. I dislike questions which could be answered in many different ways.
3. I find that a well ordered life with regular hours suits my temperament.
4. I feel uncomfortable when I don't understand the reason why an event occurred in my life.
5. I feel irritated when one person disagrees with what everyone else in a group believes.
6. I don't like to go into a situation without knowing what I can expect from it.
7. When I have made a decision, I feel relieved.
8. When I am confronted with a problem, I'm dying to reach a solution very quickly.
9. I would quickly become impatient and irritated if I would not find a solution to a problem immediately.
10. I don't like to be with people who are capable of unexpected actions.

11. I dislike it when a person's statement could mean many different things.
12. I find that establishing a consistent routine enables me to enjoy life more.
13. I enjoy having a clear and structured mode of life.
14. I do not usually consult many different opinions before forming my own view.
15. I dislike unpredictable situations.

14-item Measure of the Need for Cognitive Closure (NFCC), 2008 Knowledge Networks Survey (alpha = 0.81)

Read each of the following statements and decide how much you would agree with each according to your attitudes, beliefs, and experiences. Please respond according to the following scale, using only one number for each statement. (Strongly disagree—Strongly agree)

1. In case of uncertainty, I prefer to make an immediate decision, whatever it may be.
2. When I find myself facing various, potentially valid alternatives, I decide in favor of one of them quickly and without hesitation.
3. I prefer to decide on the first available solution rather than to ponder at length what decision I should make.
4. I get very upset when things around me aren't in their place.
5. Generally, I avoid participating in discussions on ambiguous and controversial problems.
6. When I need to confront a problem, I do not think about it too much and I decide without hesitation.
7. When I need to solve a problem, I generally do not waste time in considering diverse points of view about it.
8. I prefer to be with people who have the same ideas and tastes as myself.
9. Generally, I do not search for alternative solutions to problems for which I already have a solution available.
10. I feel uncomfortable when I do not manage to give a quick response to problems that I face.
11. Any solution to a problem is better than remaining in a state of uncertainty.
12. I prefer activities where it is always clear what is to be done and how it needs to be done.
13. After having found a solution to a problem, I believe that it is a useless waste of time to take into account diverse possible solutions.
14. I prefer things that I am used to over things I am unfamiliar with.

Measures of Political Attention and Partisan Group-Centrism in the 2008 Knowledge Networks Study

Interest in Politics

1. Some people seem to follow what's going on in government and public affairs most of the time, whether there's an election going on or not. Others aren't that interested. Would you say you follow what's going on in government and public affairs most of the time, some of the time, only now and then, or hardly at all?

General Political Knowledge (alpha = 0.65)

1. What job or political office does DICK CHENEY currently hold?
2. What job or political office does JOHN ROBERTS currently hold?
3. What job or political office does GORDON BROWN currently hold?
4. What job or political office does NANCY PELOSI currently hold?
5. Which political party currently has the most members in the Senate in Washington?
6. Which political party currently has the most members in the House of Representatives in Washington?
7. How long is the term of office for a U.S. Senator?
8. Whose responsibility is it to nominate judges to the Federal Courts—the President, the Congress, or the Supreme Court?

Political Identity Centrality (alpha = 0.84)

1. My political attitudes and beliefs are an important reflection of who I am. (Strongly disagree—Strongly agree).
2. In general, my political attitudes and beliefs are an important part of my self-image. (Strongly disagree—Strongly agree).

Group-Centric Partisanship

1. Generally speaking, do you usually think of yourself as a Republican, a Democrat, an independent, or what?
   If Republican or Democrat
   i) Would you call yourself a strong [Republican/Democrat] or a not very strong [Republican/Democrat]?

Measures of Political Attention and Partisan Group-Centrism in the 2014 YouGov Study

Interest in Politics

1. How often do you pay attention to politics and elections?

General Political Knowledge (alpha = 0.70)

1. Do you happen to know what job or political office is now held by Harry Reid?
2. Whose responsibility is it to determine if a law is constitutional or not? Is it the president, the Congress, or the Supreme Court?
3. How much of a majority is required for the U.S. Senate and House to override a presidential veto?
4. Which of the two major parties would you say is more conservative?
5. Do you happen to know what job or political office is now held by Jack Lew?

Group-Centric Partisanship

1. Partisan social identity strength (alpha = 0.85)
   a. How important is being a [Democrat/Republican] to you?
   b. How well does the term [Democrat/Republican] describe you?
   c. When talking about [Democrats/Republicans], how often do you use "we" instead of "they"?
   d. To what extent do you think of yourself as being a [Democrat/Republican]?
2. Party Feeling Thermometer Difference
   a. Respondents are asked to rate both the Democrats and the Republicans on a feeling thermometer scale that ranges from 0 to 100, where ratings between 50 degrees and 100 degrees mean they feel favorably and warm toward the group; ratings between 0 and 50 degrees mean they don't feel favorably toward the group and don't care too much for them.
      i. I then calculate a difference score by subtracting ratings of the outparty from ratings of the inparty. Higher values indicate greater affect toward the inparty than toward the outparty.

Measures of Political Attention and Partisan Group-Centrism in the 2018 SSI Study

Interest in Politics

1. How often do you pay attention to politics and elections?

General Political Knowledge (alpha = 0.46)

1. Do you happen to know what job or political office is now held by Paul Ryan?
2. How much of a majority is required for the U.S. Senate and House to override a presidential veto?
3. Which of the two major parties would you say is more conservative?
4. Do you happen to know what job or political office is now held by John Roberts?

Political Identity Centrality (alpha = 0.90)

1. My political attitudes and beliefs are an important reflection of who I am. (Strongly disagree—Strongly agree).
2. In general, my political attitudes and beliefs are an important part of my self-image. (Strongly disagree—Strongly agree).

Preference for Like-Minded Media

1. In today's media marketplace, there are many different kinds of networks with different kinds of news shows that people might like to watch. For example, some people might like to watch a show from PBS, another might like to watch a show from Fox News, and another a show from MSNBC. If you had to pick, which of the following types of news show would you most like to watch?

Group-Centric Partisanship: Interparty Marriage (analysis combines all three question wordings)

1.
    a. How would you feel if you had a son or daughter who married someone who votes for the Democratic Party? Would you feel happy or unhappy?

b. How would you feel if you had a son or daughter who married some-one who votes for the Republican Party? Would you feel happy or unhappy?

2.

c. How would you feel if you had a son or daughter who married some-one who votes for the Democratic Party but who RARELY talks about politics? Would you feel happy or unhappy?

d. How would you feel if you had a son or daughter who married some-one who votes for the Republican Party but who RARELY talks about politics? Would you feel happy or unhappy?

3.

e. How would you feel if you had a son or daughter who married some-one who votes for the Democratic Party and who FREQUENTLY talks about politics? Would you feel happy or unhappy?

f. How would you feel if you had a son or daughter who married some-one who votes for the Republican Party and who FREQUENTLY talks about politics? Would you feel happy or unhappy?

Measures of Key Variables in the 2016 MN Panel Study

Need for Cognitive Closure (alpha = 0.87), Wave 1 (Strongly disagree—Strongly agree)

1. In case of uncertainty, I prefer to make an immediate decision, whatever it may be.
2. When I find myself facing various, potentially valid, alternatives, I decide in favor of one of them quickly and without hesitation.
3. I prefer to decide on the first available solution rather than to ponder at length what decision I should make.
4. When I need to confront a problem, I do not think about it too much and I decide without hesitation.
5. When I need to solve a problem, I generally do not waste time in considering diverse points of view about it.
6. Any solution to a problem is better than remaining in a state of uncertainty.

Group-Centric Partisanship (Waves 1, 2, and 3)

1. Partisan strength categorization
   a. Generally speaking, do you usually think of yourself as a Republican, a Democrat, an independent, or what?
   If Republican or Democrat
   i. Would you call yourself a strong [Republican/Democrat] or a not very strong [Republican/Democrat]?
2. Partisan social identity strength (alpha = 0.85 Democrats; alpha = 0.92 Republicans)
   a. How important is being a [Democrat/Republican] to you?
   b. How well does the term [Democrat/Republican] describe you?
   c. When talking about [Democrats/Republicans], how often do you use "we" instead of "they"?
   d. To what extent do you think of yourself as being a [Democrat/Republican]?
3. Alternative partisanship
   a. I identify with [Democrats/Republicans] (Strongly disagree—Strongly agree)
4. Party Feeling Thermometer Difference

a. Respondents are asked to rate both the Democrats and the Republicans on a feeling thermometer scale that ranges from 0 to 100, where ratings between 50 degrees and 100 degrees mean they feel favorably and warm toward the group; ratings between 0 and 50 degrees mean they don't feel favorably toward the group and don't care too much for them.

   i. I then calculate a difference score by subtracting ratings of the outparty from ratings of the inparty. Higher values indicate greater affect toward the inparty than toward the outparty.

5. Partisan certainty

   a. To what extent do you feel certain about your [Democratic/Republican] political outlook?

6. Partisan morality (alpha = 0.85 Democrats; alpha = 0.92 Republicans)

   a. To what extent is your [Democratic/Republican] political outlook deeply connected to your beliefs about fundamental questions of right and wrong?

   b. To what extent is your [Democratic/Republican] political outlook deeply a reflection of your core moral beliefs and reflections?

TABLES

Chapter 2

TABLE B2.1 The effect of NFCC on partisan strength—Republicans, 2008 GfK

VARIABLES	(1)	(2)	(3)
	STRONG PARTISANSHIP	STRONG PARTISANSHIP	STRONG PARTISANSHIP
NFCC	−2.05	−0.17	−7.10**
	(3.181)	(4.916)	(2.224)
NFCC × Political interest	3.24		
	(4.043)		
NFCC × Political knowledge		1.03	
		(5.815)	
NFCC × Political-identity centrality			12.39**
			(3.218)
Attention to politics	2.28	1.45**	1.07**
	(3.627)	(0.534)	(0.529)
Political-identity centrality	1.20*	1.33**	−5.19
	(0.650)	(0.608)	(3.664)
Political knowledge	−0.48	−6.37	−0.24
	(0.629)	(4.374)	(0.618)
Income	0.87	0.81	1.21*
	(0.663)	(0.657)	(0.629)
Education	−1.61*	−1.73*	−1.65*
	(0.933)	(0.966)	(0.944)
Age	−0.02**	−0.02**	−0.01*
	(0.008)	(0.008)	(0.008)

(continued)

TABLE B2.1 (continued)

VARIABLES	(1)	(2)	(3)
	STRONG PARTISANSHIP	STRONG PARTISANSHIP	STRONG PARTISANSHIP
White	0.21	0.25	0.41
	(0.489)	(0.478)	(0.448)
Black	1.92	1.90	2.82**
	(1.325)	(1.296)	(1.243)
Female	0.63**	0.67**	0.67**
	(0.240)	(0.246)	(0.236)
Ideology	7.55**	3.37	4.86*
	(2.453)	(2.692)	(2.501)
Ideology × Attention to politics	−2.65		
	(2.970)		
Policy extremism	0.95	−2.34	0.65
	(1.567)	(1.844)	(1.583)
Policy extremism × Attention to politics	0.15		
	(1.991)		
Ideology × Political knowledge		3.08	
		(3.648)	
Policy extremism × Political knowledge		4.77**	
		(2.352)	
Ideology × Political-identity centrality			1.02
			(3.631)
Policy extremism × Political-identity centrality			0.79
			(2.452)
Constant	−6.91**	−2.27	−2.87
	(2.890)	(3.535)	(2.390)
Observations	626	626	626

Logistic regression model coefficients; standard errors in parentheses.

** $p < 0.05$, * $p < 0.10$

TABLE B2.2 The effect of NFCC on partisan strength—Democrats, 2008 GfK

VARIABLES	(1)	(2)	(3)
	STRONG PARTISANSHIP	STRONG PARTISANSHIP	STRONG PARTISANSHIP
NFCC	−3.86*	−3.75*	−3.67*
	(2.138)	(2.151)	(2.027)
NFCC × Political interest	5.85**		
	(2.672)		
NFCC × Political knowledge		5.80**	
		(2.871)	
NFCC × Political-identity centrality			6.57**
			(2.941)

VARIABLES	(1)	(2)	(3)
	STRONG PARTISANSHIP	STRONG PARTISANSHIP	STRONG PARTISANSHIP
Attention to politics	0.47	1.50**	1.44**
	(1.877)	(0.446)	(0.456)
Political-identity centrality	1.61**	1.59**	−0.44
	(0.492)	(0.488)	(2.150)
Political knowledge	−0.23	−2.02	−0.20
	(0.640)	(2.243)	(0.634)
Income	−0.37	−0.42	−0.40
	(0.617)	(0.611)	(0.613)
Education	0.57	0.44	0.45
	(0.793)	(0.798)	(0.775)
Age	0.01	0.01	0.01
	(0.008)	(0.008)	(0.008)
White	0.29	0.28	0.33
	(0.332)	(0.321)	(0.327)
Black	1.18**	1.22**	1.26**
	(0.562)	(0.556)	(0.572)
Female	0.42*	0.37	0.37
	(0.246)	(0.240)	(0.244)
Ideology	0.42	−0.65	−1.92*
	(1.238)	(1.608)	(1.103)
Ideology × Attention to politics	−3.67**		
	(1.703)		
Policy extremism	0.86	0.32	0.87
	(1.689)	(1.654)	(1.598)
Policy extremism × Attention to politics	−0.72		
	(2.145)		
Ideology × Political knowledge		−2.47	
		(2.259)	
Policy extremism × Political knowledge		−0.02	
		(2.383)	
Ideology × Political-identity centrality			−0.68
			(1.725)
Policy extremism × Political-identity centrality			−0.81
			(2.337)
Constant	−2.29	−1.52	−1.70
	(1.638)	(1.825)	(1.593)
Observations	650	650	650

Logistic regression model coefficients; standard errors in parentheses.

** $p < 0.05$, * $p < 0.10$

TABLE B2.3   The effect of NFCC on partisan group-centrism—Republicans, 2014 YouGov

VARIABLES	(1)	(2)	(3)	(4)
	PARTISAN SOCIAL ID	PARTISAN SOCIAL ID	PARTY FEELING THERMOMETER DIFFERENCE	PARTY FEELING THERMOMETER DIFFERENCE
NFCC	−0.51*	−0.34**	0.03	−0.15
	(0.278)	(0.146)	(0.244)	(0.150)
NFCC × Political knowledge	0.65*		0.07	
	(0.335)		(0.288)	
NFCC × Political interest		0.50**		0.35*
		(0.200)		(0.201)
Political knowledge	−0.27	0.11*	0.09	0.19**
	(0.394)	(0.065)	(0.278)	(0.063)
Political interest	0.09	−0.11	0.03	−0.25
	(0.053)	(0.224)	(0.037)	(0.196)
Income	0.08	0.09	0.16**	0.15**
	(0.056)	(0.057)	(0.050)	(0.049)
Education	−0.18**	−0.17**	−0.08**	−0.07*
	(0.043)	(0.044)	(0.039)	(0.038)
Age	0.00	0.00	0.00	0.00
	(0.001)	(0.001)	(0.001)	(0.001)
Female	0.05**	0.04**	0.03	0.03
	(0.021)	(0.022)	(0.020)	(0.021)
Black	0.06	0.08	−0.06	−0.06
	(0.065)	(0.059)	(0.061)	(0.058)
White	−0.07**	−0.07**	−0.04	−0.03
	(0.032)	(0.031)	(0.031)	(0.031)
Ideology	0.12	0.32**	0.20	0.19
	(0.229)	(0.155)	(0.185)	(0.127)
Ideology × Political knowledge	0.09		0.13	
	(0.338)		(0.237)	
Policy extremism	0.17	0.01	0.13	0.15*
	(0.142)	(0.083)	(0.142)	(0.092)
Policy extremism × Political knowledge	−0.16		−0.06	
	(0.183)		(0.184)	
Ideology × Political interest		−0.22		0.15
		(0.218)		(0.176)
Policy extremism × Political interest		0.08		−0.11
		(0.122)		(0.131)
/cut1				
/cut2				
Constant	0.69**	0.51**	0.26	0.36**
	(0.262)	(0.157)	(0.228)	(0.132)
Observations	373	373	373	373
R-squared	0.18	0.19	0.24	0.25

OLS coefficients (1–4); ordinal logistic coefficients (5–6); standard errors in parentheses.

** $p < 0.05$, * $p < 0.10$

TABLE B2.4 The effect of NFCC on partisan group-centrism—Democrats, 2014 YouGov

VARIABLES	(1)	(2)	(3)	(4)
	PARTISAN SOCIAL ID	PARTISAN SOCIAL ID	PARTY FEELING THERMOMETER DIFFERENCE	PARTY FEELING THERMOMETER DIFFERENCE
NFCC	−0.40*	−0.17	−0.53**	−0.17
	(0.227)	(0.183)	(0.134)	(0.142)
NFCC × Political knowledge	0.68**		0.90**	
	(0.283)		(0.180)	
NFCC × Political interest		0.43		0.42**
		(0.263)		(0.196)
Political knowledge	−0.33*	−0.18**	−0.23	−0.06
	(0.195)	(0.056)	(0.156)	(0.053)
Political interest	0.13**	−0.02	0.10**	−0.00
	(0.037)	(0.170)	(0.044)	(0.137)
Income	0.01	0.01	0.05	0.03
	(0.047)	(0.053)	(0.040)	(0.050)
Education	0.01	−0.00	0.01	−0.00
	(0.047)	(0.050)	(0.036)	(0.039)
Age	0.00**	0.00**	0.00**	0.00**
	(0.001)	(0.001)	(0.001)	(0.001)
Female	0.04**	0.04**	0.03	0.03
	(0.020)	(0.020)	(0.022)	(0.024)
Black	0.09**	0.09**	−0.05	−0.04
	(0.031)	(0.033)	(0.036)	(0.040)
White	0.01	0.01	−0.05*	−0.05
	(0.029)	(0.030)	(0.027)	(0.032)
Ideology	0.14	−0.06	0.09	−0.14
	(0.156)	(0.112)	(0.155)	(0.134)
Ideology × Political knowledge	−0.47**		−0.49**	
	(0.201)		(0.200)	
Policy extremism	0.18*	0.07	0.44**	0.16
	(0.099)	(0.073)	(0.069)	(0.100)
Policy extremism × Political knowledge	−0.18		−0.47**	
	(0.156)		(0.110)	
Ideology × Political interest		−0.22		−0.19
		(0.155)		(0.194)
Policy extremism × Political interest		−0.04		−0.12
		(0.123)		(0.124)
/cut1				
/cut2				

(continued)

TABLE B2.4   (continued)

VARIABLES	(1)	(2)	(3)	(4)
	PARTISAN SOCIAL ID	PARTISAN SOCIAL ID	PARTY FEELING THERMOMETER DIFFERENCE	PARTY FEELING THERMOMETER DIFFERENCE
Constant	0.65**	0.66**	0.73**	0.71**
	(0.157)	(0.142)	(0.118)	(0.109)
Observations	508	508	508	508
R-squared	0.20	0.18	0.30	0.22

OLS coefficients (1–4); ordinal logistic coefficients (5–6); standard errors in parentheses.

** $p < 0.05$, * $p < 0.10$

TABLE B2.5   The effect of NFCC on partisan group-centrism—Republicans, 2018 SSI

VARIABLES	(1)	(2)	(3)	(4)	(5)
	PREFERENCE FOR INPARTY VS. OUTPARTY MARRIAGE	PREFERENCE FOR INPARTY VS. OUTPARTY MARRIAGE	PREFERENCE FOR INPARTY VS. OUTPARTY MARRIAGE	PREFERENCE FOR INPARTY VS. OUTPARTY MARRIAGE	PREFERENCE FOR INPARTY VS. OUTPARTY MARRIAGE
NFCC	0.76**	-0.56	-1.18	0.17	-0.92
	(0.310)	(0.741)	(0.816)	(0.452)	(0.826)
NFCC × Political interest		2.15**			
		(1.070)			
NFCC × Identity centrality			3.02**		
			(1.147)		
NFCC × Like-minded news preference				1.12*	
				(0.616)	
NFCC × Political knowledge					2.57**
					(1.161)
Attention to politics	-0.19	-2.69**	-0.19	-0.23	-0.20
	(0.234)	(0.825)	(0.229)	(0.234)	(0.234)
Identity centrality	1.08**	1.08**	-3.43**	1.10**	1.09**
	(0.251)	(0.249)	(0.931)	(0.252)	(0.249)
Like-minded news preference	0.32**	0.30**	0.32**	-0.72	0.30**
	(0.105)	(0.104)	(0.102)	(0.479)	(0.104)
Political knowledge	0.29	0.34	0.38*	0.31	-2.48**
	(0.215)	(0.215)	(0.211)	(0.215)	(0.888)
Age	-0.00	-0.00	-0.00	-0.00	-0.00
	(0.004)	(0.004)	(0.004)	(0.004)	(0.004)
Education	-0.32	-0.30	-0.31	-0.33	-0.30
	(0.226)	(0.225)	(0.222)	(0.226)	(0.225)

VARIABLES	(1)	(2)	(3)	(4)	(5)
	PREFERENCE FOR INPARTY VS. OUTPARTY MARRIAGE	PREFERENCE FOR INPARTY VS. OUTPARTY MARRIAGE	PREFERENCE FOR INPARTY VS. OUTPARTY MARRIAGE	PREFERENCE FOR INPARTY VS. OUTPARTY MARRIAGE	PREFERENCE FOR INPARTY VS. OUTPARTY MARRIAGE
Sex	−0.06	−0.06	−0.07	−0.05	−0.06
	(0.102)	(0.102)	(0.100)	(0.102)	(0.102)
White	0.10	0.12	0.10	0.10	0.16
	(0.192)	(0.192)	(0.188)	(0.192)	(0.193)
Black	−0.02	0.05	0.01	0.10	0.13
	(0.421)	(0.420)	(0.412)	(0.425)	(0.421)
Ideology	1.22**	0.50	−0.77	0.97**	0.21
	(0.223)	(0.492)	(0.656)	(0.321)	(0.535)
Ideology × Attention to politics		1.15*			
		(0.665)			
Policy extremism	0.39	−0.08	−0.72	0.23	−0.02
	(0.269)	(0.602)	(0.706)	(0.430)	(0.735)
Policy extremism × Attention to politics		0.85			
		(0.931)			
Ideology × Identity centrality			2.80**		
			(0.839)		
Policy extremism × Identity centrality			1.69		
			(1.052)		
Ideology × Like-minded news preference				0.38	
				(0.420)	
Policy extremism × Like-minded news preference				0.29	
				(0.527)	
Ideology × Political knowledge					1.56**
					(0.793)
Policy extremism × Political knowledge					0.57
					(0.998)
Constant	−1.63**	−0.15	1.36**	−1.06**	0.16
	(0.359)	(0.587)	(0.690)	(0.444)	(0.663)
Observations	471	471	471	471	471
R-squared	0.22	0.23	0.26	0.22	0.23
Pseudo R-squared	0.19	0.21	0.23	0.20	0.21

OLS regression coefficients; standard errors in parentheses.

** $p < 0.05$, * $p < 0.10$

TABLE B2.6 The effect of NFCC on partisan group-centrism—Democrats, 2018 SSI

VARIABLES	(1)	(2)	(3)	(4)	(5)
	PREFERENCE FOR INPARTY VS. OUTPARTY MARRIAGE	PREFERENCE FOR INPARTY VS. OUTPARTY MARRIAGE	PREFERENCE FOR INPARTY VS. OUTPARTY MARRIAGE	PREFERENCE FOR INPARTY VS. OUTPARTY MARRIAGE	PREFERENCE FOR INPARTY VS. OUTPARTY MARRIAGE
NFCC	0.74**	−1.40	0.81	0.67	−1.25
	(0.363)	(0.961)	(1.088)	(0.446)	(0.795)
NFCC × Political interest		3.13**			
		(1.293)			
NFCC × Identity centrality			−0.10		
			(1.424)		
NFCC × Like-minded news preference				0.23	
				(0.757)	
NFCC × Political knowledge					3.32**
					(1.122)
Attention to politics	0.05	−1.31	0.07	0.05	0.11
	(0.270)	(0.912)	(0.272)	(0.272)	(0.267)
Identity centrality	0.82**	0.90**	1.18	0.84**	0.76**
	(0.299)	(0.303)	(1.047)	(0.300)	(0.298)
Like-minded news preference	0.12	0.11	0.11	−0.24	0.09
	(0.116)	(0.116)	(0.116)	(0.550)	(0.114)
Political knowledge	0.49**	0.53**	0.49**	0.50**	−0.36
	(0.216)	(0.216)	(0.218)	(0.216)	(0.880)
Age	0.00	0.00	0.00	0.00	0.00
	(0.004)	(0.004)	(0.004)	(0.004)	(0.004)
Education	0.18	0.10	0.20	0.18	0.22
	(0.265)	(0.267)	(0.266)	(0.266)	(0.262)
Sex	−0.03	−0.03	−0.03	−0.03	−0.03
	(0.112)	(0.112)	(0.112)	(0.112)	(0.110)
White	0.23	0.25	0.22	0.22	0.23
	(0.176)	(0.177)	(0.176)	(0.176)	(0.174)
Black	0.44**	0.47**	0.42**	0.45**	0.46**
	(0.209)	(0.211)	(0.210)	(0.210)	(0.207)
Ideology	−0.76**	−0.57	0.01	−0.89**	0.64
	(0.264)	(0.634)	(0.721)	(0.309)	(0.547)
Ideology × Attention to politics		−0.37			
		(0.843)			
Policy extremism	0.69**	1.14*	0.59	0.61*	0.99
	(0.299)	(0.692)	(0.812)	(0.359)	(0.690)
Policy extremism × Attention to politics		−0.62			
		(1.039)			
Ideology × Identity centrality			−1.06		
			(0.923)		
Policy extremism × Identity centrality			0.14		
			(1.173)		

VARIABLES	(1)	(2)	(3)	(4)	(5)
	PREFERENCE FOR INPARTY VS. OUTPARTY MARRIAGE	PREFERENCE FOR INPARTY VS. OUTPARTY MARRIAGE	PREFERENCE FOR INPARTY VS. OUTPARTY MARRIAGE	PREFERENCE FOR INPARTY VS. OUTPARTY MARRIAGE	PREFERENCE FOR INPARTY VS. OUTPARTY MARRIAGE
Ideology × Like-minded news preference				0.43 (0.524)	
Policy extremism × Like-minded news preference				0.18 (0.632)	
Ideology × Political knowledge					−2.41** (0.803)
Policy extremism × Political knowledge					−0.51 (0.976)
Constant	−1.11** (0.423)	−0.25 (0.702)	−1.38* (0.793)	−0.98** (0.468)	−0.64 (0.630)
Observations	490	490	490	490	490
R-squared	0.14	0.15	0.14	0.14	0.17
Pseudo R-squared	0.11	0.12	0.11	0.11	0.14

OLS regression coefficients; standard errors in parentheses.

** $p < 0.05$, * $p < 0.10$

Chapter 3

TABLE B3.1   Effect of NFCC on identifying as a partisan among respondents with more than a high school degree

VARIABLES	1988	2006–10
	PARTISAN IDENTIFIER	PARTISAN IDENTIFIER
NFCC	−0.29 (0.416)	0.40** (0.172)
Age	0.01 (0.008)	0.00 (0.003)
White	−0.21 (0.337)	−0.07 (0.135)
Income	−0.04 (0.079)	0.07** (0.030)
Female	0.42* (0.231)	0.34** (0.101)
Constant	0.58 (0.951)	−0.58 (0.392)
Observations	328	2,419

Logit coefficient estimates; robust standard errors in parentheses.

** $p < 0.05$, * $p < 0.10$

TABLE B3.2   Effect of NFCC on identifying as a strong partisan among respondents with more than a high school degree

VARIABLES	1988	2006–10
	STRONG PARTISAN	STRONG PARTISAN
NFCC	−0.12	0.38*
	(0.573)	(0.207)
Age	0.02**	0.02**
	(0.010)	(0.004)
White	−1.01**	−0.29*
	(0.408)	(0.157)
Income	0.13	−0.07*
	(0.115)	(0.039)
Female	0.02	0.26**
	(0.310)	(0.122)
Constant	−2.20	−0.07
	(1.352)	(0.504)
Observations	201	1,567

Logit coefficient estimates; robust standard errors in parentheses.

** $p < 0.05$, * $p < 0.10$

TABLE B3.3   The effect of NFCC on partisan strength is conditional on political attention (Education)

VARIABLES	1988	2006–10
	PARTISAN STRENGTH	PARTISAN STRENGTH
NFCC	0.02	−0.09
	(0.256)	(0.148)
Education	−0.01	0.12**
	(0.057)	(0.029)
NFCC × Education	−0.13	0.17**
	(0.166)	(0.074)
Age	0.02**	0.02**
	(0.003)	(0.002)
White	−0.58**	−0.33**
	(0.152)	(0.066)
Income	0.03	0.06**
	(0.020)	(0.012)
Female	0.10	0.18**
	(0.101)	(0.052)
/cut1	−1.37**	−0.07
	(0.289)	(0.160)
/cut2	−0.04	1.00**
	(0.283)	(0.159)
/cut3	1.75**	2.42**
	(0.286)	(0.162)
Observations	1,420	6,694

Robust standard errors in parentheses; ordinal logit model predicting strength of partisanship on a 4-point scale.

** $p < 0.05$, * $p < 0.10$

TABLE B3.4 The effect of NFCC × political attention on partisan opinion uniformity across environments of low and high polarization

VARIABLES	(1)	(3)
	PARTISAN OPINION UNIFORMITY	PARTISAN OPINION UNIFORMITY
	LOW POLARIZATION	HIGH POLARIZATION
NFCC	0.81	−3.02*
	(2.034)	(1.833)
Political Attention	−1.36	−5.01**
	(1.860)	(1.768)
NFCC ×	1.11	7.32**
Political Attention	(2.839)	(2.813)
Mining issue	0.41	0.16
	(0.324)	(0.273)
Medicaid issue	0.63*	0.63**
	(0.360)	(0.289)
Affirmative action issue	1.23**	0.89**
	(0.335)	(0.293)
Constant	−3.05**	0.05
	(1.372)	(1.188)
Observations	918	928

Logit coefficient estimates; robust standard errors in parentheses.

** $p < 0.05$, * $p < 0.10$

Chapter 4

TABLE B4.1 The relationship between NFCC and partisan group-centrism, wave 1—Democrats

VARIABLES	(1)	(2)	(3)	(4)	(5)	(6)
	PARTISAN STRENGTH	PARTISAN SOCIAL IDENTITY	ALTERNATIVE PARTISAN STRENGTH	PARTY FEELING THERMOMETER DIFFERENCE	CERTAINTY IN PARTISAN IDENTITY	PARTISAN MORALITY
NFCC	0.94**	0.26**	0.18**	0.02	0.14**	0.14**
	(0.372)	(0.033)	(0.044)	(0.042)	(0.029)	(0.030)
Political interest	2.80**	0.46**	0.16**	0.04	0.31**	0.29**
	(0.397)	(0.034)	(0.035)	(0.031)	(0.034)	(0.033)
Political knowledge	−0.64**	−0.17**	−0.02	0.04	−0.09**	−0.07**
	(0.291)	(0.025)	(0.029)	(0.028)	(0.023)	(0.021)
Education	0.06	−0.02	0.02	−0.01	0.01	−0.01
	(0.343)	(0.031)	(0.035)	(0.033)	(0.029)	(0.027)
Income	0.09	0.05	0.01	0.00	0.03	0.06**
	(0.340)	(0.033)	(0.039)	(0.038)	(0.033)	(0.030)

(continued)

TABLE B4.1 (continued)

VARIABLES	(1)	(2)	(3)	(4)	(5)	(6)
	PARTISAN STRENGTH	PARTISAN SOCIAL IDENTITY	ALTERNATIVE PARTISAN STRENGTH	PARTY FEELING THERMOMETER DIFFERENCE	CERTAINTY IN PARTISAN IDENTITY	PARTISAN MORALITY
Age	0.00	0.00	0.00	0.00	0.00	0.00
	(0.005)	(0.000)	(0.000)	(0.000)	(0.000)	(0.000)
White	0.16	−0.01	0.06**	0.01	−0.03*	−0.00
	(0.252)	(0.024)	(0.025)	(0.017)	(0.019)	(0.017)
Black	0.93**	0.09**	0.09**	0.05**	0.04*	0.06**
	(0.283)	(0.027)	(0.030)	(0.023)	(0.022)	(0.021)
Ideology	−2.44**	−0.16**	−0.04	−0.15**	−0.12**	−0.14**
	(0.345)	(0.034)	(0.031)	(0.033)	(0.029)	(0.028)
Policy extremism	0.37	0.04	0.17**	0.10**	0.12**	0.11**
	(0.352)	(0.035)	(0.036)	(0.032)	(0.032)	(0.030)
Constant	−1.89**	0.22**	0.44**	0.62**	0.46**	0.41**
	(0.471)	(0.044)	(0.046)	(0.041)	(0.041)	(0.036)
Observations	1,702	1,700	1,578	1,654	1,668	1,676
R-squared	N/A	0.29	0.16	0.09	0.21	0.21

Standard errors in parentheses; column 1 contains logistic regression coefficient estimates. Remaining columns present OLS regression coefficient estimates.

** $p < 0.05$, * $p < 0.10$

TABLE B4.2 The relationship between NFCC and partisan group-centrism, wave 1—Republicans

VARIABLES	(1)	(2)	(3)	(4)	(5)	(6)
	PARTISAN STRENGTH	PARTISAN SOCIAL IDENTITY	ALTERNATIVE PARTISAN STRENGTH	PARTY FEELING THERMOMETER DIFFERENCE	CERTAINTY IN PARTISAN IDENTITY	PARTISAN MORALITY
NFCC	1.75**	0.22**	0.12**	0.00	0.11**	0.09**
	(0.433)	(0.031)	(0.025)	(0.021)	(0.030)	(0.028)
Political interest	2.22**	0.35**	0.15**	0.11**	0.34**	0.28**
	(0.474)	(0.031)	(0.026)	(0.022)	(0.030)	(0.029)
Political knowledge	−1.17**	−0.15**	−0.07**	−0.03	−0.12**	−0.09**
	(0.338)	(0.026)	(0.021)	(0.018)	(0.025)	(0.023)
Education	0.71*	−0.05*	−0.00	−0.04*	−0.01	−0.02
	(0.366)	(0.029)	(0.023)	(0.020)	(0.027)	(0.026)
Income	−0.30	0.02	0.04	0.02	0.02	0.03
	(0.416)	(0.031)	(0.025)	(0.022)	(0.030)	(0.028)
Age	−0.00	−0.00**	−0.00	0.00**	−0.00*	0.00
	(0.006)	(0.000)	(0.000)	(0.000)	(0.000)	(0.000)
White	0.59*	0.01	0.05**	0.05**	0.05*	0.03
	(0.357)	(0.026)	(0.021)	(0.018)	(0.025)	(0.024)
Black	−0.03	−0.04	−0.04	−0.01	0.05	0.10**
	(0.652)	(0.052)	(0.041)	(0.037)	(0.053)	(0.050)
Ideology	3.31**	0.27**	0.27**	0.28**	0.19**	0.26**
	(0.489)	(0.031)	(0.025)	(0.021)	(0.030)	(0.028)
Policy extremism	0.98**	0.05	0.13**	0.10**	0.09**	0.09**
	(0.426)	(0.033)	(0.027)	(0.023)	(0.032)	(0.030)

VARIABLES	(1)	(2)	(3)	(4)	(5)	(6)
	PARTISAN STRENGTH	PARTISAN SOCIAL IDENTITY	ALTERNATIVE PARTISAN STRENGTH	PARTY FEELING THERMOMETER DIFFERENCE	CERTAINTY IN PARTISAN IDENTITY	PARTISAN MORALITY
Constant	−5.40**	0.11**	0.34**	0.31**	0.29**	0.23**
	(0.631)	(0.047)	(0.038)	(0.032)	(0.045)	(0.042)
Observations	1,318	1,318	1,215	1,282	1,296	1,300
R-squared	N/A	0.21	0.19	0.22	0.17	0.19

Standard errors in parentheses; column 1 contains logistic regression coefficient estimates. Remaining columns present OLS regression coefficient estimates.

** $p < 0.05$, * $p < 0.10$

TABLE B4.3 The effect of NFCC (wave 1) on change in partisan group-centrism (wave 1–wave 2)—Democrats

VARIABLES	(1)	(2)	(3)	(4)	(5)
	PARTISAN STRENGTH, W2	PARTY FEELING THERMOMETER DIFFERENCE, W2	PARTISAN CERTAINTY, W2	PARTISAN MORALITY, W2	PARTISAN SOCIAL IDENTITY, W2
Lagged DV	4.27**	0.44**	0.44**	0.43**	0.74**
	(0.240)	(0.031)	(0.051)	(0.053)	(0.024)
NFCC, W1	2.17**	0.03	−0.00	−0.03	0.07**
	(0.578)	(0.025)	(0.053)	(0.051)	(0.027)
Political interest, W1	1.42**	0.00	0.04	0.07	0.11**
	(0.563)	(0.025)	(0.053)	(0.052)	(0.028)
Political knowledge, W1	−0.31	−0.00	0.07*	0.06	−0.04*
	(0.453)	(0.021)	(0.043)	(0.042)	(0.022)
Education, W1	0.66	0.02	−0.02	0.01	0.02
	(0.523)	(0.024)	(0.049)	(0.048)	(0.025)
Income, W1	−0.04	0.02	0.10*	0.08	−0.01
	(0.543)	(0.025)	(0.052)	(0.050)	(0.026)
Age	0.01	0.00	0.00	−0.00	0.00
	(0.008)	(0.000)	(0.001)	(0.001)	(0.000)
White	−0.20	0.03	0.03	0.06	−0.03
	(0.426)	(0.020)	(0.042)	(0.040)	(0.021)
Black	0.73	0.05**	0.01	0.04	0.01
	(0.461)	(0.022)	(0.045)	(0.043)	(0.023)
Ideology, W1	−1.20**	−0.06**	−0.03	−0.05	−0.04
	(0.521)	(0.023)	(0.047)	(0.046)	(0.024)
Policy extremism, W1	−0.29	0.09**	−0.01	0.02	−0.04
	(0.556)	(0.026)	(0.053)	(0.052)	(0.027)
Constant	−4.18**	0.25**	0.17**	0.19**	0.09**
	(0.870)	(0.042)	(0.082)	(0.079)	(0.041)
Observations	908	890	870	865	904
R-squared	N/A	0.28	0.12	0.12	0.62
Adj. R-squared	N/A	0.28	0.11	0.11	0.62

Standard errors in parentheses; column 1 contains logistic regression coefficient estimates. Remaining columns present OLS regression coefficient estimates.

** $p < 0.05$, * $p < 0.10$

TABLE B4.4 The effect of NFCC (wave 1) on change in partisan group-centrism (wave 1–wave 2)—Republicans

VARIABLES	(1)	(2)	(3)	(4)	(5)
	PARTISAN STRENGTH, W2	PARTY FEELING THERMOMETER DIFFERENCE, W2	PARTISAN CERTAINTY, W2	PARTISAN MORALITY, W2	PARTISAN SOCIAL IDENTITY, W2
Lagged DV	4.29**	0.60**	0.42**	0.41**	0.70**
	(0.284)	(0.033)	(0.047)	(0.045)	(0.027)
NFCC, W1	0.72	0.00	−0.01	−0.01	0.09**
	(0.706)	(0.025)	(0.051)	(0.046)	(0.031)
Political inter-	1.99**	0.03	0.09*	0.14**	0.15**
est, W1	(0.758)	(0.026)	(0.054)	(0.049)	(0.033)
Political knowl-	−0.96	0.00	0.05	0.01	−0.05*
edge, W1	(0.592)	(0.021)	(0.043)	(0.039)	(0.026)
Education, W1	−0.12	−0.03	0.03	0.02	−0.04
	(0.641)	(0.023)	(0.046)	(0.042)	(0.028)
Income, W1	−0.21	0.03	0.01	0.03	0.06**
	(0.666)	(0.025)	(0.049)	(0.045)	(0.030)
Age	−0.01	0.00**	0.00	0.00*	−0.00**
	(0.011)	(0.000)	(0.001)	(0.001)	(0.000)
White	0.71	−0.04*	−0.01	0.03	0.04
	(0.594)	(0.023)	(0.045)	(0.041)	(0.028)
Black	−0.75	−0.07	−0.36**	−0.21**	0.05
	(1.227)	(0.043)	(0.097)	(0.089)	(0.057)
Ideology, W1	2.03**	0.07**	0.07	0.21**	0.06*
	(0.723)	(0.027)	(0.052)	(0.049)	(0.033)
Policy extrem-	0.75	0.03	0.08	0.05	−0.02
ism, W1	(0.724)	(0.027)	(0.055)	(0.050)	(0.033)
Constant	−5.42**	0.14**	0.09	−0.04	0.01
	(1.155)	(0.042)	(0.083)	(0.077)	(0.050)
Observations	668	690	651	645	668
R-squared	N/A	0.46	0.20	0.26	0.63
Adj. R-squared	N/A	0.45	0.18	0.24	0.62

Standard errors in parentheses; column 1 contains logistic regression coefficient estimates. Remaining columns present OLS regression coefficient estimates.

** $p < 0.05$, * $p < 0.10$

TABLE B4.5 The effect of NFCC (wave 1) on change in partisan group-centrism (wave 2–wave 3)—Democrats

VARIABLES	(1)	(2)	(3)	(4)	(5)
	PARTISAN STRENGTH, W2	PARTY FEELING THERMOMETER DIFFERENCE, W2	PARTISAN CERTAINTY, W2	PARTISAN MORALITY, W2	PARTISAN SOCIAL IDENTITY, W2
Lagged DV	5.86**	0.51**	0.20**	0.25**	0.78**
	(0.544)	(0.050)	(0.030)	(0.031)	(0.032)
NFCC, W1	−0.59	−0.03	0.08*	0.13**	0.05
	(1.106)	(0.044)	(0.049)	(0.050)	(0.040)
Political interest, W1	−0.38	0.03	0.19**	0.19**	0.03
	(1.079)	(0.040)	(0.045)	(0.047)	(0.038)
Political knowledge, W1	−1.80*	0.02	−0.01	−0.02	−0.01
	(0.946)	(0.036)	(0.040)	(0.041)	(0.031)
Education, W1	−0.68	−0.04	−0.03	−0.03	−0.01
	(1.025)	(0.039)	(0.044)	(0.045)	(0.035)
Income, W1	−0.95	−0.00	0.01	0.00	−0.01
	(1.058)	(0.043)	(0.047)	(0.048)	(0.037)
Age	−0.02	0.00	−0.00	0.00	−0.00*
	(0.017)	(0.001)	(0.001)	(0.001)	(0.001)
White	0.15	−0.04	−0.02	−0.03	0.05
	(1.097)	(0.040)	(0.043)	(0.044)	(0.034)
Black	0.68	0.01	0.06	0.02	0.04
	(1.157)	(0.043)	(0.046)	(0.047)	(0.036)
Ideology, W1	−1.63*	−0.07*	−0.16**	−0.21**	−0.02
	(0.982)	(0.038)	(0.042)	(0.043)	(0.034)
Policy extremism, W1	1.48	0.11**	0.11**	0.11**	0.10**
	(1.070)	(0.044)	(0.047)	(0.049)	(0.037)
Constant	−0.20	0.32**	0.49**	0.40**	0.08
	(1.813)	(0.075)	(0.078)	(0.080)	(0.062)
Observations	392	379	381	379	392
R-squared	N/A	0.34	0.29	0.33	0.69
Adj. R-squared	N/A	0.32	0.27	0.31	0.69

Standard errors in parentheses; column 1 contains logistic regression coefficient estimates. Remaining columns present OLS regression coefficient estimates.

** $p < 0.05$, * $p < 0.10$

TABLE B4.6 The effect of NFCC (wave 1) on change in partisan group-centrism (wave 2–wave 3)—Republicans

VARIABLES	(1)	(2)	(3)	(4)	(5)
	PARTISAN STRENGTH, W2	PARTY FEELING THERMOMETER DIFFERENCE, W2	PARTISAN CERTAINTY, W2	PARTISAN MORALITY, W2	PARTISAN SOCIAL IDENTITY, W2
Lagged DV	5.29**	0.50**	0.22**	0.27**	0.79**
	(0.529)	(0.049)	(0.035)	(0.036)	(0.034)
NFCC, W1	0.36	0.08**	0.03	−0.03	−0.02
	(1.118)	(0.042)	(0.051)	(0.048)	(0.039)
Political inter-est, W1	3.39**	0.02	0.06	0.10**	0.01
	(1.265)	(0.041)	(0.050)	(0.047)	(0.039)
Political knowl-edge, W1	−0.95	−0.01	−0.04	−0.11**	−0.04
	(0.945)	(0.033)	(0.040)	(0.037)	(0.031)
Education, W1	−0.85	−0.09**	−0.11**	−0.08**	−0.01
	(1.024)	(0.035)	(0.043)	(0.040)	(0.032)
Income, W1	−0.63	0.05	0.11**	0.05	−0.02
	(1.111)	(0.039)	(0.048)	(0.045)	(0.036)
Age	−0.06**	−0.00**	−0.00	−0.00	−0.00**
	(0.021)	(0.001)	(0.001)	(0.001)	(0.001)
White	0.40	0.06	0.00	0.04	−0.05
	(1.115)	(0.038)	(0.049)	(0.045)	(0.037)
Black	0.22	0.00	−0.03	0.10	−0.08
	(2.472)	(0.084)	(0.116)	(0.128)	(0.088)
Ideology, W1	3.90**	0.26**	0.40**	0.40**	0.17**
	(1.450)	(0.047)	(0.056)	(0.054)	(0.044)
Policy extrem-ism, W1	−1.69	−0.00	0.08	0.04	0.02
	(1.304)	(0.046)	(0.056)	(0.052)	(0.043)
Constant	−2.95	0.14**	0.25**	0.26**	0.16**
	(1.913)	(0.068)	(0.082)	(0.077)	(0.062)
Observations	345	341	340	334	345
R-squared	N/A	0.42	0.32	0.41	0.71
Adj. R-squared	N/A	0.40	0.30	0.39	0.70

Standard errors in parentheses; column 1 contains logistic regression coefficient estimates. Remaining columns present OLS regression coefficient estimates.

** $p < 0.05$, * $p < 0.10$

Notes

INTRODUCTION

1. *Saturday Night Live*, "The Bubble," YouTube video, 2:20, November 20, 2016, https://www.youtube.com/watch?v=vKOb-kmOgpI.

2. "Partisan stereotypes, views of Republicans and Democrats as neighbors," *Partisanship and political animosity in 2016*, Pew Research Center, June 22, 2016, https://www.pewresearch.org/politics/2016/06/22/4-partisan-stereotypes-views-of-republicans-and-democrats-as-neighbors/.

3. While many applications of Big Five personality traits to political attitudes exclude explicitly political questions in the measurement of openness to experience, this does not completely eliminate the problems, since the openness trait was conceptualized partly in terms of political beliefs (see Brad Verhulst's comments in Maria Konnikova, "Politics and personality: Most of what you read is malarkey," *New Yorker*, August 23, 2016, https://www.newyorker.com/science/maria-konnikova/politics-and-personality-most-of-what-you-read-is-malarkey).

4. There are other potential challenges with the child-rearing measure of authoritarianism—namely, that it could be endogenous to political preferences (Bakker, Lelkes, and Malka 2021; Goren and Chapp 2019; Luttig 2021; Smith et al. 2021) or that it lacks construct validity (Pietryka and MacIntosh 2022).

5. Other research has shown, however, that the effects of NFCC—in this case on intergroup conflict and hostility—are concentrated more among conservatives than liberals (De Zavala et al. 2010).

1. THE CLOSING OF THE PARTISAN MIND

1. This statistic is taken from Knight Foundation, "Indicators of news media trust," September 11, 2018, https://www.knightfoundation.org/reports/indicators-of-news-media-trust.

2. Johnston, Lavine, and Federico (2017, 47) note that the correlation between a scale based on these two survey questions of political self-expression and an index based on measures of political interest and political knowledge is a moderately strong 0.49.

3. Anthony Salvanto, Jennifer De Pinto, Fred Backus, and Kabir Khanna, "Mueller report: Majorities across party lines want full report released, CBS News poll says," CBS News, March 27, 2019, https://www.cbsnews.com/news/mueller-report-majorities-across-party-lines-want-full-report-released-says-cbs-news-poll/.

2. THE NEED FOR COGNITIVE CLOSURE AND PARTISAN GROUP-CENTRISM

1. The type of analysis varies depending on the structure of the dependent variable. If the dependent variable is continuous or resembles a continuous variable (such as the feeling thermometer, which ranges from 0 to 100), I use OLS regression. If the dependent variable is binary or has limited response options (such as those that distinguish strong partisans from not-strong partisans and partisan leaners), I use MLE models like logistic regression.

2. The measure uses a "branching" structure, such that people are first asked which party, if any, they identify with, then subsequently asked the strength of their

identification (if they indicate a partisan identity in response to the first question) or whether or not they lean toward a party (if they claim not to identify with either party in response to the first question).

3. In the Knowledge Networks survey, the policy extremism index is based on preferences regarding eight issues: government services, defense spending, government jobs, government aid to Black people, gender equality, government regulation on business, abortion rights, and protection for gays and lesbians from discrimination

4. YouGov uses sample matching techniques to generate "representative" samples from nonrandomly selected pools of respondents. For this study, YouGov interviewed 1,358 respondents who were then matched down to 1,200 respondents on the basis of gender, age, race, education, party identification, ideology, and political interest. The frame was constructed by stratified sampling from the full 2010 American Community Survey. Although YouGov samples contain nonrandomly selected respondents, they can in some respects be treated like random samples and frequently produce estimates comparable to random samples, such as the American National Election Studies (Ansolabehere and Rivers 2013; Vavreck and Rivers 2008). In all of the following analyses, I apply the available survey weights.

5. The survey questions also included an experimental component that varied the frequency with which the hypothetical marital partner discussed politics (Klar, Krupnikov, and Ryan 2018). One-third of respondents were told that the marital partner discussed politics rarely, one-third that the partner discussed politics frequently, and one-third contained no information. Consistent with Klar, Krupnikov, and Ryan (2018), I find that people are more accepting of interparty marriage if politics is discussed rarely. This manipulation, however, did not consistently alter the relationship between the need for closure and attitudes toward partisanship and marriage. Therefore, for the purposes of this analysis I include all three experimental manipulations in the analysis.

6. The interaction between NFCC and political interest, as well as the interaction between NFCC and political-identity centrality, is insignificant in this data set. There is also not a significant main effect of NFCC on pure partisan identification in this data set. For this reason, I urge viewing these findings as suggestive rather than definitive.

3. CLEAR CHOICES, GROUP-CENTRIC PARTISANS

1. Analyses based on the GSS data make use of the survey weights provided by the GSS in its cumulative data file.

2. Empirical models, available in full in appendix B, tables 7–9, also include control variables for demographics: age, race, income, and sex.

3. I code "leaners" as independents in this analysis, to distinguish most clearly between those who identify as partisans and those who do not but who may lean toward a party. The results do not change, however, if leaners are instead classified as partisans.

4. I slightly changed the manipulations across issues to increase the believability of the experiment. The full manipulations for each issue are available upon request.

5. Interested readers can consult Luttig (2018) for a look at the graphical representations of low and high polarization that accompanied these verbal descriptions.

6. For a similar approach, see Johnston, Lavine, and Federico (2017, 65). Running the analyses on both variables separately reports essentially identical findings (in both cases the coefficient for the interaction term is $p < 0.05$).

4. THE DYNAMICS OF PARTISAN CLOSURE AND THE 2016 PRESIDENTIAL CAMPAIGN

1. A *Washington Post*/ABC News poll from 2016 found that 65 percent of registered voters viewed Trump as not having "the kind of personality and temperament to serve

effectively as president." Dan Balz and Scott Clement, "Poll finds Clinton has widened lead ahead of Trump to 8 points," *Washington Post*, August 7, 2016, https://www.washington post.com/politics/poll-after-conventions-clinton-leads-trump-by-8-points/2016/08/06/5 17999c0-5b33-11e6-9aee-8075993d73a2_story.html.

2. A *Washington Post*/ABC News poll from 2016 found that 60 percent of registered voters viewed Clinton as not "honest and trustworthy." Balz and Clement, "Poll finds Clinton has widened lead."

3. The first virtue is that panel data provide multiple measures of the same construct, which can reduce measurement error that emerges from a single measure. This virtue is not irrelevant, but all of the measures included in this study are based on multiple questions and have high internal reliability, or measure attitudes that tend to be highly stable over time (e.g., partisanship) and that are thus less vulnerable to problems that emerge due to poor measurement.

4. The fourth wave, however, did not include the relevant measures of partisan group-centrism. Therefore, I focus below on analysis of the first three waves of the study.

5. In addition, the analyses reported below include similar control variables as before: demographic characteristics, ideological self-identification, and policy extremism. In the 2016 Minnesota panel study, there are ten policy issues included in the policy extremism scale: raising taxes to support Social Security and Medicare, raising taxes to reduce income inequality, raising the federal minimum wage, requiring employers to offer paid leave, banning Muslims from entering the United States, deporting undocumented immigrants, allowing transgender individuals to use bathrooms corresponding to their identity, instituting a ban on assault weapons, restricting suspects on the "no-fly list" from purchasing guns, and imposing tariffs on China.

6. Wave 1 was in the field from July 1, 2016, to July 18, 2016.

CONCLUSION

1. The 2014 YouGov study described at various points throughout this book included a five-item measure of the need for cognition. This construct correlates with the need-for-cognitive-closure measure at only −0.11. Therefore, people with a high need for closure tend to have a lower need for cognition. But the two constructs are by no means interchangeable with each other.

2. Woolf to Ethel Smyth, July 29, 1934, in *The Letters of Virginia Woolf*, vol. 5, *1932–1935*, ed. Nigel Nicolson and Joanne Trautmann (Harcourt Brace Jovanovich, 1975), 319.

References

Abramowitz, Alan I. 2010. *The disappearing center.* Yale University Press.

Adorno, Theodor, Else Frenkel-Brenswik, Daniel J. Levinson, and R. Nevitt Sanford. 1950. *The authoritarian personality.* Verso Books.

Ahler, Douglas J., and Gaurav Sood. 2018. "The parties in our heads: Misperceptions about party composition and their consequences." *Journal of politics* 80, no. 3: 964–81.

Aldrich, John H., and David W. Rohde. 2019. "Congressional committees in a continuing partisan era." In *Principles and practice of American politics: Classic and contemporary readings,* 7th ed., edited by Samuel Kernell and Steven S. Smith, 171–85. SAGE.

Altemeyer, Bob. 1988. *Enemies of freedom: Understanding right-wing authoritarianism.* Jossey-Bass.

American Political Science Association. 1950. "A report of the committee on political parties: Toward a more responsible two-party system." *American political science review* 44, no. 3, part 2: i–99.

Ansolabehere, Stephen, and Douglas Rivers. 2013. "Cooperative survey research." *Annual review of political science* 16:307–29.

Arceneaux, Kevin, and Ryan J. Vander Wielen. 2017. *Taming intuition: How reflection minimizes partisan reasoning and promotes democratic accountability.* Cambridge University Press.

Bakker, Bert N., Yphtach Lelkes, and Ariel Malka. 2021. "Rethinking the link between self-reported personality traits and political preferences." *American political science review* 115, no. 4: 1482–98.

Baldner, Conrad, Antonio Pierro, Marina Chernikova, and Arie W. Kruglanski. 2018. "When and why do liberals and conservatives think alike? An investigation into need for cognitive closure, the binding moral foundations, and political perception." *Social psychology* 49, no. 6: 360–68.

Barber, Michael, and Jeremy C. Pope. 2019. "Does party trump ideology? Disentangling party and ideology in America." *American political science review* 113, no. 1: 38–54.

Bartels, Larry M. 2002. "Beyond the running tally: Partisan bias in political perceptions." *Political behavior* 24, no. 2: 117–50.

Bartels, Larry M. 2006. "Three virtues of panel data for the analysis of campaign effects." In *Capturing campaign effects,* edited by Henry E. Brady and Richard Johnston, 134–63. University of Michigan Press.

Beauchamp, Zack. 2019. "Robert Mueller and the collapse of American trust." Vox, March 25, 2019. https://www.vox.com/policy-and-politics/2019/3/25/18280802/donald-trump-mueller-report-barr-news-trust.

Bonilla-Silva, Eduardo. 2006. *Racism without racists: Color-blind racism and the persistence of racial inequality in the United States.* Rowman & Littlefield.

Boston, Joshua, Jonathan Homola, Betsy Sinclair, Michelle Torres, and Patrick D. Tucker. 2018. "The dynamic relationship between personality stability and political attitudes." *Public opinion quarterly* 82, no. S1: 843–65.

Bougher, Lori D. 2017. "The correlates of discord: Identity, issue alignment, and political hostility in polarized America." *Political behavior* 39, no. 3: 731–62.

Brandt, Mark J., and Christine Reyna. 2010. "The role of prejudice and the need for closure in religious fundamentalism." *Personality and social psychology bulletin* 36, no. 5: 715–25.

Brewer, Judson A., Patrick D. Worhunsky, Jeremy R. Gray, Yi-Yuan Tang, Jochen Weber, and Hedy Kober. 2011. "Meditation experience is associated with differences in default mode network activity and connectivity." *Proceedings of the National Academy of Sciences* 108, no. 50: 20254–59.

Bump, Philip. 2019. "How Fox News worked to spin Robert Mueller's public statement." *Washington Post*, May 30, 2019. https://www.washingtonpost.com/politics/2019/05/30/how-fox-news-worked-spin-robert-muellers-public-statement/.

Campbell, Angus, Philip E. Converse, Warren E. Miller, and Donald E. Stokes. 1960. *The American voter*. University of Chicago Press.

Chambers, John R., and Darya Melnyk. 2006. "Why do I hate thee? Conflict misperceptions and intergroup mistrust." *Personality and social psychology bulletin* 32, no. 10: 1295–311.

Chirumbolo, Antonio, Stefano Livi, Lucia Mannetti, Antonio Pierro, and Arie W. Kruglanski. 2004. "Effects of need for closure on creativity in small group interactions." *European journal of personality* 18, no. 4: 265–78.

Choi, Jong An, Minkyung Koo, Incheol Choi, and Seigyoung Auh. 2008. "Need for cognitive closure and information search strategy." *Psychology & marketing* 25, no. 11: 1027–42.

Converse, Philip E. "The nature of belief systems in mass publics (1964)." 2006. *Critical review* 18, no. 1–3: 1–74.

Crescentini, Cristiano, and Viviana Capurso. 2015. "Mindfulness meditation and explicit and implicit indicators of personality and self-concept changes." *Frontiers in psychology* 6:1–6.

De Zavala, Agnieszka Golec, Aleksandra Cislak, and Elzbieta Wesolowska. 2010. "Political conservatism, need for cognitive closure, and intergroup hostility." *Political psychology* 31, no. 4: 521–41.

Delli Carpini, Michael X., and Scott Keeter. 1996. *What Americans know about politics and why it matters*. Yale University Press.

Djikic, Maja, Keith Oatley, and Mihnea C. Moldoveanu. 2013. "Opening the closed mind: The effect of exposure to literature on the need for closure." *Creativity research journal* 25, no. 2: 149–54.

Druckman, James N., Erik Peterson, and Rune Slothuus. 2013. "How elite partisan polarization affects public opinion formation." *American political science review* 107, no. 1: 57–79.

Dweck, Carol S. 2008. *Mindset: The new psychology of success*. Random House Digital.

Eady, Gregory, Jonathan Nagler, Andy Guess, Jan Zilinsky, and Joshua A. Tucker. 2019. "How many people live in political bubbles on social media? Evidence from linked survey and Twitter data." *Sage open* 9, no. 1: 1–21.

Egan, Patrick J. 2020. "Identity as dependent variable: How Americans shift their identities to align with their politics." *American journal of political science* 64, no. 3: 699–716.

Engelhardt, Andrew M. 2018. "Racial attitudes through a partisan lens." *British journal of political science* 51, no. 3: 1062–79.

Federico, Christopher M. 2021. "When do psychological differences predict political differences? Engagement and the psychological bases of political polarization."

In *The psychology of political polarization*, edited by Jan-Willem van Prooijen, 17–37. Routledge.

Federico, Christopher M., and Grace Deason. 2012. "Uncertainty, insecurity, and ideological defense of the status quo: The extremitizing role of political expertise." In *Extremism and the psychology of uncertainty*, edited by Michael A. Hogg and Danielle L. Blaylock, 197–211. Wiley-Blackwell.

Federico, Christopher M., Grace Deason, and Emily L. Fisher. 2012. "Ideological asymmetry in the relationship between epistemic motivation and political attitudes." *Journal of personality and social psychology* 103, no. 3: 381–98.

Federico, Christopher M., Agnieszka Golec, and Jessica L. Dial. 2005. "The relationship between the need for closure and support for military action against Iraq: Moderating effects of national attachment." *Personality and social psychology bulletin* 31, no. 5: 621–32.

Federico, Christopher M., and Ariel Malka. 2018. "The contingent, contextual nature of the relationship between needs for security and certainty and political preferences: Evidence and implications." *Political psychology* 39:3–48.

Federico, Christopher M., and Michal Reifen Tagar. 2014. "Zeroing in on the right: Education and the partisan expression of authoritarianism in the United States." *Political behavior* 36, no. 3: 581–603.

Feldman, Stanley, and Karen Stenner. 1997. "Perceived threat and authoritarianism." *Political psychology* 18, no. 4: 741–70.

Festinger, Leon. 1950. "Informal social communication." *Psychological review* 57, no. 5: 271–82.

Fiorina, Morris P., Samuel J. Abrams, and Jeremy C. Pope. 2011. *Culture war? The Myth of a Polarized America*. 3rd ed. Longman.

Fowler, James H., and Cindy D. Kam. 2007. "Beyond the self: Social identity, altruism, and political participation." *Journal of politics* 69, no. 3: 813–27.

Garrison, Kathleen A., Thomas A. Zeffiro, Dustin Scheinost, R. Todd Constable, and Judson A. Brewer. 2015. "Meditation leads to reduced default mode network activity beyond an active task." *Cognitive, affective, & behavioral neuroscience* 15, no. 3: 712–20.

Goren, Paul, and Christopher Chapp. 2019. "When worldviews collide: Authoritarianism is endogenous to culture war issues." Paper presented at the Annual Meeting of the Midwest Political Science Association, Chicago, April 4–7, 2019.

Green, Donald P., Bradley Palmquist, and Eric Schickler. 2002. *Partisan hearts and minds: Political parties and the social identities of voters*. Yale University Press.

Greenberg, Jeff, and Eva Jonas. 2003. "Psychological motives and political orientation— the left, the right, and the rigid: Comment on Jost et al. (2003)." *Psychological Bulletin* 129, no. 3: 376–82.

Greene, Steven. 2004. "Social identity theory and party identification." *Social science quarterly* 85, no. 1: 136–53.

Grieve, Paul G., and Michael A. Hogg. 1999. "Subjective uncertainty and intergroup discrimination in the minimal group situation." *Personality and social psychology bulletin* 25, no. 8: 926–40.

Groenendyk, Eric. 2013. *Competing motives in the partisan mind: How loyalty and responsiveness shape party identification and democracy*. Oxford University Press.

Grossmann, Matt, and David A. Hopkins. 2016. *Asymmetric politics: Ideological Republicans and group interest Democrats*. Oxford University Press.

Guess, Andy. 2021. "(Almost) everything in moderation: New evidence on Americans' online media diets." *American journal of political science* 65, no. 4: 1007–22.

Harbridge, Laurel, and Neil Malhotra. 2011. "Electoral incentives and partisan conflict in Congress: Evidence from survey experiments." *American journal of political science* 55, no. 3: 494–510.

Hardin, Curtis D., and E. Tory Higgins. 1996. "Shared reality: How social verification makes the subjective objective." In *Handbook of motivation and cognition*, vol. 3., *The interpersonal context*, edited by Richard M. Sorrentino and E. Tory Higgins, 28–84. Guilford.

Hatemi, Peter K., Charles Crabtree, and Kevin B. Smith. 2019. "Ideology justifies morality: Political beliefs predict moral foundations." *American journal of political science* 63, no. 4: 788–806.

Hetherington, Marc J. 2001. "Resurgent mass partisanship: The role of elite polarization." *American political science review* 95, no. 3: 619–31.

Hoffer, Eric. 1951. *The true believer*. Perennial.

Hogg, Michael A. 2007. "Uncertainty-identity theory." *Advances in experimental social psychology* 39:69–126.

Hogg, Michael A., Janice R. Adelman, and Robert D. Blagg. 2010. "Religion in the face of uncertainty: An uncertainty-identity theory account of religiousness." *Personality and social psychology review* 14, no. 1: 72–83.

Hogg, Michael A., and Paul Grieve. 1999. "Social identity theory and the crisis of confidence in social psychology: A commentary, and some research on uncertainty reduction." *Asian journal of social psychology* 2, no. 1: 79–93.

Huddy, Leonie, Lilliana Mason, and Lene Aarøe. 2015. "Expressive partisanship: Campaign involvement, political emotion, and partisan identity." *American political science review* 109, no. 1: 1–17.

Iyengar, Shanto, Gaurav Sood, and Yphtach Lelkes. 2012. "Affect, not ideology: A social identity perspective on polarization." *Public opinion quarterly* 76, no. 3: 405–31.

Jackson, Joshua J., Patrick L. Hill, Brennan R. Payne, Brent W. Roberts, and Elizabeth A L Stine Morrow. 2012. "Can an old dog learn (and want to experience) new tricks? Cognitive training increases openness to experience in older adults." *Psychology and aging* 27, no. 2: 286–92.

Johnston, Christopher D., Howard G. Lavine, and Christopher M. Federico. 2017. *Open versus closed: Personality, identity, and the politics of redistribution*. Cambridge University Press.

Jost, John T. 2006. "The end of the end of ideology." *American psychologist* 61, no. 7: 651–70.

Jost, John T., Christopher M. Federico, and Jaime L. Napier. 2009. "Political ideology: Its structure, functions, and elective affinities." *Annual review of psychology* 60:307–37.

Jost, John T., Jack Glaser, Arie W. Kruglanski, and Frank J. Sulloway. 2003. "Political conservatism as motivated social cognition." *Psychological bulletin* 129, no. 3: 339–75.

Kalmoe, Nathan P. 2020. "Uses and abuses of ideology in political psychology." *Political psychology* 41, no. 4: 771–93.

Kam, Cindy D. 2005. "Who toes the party line? Cues, values, and individual differences." *Political behavior* 27, no. 2: 163–82.

Kaplan, Jonas T., Sarah I. Gimbel, and Sam Harris. 2016. "Neural correlates of maintaining one's political beliefs in the face of counterevidence." *Scientific reports* 6, no. 1: 1–11.

Klar, Samara, and Yanna Krupnikov. 2016. *Independent politics: How American disdain for parties leads to political inaction*. Cambridge University Press.

Klar, Samara, Yanna Krupnikov, and John Barry Ryan. 2018. "Affective polarization or partisan disdain? Untangling a dislike for the opposing party from a dislike of partisanship." *Public opinion quarterly* 82, no. 2: 379–90.

Knausgaard, Karl Ove. 2015. "Vanishing point." Translated by Martin Aitken. *New Yorker*, November 17, 2015. https://www.newyorker.com/books/page-turner/vanishing-point.

Kruglanski, Arie W. 2004. *The psychology of closed mindedness*. Psychology Press.

Kruglanski, Arie W., Antonio Pierro, Lucia Mannetti, and Eraldo De Grada. 2006. "Groups as epistemic providers: Need for closure and the unfolding of group-centrism." *Psychological review* 113, no. 1: 84–100.

Ksiazkiewicz, Aleksander, Steven Ludeke, and Robert Krueger. 2016. "The role of cognitive style in the link between genes and political ideology." *Political psychology* 37, no. 6: 761–76.

Ladd, Jonathan M. 2012. *Why Americans hate the news media and how it matters*. Princeton University Press.

Lavine, Howard G., Christopher D. Johnston, and Marco R. Steenbergen. 2012. *The ambivalent partisan: How critical loyalty promotes democracy*. Oxford University Press.

Lee, Frances E. 2009. *Beyond ideology: Politics, principles, and partisanship in the US Senate*. University of Chicago Press.

Lee, Frances. 2017. "This is how Trump turned the politics of the debt ceiling upside down." *Washington Post*, September 10, 2017. https://www.washingtonpost.com/news/monkey-cage/wp/2017/09/10/this-is-how-trump-turned-the-politics-of-the-debt-ceiling-upside-down/.

Levendusky, Matthew. 2009. *The partisan sort: How liberals became Democrats and conservatives became Republicans*. University of Chicago Press.

Levitsky, Steven, and Daniel Ziblatt. 2018. *How democracies die*. Broadway Books.

Luttig, Matthew D. 2017. "Authoritarianism and affective polarization: A new view on the origins of partisan extremism." *Public opinion quarterly* 81, no. 4: 866–95.

Luttig, Matthew D. 2018. "The 'prejudiced personality' and the origins of partisan strength, affective polarization, and partisan sorting." *Political psychology* 39:239–56.

Luttig, Matthew D. 2021. "Reconsidering the relationship between authoritarianism and Republican support in 2016 and beyond." *Journal of politics* 83, no. 2: 783–87.

Malka, Ariel, Yphtach Lelkes, and Nissan Holzer. 2017. "Rethinking the rigidity of the right model: Three suboptimal methodological practices and their implications." In *Politics of social psychology*, edited by Jarret T. Crawford and Lee Jussim, 126–46. Psychology Press.

Malka, Ariel, Christopher J. Soto, Michael Inzlicht, and Yphtach Lelkes. 2014. "Do needs for security and certainty predict cultural and economic conservatism? A cross-national analysis." *Journal of personality and social psychology* 106, no. 6: 1031–51.

Mar, Raymond A. 2004. "The neuropsychology of narrative: Story comprehension, story production and their interrelation." *Neuropsychologia* 42, no. 10: 1414–34.

Mar, Raymond A., Keith Oatley, and Jordan B. Peterson. 2009. "Exploring the link between reading fiction and empathy: Ruling out individual differences and examining outcomes." *Communications* 34, no. 4: 407–28.

Marchlewska, Marta, Aleksandra Cichocka, and Małgorzata Kossowska. 2018. "Addicted to answers: Need for cognitive closure and the endorsement of conspiracy beliefs." *European journal of social psychology* 48, no. 2: 109–17.

Margolis, Michele F. 2018. *From politics to the pews: How partisanship and the political environment shape religious identity.* University of Chicago Press.

Mason, Lilliana. 2015. "'I disrespectfully agree': The differential effects of partisan sorting on social and issue polarization." *American journal of political science* 59, no. 1: 128–45.

Mason, Lilliana. 2018. *Uncivil agreement: How politics became our identity.* University of Chicago Press.

McCarty, Nolan, Keith T. Poole, and Howard Rosenthal. 2016. *Polarized America: The dance of ideology and unequal riches.* MIT Press.

Miller, Joanne M., Kyle L. Saunders, and Christina E. Farhart. 2016. "Conspiracy endorsement as motivated reasoning: The moderating roles of political knowledge and trust." *American journal of political science* 60, no. 4: 824–44.

Mullin, Barbara-Ann, and Michael A. Hogg. 1998. "Dimensions of subjective uncertainty in social identification and minimal intergroup discrimination." *British journal of social psychology* 37, no. 3: 345–65.

Neuberg, Steven L., T. Nicole Judice, and Stephen G. West. 1997. "What the need for closure scale measures and what it does not: Toward differentiating among related epistemic motives." *Journal of personality and social psychology* 72, no. 6: 1396–412.

Paluck, Elizabeth Levy, and Donald P. Green. 2009. "Deference, dissent, and dispute resolution: An experimental intervention using mass media to change norms and behavior in Rwanda." *American political science review* 103, no. 4: 622–44.

Panno, Angelo, Giuseppe Carrus, Ambra Brizi, Fridanna Maricchiolo, Mauro Giacomantonio, and Lucia Mannetti. 2018. "Need for cognitive closure and political ideology: Predicting pro-environmental preferences and behavior." *Social psychology* 49, no. 2: 103–12.

Peterson, Benjamin, J. Allegra Smith, David Tannenbaum, and Moira P. Shaw. 2009. "On the 'exporting' of morality: Its relation to political conservatism and epistemic motivation." *Social justice research* 22, no. 2–3: 206–30.

Pierro, Antonio, and Arie W. Kruglanski. 2006. "Validation of a revised need for cognitive closure scale." Unpublished data, Sapienza University of Rome.

Pietryka, Matthew T., and Randall C. MacIntosh. 2022. "ANES scales often don't measure what you think they measure." *Journal of politics* 84, no. 2: 1074–90.

Pokorski, Mieczyslaw, and Anna Suchorzynska. 2017. "Psychobehavioral effects of meditation." In *Pulmonary Disorders and Therapy*, edited by Miecyslaw Pokorski, 85–91. Springer, Cham.

Pollan, Michael. 2019. *How to change your mind: What the new science of psychedelics teaches us about consciousness, dying, addiction, depression, and transcendence.* Penguin.

Posner, Daniel N. 2004. "The political salience of cultural difference: Why Chewas and Tumbukas are allies in Zambia and adversaries in Malawi." *American political science review* 98, no. 4: 529–45.

Prior, Markus. 2007. *Post-broadcast democracy: How media choice increases inequality in political involvement and polarizes elections.* Cambridge University Press.

Roets, Arne, and Alain Van Hiel. 2011a. "Allport's prejudiced personality today: Need for closure as the motivated cognitive basis of prejudice." *Current directions in psychological science* 20, no. 6: 349–54.

Roets, Arne, and Alain Van Hiel. 2011b. "Item selection and validation of a brief, 15-item version of the Need for Closure Scale." *Personality and individual differences* 50, no. 1: 90–94.

Rohde, David W. 1991. *Parties and leaders in the postreform house.* University of Chicago Press.

Rokeach, Milton. 1960. *The open and closed mind: Investigations into the nature of belief systems and personality systems.* Basic Books.

Rosenfeld, Sam. 2018. *The polarizers: Postwar architects of our partisan era.* University of Chicago Press.

Saroglou, Vassilis. 2002. "Beyond dogmatism: The need for closure as related to religion." *Mental health, religion & culture* 5, no. 2: 183–94.

Sherif, Muzafer. 1936. *The psychology of social norms.* Harper.

Sherif, Muzafer. 1954. *Experimental study of positive and negative intergroup attitudes between experimentally produced groups: Robbers cave study.* University of Oklahoma.

Shils, Edward. 1954. *Authoritarianism "right" and "left."* Free Press.

Smidt, Corwin D. 2017. "Polarization and the decline of the American floating voter." *American journal of political science* 61, no. 2: 365–81.

Smith, Amy Erica, Mollie Cohen, Mason Moseley, and Matthew Layton. 2021. "Rejecting authoritarianism: When values are endogenous to politics." Unpublished paper, February 19, 2021. http://amyericasmith.org/wp-content/uploads/2021/04/Smith-et-al_Rejecting-Authoritarianism_2.19.21.pdf.

Sniderman, Paul M., and Edward H. Stiglitz. 2012. *The reputational premium: A theory of party identification and policy reasoning.* Princeton University Press.

Somin, Ilya. 2006. "Knowledge about ignorance: New directions in the study of political information." *Critical review* 18, no. 1–3: 255–78.

Stroud, Natalie Jomini. 2011. *Niche news: The politics of news choice.* Oxford University Press.

Sunstein, Cass R. 2018. *#Republic: Divided democracy in the age of social media.* Princeton University Press.

Taber, Charles S., and Milton Lodge. 2006. "Motivated skepticism in the evaluation of political beliefs." *American journal of political science* 50, no. 3: 755–69.

Tajfel, Henri. 1969. "Cognitive aspects of prejudice." *Journal of biosocial science* 1, no. S1: 173–91.

Tajfel, Henri. 1972. "La categorization sociale." In *Introduction à la psychologie sociale,* edited by Serge Moscovici, 272–302. Larousse.

Tajfel, Henri. 1974. "Intergroup behaviour, social comparison and social change." Unpublished Katz Newcomb Lectures, University of Michigan, Ann Arbor.

Tajfel, Henri, and Michael Billic. 1974. "Familiarity and categorization in intergroup behavior." *Journal of experimental social psychology* 10, no. 2: 159–70.

Tajfel, Henri, John C. Turner, William G. Austin, and Stephen Worchel. 1979. "An integrative theory of intergroup conflict." In *Organizational identity: A reader,* edited by Mary Jo Hatch and Majken Schultz, 56–65. Oxford University Press.

Tamir, Diana I., Andrew B. Bricker, David Dodell-Feder, and Jason P. Mitchell. 2016. "Reading fiction and reading minds: The role of simulation in the default network." *Social cognitive and affective neuroscience* 11, no. 2: 215–24.

Tesler, Michael. 2018. "Elite domination of public doubts about climate change (not evolution)." *Political communication* 35, no. 2: 306–26.

Turner, John C. 1975. "Social comparison and social identity: Some prospects for intergroup behaviour." *European journal of social psychology* 5, no. 1: 1–34.

van den Hurk, Paul A. M., Tom Wingens, Fabio Giommi, Henk P. Barendregt, Anne E. M. Speckens, and Hein T. van Schie. 2011. "On the relationship between the practice of mindfulness meditation and personality—an exploratory analysis of the mediating role of mindfulness skills." *Mindfulness* 2, no. 3: 194–200.

Vavreck, Lynn, and Douglas Rivers. 2008. "The 2006 cooperative congressional election study." *Journal of elections, public opinion and parties* 18, no. 4: 355–66.

Webster, Steven W., and Alan I. Abramowitz. 2017. "The ideological foundations of affective polarization in the US electorate." *American politics research* 45, no. 4: 621–47.

Zajonc, Robert B. 1980. "Feeling and thinking: Preferences need no inferences." *American psychologist* 35, no. 2: 151–75.

Zaki, Jamil. 2020. *The war for kindness: Building empathy in a fractured world*. Broadway Books.

Zaller, John R. 1992. *The nature and origins of mass opinion*. Cambridge University Press.

Zmigrod, Leor, Peter Jason Rentfrow, and Trevor W. Robbins. 2019. "Cognitive inflexibility predicts extremist attitudes." *Frontiers in psychology* 10:1–13.

Index

Page numbers in *italics* refer to figures and tables.